9B 15
CW00409077

Leominster Minster, Priory and Borough c660–1539

Leominster Minster, Priory and Borough
c660–1539

by

Joe & Caroline Hillaby

The Friends of Leominster Priory
in association with
Logaston Press

LOGASTON PRESS
Little Logaston Woonton Almeley
Herefordshire HR3 6QH
logastonpress.co.uk

First published in 2006
Copyright © Joe & Caroline Hillaby 2006

All rights reserved. No part of this publication
may be reproduced, stored in a retrieval system,
or transmitted, in any form or by any means,
electronic, mechanical, photocopying, recording
or otherwise, without the prior permission,
in writing, of the publisher
ISBN 1 904396 56 9

Set in Baskerville and Times by Logaston Press
and printed in Great Britain by
Biddles Ltd., King's Lynn

Contents

List of Tables

Acknowledgements

Our thanks go first to Bishop Michael, much loved and respected in Leominster, as in the diocese, for his foreword, produced in the very short time between submission of text and publication. Next we all owe a great debt of gratitude to both John Campbell and Don King, as initiators of the extraordinarily successful 'Operation Leofric' project. Congratulations go to Ann and Tony Malpas and the Leominster Historical Society who, through the organisation of the 2005 conference and publication of *The Early Church in Herefordshire*, kept the torch burning. To Muriel Tonkin's persuasive power we owe the gift to HRO by Stephen Millett of Rhode Island of Coningsby's *Register*. Without the *Register* chapters 19 and 20, and significant sections of other chapters, would not have been written. For important cartographic material and fruitful discussion, we are indebted to Eric Turton. Much of the interest in the section on the Leominster missal and breviary is due to the enthusiasm and specialist knowledge of the Revd Ian Gibbs. Duncan James' contribution on the 15th-century School Lane project is manifest in his plan, elevation and sketch in the Urban Development section of Chapter 23. We also enjoyed many interesting, wide-ranging discussions on vernacular buildings, and the Leominster chalice. With Prof David Wulstan there was much lively debate about the cuckoo!

Thanks also to Duncan Brown, Special Projects Officer, National Monuments Record Centre, Swindon, formerly Field Officer with the Hereford and Worcester County Archaeological Service, for exchange of emails on the priory in general, and the tile survey in particular; John Freeman for an enthusiastic discussion on place-names and allied matters; and to Michael Faraday for select Leominster items, from the *De Banco, Coram Rege* and the uncalendared *Curia Regis Rolls,* Feet of Fines and Chancery Master's Exhibits: Duchess of Norfolk Deeds, just prior to his departure in 1986/7 from 'WC2 and the vicinity of the record repositories'; and later further items from the Ludlow Palmer's Guild Muniments of Title at Salop CRO. For errors and inadequacies we alone are responsible.

This book could not have been written without the facilities available at the British Library and the libraries of the University of Bristol, University College London, Hereford City and Cathedral — and Great Malvern Library for access to Eames' *Catalogue of Tiles*; not forgetting the London Library, with its unparalleled service and splendid collection of archaeological and county journals, and Herefordshire Record Office. The whole has been brought together by Andy Johnson, with infinite patience and good humour.

Our thanks go to many people for illustrative material, notably to Norman Childs, working with Pat Shirreff-Thomas, whose comissioned photographs include front and back covers, Figs 1.5, 7.2-3, 8.3-5, 9.1-2, 9.4-7, 9.14, 10.2-3, 15.1-3, 15.5, 15.7, 15.9-11, 18.3, 22.2 and 24.6. together with Plates 5 to 15 and 17b; Duncan Brown for the tile drawings; Derek Hurst for Fig 18.6 (tile from 2005 excavations similar to that rescued by G.G.Scott); Duncan James for photography showing replacement side of base of Leominster chalice (Fig 22.5b) and the dawings 23.2 and 23.3; Dave Lovelace for images of Leominster parliamentary returns in the National Archives (Fig 16.10); Joyce Marston for Stockton dovecote and barn (Fig 19.4); Chris Musson and Ruth Richardson for aerial photographs from the Woolhope Club Millennium Air Survey; Tony Reeve for the photograph of the Ionic/Green Man capital, probably from the minster (Plate 18); Richard Sermon for the photograph of dole window at Gloucester (Fig 11.7) and help with procuring others from Gloucester; Tim Ward for postcards of Corn Square (Figs 23.4 and 23.5); Bruce Watson for photographs of 2005 excavation (Figs 1.1 and 24.1); all other photographs, Joe & Caroline Hillaby, with thanks to Richard Winterbourn for access for photography at Crowards Mill. Thanks are due to Catherine Hall for the index.

Foreword

One of the most significant moments of my life was when I was offered the post of Vicar of Leominster by the Bishop of Hereford in 1979. I have never forgotten my first visit to the Priory where I soon realised that I was entering a huge heritage. The foundation of this holy place goes back to 660AD and there was probably a Christian presence or church even earlier. This holy place surrounded by water where four rivers meet was where baptisms took place as the first people embraced the Christian faith. This has been a place of worship and prayer for over 1,300 years. Although it is comparatively unknown it ranks alongside St David's Cathedral, Iona and other great places of pilgrimage. It is a liminal place where the boundaries of earth and heaven are very close. Worship and prayer continue to be at the very heart of Leominster Priory in the 21st Century and is there for people today who have a great hunger for spiritual things.

It is fascinating to read the detail of the late Anglo-Saxon prayer book which belonged to Leominster Priory. It is good that this has now been recognised because prayer has been at the very heart of this foundation which has had such an important influence on the Diocese of Hereford. It is both exciting and intriguing to read the detail of the history of this book and its proper attribution to Leominster Priory where it belongs.

Leominster is fortunate that the parochial church remained a part of the conventual building. Joe points out that conflict which arose between monks and parishioners often led to the building of separate parish churches. This did not happen in Leominster and I believe has helped the town to have a sense of unity because there has been no conflict between two separate parish churches. The conflict in Leominster has always been contained in one place.

Leominster Priory deserves a scholarly book of this nature which Joe and Caroline Hillaby have written. There are so many puzzles about this building and how it was intended to be, which are carefully explored. The destruction of the east end and the monastic church at the dissolution of the monasteries make it more difficult in trying to solve the mystery of the intentions of the original architect. As you read you can hear the infectious enthusiasm with which Joe and Caroline speak about Leominster Priory.

Like the Priory itself, *Leominster Minster, Priory and Borough* points to something beyond, far greater than anything we can imagine; the transcendent God but also the immanent God who is in our midst, Emmanuel, has promised to be with us to the end of time. This book has an eternal dimension like its subject and I hope many will have the joy and benefit of reading it and seeing to the heart of what Leominster Priory represents.

+Michael Ludlow

The Feast of the Transfiguration
6 August 2006

The Right Reverend Michael Hooper, Bishop & Archdeacon of Ludlow

Introduction

Founded about 660, Leominster's church originally served the spiritual needs of the people living in much of Herefordshire north of Dinmore. This role was assumed by its successors, the vicars and chaplains of the parochial church established in the nave of the Benedictine priory, c1123. The borough of Leominster, founded shortly after, quickly became the economic, commercial and cultural focus for that district.

Don King first suggested an application to the Local Heritage Initiative to fund a project on Leominster priory. The LHI is a national grant scheme to help community groups to investigate, explain and care for their local landscape, landmarks, traditions and culture. Although the Heritage Lottery Fund provides the grant, the scheme is a partnership, administered by the Countryside Agency with additional funding from the Nationwide Building Society. John Campbell's application, code-named 'Operation Leofric', was successful. It originally comprised four elements: a geophysical survey north of the priory, to identify the site of the conventual buildings about the cloister, and facilitate the construction of a model of the monastery, with its ancillary buildings. The third element was to be a comprehensive history of the priory, to engage that wider community which Leominster had served for more than 13 centuries as religious centre, and for some nine centuries as market town. To stimulate involvement, a highly successful play on the early history of the monastery was produced. With a cast of more than 50, it was enjoyed by an audience of some 450 people.

The geophysical survey was carried out in 2003, in two stages: a resistivity survey followed by a radar survey. The *Report* presented both disappointed and surprised. Survival of archaeology in the cloister area was in no way as good as at the east end of the priory, surveyed in 1997, and revealed little if anything of the layout of the monastery, giving no indication of the walls of the north transept or its semi-circular chapel. On the other hand, the survey did reveal what appeared to be a substantial circular building, some 17 metres across. Such a structure is quite alien to a cloister garth. It thus either pre- or post-dated the cloister.

With no details of claustral and other monastic buildings, the model project had to be abandoned. Given LHI agreement, funds were transferred to an excavation to determine the nature, and date, of the circular structure, provisionally interpreted as a Saxon rotunda. Permission was granted by English Heritage and Herefordshire Council, and support from the British Archaeology Challenge fund, for an evaluation dig under the auspices of the Museum of London Archaeological Service. This was undertaken in August 2005 by the Friends and local volunteers. It emerged that there was a serious error in the ground radar data, and that the rotunda structure did not exist. Nevertheless, carbon-dating of some of the excavation finds provided invaluable archaeological evidence to support the documentary dating of the minster site. It indicated two periods of occupation, 655–775 and 775–900, and provided evidence relating to it successor, the priory, founded c1123.

The lively response to the challenge offered by the geophysical survey is not surprising, for it fell on fertile ground. An extended version of the author's 1986/7 presidential address to the Woolhope Club, the county's archaeological, local and natural history society, published in the Club's *Transactions* for 1987, argued, in some detail, that the, then, British Museum's Nero Aii/ Galba Axiv prayer book was in fact a single volume, and that its place of origin was not the famous Winchester nun-minster founded by King Alfred c900, but the Leominster nunnery recorded in Domesday Book. The following year, B.J. Muir's edition of the Nero/Galba prayer book was published by the Henry Bradshaw Society. Muir also firmly believed that Nero and Galba were in origin one manuscript, but that it was 'probably used at St Mary's convent, Winchester'. This stimulated further debate at the British Archaeological Association Hereford Conference in 1995, leading to a weekend school and a series of lectures on the Saxon minster, its foundation legend and the prayer book, events which culminated in June 2000 in a conference, organised by the Leominster Historical Society and Leominster History Study Group, on 'The Early Church in Herefordshire', attended by over 200 people. Speakers included John Blair, Fellow of Queens College, Oxford, and John Harper, Director General of the Royal School of Church Music. The LHS summer visit that year was to Reading, to see the abbey and its capitals in the town's museum, to compare the early topography of the two medieval boroughs, and to visit Cholsey, the other Saxon nunnery granted, with its lands, by Henry I to his foundation at Reading.

John Blair underlined Leominster's status in the 7th–8th centuries in no uncertain fashion. 'If minsters were few and far between (west of the Severn, c650–750), one was outstandingly important … from a national perspective, the place looks highly exceptional. Leominster's area of parochial dependence was at least 12 miles across, one of the biggest mother parishes known in England'. In the book it is argued that originally it was even larger. 'It had three Anglo-Saxon saints, which is most unusual for a non-cathedral site before the (10th-century) Benedictine Reform; and the area around the monastic centre was articulated by complex territorial divisions and satellite settlements', a reference to its four *herneys*, based on burys, monastic granges, at Luston, Ivington, Stockton and Stoke. Blair concluded, 'whatever the reasons for Leominster's exceptional character, it is an early medieval centre of not merely local but national significance, which deserves far more archaeological investigation than it has yet received'. He has even suggested that Hereford may have been inserted 'into an older religious landscape dominated by minsters' such as Leominster and Ledbury.

Two years later, Blair included Leominster's three unique saints — Edfrith, founder of the minster, Haemma, first abbot of the monastery, and the mysterious Aethelmod — in his *Handlist of Anglo-Saxon Saints*. The trio are to be found in both the Calendar of saints in the Nero Aii section of the Leominster prayer book, and in the lengthy litany which forms an important element amongst the Galba Axiv prayers, thus proving not only that the two manuscripts are indeed, as Muir believed, a unity, but that both emanated from the minster beside the Lugg, founded by King Merewalh. At the same time, the 'compelling argument' put forward in 1987 was reviewed by Rebecca Rushforth, who pointed out that 'the manuscripts (of Nero and Galba) were written in very interesting script, both Insular and Caroline, with high-grade intentions but seemingly from without what we understand as the mainstream scribal traditions of the period; this argues against a Winchester origin'. Doubts remain. At Winchester, the case for the Galba prayer book being from Leominster 'has not been generally accepted'.

The book is intended to be of interest to both the local, lay reader and, given the importance of the minster's early history and its Anglo-Saxon prayer book, to a wider, specialist audience. As far as possible, a number of the principal characters in the story have been enabled to speak in their own words. These include the canons or nuns who wrote some remarkable prayers in the Nero/Galba prayer book; the author of the *Life* of St Mildburg of Wenlock, who provides our only account of the foundation of the minster by the Lugg, c660; such leading figures as King Henry I, bishops Robert de Bethune, St Thomas Cantilupe, Richard Swinfield and John Trillek; as well as the words used at his show trial in the cathedral by that severe local critic of the medieval church, the Welsh Lollard, Walter le Brut, whose spiritual successors were to play such a prominent role in the history of the borough in the mid 17th century.

The inter-library loan service, based on the British Library at Boston Spa, makes almost all books and periodical literature available for home reading. In order that readers can pursue their personal interests, many references include suggestions for further reading. A copy of both volumes of Kemp's *Reading Abbey Cartularies* has been deposited in Leominster Library. It is hoped these can be supplemented by Muir's edition of the Nero/Galba prayer book.

1 The Foundation and Site of the Minster on the Lugg, c660

Foundation

The conversion of Merewalh, ruler of the folk west of the Severn, by Edfrith, a Northumbrian monk, and the foundation of the minster on the banks of the Lugg, form part of the *Life* of St Mildburg. She was one of Merewalh's three daughters by his marriage to the Kentish princess, Eafe. Merewalh, we are told, 'royally endowed' his minster. The *Life* first describes the royal lineage of Mildburg's parents, and then recounts the Leominster foundation legend. 'Merewalh, king of the Mercians, was completely devoted to paganism when the holy Edfrith, famous for his learning and warned by a heavenly vision, came from Northumbria to convert him. Having received divine bidding, he made his way to the land of the Mercians, to a place called *Reodesmuthe*. On arrival he prayed before eating. A huge lion, with bristling mane, appeared. Quite unperturbed, Edfrith offered it bread which it ate at his feet, like a lamb. The lion then disappeared'.

Shortly after, Edfrith was invited into Merewalh's presence to interpret a dream, which troubled the king sorely and none could explain. Two enormous and hideous dogs were about to go for his throat, but a venerable person, with hair cut above his ears in the shape of a crown, snatched him from the dogs' jaws, aided by a golden key. Edfrith explained he should not be troubled by the dream, for it betokened his salvation. 'Listen therefore my king, to understand the horrendous aspect of the dogs that attacked you and the benign face of the key bearer, your saviour. The hideous dogs are the soot-black attendants of Satan, enemies of life and salvation. They bring death and in their jaws you would be prey to be devoured and, having been devoured, to be eaten again forever. Thus, always dying but never completely dead, with those in the midst of hell you will be tortured by perpetual terrors, fumes of sulphur, gnashings of teeth, burning of the fire and terrible and unbearable punishments, unless you wholeheartedly deny your pagan beliefs and, from the depths of your soul, turn to Christ the Son of the living God.

'The key bearer by whose power you were saved from these dogs is the keeper of the gates of heaven, leader of the heavenly host, and on earth the vicar of Christ, Saviour of the world. His golden key is the heavenly power by which he binds whatever is bound and frees whatever is free. Build a church to him in your realm, so that praise and thanks be given day and night to the King on High. Believe in Him in your heart, profess your faith in Him with your mouth, and wear the garb of His baptism. Once you have denied the devilish rites of the pagan life and the profane cults of idolatry, you will become acceptable to the heavenly kingdom where eternal and blessed joy knows nought of failure and death. Freed from the fangs of the hounds by acceptance of the faith of your deliverer, the Blessed Peter, you will be an heir, joyous and everlasting, to this kingdom.'

With these and other essentials of the faith, Edfrith brought the good news of Christ to the king who, having listened carefully, said: 'if I can avoid being torn and devoured by such terrible beasts, I accept with devoted submission whatsoever your Christian doctrine teaches me'. Overcome by heaven's mercy, the king destroyed every one of his idols. Crying out in lamentation, he was driven to total repentance. He set aside the insignia of kingship — the sceptre, the purple and the crown — putting on sackcloth and ashes. Throwing himself at the feet of the saint, he abjured his paganism, professing the worship of God. Reborn in the sacred water, he offered devotion to all his evangelist had taught him. King Merewalh's baptism took place '660 years after Our Lord's incarnation'.

'Thus the king, hitherto like the lion that appeared to Edfrith, became meeker than a lamb, receiving the true faith, the bread of life, from his guest and teacher. At the site where Merewalh's conversion had been foretold by the Lord, in the form of the lion which had appeared to Edfrith, a church was built, dedicated to Peter, the king's deliverer and the gatekeeper of heaven. The house thus founded was richly furnished and royally endowed from the king's wealth. Placed under Edfrith's authority, it later became the monastery of the lion. May the memory of the blessed Edfrith, the saint who first brought the grace of the true light to shine brightly on the western shores of Mercia, be honoured, world without end. Amen.'[1]

Mildburg's convent at Much Wenlock was refounded as a Cluniac priory, 1080–81. The *Vita Sancte Milburge verginis* was written at the time of the translation of her relics into a new shrine at Wenlock c1101. There was apparently a rival cult at Leominster, which also held her relics (Table 6, no 36), and celebrated her festival on 23 February. There are two extant copies of the full text of the *Life*. One is in the 13th-century British Library Additional MS 34,633, where it is the second of six items. This manuscript had belonged to the Augustinian priory of St Mary at Beddgelert, Gwynedd. The second copy, together with *The Miracles of Mildburg*, is in the 14th-century *Forschungs-bibliothek Gotha*, MS. I, 81, f166v-175r. Both are derived, ultimately, from a lost Wenlock original. Variations between the texts are minor.[2] The early 14th-century BL Harley MS 2253 contains the passage from Mildburg's *Life* on *The Legend of St Etfrid, Priest of Leominster* (see Fig 25.2). There are also two brief lectionary versions, to be read during Divine Office on the occasion of her festival.[3]

In so far as it 'displays the role of the king as the converter of his people', the conversion of Merewalh and his folk west of the Severn is 'typical of the history of the coming of Christianity to Anglo-Saxon England. In no kingdom did the conversion occur without such royal leadership, and in none do we hear of the conversion of the folk without that of the monarch previously', for the pagan kings were intermediaries between their folk and their gods. It was part of the rapid process described by Bede of the formal acceptance of Christianity throughout most of greater Mercia by 660. This was the work of the Columban church of Northumbria, from its base at Lindisfarne, Holy Island, founded by St Aidan from Iona in 635 — not of the Roman church, founded in 597 by Augustine in the kingdom of Kent. Paulinus, first bishop of York, came to England in the entourage of Augustine. He accompanied Aethelburg, daughter of King Aethelbert, to Northumbria following her betrothal to the Northumbrian king Edwin, whom he baptised at York in 627. After the victory of Penda, pagan king of Mercia c632–55, and the death of Edwin, Paulinus fled back to Kent in 633.[4]

According to Bede, Penda did not forbid the preaching of the faith in Mercia, and his son, Peada, ruler of the Middle Angles, was baptised on his marriage to the daughter of the

Northumbrian King Oswy in 653, 'with all his companions, thegns and servants'. Peada then 'arranged for four priests, chosen for their learning and holy life, to instruct and baptise his people'. Formal introduction of Christianity into Mercia came after Penda's defeat and death in 655, after which Oswy ruled Mercia for three years. On the accession of Penda's son, Wulfhere, 658–74, a Northumbrian, Trumhere, served as his first bishop (see Fig 2.1). Bede recounts in detail the conversion of the Northumbrian folk following Edwin's baptism. At Yeavering Paulinus was constantly 'occupied for 36 days in instructing and baptising the common people and then washing them in the cleansing water of baptism in the nearby river of Glen'. The Lugg at Leominster, by the newly-founded church of St Peter, would have provided an ideal site for such a spectacular folk baptism.[5]

If the conversion of Merewalh's folk was c660, what confidence can be attributed to Edfrith's primary role? There is early evidence from the church of Leominster itself. Amongst the British Library's Cottonian manuscripts is an Anglo-Saxon prayer book, Nero Aii/Galba Axiv, discussed more fully in Chapter 3. Some of its contents were garnered over a very long period; a few may go back to the minster's earliest years. The prayer book includes, as its first item, a calendar that lists, month by month, the saints' days to be commemorated. On 26 October is the feast of *sci eadfridi. conf.*, Edfrith the confessor, sanctified for the holiness of his life. He is also invoked, as *Sancte Entferth*, in a long litany of saints, between *Sancte Aethelmod* and *Sancte Hemma*, Leominster's two other saints (Fig 3.2). These point to an unbroken tradition at the minster church of liturgical observance, particularly of Edfrith and his cult, from the 7th century. The evidence for such continuity is considered in Chapter 2.[6]

Excavations were conducted on the site of the priory cloister during August 2005 by Bruce Watson of the Museum of London Archaeological Service and Peter Busby of English Heritage, assisted by a number of volunteers. These were funded by the Friends of Leominster Priory through the Local Heritage Initiative. An evaluation trench, 16.85m long and 5m wide, was opened up within the south-west portion of the Old Priory Buildings car park. Two residual struck flints indicated some prehistoric activity on the site. Parts of a small pit of Roman date, but uncertain function, were found. Two residual Roman tile fragments were also found, in a Saxon

Fig. 1.1 The excavation of 2005 showing the line of the Saxon ditch indicated between the arrows

context, indicating some Roman presence, unless they were brought to the site during the Saxon period for re-use.[7]

Initial Saxon activity probably consisted of dumping subsoil and marl to level up the natural south/north ground slope. The earliest features were a series of ditches and pits, which contained numerous animal and fish bones and daub. Fig 1.1 shows the line of the early Saxon ditch, where the pits were discovered. The wide variety of large and small bones present suggests that the area excavated was used for rubbish disposal, probably for the small community of priests or monks caring for the spiritual needs of the people of the surrounding area, the *parochia*. The ditches and pits were sealed by a series of levelling dumps, also rich in animal bones. A sample from the next-to-top spit produced a further date. Radiocarbon dates were obtained from four animal bone samples. A chronological model for the radiocarbon dates by Alex Bayliss, English Heritage Scientific Dating Co-ordinator, indicates two periods of occupation: AD 655–775 (95% probability) and AD 775–900 (95% probability). This confirms late 7th-8th century occupation, continuing for some 200 years.[8] The excavation also provided evidence relating to the priory, founded c1123, which is described in later chapters.

The Cult of Edfrith

Edfrith's cult continued to flourish after the foundation of Leominster Priory as a cell of Henry I's great Benedictine abbey of Reading. In the 1290s Leominster's great autumn fair, which attracted clients from as far as central Wales, was held on the vigil and feast of St Edfrith, 26 October, and four days following. Some 50 years later the brief section, now called *The Legend of St Etfrid, Priest of Leominster*, was copied from Wenlock Abbey's copy of Mildburg's *Life* into what is now BL Harley MS 2253, which also includes an abbreviated *Life* of St Aethelbert, patron of Hereford cathedral, and a *Martyrdom* of the north Worcestershire saint, Wistan. This and other internal evidence suggest the manuscript was compiled for Adam de Orleton, bishop of Hereford 1317–27, while he held the see of Worcester, 1327–33. John Trillek, bishop of Hereford 1344–61, borrowed Wenlock's copy of Mildburg's *Life*, evidently to make his own, giving a written bond as security for its return. In 1433 Bishop Spofford's Register records that the, undated, principal festivals of Leominster Priory included that of St Edfrith. The date is confirmed, however, by its position, after the dedication of the priory's relics, on 10 October, and before the feast of SS Simon and Jude, 28 October. Edfrith's cult survived both Dissolution and Reformation, for another *Life*, in the vernacular, was published in 1605. Its purpose was not to attract pilgrims but to foster civic pride, by stressing the antiquity of the borough to which Queen Mary had granted a charter in 1554.[9]

The Place-name

Leomynstre, in the will of Wulfgeat of Donnington, c975, in which he left the minster four full-grown bullocks, is the earliest form of the place-name. It is found in a similar form, as *Leomynster* in the *Anglo-Saxon Chronicles*: in the C, Abingdon Abbey, version for 1046, when Earl Swein 'commanded the abbess to be fetched to him'; and in the D, Worcester Priory, version for 1052, when the Welsh under Gruffudd ap Llywelyn came 'very near' to Leominster; and as *Leuministre* in the mid-12th century Latin text of Rhigyfarch's *Life* of St David, of 1056/7–99. The first element is the Old English *leon*, which occurs in other local place-names: Lyonshall, *Lenehalle* of Domesday Book, and Leen Farm, Pembridge, close to the place where Rowe Ditch crosses the Arrow. It is the second element in Eardisland, Kingsland, Monkland and Nokelane in Pembridge. In all cases *leon* refers to the lowland district watered by the Lugg and Arrow, with their tributaries, the Pinsley, Ridgemoor and (western) Stretford brooks. It also occurred as the name of a Herefordshire Domesday hundred, when *Lene* was a much smaller area. The place-name Leominster may have inspired Mildburg's hagiographer to include the episode of Merewalh and the lion, as it apparently incorporated the genitive of *leo*, 'of the lion'. But to locals it represented something of much more practical significance. The land of Lene was the distinctive name of their district, from which they gained their sense of identity.[10]

The Old English *leon* comes from the Old Welsh *lion* or *lian*, from the root *lei*, 'to flow, to water', as in the Welsh *lliant*, a torrent or stream. These two forms are found in a Staunton-on-Arrow charter of 958, which refers to the bounds of *Lionhina* or Leonhiena *gemæres*, the (religious) community of *Lion* or *Leon*. This Old Welsh district name would therefore be 'the streams', that is the Lugg, Kenwater, Pinsley and Arrow, and Leominster 'the minster on the streams' or 'the minster of the district of the streams'. However, William Owen Pughe's *Welsh and English Dictionary* (1803) goes further. Having explained that *llion* is the plural form of *lli*, 'a multitudinous flux, an aggregate of floods', he refers to *Llyn llion* as 'the lake of streams, an inexhaustible collection of waters, popularly supposed to be in the earth', with his example from Taliesin. For R.J. Thomas, in view of the noun *lliant*, 'sea, flood', *llieni* is 'watery region'. A more satisfactory interpretation is thus probably, 'the minster of the district of floods'. Leland reported in 1535–43 that Leominster was 'caullyd in Walche *Llan-llieny*' and elsewhere '*Llinlini*'. As late as 1893, J.E. Southall heard an old woman from Abbey Cwmhir recite a doggerel she had first heard many years earlier:

How many miles, how many
Is it from Leominster to Llanllieni?

and was assured, despite the disappearance of Welsh from Radnorshire in the 18th century, that it was still so known by some Welsh people.[11]

An island site

Island sites were dear to the heart of the monks of the early Irish church. Skellig Michael, off the coast of Kerry, is the most spectacular example, but St Columba's church at Iona in Scotland, and St Aidan's at Lindisfarne, Holy Island in Northumbria, are, from our point of view, the most significant. Such islands were not always sea-girt. Clonmacnoise, founded in the 6th century by St Kieran, had the Shannon on one side and marshland on the other. At Glastonbury, the 'royal island', it would be difficult to determine where sea ended and marsh began.

Of the local saints mentioned in the longer litany of the Leominster Anglo-Saxon prayer book, St Cynidr had an island hermitage in the Wye near Bredwardine whilst St Triac gave his name to the tiny island still to be seen off Beachley Point when bound for Wales on the old Severn bridge.[12] The hermitage of St Guthlac (673–714) at Crowland could be reached only by boat, and St Aetheldreda (d679) also chose a place in the Fens, the isle of Ely. Less intimidating but nevertheless island sites, on Thanet and Sheppey in the Thames estuary, were adopted by Merewalh's wife, Eafe, and her aunt, Sexburg (dc700), for their princess minsters. Another, at Barking, must have had a similar situation.

Surrounded on all sides by water and marsh, Leominster was virtually an island site at the time of Edfrith's arrival. It was connected with the world beyond merely by a narrow neck of flood-free land at Cholstrey. Even today the impact of the drainage pattern on Leominster's imme-

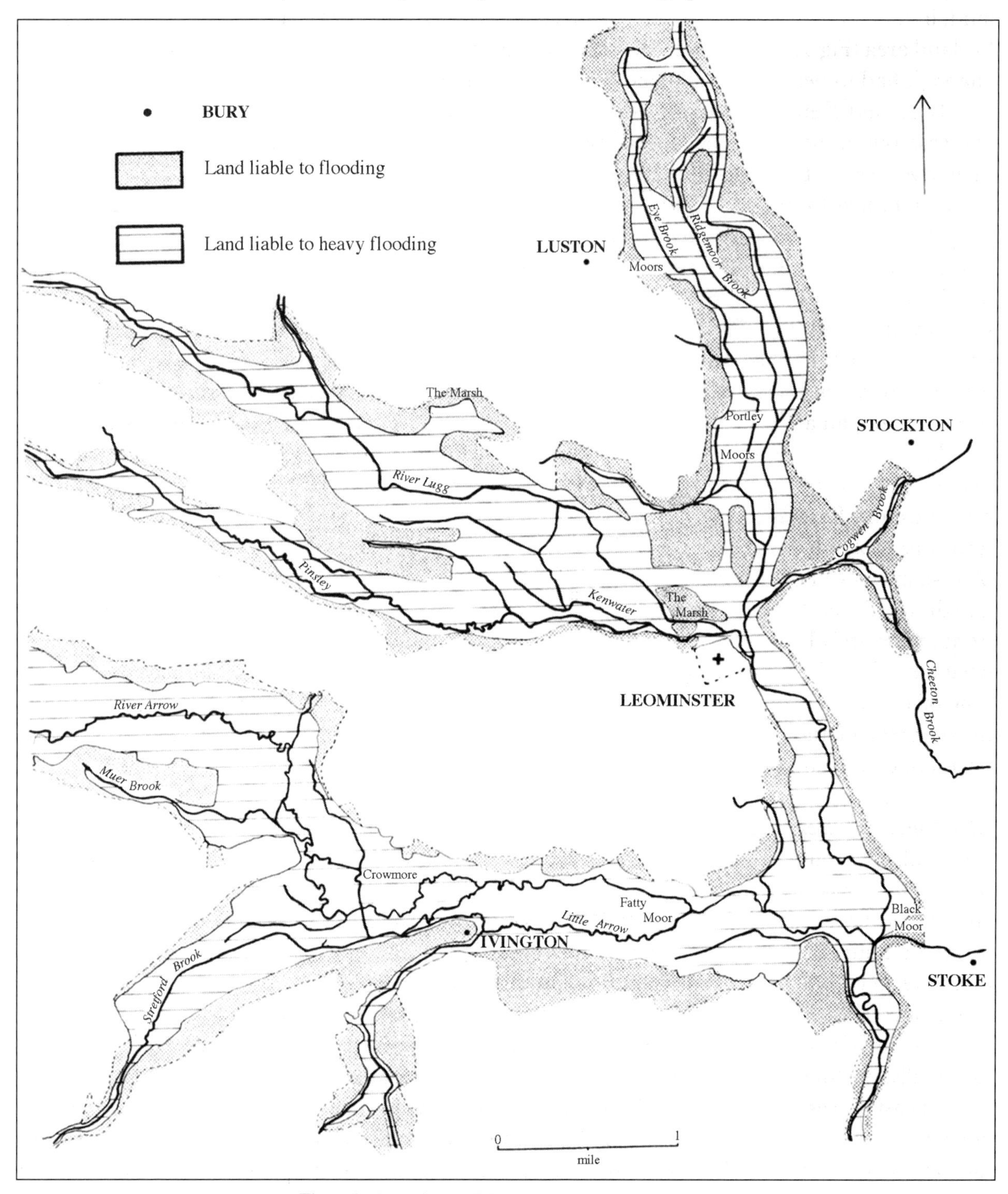

Fig 1.2 Leominster District: lands liable to flood

diate neighbourhood can be starkly illustrated by reference to the Ordnance Survey Agricultural Land Classification Map, where liability to flooding is an important factor in the fivefold grading of agricultural land. Except at Cholstrey the town is surrounded by the yellow fingers of Grade 4 land, in marked contrast to the predominant blue of the superior Grade 2 land of the rest of the lowland area (Fig 1.2). As late as the reign of Edward VI, the borough was able to claim the great charge it had to bear 'with ten stone bridges to maintain'.[13]

Lugg and Kenwater still provide natural boundaries for the minster's precinct on the north and east, but in the 7th century they flowed through extensive tracts of marsh, fed not only by the main river system but also by the Eye and Ridgemoor brooks from the north, and the Cogwell and Cheaton brooks from the east. About a mile to the south flowed the Arrow, with its tributaries, the Tippet and Stretford brooks. The area immediately north of the Kenwater has always been called, as today, the Marsh. Beyond lay the Broad, a term originally meaning 'lake' or 'expanse of water', but the wetlands extended much further north. The ancient church at Eye was built on what was virtually an island just above the 75m contour between the Ridgemoor and Eye brooks. A mile beyond is Marsh Hill between Ashton and Orleton, '*tun*, amongst the alders'. To the west fenland extended between Lugg and Pinsley as far as Cobnash, Holgate and Lugg Green, half a mile north of Kingsland, an area carefully avoided by the Roman road going north to Mortimer's Cross.

Locally, since the first records, such land liable to flood has been called 'more'. Originally 'barren waste-land', in the north it became 'barren, uncultivated high ground', but in the south, midlands and East Anglia, 'marshland', as in Sedgemoor and Wedmore — and moorhen. The term was probably current to the end of the 9th century. When these lands were drained, the old place-names lived on. They thus came to mean 'a low flat level of former marshland, reclaimed and drained', and 'marsh' became pasture or even arable, as entries in Coningsby's *Register*, drawn from the priory's 14th-century court rolls, reveal. The number and range of such references show what a marked characteristic of the landscape of Lene these marshlands would have been at the time of the minster's foundation, and how far they had been transformed in the 700 years before the outbreak of the Black Death. In Edfrith's day the setting of the monastic enclosure will have been not dissimilar to that at Glastonbury.[14]

The Sacred Enclosure

Even today, the outstanding landscape feature of Leominster as a town is the precinct of its Anglo-Saxon minster, which proclaims its original role of dividing the sacred from the profane. As the church was built at the north-east end of its island site, the Lugg, its tributaries and marshlands formed a natural boundary on those two sides. A bank and outer ditch, a *vallum monasterii*, had therefore to be built only on the south and west. A watercourse flowed down a ditch outside the south bank to the Pinsley. 16th- and 17th-century court leet records are full of presentments of residents on the north side of Etnam Street for failing to 'scour the Town Ditch against their gardens'. Originally, marshes, watercourses, ditch and bank together formed a trapezoidal enclosure, some 1,200ft east to west and 1,100 north to south, approximately 150,000 square yards in area. By the cricket ground, a considerable part of the great earthen bank can still be seen. This gives some indication of how impressive it must once have been. Yet air photographs and the current 25" OS plan indicate how woefully eroded this division between precinct and secular world beyond has

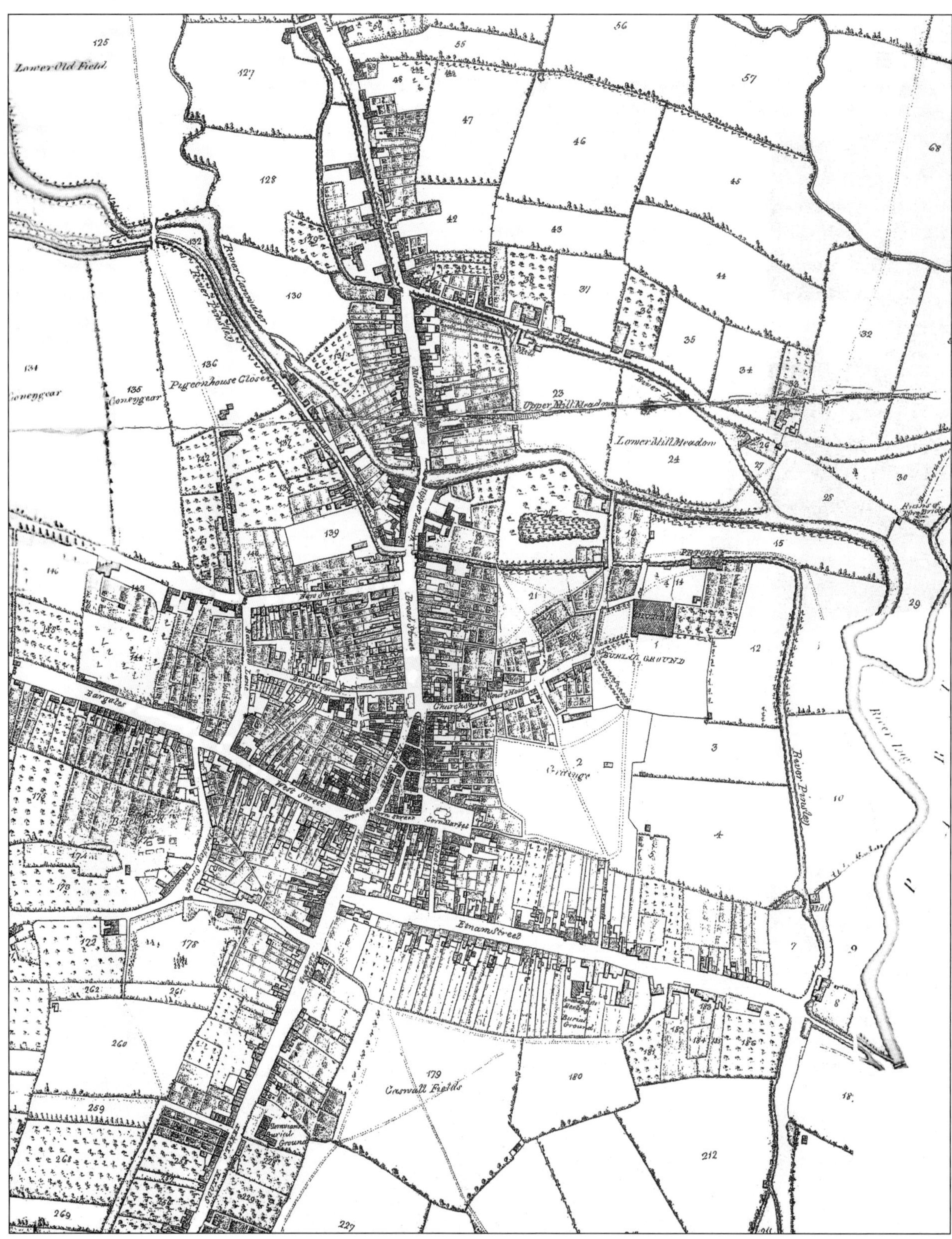

Fig 1.3 Gallier's 25" Plan of Leominster, *'ordered to be made Sept 26,1832 at a cost of £150'*

Fig 1.4 Aerial photo showing the precinct from the east (99-MB-0234)

become, as compared to the closes of many of our major cathedrals. Nevertheless, it remains one of the most notable enclosures of any of our greater Anglo-Saxon non-cathedral minster churches. Its only serious rival is Glastonbury (Figs 1.3 – 1.4).

As early as 1808 this striking feature aroused the curiosity of the Rev Jonathan Williams. In his *Historical and Topographical View of the Ancient and Present State of Leominster* he drew attention to the fact that even then 'only a part of the southern side remains now in a state of perfection, the other sides having been levelled ... partly for the formation of private gardens and the foundations of houses and partly for dividing the course of the Pinsley'. 'Its *vallum* and *fossa*, its square figure, its rectilinear sides, its elevated praetorian station' were, he suggested, 'strong indications of Roman art

Fig 1.5 The south-west corner of the monastic precinct with recent brick wall

and construction'. This is not the case. A camp with ramparts on but two sides would be in total conflict with the Roman military handbooks, and the two Roman roads running north-south, reflected in the place-names Stretford, carefully avoid the marshy ground about Leominster, passing 1½ and 4 miles to the east and west respectively. Since Williams' comments, the *vallum monasterii* has been overlooked by both historians and archaeologists. No part of the *vallum monasterii*, and only a small part of the precinct, has been included in the scheduling of the priory by English Heritage.

Construction of bank and ditch took place long before the priory's foundation c1123, for these were not characteristic of Benedictine precinct planning. The burgage plots on the east of Broad Street and Drapers Lane had to terminate at the ditch and bank, subsequently strengthened by the priory wall, as did the later burgage plots of Etnam Street. At Reading, no such earthworks protected the abbey from the considerable borough at its gates. A bank marked off part of the precinct at the Cistercian abbey of Bordesley near Redditch, but did not 'serve as a *vallum monasterii* as in earlier monasteries, for it did not surround the whole monastic area'. It was built 'to protect the low-lying land near the river from flooding'. At Leominster the bank was quite different. On the south and west, away from the Lugg and Pinsley to the north and east, it could not have served this purpose.[15]

Did Merewalh, or his sons, command the resources to construct some 500 yards of bank and ditch about the site of Edfrith's church? Were such banks and ditches part of contemporary culture? The answer to both questions is undoubtedly in the affirmative. Rowe Ditch, west of Pembridge, 'the most obvious feature of the early Anglo-Saxon period' in this area, extends some 2¼ miles across the valley of the Arrow and Curl brooks between Vallet Covert and Pitfield Farm. It has a ditch in places over 2m deep and 5m wide, and a bank of considerable height. Hill and Worthington concluded that Rowe Ditch was pre-Offan. Excavations in 2003 suggest that the Ditch 'dates from the earliest arrival of the English in numbers in the Arrow valley, cAD 650,' for, whereas Offa's Dyke west of Lyonshall seems to have been slotted into the field patterns, Rowe Ditch cuts through earlier settlement and landscape boundaries and 'considerable Roman remains', including 'Roman material redeposited in the bank'. With no apparent strategic advantage, the Ditch is believed to represent 'a line of occupation'. In this case it is a formidable tribute to the resources at the disposal of the incoming Anglian ruler.[16]

The church had, from the earliest times, marked off its sacred enclosures from the profane world beyond by bank and ditch, an inheritance from the pagan past, stretching back as far as Avebury and Stonehenge. In Adomnán's *Life* of Columba are repeated references to the *vallum monasterii*. The ideal enclosure was circular, but 'an ideal rarely attained on the ground'.[17] In Ireland curvilinear enclosures were the norm. Armagh is one of the few to have been excavated and subjected to detailed survey. An early 17th-century plan revealed the cathedral at the centre of two concentric enclosures. The 1968 excavation showed the ditch of the inner enclosure to be some 6.5m wide and 2 to 3m deep. The Welsh church also had a predilection for curvilinear enclosures, and a recent survey has even identified a number of largely curved churchyards in north-east Herefordshire, including Pencombe, Much Cowarne, Mathon and Castle Frome.[18]

Rectangular Enclosures

The only major rectangular ecclesiastical enclosures to be subjected to detailed archaeological investigation are those at Iona and Glastonbury. Elsewhere, at Clonmacnoise, Charles Thomas's 1958 and 1963 field surveys show a rectangular enclosure of 11 acres, with remnants of a bank of some 1,200ft on the east and 1,200ft or more to the south, with marshland and Shannon to the north and west. This, we are told, is not substantiated by later fieldwork and air photography. Yet for Nancy Edwards in 1989 such earthworks were still 'clearly visible' beside the river, and on the ridge to the south and east of the ruins.[19]

At Iona, founded by St Columba c563, the monastery from which St Aidan set out in 635 to evangelise Northumbria, traces of more than one *vallum* have been found by a combination of excavation, air photography and geophysical surveys. These extend some1,200ft on the north-north-east/south-south-west axis and a maximum of c1,000ft on the west-north-west/east-south-east axis. Radiocarbon dating shows that at least part of one of the *valla*, on the south, predates St Columba's arrival. As there was no such evidence fronting the shore, these earthworks were of a religious, not defensive, character. Documentary evidence supports the archaeological. In his *Life* of Columba, Adomnán refers to a monk going outside the 'monastery rampart', *vallum monasterii*, to kill a cow. In his description of Columba's visit to Clonmacnoise, Adomnán writes of the abbot and his monks 'passing outside the *vallum monasterii* to meet him', and elsewhere 'to certain places frequented by angels' as being 'within the enclosure, *cenubii septa*'. At Iona, there is, in addition, archaeological evidence of a cemetery, *Reilig Odhráin*, with its own chapel in an adjoining enclosure to the south, linked by a stone causeway to the main enclosure. The belief, as late as the 9th century in Ireland, that one could be defiled by contact with the dead, may well explain this separate cemetery.[20]

Deirdre O'Sullivan has extended the debate, by seeking to establish whether St Aidan took the Iona rectangular plan south to Lindisfarne. Certainly, relations with the mother house remained close after Aidan's death, for his two immediate successors as abbot, Finan and Colman, were both Iona monks. Here, as at Iona, the eastern edge of the enclosure fronted the shoreline. On Heugh Hill are the remains of structures, similar to those of the dispersed Irish type of monastery, below which, to the south, lies the shore. To the north is the present priory site; further north, Marygate, and to the west another lane, The Green. These, O'Sullivan suggests, reflect the bounds of a larger enclosure, comparable in size to that on Iona. Additionally Lindisfarne provides a particularly good example of the 'twinning' of an early minster with a royal centre, some three miles away. Here the link was by a causeway, even today passable only at low tide; at Leominster there is evidence of a royal centre at Kingsland, connected by the narrow Cholstrey land bridge between marsh and more.[21]

'The most convincing *vallum* of any Anglo-Saxon monastery' yet excavated is at Glastonbury. There in 1956–7 Ralegh Radford revealed part of both a bank and ditch, running north-south across the ruins of the 12th-century chapter-house, extending at least 200 feet. The V-shaped ditch was some 15ft wide and 7ft 6in. deep. The bank was to the west, 20 foot at the base and of an 'estimated' original height of almost 9 feet. These he interpreted as the vallum. In 1978 Leach and Ellis excavated a bank and ditch, running north-south, which they regarded as the north-east corner of the precinct. The radiocarbon dating of stakes, probably part of the palisade, was between c610 and 670, indicating that the bank and ditch may predate West Saxon control, for which the earliest evidence is a charter of 670 when the West Saxon king, Coenwealh, granted land at Meare to Abbot Beorhtwald. According to the Winchester manuscript of the Anglo-Saxon Chronicle, King Ine 'built the minster at Glastonbury' in 688. From the excavation data Rodwell postulates three possible circuits: the smallest, the least favoured, a precinct of 984 square feet; the second 984 x 1,180 feet; and the third 1,047 x 1,080 feet. In 1987 Humphrey Woods found a second, northern, line of the 1957 bank and ditch, confirming Radford's interpretations of the V-shaped ditch as the early *vallum monasterii*. The most recent indication of the width of the ditch is 13ft, and of the internal bank, 20ft. A firm date has yet to be established.[22]

Leominster's rectangular enclosure, unrecognised in any of the literature, is similar in its dimensions, some 1,100 x 1,200 feet, to Rodwell's second and third circuits. An early banked and ditched enclosure is not the only feature which the two monasteries have in common. Acording to Rhigyfarch, in his *Life* of the saint, both were founded by David. Both houses claimed some of his relics, but only at Leominster was his feast, on 1 March, included in the Calendar. Furthermore, in the longer litany of Leominster's prayer book a unique reference links St Indract and St Patrick. Their tombs, marked by 'pyramids', stone crosses, were the dominant features in the 'Old Church' at Glastonbury. However, probably the most significant link is the congruence, in terms of both entries and omissions, between Leominster's early 11th-century Calendar and those of the pre-Conquest group, emanating from Glastonbury (see Table 2).[23]

It has been assumed that rectangular minster enclosures were a rare phenomenon in England, but a recent and detailed study of Dorset minsters has revealed the predominance of strongly rectilinear areas surrounding most of the county's minsters, suggesting that the '*vallum monasterii*' of their precincts must also have been rectilinear. Roads and boundaries associated with such enclosures are aligned roughly north-south and east-west, with the minster and its precinct being accommodated in one of the angles formed by the crossroads.[24] A remarkably similar layout is to

Fig 1.6 Aerial photo showing the crossroads, the broken white line indicating the precinct boundary (99-MB-0232)

be found at the royal minsters of Leominster and Hereford, and episcopal minster of Ledbury. At all three the shape of the precinct is rectilinear, defined by the intersection of north-south and east-west roads.

At Leominster the north-south route was along the line of Broad Street, High Street and South Street, whilst the east-west route crossed the Lugg just below Pinsley mill, in a straight line to Corn Square, the Iron Cross and West Street (Fig 1.6). At the foundation of the borough in the 12th century, the eastern section of this route was realigned by one burgage length to create Etnam Street. The enclosure thus lay within the north-east angle of the cross. At Hereford the pattern was replicated when the minster church was founded, prior to 690. The north-south route is marked today by the line of Broad Street, down Gwynne Street to the Wye ford, and the east-west route by Castle Street, King Street and St Nicholas Street. Originally the cathedral was thus situated in the south-east angle of the crossroads, but the ground plan of the town was altered dramatically by William fitz Osbern, who created a vast new wedge-shaped market, delineated today by High Town, Commercial Street and Union Street. To deflect all traffic into his market, fitz Osbern closed the original east-west route by extending the Cathedral Close much further north (Fig 1.7). At Ledbury also the minster was within the south-east angle of a crossroads. The north-south route remains as Homend, High Street and the Southend. The east-west route came down from Dog Hill and Back Lane to the Lower Cross and Bye Street. Worcester Road, at the southern, narrower, end of the High Street, today the main road to the east, was a creation of the turnpike era.[25]

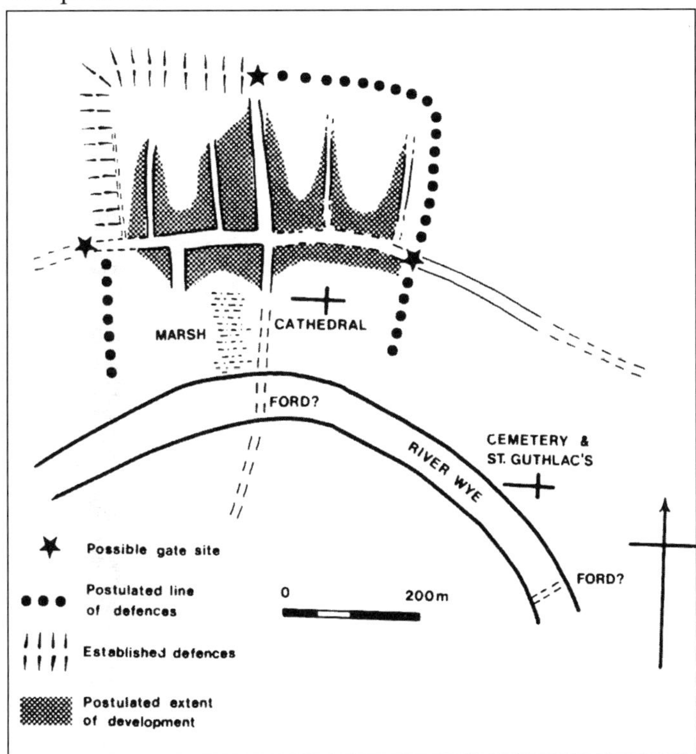

Fig 1.7 Hereford showing the central crossroads and initial defences with the cathedral in one of the subsequent qudrants

At all three sites the minster rapidly became the defining focus of its region, in economic and social as well as religious terms. For the folk of the district, Sunday attendance at the minster would be combined with all manner of buying and selling, for this became market day. Similarly, the principal festivals of the church year were also scenes of intense activity. On these occasions the area about *Corncepyng*, now contracted to Corn Square, and the Iron Cross would be full of sheep, cattle, poultry and farm produce, with craftsmen and pedlars selling their wares. The specialist requirements of the minster and the religious served to generate further economic activity. Similar scenes on a larger scale would be witnessed at the bishop's market-place about Broad Street in Hereford. At Leominster and Hereford such marketing was kept strictly beyond the ditch and bank of the enclosures. At Ledbury, however, the markets and fairs apparently encroached on the north-east angle of the minster enclosure, for the outline of the first market-place is betrayed even today by the lines of Church Street and Back Lane. These show that buying and selling on Sundays and festivals extended from the narrow end of the wedge, by the Lower Cross, to the broad end, by the present church gates.[26]

2 Merewalh, Eafe and their Children

Merewalh and his realm

Since Finberg's outstanding work on the *Life* and *Testament* of St Mildburg, the concern of historians has been with Merewalh's lineage, not his historicity. Was he Anglian or Welsh? Was he the son of the pagan Penda, king of Mercia c632–55, as the *Life* unambiguously proclaims? He was apparently recognised as of the line of Penda by Aethelbald, king of Mercia 716–57, who claimed consanguinity with Merewalh's daughter, Mildred, abbess of Minster-in-Thanet and later saint; Mildburg herself refers to Aethelred, king of Mercia, another of Penda's sons, as her uncle[27] (Fig 2.1).

In almost all texts, other than Mildburg's *Life*, her father's name is Merewalh, and this may throw some light on his ancestry. Merewalh, Gelling has suggested, means 'famous Welshman'. However, the Old English *walh* or *wealh*, from which the word 'Welsh' has been derived, was also a term for a man who spoke a Celtic language. Thus *Wealhstod*, the fourth bishop of Hereford, was a man who understood the language of a *wealh*. Additionally, *-wealh* names could be 'borne

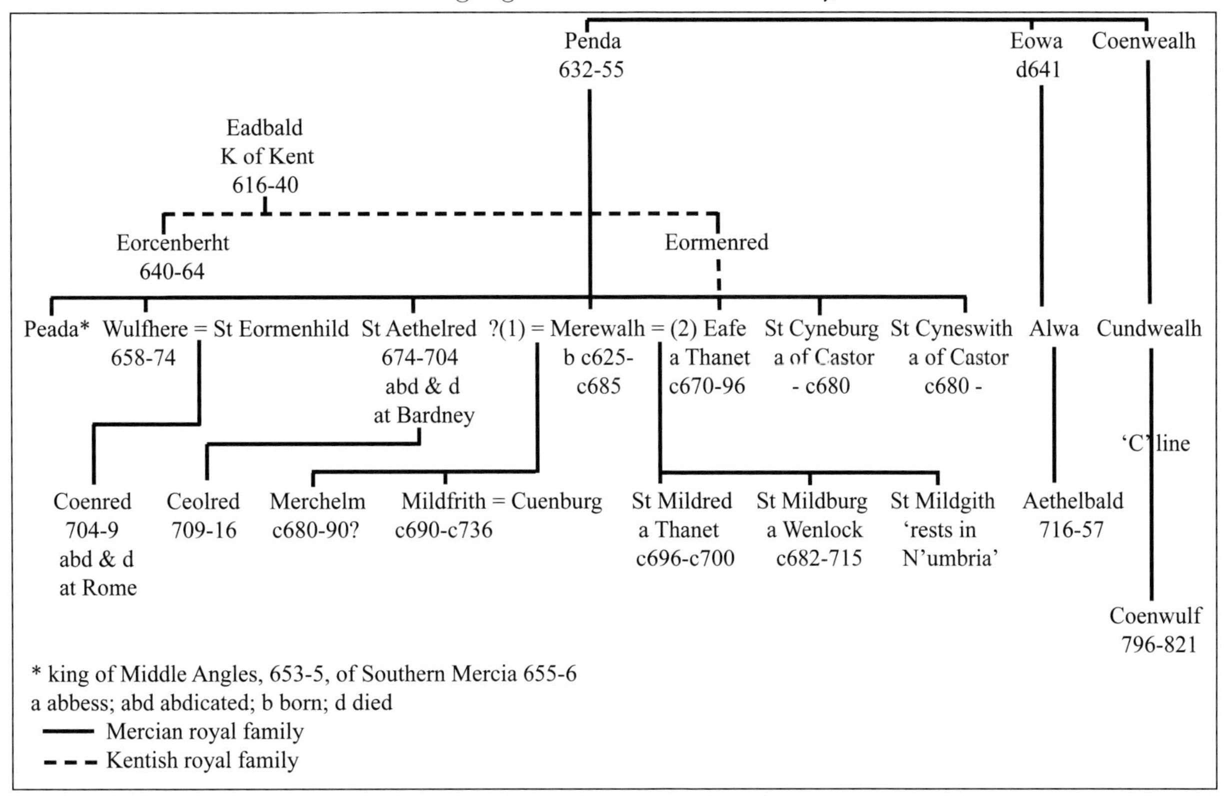

Fig 2.1 The Mercian Royal Family, 632–757

by English people of rank at an early date', and 'the use of this element should indicate that the holder had some Celtic blood'. Merewalh shared this second element with four other members of the 7th-century Mercian royal family, including his uncle, Penda's brother, Coenwealh, and his son, Cundwealh, of the 'C' line of the dynasty. Further 7th-century examples in other Anglo-Saxon dynasties include Cenwalh, king of the West Saxons 643–74, who founded the see of Winchester, and Aethelwalh, king of the South Saxons c674–85, baptised c674, and the godson of King Wulfhere of Mercia. In such names *walh* was compounded with an element of complement. Thus *cene*, as in Coenwealh, was 'fierce or bold', *cuth*, as in Cuthwalh or Cundwealh, was 'well-known, famed', and *aethel* 'noble born or brave'.[28]

If, as his name suggests, Merewalh had Welsh blood, it could have been through an early, or irregular, marriage between Penda and a Welsh princess, for a strong military alliance between Penda and Cadwallon, king of Gwynnedd, had led to the defeat and death of Edwin of Northumbria at Hatfield in 633. Now the senior partner, Penda maintained this alliance for more than 20 years, and Cadafael, Cadwallon's successor, with other Welsh princes, joined him on the campaign that led to Penda's death at Winwaed in 655. Marriage into a Welsh ruling family may have been a formal expression of this alliance, and have facilitated Penda's establishment of a satellite, but still predominantly Welsh, principality, for his son, Merewalh, between the Severn in the north and the Wye in the south. This offers an explanation for what is generally accepted as the peaceful nature of Anglian colonisation across the Severn.[29]

River-names throw light on the origins of Merewalh's realm. They show that the Severn once formed a boundary between English and Welsh. The loss of Celtic river-names to the east is taken as evidence of Anglian settlement between 550 and 650. Their survival to the west indicates Angles did not penetrate until c650. In Herefordshire practically all river names are Celtic, the exceptions being

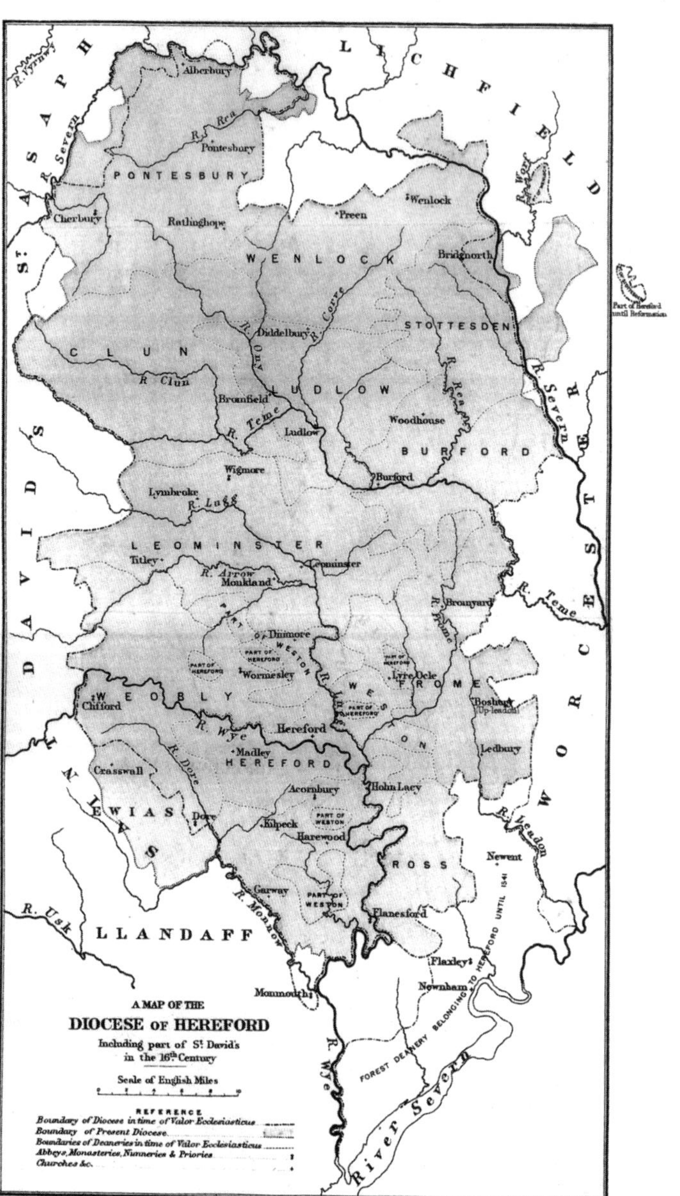

Fig 2.2 The diocese of Hereford showing the later extension south of the rivers Wye and Frome

two small brooks, both associated with early Anglian settlement: the Curl and Summergil, the first element of which is English, tributaries of the Arrow and Lugg. A date of c660 for Merewalh's rule, as indicated in Mildburg's *Life*, is thus not unreasonable.[30]

The lands ruled by Merewalh, and his sons, Merchelm and Mildfrith, lay west of the Shire Ditch that ran along the top of the Malverns, which was to become the formal boundary with the *Hwicce*, the folk to the east of the Severn. It also became the boundary of the diocese of Hereford when Archbishop Theodore of Tarsus formalised English dioceses on the basis of tribal territories. To the north Merewalh's lands extended, in an irregular fashion, to the Severn. Beyond lay the territory of the *Wreocensaetan*, the folk about the Wrekin and north Shropshire, which became part of Lichfield diocese (Fig 2.2).[31]

The heart of Merewalh's kingdom was the land of Lene, the northern part of the Herefordshire Lowlands, dominated by the Lugg, Arrow and their tributaries, with their rich meadows and pastures. To the south only Dinmore and Wormsley hills separated Lene from the southern Herefordshire Lowlands. To its east was the Herefordshire Plateau, about Bromyard. North and north-west of Lene were the North-west Herefordshire Hills, stretching from the hills about Kington as far as Ludlow and rising to 1,000ft; beyond Ludlow his realm stretched across the Shropshire Hills to the Severn. Merewalh's political centre in the land of Lene was between the Lugg and Pinsley, probably at Kingsland. Here the royal food rents would be collected, and close by, at Leominster, was his first church, dedicated to St Peter. Domesday Book and a charter of c1123 provide firm evidence that this church had indeed been 'royally endowed'. They show that most of Lene to the west, together with much of the Herefordshire Plateau to the east, formed its *parochia*, the area for which, since foundation, the ancient minster had had spiritual responsibility (see Fig 6.3).[32]

Coningsby's *Register* shows that Leominster Priory's estates ranged on all sides, with one exception: the lands between Lugg and Pinsley never formed part of the priory's lordship. Studies elsewhere have shown that minsters were frequently founded close to the 'central place' of large, royal (and later, episcopal) estates, as at Lindisfarne and sites in Kent and Dorset, and to Roman roads. The royal centre with which they were 'twinned' was often 'no more than two miles away'. Kingsland is only 3 miles west of Leominster, and a mile to the east was the strategic Roman road that traversed the Marches, from Caerleon to Chester via Wroxeter. The tradition of Kingsland as the royal centre lived on to the 1530s, when John Leland reported that Merewalh had endowed his minster 'with all territoris thereabout savynge only the lordshipe now caulyd Kingsland'. A second major royal centre lay in the Lugg valley to the south of Dinmore Hill, in the clutch of manors between Marden and Lugwardine, by the confluence of Lugg and Frome. These continued to be categorised as ancient demesne until the end of the Middle Ages. The precise site has yet to be identified.[33]

If the Staunton-on-Arrow charter of 958 is correctly interpreted, at least part of Merewalh's enclave about Kingsland was still in royal hands during the reign of Edgar, 957–9. The new dynasty which, it is generally agreed, achieved control through peaceful rather than violent means, could hardly have taken measures which would reduce its ability to draw food rents from its newly-acquired lands. Early evidence of agricultural change, especially drainage of 'more', marshy lands, extends to the Lugg valley, south of Dinmore Hill at Wellington quarries.[34]

The name of Merewalh's folk is problematic. Of them even Bede had no knowledge. For him they were merely the 'people living beyond the river Severn to the west'. Indeed all he knew of Mercia he had 'learned from the brethren of the monastery of Lastingham, founded by Chad and Cedd, (and) how through their ministry ... north Mercia achieved the faith of Christ which it had never known'; but neither Chad nor Cedd was Mercian. There is no Mercian chronicle, and even today its early history 'remains obscure'. In early Mercian episcopal lists they are '*Uestor E...*', the second word being lost, but in a second the folk are '*Uestor Elih*'.[35] In the *Life* of Mildburg Merewalh is *rex Westehanorum*, but in John of Worcester's 'List of Kings of the Angels' he is *Westan-Hecanorum rex*; elsewhere king of the *West Angli*. In the 11th-century copy of the *Tribal Hidage* they are merely '*Westerne*'. Although late sources, of the late 11th and early 12th century, these are local. West Angles, even if not the original title, is appropriate, completing the sequence running westwards from East Anglia, through Middle Anglia and Mercia to West Anglia.[36]

To add to the difficulty, another, quite different, term was used for the folk west of the Severn, the *Magonsaete*, the people of *Magana*, Maund. In her so-called *Testament* St Mildburg was granted by her family, amongst other lands, a five-hide estate at *Magene*, possibly an Old English name for the Lugg flood plain about Maund Bryan and Rosemaund, corresponding quite closely to the Domesday hundred of Cutsthorn.[37] The traditions of a royal complex in the area of Marden and Sutton Walls suggest 'Maund' may have been a considerably wider area than the place-name evidence indicates. Subsequently the term was applied to an even more extensive area. The earliest secure reference to *Magonsetum* is in a charter of 811. By 958 Staunton-on-Arrow, west of Leominster, was in the pagus, province, of the *Magonsaete*. In 1016 comes the first reference to Hereford as a 'shire'. In that year, at the battle of Assandun, the Anglo-Saxon Chronicle tells us, ealdorman Eadric (of Mercia) 'did as he so often did before, first started the flight', with his men. On this occasion, however, they are called the *Magonsaete*, not the men of Herefordshire. These Mercian counties had been 'in existence in the 10th century'. The realm of Merewalh and his successors had long since disappeared as a political unit — replaced by the lands subject to the *burhs* at Hereford and Shrewsbury.[38]

The evidence thus points to the peaceful penetration of the lands south and west of the Severn in the mid 7th century, by an Anglian folk, later known as the Magonsaete. They were led by Merewalh, a son of Penda, probably of partly Welsh extraction. The principal archaeological evidence is apparently Rowe Ditch, across the Arrow valley some 3 miles south-west of Kingsland.

The Kentish Marriage: Eafe, Mildred, Mildburg and Mildgith

After describing Merewalh's conversion by Edfrith, Mildburg's *Life* includes an account of his marriage to the Kentish princess, Eafe, great-granddaughter of St Augustine's royal convert, King Aethelbert of Kent, died 616. In this the *Life* follows a series of other *Lives* concerning Mildburg's elder sister, St Mildred, the central figure in what came to be called the Kentish Royal Legend (Fig 2.2).[39]

By an earlier marriage Merewalh already had two sons, Merchelm and Mildfrith. By his second marriage, to Eafe, he had three daughters, and a son who died in infancy. After the birth of the last child, the royal couple 'began to turn away from normal embraces' and eventually 'for

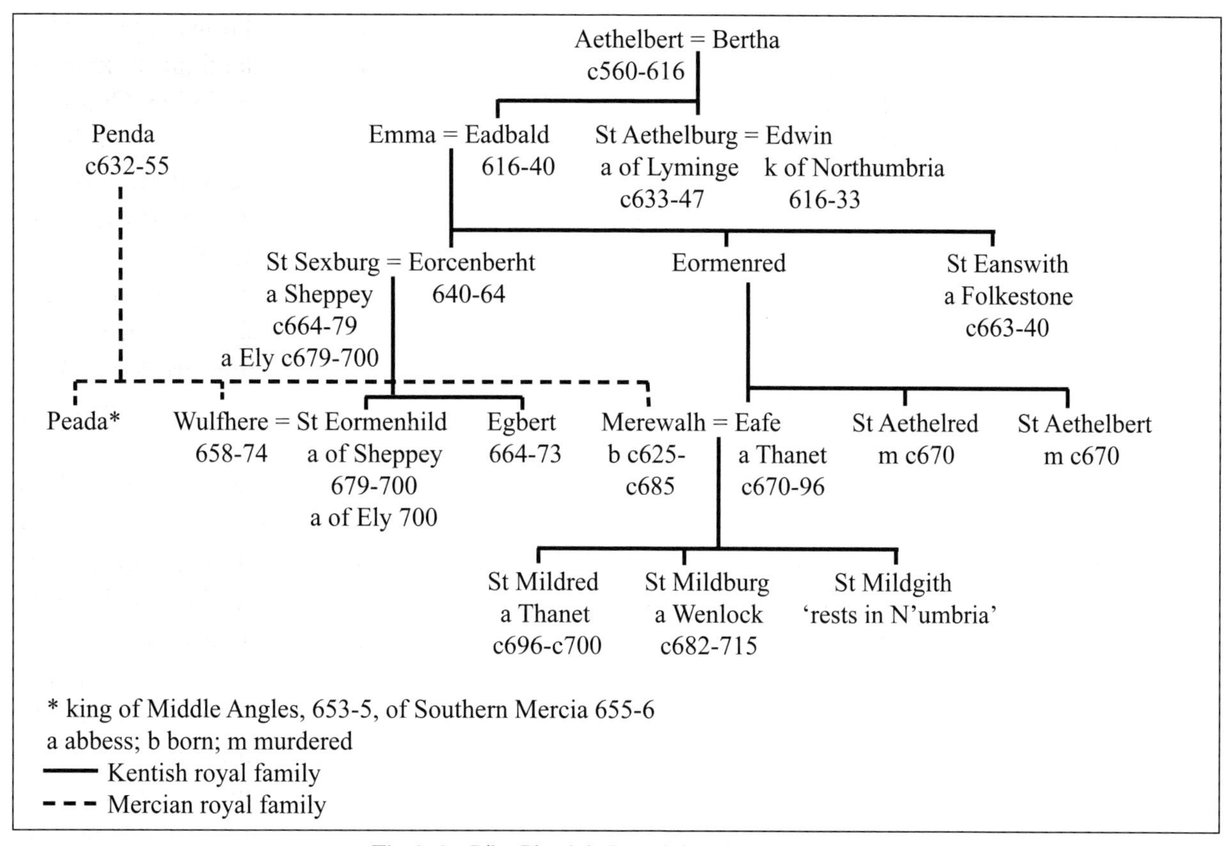

Fig 2.3 The Kentish Royal family, 560–c715

the love of God and of mankind separated from their conjugal estate'. In 7th-century England this was not unusual, for the earliest Kentish laws state, 'if a wife wishes to depart with her children she shall have half the goods. If the husband wishes to keep the children she should have a share of the goods equal to a child's.' Even Archbishop Theodore compromised with Corinthians 7:10-11: 'the Lord commanded the wife depart not from her husband and the husband put not away his wife', by stating, 'a woman could not reject her husband — unless perchance, to enter a monastery'. This is precisely what Eafe, like a number of other royal consorts, chose to do.[40]

Eafe returned to Canterbury. 'Just as a dove, freed from the snare, flies to her beloved cote, so the noble queen, free from the ties of the flesh, went to her native Kent.' There, we are told, she 'enjoyed the company of the great men of Heaven, the holy Theodore, archbishop, and the blessed Hadrian, abbot'. But not for long. Granted land by her cousin, King Egbert (664–73), Eafe founded a princess-minster on the isle of Thanet, where she brought up her three daughters: St Mildred, her successor as abbess; St Mildburg, who became abbess of Much Wenlock; and St Mildgith. Women invariably ruled such houses, where adjacent communities of chaplains served the altars. There were princess-minsters at Lyminge, founded c633 by St Aethelburg, daughter of King Aethelbert, and at Folkestone, founded by Eafe's aunt, St Eanswith, daughter of King Eadbald of Kent, Aethelbert's successor.[41]

A recent study has shown that the essential elements of the earliest *Life* of St Mildred, and thus the details of the marriage of Merewalh to Eafe, can be attributed to Mildred's successor as abbess at Thanet, Eadburg, c732–51. The relics of a Saint Eadburg were held at Leominster (Table 6, no 37). A woman of wide culture, Eadburg corresponded with Boniface, the most famous of all the Anglo-Saxon missionaries to Germany and first archbishop of Mainz. Eadburg sought to provide security for her convent and its lands in an unruly world by the promotion of a powerful local cult. This proved to be remarkably successful. First she enshrined the incorrupt body of Mildred, in practice a form of canonisation, in her new conventual church of SS Peter and Paul. From the earliest days, the shrine was the scene of numerous miracles. Secondly, she was responsible for the compilation of a *Life*.

In the mid-11th-century manuscript, BL Cotton Caligula Axiv, is an Old English fragment, ff121v-124v. This Stephanie Hollis has shown to be the closest surviving representative of Eadburg's *Life* of Mildred, for it embodies ideas that predate the Benedictine reform movement of the 10th century. Eadburg had 'created a female monastic version of the dynastic legend', with Eafe as the 'hero-protagonist'. The original, written at the most only some 50 years after Eafe's death in 694 and merely a few years after the death of her daughter, the abbess Mildred, c732, provided a reliable witness for Eafe and her marriage to Merewalh. Mildred's *Life* underwent a renaissance on the translation of her body from Minster to St Augustine's Abbey, Canterbury, in 1035. However, the emphasis of the flurry of *Lives* published by monks to arouse interest and offerings at her new shrine in St Augustine's was on Mildred's patriarchal rather than her matriarchal forebears.[42]

It is a measure of Eadburg's success with the canonisation and *Life*, that a third of the 30 earliest extant charters of the Kentish kings either grant or confirm privileges to Minster-in-Thanet. Evidence in some of these charters also throws light on Merewalh's lineage. Given the political circumstances, when all the kingdom south of the Humber acknowledged the supremacy of Aethelbald of Mercia, mightiest of the Mercians kings (716–57), Eadburg's *Life* stressed the royal lineage of Mildred on the Mercian as well as the Kentish side. In 733, whilst in control of Kent, Aethelbald granted St Mildred and her church at Thanet the tolls due on one ship. In a further grant to the church, in 748, he explained that this he made not only for 'eternal reward', but 'in consideration of the blood link with abbess Mildred whose body had been translated into the minster of the apostles', at Thanet. Such a reference to consanguinity indicates Merewalh was indeed a son of Penda, for Aethelbald was the grandson of Penda's brother, Eowa[43] (see Fig 2.1),

Now the Mercian royal family, as well as the Kentish royal house, laid claims to sanctity. Merewalh's sisters, Cyneburg and Cyneswith, were saints. So also were his daughters, Mildred of Thanet and Milburg of Wenlock, and even the obscure youngest daughter, Mildgith, of whom all we otherwise know is that she 'rested' in Northumbria. The only extant reference to Mildgith, other than those in the Kentish Royal Legend, is in the Leominster prayer book. There she is included amongst 'the holy virgins' invoked by the minster's nuns in their longer litany. As this was composed almost a century earlier than Mildburg's *Life*, it is witness to the vitality as well as the independence of Leominster's own tradition concerning Merewalh, Eafe and their three daughters.[44]

The Adoption of Roman Ways west of the Severn

Mildburg left Thanet and returned to her father's lands beyond the Severn, to become a nun at Wenlock, in their northernmost reaches. Shortly afterwards she succeeded as abbess. Finberg explains that Mildburg's 'fugitive and cloistered virtue' probably left her hagiographer scope for little more than family history, pious rhetoric and one or two miracle stories. To give weight to the *Life*, he copied out a document allegedly dictated by Mildburg. This, which he called her *Testament*, gives what claims to be the text of early charters granting estates to her monastery, in the south as well as the north of the territory of the West Angles: 5 hides at *Magana* (Maund) and 30 in Lydas, Lyde, some 3 miles north of Hereford, as well as 97 hides at Wenlock. The hide, ploughland or carucate was a customary measure, consisting of 4 virgates. In Herefordshire the hide on the episcopal estates was 240 acres. *Lydas*, Coplestone-Crow suggests, may have been a Welsh multiple estate or commote, demarcated on the south by the Wye between Hampton Bishop and Breinton, and on the east by the Lugg, from Marden in the north to Hampton Bishop in the south. This included the area about the Wye ford at what was soon to become Hereford. If we can trust her *Testament*, Mildburg ruled Wenlock as a princess minster of the Kentish type until the episcopate of Bishop Wealhstod of Hereford (727–36). Her return to the land of her birth was at a time of rapid change, in which she played a major role.[45]

According to tradition, Edfrith ruled his church for fifteen years. As a Northumbrian monk he would have established at Leominster the customs and uses of the Columban church, as they had been brought from Ireland to Lindisfarne by way of Iona. There lay the roots of the zeal, humility and asceticism which characterised the early Northumbrian missionaries, qualities exemplified by the story of St Chad who, forbidden to continue making visitations of his diocese on foot, was lifted onto a horse by Archbishop Theodore's own hands. Roman ways, in particular over the observation of Easter, were accepted by the Northumbrian king, Oswy, at the Synod of Whitby in 664. They were firmly established in Mercia during the reigns of Merewalh's brother, Wulfhere (658–74), with Theodore's reconsecration of St Chad as bishop of Mercia according to Catholic rites in 669. Merewalh's sisters, Cyneburg and Cyneswith, founded a double house of the Kentish type at Castor in Northamptonshire (see Fig 2.1). The church in the lands west of the Severn could not cut itself off from such events.[46]

Merewalh, faithful to Edfrith, may have held out in the isolated, half-Welsh western Marches for the old ways of the Northumbrian church, but after the accession of his son events moved swiftly. Merchelm, with his brother, Mildfrith, witnessed two charters in the *Testament*. In the first, c680, where Merchelm is described as king, they granted lands, including estates at Maund and Lydas, to their half-sister, Mildburg, for the benefit of her convent at Wenlock. Merchelm was succeeded by Mildfrith, who was buried c736 at Hereford cathedral, by the side of his 'beautiful wife Cuenburga' in a mausoleum that also held the bodies of the first three bishops. By 693 the interests and ambitions of the dynasty had been drawn from Leominster to Hereford, in all probability for military reasons. The 7th century, especially under Penda, had been characterised by accommodation and even co-operation with the Welsh, especially of Gwynedd, but the 8th century witnessed increasing confrontation and Anglian penetration of lands south of the Wye. Whether the adoption of Hereford as the dynasty's political centre was cause or effect it is difficult to say.[47]

The loose structure of the Columban monastic church, developed within a pastoral and hunting society, was now abandoned. Its place was taken by an institutional church, organised on Roman lines, reflecting the forms of an ancient urban civilisation. Ecclesiastical jurisdiction was now exercised by a bishop within a diocese, itself a term derived from the late imperial administration. One of Merewalh's sons, probably Mildfrith, acquired the 30 hides at Lydas from Mildburg. At the new dynastic centre on the banks of the Wye c693 Tyrthel, the earliest documented bishop west of the Severn, established his *cathedra*, or seat.[48] According to Leland 'Milfridus Regulus and Quenburg his wyfe' were 'first founders of the cathedral church of Hereford'. The bounds of the diocese, following those of the folk ruled by Merewalh and his sons, lay west of the Malverns and between Severn and Wye. William of Malmesbury records that Bishop Cuthbert (736–40), later archbishop of Canterbury (740–58), erected the 'high roofed mausoleum of wondrous beauty' for Mildfrith, Cuenburg and Osric, presumably Mildfrith's successor, as well as his own three predecessors in the see. These, his inscription informs us, were '*Walhstodus*, *Torhtere* and *Torhtil*'. There is no mention of the supposed founder, Putta, who fled Rochester cathedral when his see was devastated by Aethelred in 676. In this way Leominster was replaced by Hereford as the political and religious centre of the lands west of the Severn.[49]

Continuity as a Religious Site

Despite this transfer of power to Hereford, and the foundation of a cathedral, Leominster remained a major religious centre throughout the Saxon period. Edfrith's church will have been reformed, to become a house firmly in the Roman Benedictine tradition. Evidence in the minster's late Anglo-Saxon prayer book makes this clear. Although compiled in the early 11th century, at its core one finds the observance of the cults of saints who reigned supreme at Rome in the 7th and early 8th centuries, indicating the adoption of the Roman liturgy at this time. It is sometimes assumed that a double house or princess minster, as at Wenlock, Minster-in-Thanet, Folkestone etc, replaced Edfrith's church. There is no evidence to support this, nor of nuns at Leominster until c1000. It is possible, however, that they were introduced during the Benedictine revival of the second half of the 10th century.[50]

What is certain is that in the early 11th century the nuns cherished the memory of a certain St *Haemma* (see Fig 3.2). His feast is found on 25 May in the Calendar of the Nero/Galba prayer book, where he is described as *Haemma, Abbatis*. The last folios of the prayer book include a short prayer of intercession, to Haemma, 'to succour and preserve me from all my adversaries'. His 'body' is first in Bishop Swinfield's list of all the relics held at Leominster Priory in 1286, where he is described as 'abbot of this church', and the Reading relic list of 1190 records 'one large bone and two ribs of St Haemma, first abbot of Leominster'. The assumption must be that Haemma became the first abbot of a Roman monastery that succeeded Edfrith's minster on the acceptance of Roman ways west of the Severn. This, one also assumes, took place about the time of the foundation of Hereford cathedral, of which the first securely recorded bishop was Tyrhtel, 688–705x710. Hereford lost all its literary treasures in the destruction wrought by Gruffudd ap Llywelyn in 1055. In consequence, Leominster's late Anglo-Saxon prayer book is our sole source for the liturgy of the church west of the Severn prior to the Norman Conquest.[51]

Between the early 8th and the 11th century only two documents refer to Leominster. Neither indicates whether it was a house of monks or of nuns. An early 11th-century *List of Saints' Resting-Places* provides details for 89 saints. Rollason has shown that it was composed in two sections. The first names 25 saints, almost all defined by reference to rivers or the sea. Very few saints of this early group were translated to their resting-place later than the end of the 9th century. In this group is 'Aethelred who rests by the Lugg', for whom 'there is no reason to assign a late rather than early date'. As will be shown, this was a copyist error for Aethelmod. Other saints in this early group include Alban at St Albans on the Ver, Columcille at Dunkeld on Tay, Cuthbert at Norham on Tweed, Chad at Lichfield on the Tame and Guthlac at Crowland on Gyrwan Fen. This group of early saints was evidently copied from a 9th-century list. Such lists are in the spirit of the Roman tradition, since 'their form implies they are dealing predominantly with whole saints, not with small corporeal relics'. The second section of the *List* is composed of saints of the late Saxon period, especially the 10th century, but without reference to rivers. The *List* shows that Leominster, like Hereford with St Aethelbert, had the distinction of a shrine of national repute before 900. Possession of such relics was an indication of prestige and power. Equally important, the presence of a shrine at Leominster indicates the existence of a community, appropriately organised to house the shrine and administer the cult.[52]

The second document is a charter that records the sale in 958 of six *manentes* of land in *Stanton*, Staunton-on-Arrow, by King Edgar of the Mercians, to his thegn, Ealhstan. The bounds, which are described in detail, refer in one place to the boundary of *lionhina* or *leonhiena*. Here the first element is *lene*, and the second signifies 'a community of some sort, especially a religious community'. Thus we have the religious community of the Lene district. The boundary of nearby Titley is referred to in the 958 charter, and in Bishop Capella's 1123 charter as part of the *parochia* of the minster church founded by Edfrith at Leominster. North of Staunton lies *Wapletone* (Wapley), recorded in Domesday Book as part of the great manor of Leominster 'before 1066' (see Map 3). Here then is as firm evidence as one can anticipate at this date of the religious community, and much of its estates, that administered the shrine of St Aethelmod. Leominster had successfully weathered the Viking invasions of 866–95.[53]

Leland reports 'that the nunnery was ... in the Danes warres destroyed and after a college of prebendaries sett there'. This is qualified by 'some say', evidently referring to his, not altogether reliable though knowledgeable, local correspondent Thomas Hackluyt of Eaton. It may have been the case that Haemma's monastery had declined into 'a college of prebendaries' and later been converted into a nun-minster, but the minster at Leominster was certainly not destroyed 'in the Danes warres'. Not only is there evidence of the existence of a major shrine before 900, and of a religious community in 958, but also, as Leominster's late-Anglo-Saxon prayer book shows, a number of major Breton and other cults, closely associated with King Athelstan (924–39), were venerated here. To be the recipient of such royal patronage, the community must have been flourishing.[54]

There is no evidence of any significant Danish attacks on Herefordshire. The Anglo-Saxon Chronicle records one incident, vaguely identified as in Archenfield in 914, when they settled at the mouth of the Severn, whence they raided adjacent parts of Wales, along the banks of rivers. Here they took prisoner Cameleac, bishop of Archenfield, for whom King Edward paid a ransom of £40. On the Severn, although Gloucester had fallen, Worcester remained secure. The lands west of the Severn were never subjected to attack. When the Danish army overwintered at Buttington, near Welshpool, in 893, they were 'weighed down with lack of food and had to devour the greater part of their horses'.[55]

Blair provides three indicators as to continuity. He has expressed the incidence of identifiable continuity between pre-Viking minsters and mother churches of c950–1200 in map form. On a scale of 1 to 5, Herefordshire rates highly, as level 4. Secondly, in discussing the cults of very minor local saints, known or inferred to be of pre-Viking origin and attested in post-Viking sources, he has observed that 'the more obscure the saint the stronger the likelihood of genuine continuity'. Of Leominster's three such saints, Edfrith, Haemma and Aethelmod, the last was 'obscure' even to the author of the *List of Saints' Resting-Places*. Thirdly, Blair confirms that 'the old territories of the Hwicce and Magonsaete ... remained an abnormally stable region, neither overrun by the Vikings nor subjected to undue pressure from the West Saxon court'. One of the characteristics of the minsters of this area is their huge mother-parishes (see Fig 6.3 & Table 5).[56] On all three counts, the evidence for Leominster's continuity is formidable.

3 The Late Anglo-Saxon Prayer Book, Nero Aii/Galba Axiv

A late Anglo-Saxon prayer book is the second major source for the history of the minster. This was edited in 1988 by Bernard Muir, who points out that the manuscript was in origin a blank book, which passed through a number of hands, both male and female. It was used to collect texts of general interest to the community, becoming in effect a commonplace book. The texts range widely, and many are removed from their original context. The material is formal, informal and composite.

Before the prayer book was acquired by the great antiquary, Sir Robert Cotton (1571–1631), it had been split into two parts, Nero Aii, f3-13, and Galba Axiv, as his earliest catalogue shows. A disastrous fire in 1751 destroyed or damaged nearly a quarter of Cotton's manuscripts. Nero was unaffected, but Galba suffered badly from fire and water; a number of the leaves, particularly at the end, are wholly or partly illegible. The original order of the leaves has thus been lost, so the sequence of handwriting, and thus the changing ownership of the book, is difficult to establish. Muir has reconstructed a number of the prayers, either from analogous texts or from Humfrey Wanley's *Catalogue* of the Cottonian collection, written prior to the fire. This has helped with some restoration of the sequencing, and thus analysis of the various hands through which the book passed.

In 1908 Edmund Bishop, the eminent liturgiologist, pointed out that the Nero Calendar, although written in the early 11th century, is full of archaisms drawn from 'our earliest extant hagiographical records'. With remarkable insight, he continued, 'this is easily explained. It comes not merely from the most remote, but from the most Celtic, backward part of the country'. Such a description could easily well fit Herefordshire, but Bishop hazarded the guess that it came from 'furthermost Wessex, being the type of calendar in use in Devonshire before (Bishop) Leofric (1046–72) took the Church (of Exeter) in hand'. However, the presence of the feminine as well as masculine singular forms in Galba, and of prayers to nine of Winchester's saints in its longer litany, persuaded Bishop that Galba was 'the work of a nun of St Mary's convent, Winchester'. Bishop's judgement on what appeared to him to be the quite distinct characters of Nero Aii and Galba Axiv was generally accepted by later scholars, and has cast a long shadow, which it has been difficult to dispel.[57]

In 1957 N.R. Ker, one of our most eminent palaeographers, examined both the handwriting and content of the two manuscripts. For Ker, 'the evidence that the leaves containing a Calendar and tables (Nero Aii, f3-13) have been detached from Galba (Axiv) seems fairly conclusive'. Two of the hands in Nero are also in Galba, the format is the same, both manuscripts contain notes by John Joscelin (1529–1603), the scholar who assisted Cotton with his collection, and 'both have the same, curiously comprehensive character and come evidently from the same region'. Nevertheless others have insisted that Nero and Galba were the products of different houses.[58] However, in her recent *Atlas of Saints in the Anglo-Saxon Calendar* (2002), Rebecca Rushforth concludes that 'the (Nero and Galba) manuscripts are written in very interesting script ... seemingly from without ... the mainstream scribal traditions of the period; this argues against a Winchester origin'. Most of the Galba entries are in Latin, but some are in Old English. These were studied in 1965 by Banks, who drew particular attention to the form of alliteration and end-rhyme used. He points out that they belong to a type of Old English rhythmical writing employed over a large part of the midland area in the late 10th and early 11th centuries.[59]

The relationship of Nero Aii to Galba Axiv is discussed by Muir in his introduction to *A Pre-Conquest English Prayer-Book*. 'Both palaeographic and textual evidence' led him to conclude that they were 'originally one manuscript, and (subsequent) reference to the manuscript assumes this unity'. However, Muir followed Bishop in believing this was 'probably used at St Mary's Convent, Winchester'. The presence of three unique Leominster saints in both the Calendar of Nero and the longer litany of Galba not only confirms the integrity of the combined manuscript but also shows, as John Blair puts it, that it came from 'a very important community', the minster church of Leominster.[60]

Nero includes computational tables for the lunar cycle 1029–47, but there are other clues as to the dates of various entries. Ker identified five different hands, which wrote 74 of the 104 legible entries. Hands (1) and (4) are in Insular script which was developed in Ireland and adopted in England in the 6th century; it was used in the Lindisfarne Gospels and the Book of Kells. The other three are in Caroline script, developed at the court of Emperor Charles the Great, who died in 814. This was challenging Insular script in leading English monasteries by the mid 10th century. The most prolific is hand (1), to which Ker attributes forty items. This he describes as 'slightly forward sloping, delicate and rather later in date than some of the hands in the manuscript'. The feminine forms, *peccatrice*, sinner, which occurs on a number of occasions, and *ancillas tuas*, 'your handmaidens', on another, show these to be the entries of a nun. In addition, one prayer is a plea for mercy from a person describing herself as *miserulam famulam*.[61] In some entries gender alterations show they were used by a man at one time and a woman at another. Occasionally masculine and feminine forms are found virtually side by side. The Latin of hand (1), the nun, often leaves something to be desired, but this is not unusual in late Anglo-Saxon monasticism. She evidently had the book a long time, for though many pages she wrote confidently, elsewhere her hand is tremulous, as if nearing life's end. At or shortly after the death of Aethelred II, the Unready, in 1016, she wrote in such a tremulous hand, 'O God Almighty, give, we beseech Thee, rest everlasting to the soul of Thy servant King Aethelred, and to all who by their alms have increased this monastery to the praise and glory of Thy Holy Name'.[62] Hand (2) makes but one contribution, the translation of a prayer into Old English.

Ker suggests that the oldest parts were for male use. Hand (3) is responsible for at least 21 entries. The majority, nos 86–103, are at the end of the prayer book, mostly collects and prayers to individual saints. These include, significantly, the short prayer of intercession to St Haemma and a fragment of a prayer and postcommunion for the feast day of Merewalh's daughter, St Mildburg. There are also two prayers to St Edmund, the East Anglian king who died a martyr to the faith at the hands of the Danes in 869. Two other prayers have close associations with

Shaftesbury. One is to its foundress, St 'Aelfgyfe' or Elgiva, wife of the West Saxon king who died 946, whose cult developed there shortly after her death; the other to Edward, king and martyr, slain in 978 and buried at Shaftesbury. Leominster claimed relics of both.[63]

Hand (4), like the nun's hand (1), is in Insular script. It wrote, in Nero, 'A Poem from the Reign of King Æthelstan' and a prayer to God the Father and, in Galba, a prayer for the feast of the great 10th-century reforming bishop, St Aethelwold of Winchester, who died in 984.[64] As Insular script was unusual for Latin after 1000, palaeography and text suggest the Nero/Galba prayer book was built up over more than quarter of a century. Hand (5) wrote the Calendar and three computational entries in Nero, and a further computational table in Galba.[65] Meaney draws attention to a sixth hand. This provides two herbal remedies that are also to be found in Bald's *Leechbook*. Although extremely close to the text of the latter, in BL Royal 72Dxvii, they probably both go back to a common original, for Galba has preserved earlier spellings than Royal. The date of the remedies, for Meaney, could not be 'later than about the year 1000'.[66]

The Minster Churches of SS Peter and Paul, and St Andrew

That the prayer book was used by male and female members of a monastic community is evident in its wide range of prayers. A prayer of intercession to the Virgin is on behalf of 'the family of this holy monastery (*cenobium*)'. Another includes 'all who by their alms have increased this monastery (*hoc monasterium*)'.Much relates to the monastic life: the calendar of festivals observed by the house, the four computational tables, references to the *Opus Dei*, the daily cycle of liturgical prayer — prayers for the 'hours' of the monastic day and some 20 collects and two litanies — Latin texts with musical notation, and processional hymns for festivals and the weekly aspersion of buildings throughout the monastery. [67] Others are personal, including some of the prayers and hymns. One item provides texts of prayers to saints for relief of ailments of the foot. Some entries appear to us as secular, such as gall as a remedy for the eyes, and the virtues of the front teeth and the left foot. In all, more than 100 items have been established.[68]

The prayer book provides a range of evidence about the minster and its community during the reign of Athelstan (924–39) and the early years of the 11th century. A prayer to be said outside the church proclaims that it was consecrated to the blessed apostles, Peter, Paul and Andrew. The dedication of the church at Leominster to SS Peter and Paul is well attested. A charter of 1123 refers to the church as St Peter's, as does another, of Bishop Robert de Bethune c1135. In 1127 Ailward the radknight paid his 10s rent to the church at the feast of SS Peter and Paul, 29 June, the traditional date for such annual payments. Furthermore, early 13th-century indulgences of the bishops of St David's and Bangor both refer to 'the church of Peter and Paul'. The joint seal of Reading abbey and its priory at Leominster (see Fig 13.3) portrays Reading's patrons, the Virgin, James the Great and John the Evangelist, on the obverse; on the reverse is Henry I as founder, with Leominster's patrons, Peter and Paul, on either side. In 1433 the principal festivals included not only their joint feast, but also its commemoration on the octave; the only principal feast to be so honoured.[69]

The presence of a second church is not unusual. Any Anglo-Saxon religious community of importance had at least two churches, as can still be seen at St Augustine's, Canterbury. There is evidence of a 'chapel of St Andrew', close to the Leominster precinct, in both medieval and later sources. It is probable therefore that, 'weather permitting', the community would have passed in procession from the church of SS Peter and Paul to the chapel of St Andrew at Rogation, Candlemas and other festivals. In 1291–2 Isabel de Lindebrok sought sanctuary in St Andrew's church in Leominster. In 1433 the vicar had pasture at the 'chapels of St Andrew at Leominster, and at Stoke'. The 1535 *Valor Ecclesiasticus* refers to the cemetery of St Andrew, and a terrier of 1685 describes land near the Poplands, formerly Popelands, as 'St Andrew's Garth'. Access was through Paradise Meadow to the north of the minster (Fig 3.1).[70]

Fig 3.1 Poplands, close to the site of St Andrew's chapel, formerly the Harp Inn, with early 16th-century barge boards with running leaf decoration

By the early 11th century the monastery of which Haemma was first abbot had become a nunnery. To celebrate the Mass and fulfil the nunnery's wide-ranging pastoral responsibilities as successor to the minster church, the nuns would have been attended by prebendaries or canons who, like the canons of a cathedral, would have derived a living from a prebend, one of the manors of the minster church. The *parochia* extended over a very considerable area in all directions, except the royal lands between Pinsley and Arrow. The last of the priests to serve the minster was probably 'canon Ailwin', mentioned in a grant by Roger, abbot of Reading 1158–65. Ailwin having died, his *managium* in the town, evidently more than a mere house, and 42 acres outside the borough were granted to a certain Hugh for the considerable rent of 11s per annum. Such freehold benefices, held as prebends, were as much a characteristic of pre-Conquest nunneries, when they had inherited pastoral responsibilities, as they were of secular minsters. In 1086 Bromyard, documented as a secular minster in the 9th century, had three such 'canons' responsible for the spiritual well-being of the folk of its *parochia*, each enjoying his own 'portion' of the minster estates, and at Ledbury there were two such portionists.[71]

The prayer book has three principal components: the prayers, a calendar and two litanies.

The Galba Prayers

The series of prayers for the monastic hours throws light on the Opus Dei, the Divine Office, at Leominster in the early 11th century, in particular on the relationship of the nunnery to the 10th-century monastic reform movement led, in this country, by Archbishop Dunstan and bishops Aethelwold of Winchester and Oswald of Worcester. The *Regularis Concordia*, the *Monastic Agreement* approved at the Synod of Winchester c970, sought to standardise observance, 'lest by unequal and various use of one rule holy life shall be brought into disrepute'. The first chapter, following Benedict's *Rule*, prescribed eight offices or hours, seven day hours and the night office of Nocturns.

The nun, of hand (1), felt free, however, to suit her own needs. The Leominster liturgy thus consisted of only six offices. Those for the first, third, sixth and ninth hours are similar to those of the reformed liturgy of Worcester Cathedral Priory in the era of Bishop Wulstan (1062–95) and the church of Exeter during the episcopacy of Leofric (1046–72); but, with the two subsequent hours, Leominster diverges. For these the nun drew upon an earlier liturgy, of six offices. The text indicates that her source was the *Liber Sacramentorum* by Alcuin, the Northumbrian scholar who served at Charlemagne's court, c781–804. Vespers is followed by the twelfth hour, which brought together Compline, the last of the day hours, with Nocturns; and there is no Matins.[72]

Galba provides three prayers from the Good Friday ceremony for the 'veneration of the Cross' in Latin, with a translation into Old English. Of these prayers there are two versions, but the distinction is small. Here the Galba version did follow the text of the *Regularis Concordia*. From the *Agreement* we can reconstruct the ceremony within the churches of SS Peter and Paul and St Andrew as it would have been conducted more than a quarter of a century before the Conquest.[73] A processional Cross, within its shroud, was brought from the altar by two deacons or priests who halted at three stations for antiphons and responses. At each the deacons or priests sang one of three verses with words intended to be those of both Christ crucified and God to His people. The abbess, followed by the sisters, then prostrated herself, thrice, before the unveiled Cross, a ritual apparently derived from Byzantium where the Veneration took place in the emperor's presence with triple prostration. They would then say three prayers, rise and humbly kiss the Cross, the whole community walking barefoot until after the Veneration. Near the altar was 'a representation of a sepulchre hung about with a curtain'. The Holy Cross was then wrapped once more in its shroud, a napkin, and replaced in the sepulchre. There it was guarded 'with all reverence until the night of the Lord's resurrection' by pairs of nuns, 'keeping faithful watch and singing psalms'.[74]

The Asperges prayers in Galba provide basic information on the layout of Leominster's early-11th-century monastic buildings. This weekly ceremony, on Sundays before High Mass, was named from a chant based on David's prayer in Psalm 51:

'Purge me with hyssop and I shall be clean
Wash me and I shall be whiter than snow,'

The salt having been exorcised and blessed, a small quantity was sprinkled, crosswise, in the water (Plate 2a). Led by the officiating priest with cross-bearer, thurifer with censer, and candle-bearer, the whole community then moved through the church in solemn procession, blessing the altars before going outside to the monastic buildings. This completed, the procession re-entered the church to say the bidding prayer for their community, king, queen and all benefactors before the Great Rood, and then passed back into the choir.[75]

The ceremony provides firm evidence for the types of buildings within the Leominster precinct in the early 11th century, for each had its own prayer. Comparisons can be made with examples from two early liturgical books, the Sacramentary of Gellone, 772-95, and the Gregorian, c790, together with two other sources, the first from Peterborough or Canterbury, the other from Worcester. The Leominster prayers appear either incomplete or somewhat perfunctory as compared to the first three. The order in which the conventual buildings were visited was, apparently: kitchen (*coquina*), storehouse (*cellarium*), 'chimney room' (*caminita*), refectory, dormitory, larder (*lardarium*), infirmary. Two prayers, to be chanted at the gateway of the monastery and west door of the church, are now quite detached; thus the omission of other buildings may be due to loss of folios through fire damage. A diagram of St Gall, Switzerland, of c820, gives some impression of the layout of a greater monastery. Although the Galba order may represent a topographic sequence, to visit the kitchen first is somewhat eccentric. One would have expected the procession to visit the dormitory, with easy access to the church, at an early stage. For purposes of comparison, the sequence of the five series of prayers is presented in Table 1.[76]

	Gel	Greg	P/C	Worc	Leom
Church					
Sacristy	3	1		1	
Vestry	5	2			
Cloister					
Dormitory	4	4	1	2	5
Scriptorium	15	16	3		
Calefactorium	14	14	8		3
Refectory	6	3	2	3	4
Cellar	7	5	6	5	2
Dispensary	8				
Kitchen	9	12	4	4	1
Larder	10	13	5	6	6
Outer Court					
Area	13	9	10		
Granary	11	10	11		
Bakery	12	11	12		
Hospital	16	7	9		
Infirmary	17	8	7	7	7
Gatehouse	1		13	8	d
Church Door	2		14	9	d

Gel Gellone; Greg Gregorian; P/C Peterborough or Canterbury; Worc Worcester; Leom Leominster. d = displaced in text See n76

Table 1 Sequence of Monastic Buildings in the Asperges *Prayers*

Two Prayers from Iona?

Much material within the book was drawn from ancient traditions of the minster church. As the prayer book commemorates Edfrith, its founder, it may contain clues to aspects of the liturgy here in its early days. Edfrith had been a member of the Northumbrian church founded by Aidan from his island base at Iona, the church of St Columba, the English form of Colum Cille, 'dove of the church'. As Blair points out, 'it could well be that the Ionan influences found in the liturgical material from Leominster were mediated to the region by Edfrith'. However, Irish priests were active in Mercia, as well as other areas of Anglo-Saxon England, in the second half of the 7th century and later. On the other hand, the *Amra Choluimb Chille*, or *Elegy of Colum Cille,* written soon after his death in 598, and one of the earliest datable Gaelic poems, records that 'he went with two songs to Heaven after his cross'. The prayer book contains both of these 'songs': the only British exemplar of the first, and the only known example of the second.[77]

Altus Prosator

There are two Hiberno-Latin hymns in the prayer book, both of which have for long been attributed to Columba himself. The first, the *Altus Prosator*, is, and always has been, well known. It is in abecedary form (i.e. in alphabetical order), but J, V and W are omitted. Its subject is the 'great argument' of Christian cosmogony: the nature of the Godhead; the creation of the orders of angels; the fall of Lucifer (from heaven to earth); the creation of the universe; the seduction of

Adam and Eve and second fall of the devil (from earth to hell); the nature of the world and of the infernal regions; the giving of the Law to Moses; the terrors of the Judgment Day; the fate of the wicked and of the good.[78]

To appreciate the significance of their presence in the Leominster prayer book, the hymns have to be placed in the context of the other extant copies. Not one is from Britain. Of the seven other manuscripts of the *Altus*, four are continental. Known as the 'Prosperan' group, two of them are of the 9th century: a Bobbio manuscript, now in the Ambrosian Library, Milan; another at the Medical School Library, Montpellier. The other two manuscripts are of the 9th to 10th and 10th to 11th centuries. All are very similar, depending ultimately on a very early, common, exemplar, probably at Bobbio in Lombardy, the monastery founded by the great Irish monastic evangelist, Columbanus, in 614. All four of these continental manuscripts lost their Columban context, for they were attributed, incorrectly, to Prosper of Aquitaine (403–65).[79]

The three other manuscripts of the *Altus* are Irish. Only one, in the Dublin Franciscans' 8th-century manuscript of the *Liber Hymnorum*, has all 24 stanzas. All three have stanza titles several lines long, explaining the text in prose. In addition, they have prefaces in the vernacular, which describe the circumstances under which the *Altus* was composed. Colum Cille, they tell us, was expecting messengers from the pope. In preparation he carried a sack of grain on his shoulders up to the mill. When he 'put the first feed into the mouth of the mill he then began upon the *Altus*, and the composition of the hymn and the grinding of the corn were completed together'. The *Altus* was not 'the fruit of meditation but *per gratiam Dei*'. In return for Gregory the Great's gifts — a cross called *mor-Gemm*, 'the great gem', and *Hymns for each Day of the Week* — Columba sent him the *Altus*, with which the pope is said to have found no fault, except for the slightness of its praise for the Trinity.

There have been doubts about hymns attributed to Colum Cille, but most authorities have accepted as reliable the tradition that links the *Altus* with Iona. From her recent study of its style, rhyming scheme and sources, Jane Stevenson has concluded that 'it was written at Iona in the second half of the 7th century', that is at a time when, despite the decision at the Synod of Whitby, 664, the connection between Iona, the mother house, and Lindisfarne, the daughter, continued to be active. Stevenson adds, 'if the poem came from Iona, it was as good as written by Columba to an age which was less concerned with ownership than our own and very conscious of the continued, active existence (and intervention) of long-dead saintly founders'.[80]

Adiutor Laborantium (Plate 1)

The Irish prefaces also describe how Colum Cille composed a second, shorter, hymn on the same occasion. He 'felt his burden heavy so he composed a hymn in alphabetical order, from there up to the mill, *Adiutor laborantium*', 'Helper of those who toil'. No copy being known, the very existence of this second hymn was called into question. However, in 1983 Bernard Muir recognised the hymn following the *Altus* in the Leominster prayer book as the *Adiutor*. The Irish prefaces were fully vindicated, for the text confirmed both its title and abecedary form. The *Adiutor* has 26 verses, of which the first 24, each of one line, have the initial letter in alphabetical sequence, except K which is represented by two lines, both commencing with C. When he discovered it almost a century ago, Edmund Bishop was deeply moved by this hymn, although he had no suspicion of its true authorship. For him it was 'a relic of the ancient Celtic piety so widely spread in England of the 7th century'. However, his partial translation may have masked its real identity from scholars (see Appendix 1).[81]

Although both hymns are abecedary, they are quite different in form and content. *Adiutor Laborantium* is a hymn of supplication. God the Father is invoked in different ways in the first 15 of the 27 lines. 'Helper of those who toil, Ruler of all the good, Custodian of the ramparts, Defender of the believers, Exalter of the lowly, Breaker of the proud, Governor of the faithful, Enemy of the impenitent, Judge of all judges, Chastiser of those who sin, Pure life of the living, Light and father of all lights Shining with great brilliance, Denying to none who hope Your help and succour'. The hymn then arrives at the supplicant, 'me, broken and wretched little man, rowing through the storm of this infinite age', to be drawn after Him to life's most beautiful haven. Only as a result of Dr Muir's work do we know that this was possibly the prayer of Colum Cille himself.

Columba continued to be venerated at Leominster in the 11th century, for the feast of '*Collumcylle*' is recorded in the Nero Aii Calendar on 9 June. It can be found in only one other Anglo-Saxon calendar, and there it is expunged. However, it does appear in the early 8th-century calendar of Echternach, dated c703–10. This monastery was founded by St Willibrord, archbishop of the Friesians. An Englishman, he spent twelve years in exile in Ireland 678–90 before embarking on his continental mission. The Leominster calendar observed not only Columba's feast but also that of his namesake and contemporary, Columbanus. Greatest of Ireland's apostles to continental Europe, Columbanus founded a number of monasteries, including Bobbio. The strictness of his rule and his adherence to Irish customs, including the date for the celebration of Easter, together with his forthright manner, created many enemies in France, but his cult remained popular in Italy. His festival, on 21 November, is found in only one Anglo-Saxon calendar, that of Leominster.[82]

Prayers of Penitence

A number of the prayers are of great devotional intensity. They have a Celtic base, with a strong emphasis on the confession of sin. Like the *Antiphonary of Bangor*, c680, and the West Midland *Book of Cerne*, c820–49, the Galba prayer book brings together Celtic and Roman devotional material. The contrast between these two evidently disturbed Bishop, who confided that 'by excess of words and sometimes by extravagance of forms, they bring us within the verge of unreality'. Such detailed confessions emanated from 7th- and 8th-century Irish prayers. Called *Loricae*, breast plates, after the robes of the penitents, these were believed to be spiritual medicine. They had the 'peculiarly Irish trick for analysing, distinguishing and subdividing'. The first of these prayers is also found in a 9th-century Greek psalter with Latin translations and additions in Irish script, and the *Book of Cerne* and a prayer book that had belonged to Alfred the Great's queen, Ealhswith.[83] The confession lists an extraordinary range of sins: neglecting the divine commands in favour of the penitent's own wicked deeds; pride and envy; slander and covetousness; fornication and greed; false testimony and malice towards others; rapine and theft; blasphemy and carnal desire; drunkenness and gossiping; quarrelling and contentiousness; swearing and anger; earthly and transitory joys; anguish and murmuring. It then catalogues the various parts of the body through which the suppliant has sinned. This is taken further in a second prayer, *Deus inestimabilis misericordie*, copied out by the nun. Here she names each of her natural members, describing how it sustained her in sin, from her feet, 'running in wickedness', to her legs, knees, thighs, genitals, stomach, bowels, kidneys, loins, side, back, shoulders, arms, hands, mouth, throat, windpipe, ears, nostrils, eyes, head and finally to her heart, 'full of pain and malice'.[84]

This was not mere form. The prayers were included for the very way they expressed the deepest feelings of the various members of the community to whom the book had belonged. Another prayer, for reconciliation as death approached, illustrates their intense and very personal manner: 'O Lord, hear my prayers, for I know already that my time is near at hand ...Pour out to me tears of the heart, as Thou didst lay the foundations of the earth upon the waters, for my heart has grown hard as if a stone; I have sinned, O Lord, I have sinned exceedingly in my life; I acknowledge all my iniquities. I entreat of Thee, to Thee do I cry. Do stretch out Thy right hand and deliver me from my adversary as Thou didst deliver the three children from the furnace of burning fire. I pray Thee, O God, heavenly King, give me temperance and chastity, humbleness and faithfulness and truth, that I may be found worthy to persevere in good works. As indeed the desire of my heart is, whatever it be I have said or thought or done from my youth upwards ...to Thee I cry with a great cry out of my whole heart.'[85]

The *Calendar*, Nero Aii, ff3r-8v

The *Calendar* is one of the key records of any monastery. It lists, month by month, the saints' days to be commemorated in the daily service of the Mass. The Anglo-Saxon church observed the feasts of saints from many different places. The first English *Calendars* were copies of those of Gaul and Italy in the 7th century, but each church amended its *Calendar* as new influences — local, regional, national or from far beyond — made themselves felt. Saints were added as their cults came to be observed in the locality. In consequence, earlier saints came to be rejected. The Nero Aii Calendar, however, is distinctive in that it retained many of the old cults, thus revealing the antiquity of the original calendar from which it was derived, and detailed analysis of its contents can identify the major cultural influences. Almost a century ago, Bishop and Gasquet described it as 'of the old world indeed', concluding that, 'although of late date (that is, the early 11th century), it is among the most archaic of the pre-Conquest calendars'.[86]

Well over fifty of the festivals recorded in Nero Aii are found in no other extant Anglo-Saxon calendar. Many are listed in the *Hieronymian Martyrology*, erroneously attributed to St Jerome. Composed in Italy, it was based on a Greek martyrology from Asia Minor, of the mid 5th century. In the 6th century a copy was taken to Gaul. There further additions were made, including saints local to parts of Gaul and others from the Roman service books. Of the three extant texts of the *Hieronymian Martyrology*, that from Echternach, founded c700 by Willibrord, is the earliest, 'the most ancient and venerable monument of our English hagiographical tradition'. The majority of Nero's unique feasts are found in the Echternach text. The Nero Aii Calendar thus 'brings us across the centuries into direct touch with those documents and literary stores brought to this island by Benedict Biscop and Hadrian'. Hadrian, a Greek from Cyrenaica, who fled from the Arabs to Naples c645, became abbot of the monastery of SS Peter and Paul at Canterbury c670. Benedict Biscop (628–89), founder and first abbot of Wearmouth, made a series of visits to Rome to collect books for the English church, the last c672.[87] The early feasts of the Nero Calendar grant us an extraordinary glimpse of the cults brought by the Roman church to the kingdom across the Severn, and expounded by the minster clergy within their precinct and on their missions throughout its *parochia*. A number are of particular interest. St. Helen, mother of Emperor Constantine and celebrated for her part in the finding of the True Cross, was incorrectly believed to have been of British birth. Throughout the west her festival was celebrated on 18 August. It appears on that date in all the early Anglo-Saxon calendars, except that of Leominster. There, and only there, it was celebrated on 22 May, according to the custom of the eastern church.[88]

Strong on early saints, the Nero Calendar, unlike the litanies, is not so strong on those of later years. St Aldhelm (d709), abbot of Malmesbury and bishop of Sherborne, was ignored. Neither Edmund, king of East Anglia, nor Alphege, archbishop of Canterbury, both martyrs to the Danes, was acknowledged. In this way the calendar provides evidence not merely of the minster's origin,

	Date	Feast			*Leom*	*Glastonbury*					*Winchester*											Total
																	Worcester/E.Anglia					
			1	2	*3*	*4*	*5*	*6*	*7*	8	*9*	*10*	*11*	*12*	13	14	*15*	*16*	*17*	*18*	*19*	*20*	
1	9 Jan	Trans Judoc C		x						x	x	x	x	x		x			x	x	x		10
2	12 Mar	Alphega B										x		x									2
3	15 Jun	Edburga V		x			x	x			x	x	x	x		x	x	x	x		x	x	13
4	2 July	Dep Swithin B		x			x	x	x	x	x	x	x	x	x	x	x	x	x	x	x	x	17
5	7 July	Hedda B									x	x	x	x								x	5
6	8 July	Grimbald C		x	x		x	x	x	x	x	x	x	x		x	x	x			x	x	15
7	15 July	Trans Swithin B					x	x	x	x	x	x	x	x	x	x	x	x	x	x	x	x	16
8	1 Aug	Ethelwold B									x	x	x	x		x	x	x			x	x	9
9	4 Sept	Trans Birinus B			x			x	x		x	x	x	x	x	x	x	x	x	x	x		14
10	10 Sept	Trans Ethelwold B						x	x		x	x	x	x		x					x	x	9
11	18 Oct	Justus M						x		x	x	x	x	x		x		x	x	x		x	11
12	30 Oct	Ord Swithin B						x						x			x	x					4
13	4 Nov	Birnstan							x		x	x	x	x						x			6
14	3 Dec	Dep Birinus B	x	x	x			x	x	x	x	x	x	x	x	x	x	x	x	x	x	x	18
15	10 Dec	Oct Birinus B											x	x									2
16	13 Dec	Judoc C		x	x					x	x	x	x	x	x	x	x	x	x	x	x	x	15
			1	6	4	0	4	9	7	7	13	14	14	16	5	11	9	10	8	8	10	10	

B Bishop; C Confessor; L Leominster; M Martyr; V Virgin.
Dep Deposition; Oct Octave; Ord Ordination; Trans Translation.
I Oxford, Bodleian Digby MS 63 ff4Or-45v; North Country, 9th century
2 Salisbury Cathedral Library, MS 150 ff3r-8v; West Country, 969-78
3 BL, Cotton MS Nero AII ff3r-8v; Leominster, early 11th century
4 Oxford, Bodleian Bodley MS 579 ff39r-44v; Glastonbury Abbey, Leofric Missal, c980
5 BL, Add MS 37517 ff2-3; St. Augustine's Abbey, Canterbury, Bosworth Psalter,late 10th century
6 Cambridge, Un Lib, MS KkV 32 ff5Or-55v; West Country, early 11th century
7 BL, Cotton MS Vitellius AXiI ff65v-7Ir; Exeter Cathedral
8 BL, Cotton MS Vitellius AXVII ff3r-8v; Wells Cathedral, 106lx1083
9 BL, Cotton MS Titus DXXVII ff3r-8v; Hyde Abbey, Winchester, cl030
10 Cambridge, Trin Coll, MS RI5 32,15-26; Hyde Abbey, Winchester, early 11th century
11 BL, Arundel MS 60 ff2r-7v; Winchester Cathedral, cl070
12 BL, Cotton MS Vitellius EXVIII ff2r-7v; Winchester Cathedral, cl050
13 BL, Arundel MS 155 ff2r-7v; Christ Church Cathedral Priory, Canterbury
14 Cambridge, CCC, MS 422, 29-40; Sherborne Abbey, clO6O
15 Rouen, Bibl Mun MS Y6 ff6r-llv; Ely Abbey, Missal of Robert of Jumieges, early 11th century
16 Oxford, Bodleian Hatton MS 113 ff3r-8v; Evesham Abbey, 1050-1100
17 Cambridge, CCC, MS 391, 3-14; Worcester Cathedral Priory, 1050-1100
18 Cambridge, CCC. MS 9, 3-14; Worcester Cathedral Priory, 1025-50
19 Rome, Bibl Vat Reg Lat 12 ff7r-12v; Bury St. Edmunds Abbey, cl050
20 Oxford, Bodleian Douce MS 2% fflr-6v; Croyland Abbey, mid 11th century

Source : Wormald (1988) see n90

Table 2 Calendar of BL Cotton MS Nero Aii: The Winchester Saints

but also of the continuity of its liturgical life. Mildburg's convent at Wenlock, close to the Severn, may well have suffered, but Leominster, close to the Welsh border, was removed from the routes taken by the Danes in their disastrous attacks on the wealthy Anglo-Saxon monasteries. This explains a third characteristic of the Nero calendar, its extraordinary conservatism.[89]

Table 2 shows that Nero Aii is not a Winchester calendar. Of the 16 feasts of Winchester cults observed at the nun-minster in the Arundel Psalter of c1073, only four are recognised in the Nero Calendar. Of the 20 calendars listed in the table, other than the 9th-century Digby Missal, only Leofric, with a Glastonbury base, has a lower score. Moreover, Leominster's three local saints are found not only in the Calendar, Aethelmod on 9 January, Haemma on 25 May and Edfrith on 26 October, but also, together, in the longer Galba litany, indisputable evidence that the Nero Aii/Galba Axiv is a single, Leominster, prayer book.[90]

Galba Axiv: The Litanies

The prayer book's litanies are invocations for mercy and deliverance to the Trinity and for intercession to the Blessed Virgin, the archangels and angels, the patriarchs and prophets, the apostles and saints. Both are in the nun's hand. The first is quite short. The second, the longest of extant Anglo-Saxon litanies, has some 350 invocations, of which about 60 cannot be read due to fire damage.[91]

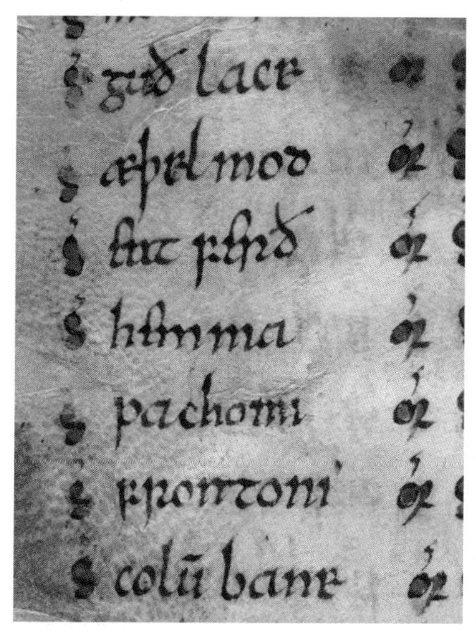

Fig 3.2 BL Cotton MS Galba, Axiv f93v. The longer litany: Invocations to Leominster's three unique saints, aethelmod, entferth (Edfrith) and hemma in company with the Mercian Guthlac, whose hermitage was at Crowland in the fens, and Columbanus, greatest of Ireland's apostles to the Continent

Reference has already been made to the longer litany's wide and indicative range of local and regional saints. 'It is a perilous business', we have been told, 'to attempt to discern evidence for the cults of local saints amongst such litanies'. This may well be the case — if there is not adequate supporting evidence. But, in Blair's words, Leominster's three saints are 'exceptionally well documented'. Edfrith, as the *Life* of St Mildburg tells us, was the founder of the minster. From 1290 Leominster's autumn fair was held on the vigil and feast of St Edfrith, 26 October, the date of his feast as recorded in the Calendar, and the four days following. The *Legend of St Etfrid, priest of Leominster* was reproduced from the Wenlock *Life* of St Mildburg, with *Lives* of St Aethelbert of Hereford and St Wistan of Worcestershire, by a scribe closely associated with Adam de Orleton, bishop of Hereford 1317–27 and of Worcester, 1327–33. The feast of St Edfrith was still recognised as a principal festival of the priory in 1433. The *Legend of St Etfrid* was to be recycled after the priory's dissolution in 1569 as a borough foundation legend. Haemma, according to the Leominster and Reading relic lists, was its first abbot (Fig 3.2).[92]

Aethelmod recorded in the 9th- and early 11th-century *List of Saints' Resting-Places*. The stark entry, 'St Ethelred rests at Leominster, near the river Lugg', indicates the national repute of his shrine. This, as later sources have shown, is a scribal error, which should read St Aethelmod. A number of guesses have been made as to his identity. For Bishop he might have been a bishop of Sherborne, but he does not appear in that abbey's calendar of c1061. The unique character of the Aethelmod entry in both *Calendar* and litany suggests a local person. Domesday Book's form of the place-name Aymestrey, *Elmodestreu*, is accepted as the Old English personal name, Aethelmod, plus Old English *treow*, a tree. For Gelling *treow* could mean 'wooden cross', or might be an internal boundary mark between the divisions of a large estate. Prior to the Conquest, Aymestrey was a Leominster estate and, originally, will have been within its *parochia*. Do we have here a reference to the saint 'who rested by the Lugg'? If *treow* was used in the sense 'the cross on which Christ was crucified', was Aymestrey the site of his martydom? Mrs Leather, the great recorder of Herefordshire folklore, records a gospel oak at the meeting point of the parishes of Aymestrey, Kingsland, Lucton and Shobdon. In medieval Latin *Lignum*, wood, was used in a similar way; thus *lignum Dominum* and *lignum Pascale*. Leland, following local tradition, refers to the monks as having the skull of 'Ethelmund, king of the Marches'.[93] The identity of St Aethelmod has yet to be adequately resolved. Nevertheless, he appears in the Leominster and Reading relic lists as martyr, and his festival was listed, with that of Edfrith, as one of the principal feasts of the priory in 1433.[94]

Most of the martyrs recorded in the longer litany are early Mediterranean saints. Only six are English. The first is Alban, protomartyr of Britain, and the only member of the group not of royal blood. He is followed by Edmund, the East Anglian king killed by the Vikings in 869, whose shrine was established at Bury St Edmunds in 915. Ignored by the Nero Calendar, his entry in the Galba litany may be due to the revival of the cult by Canute at Bury c1020.[95] The local martyr, Alkmund, 'Ealchmund', is another of Galba's unique entries. This Northumbrian prince, it is said, was murdered by the Mercian usurper, Eardwulf (796–c805). According to the earlier, 9th-century, *List of Saints' Resting Places*, Alkmund 'lies at Northworthy' (Derby). Here Ralegh Radford discovered a 9th-century sarcophagus 'elaborately carved on all sides ... the shrine prepared for the relics of St Alkmund'. Others say Alkmund died in battle against the West Saxons, his body first resting at Lilleshall, Salop. Although doubts have been cast on this, Alkmund's cult was certainly strong in west Mercia. Of the four dedications to him outside Derby, three are west of the Severn, at Shrewsbury, Whitchurch, and locally Aymestrey.[96]

The proof of the integrity of Nero and Galba lies, not only in the appearance of Leominster's three saints in both calendar and prayer book, but also in the inclusion, on the next folio of the longer litany, of a number of little-known marcher saints. St *Canidir* (Keneder) of Glasbury was reputedly son or grandson of Brychan, founder of Brycheiniog (Brecon). According to tradition, his hermitage was on an island in the Wye at Winforton, 15 miles southwest of Leominster, on one of its principal routes from Wales. His well, Ffynnon Gynidd, can still be seen on the common above Glasbury, some 10 miles further west on the same route. He gave his name to Kenderchurch (Llangynidr), close to Pontrilas, on the main road between Hereford and south Wales; and to Llangynidr between Brecon and Abergavenny. St Siloc is a hypocoristic form of the 7th-century Suliau or Tysilio, supposed son of Brochwel of the Tusks, who was prince of Powys and first cousin of SS Asaph and Deiniol. Llandysilio, near Newtown in Powys, the site of his cell, was the centre of his cult. Evidence of local observance is found in the Herefordshire place-names, Sellack, on the Wye north of Ross, and Llancillo, just off the Abergavenny to Brecon road.[97]

More than 50 of the saints invoked in the longer litany, one in six of the legible entries, are unique. They do not occur in any of the other 45 extant Anglo-Saxon litanies. Here are more obscure saints than in any other litany known from Anglo-Saxon England. They include, immediately after *Siloc*, *Triohoc*, *Tula* and *Twioric*.[98] Such invocations are highly problematic. *Triohoc* is possibly St Triac. The ruins of a chapel dedicated to him can be seen on the tiny island at the mouth of the Wye at Beachley Point. It was in use in 1290, when the Benedictine John Sterre celebrated Divine Office at 'St Tryak de Betesley'. In the 15th century it was 'rok seynt Tryacle' or 'Sancti Teriaci, Anachoritae'. Of the mysterious *Tula* all trace has been lost — unless it be a very debased form of Teilo. *Twioric* may be a reference to the north Welsh saint, Twrog, disciple and author of the now lost *Life* of St Beuno. Another saint mentioned, Geroc, could be the Gwentian saint, Garai, mentioned in the Iolo manuscript. As John Blair has remarked, 'it is this overlap of cultural and institutional origins that makes the region so fascinating'.[99] One of the saints invoked in the longer litany is particularly appropriate in terms of Blair's comment. This is Mildgith, the obscure youngest daughter of Merewalh and Eafe, who according to the *Life* of her sister, Mildred, 'rests in Northumbria', but her memory continued to be cherished, uniquely, at Leominster.[100]

Most famous of all Leominster's Welsh cults was that of St David himself. The minster claimed his arm bone, and his feast, on 1 March, continued to be celebrated as one of the priory's principal festivals throughout the Middle Ages. As well as that at Leominster, the calendars of Glastonbury, which also claimed a relic, and Sherborne included his feast. David however appears in only two other litanies, one written in Brittany c900. Three Welsh bishops, of St David's, Bangor and Elfael, granted generous indulgences to pilgrims visiting David's shrine at Leominster.[101] The relic list includes the Caerleon martyrs Julian and Aaron (Table 6, no 25).

Furthermore, two of the Galba prayers are directed to Merewalh's daughter, Mildburg of Wenlock, and another to Haemma, whilst St David's feast, on 1 March, is included in the Calendar. If Galba is indeed a Winchester nun-minster prayer book, then the nuns certainly had a marked penchant for the exotic.[102] Both calendar and prayer book are to be identified through the absence of popular saints, and the inclusion of those who are unique or unusual (Fig 3.3).

The Patronage of Athelstan?

The feasts of the Celtic saints recorded in the Calendar, litany and relic lists have a particular interest. 'Whoever approaches the Celtic saints', however, 'walks all the time on the edge of a quicksand — but a quicksand that conceals valuable treasure.' The word 'Celtic' itself is fraught with difficulties, as are such alternatives as 'Breton', 'Cornish', 'British' or 'Welsh'. An important, often troublesome, question is, at what period were the cults of the various Celtic saints adopted? One well-studied and cohesive group was introduced by Breton churchmen fleeing the Vikings during Athelstan's reign. They brought important relics, of St Samson, his companion Branwalader, and St Iwi, St Cuthbert's disciple who had ended his days in Brittany. Some of Branwalader's relics were claimed by Leominster, and Iwi's feast is celebrated on 8 October in the Nero Calendar.[103]

From an early age, Athelstan had had a passion for precious objects, relics, rare books etc. As king he sent 'true and wise men' to scour the continent on his behalf. For Christopher Brooke, Athelstan was 'the Pierpont Morgan' of his age. William of Malmesbury writes, 'there can scarcely

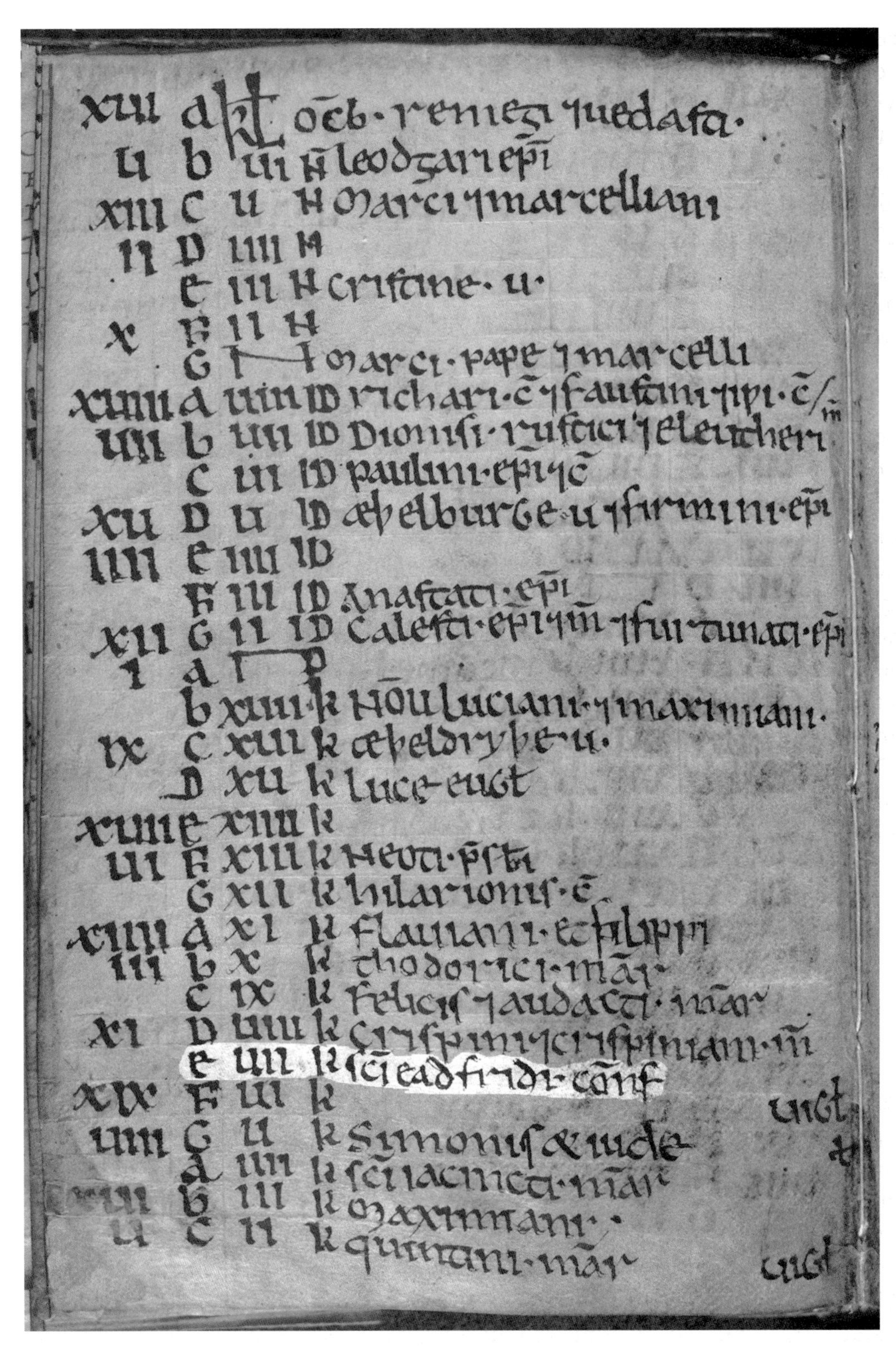

Fig 3.3 BL Cotton MS Nero Aii f7v.
*October, showing the Feast of St Edfrith on 26th (*sci eadfride conf; *highlighted above)*

have been an ancient monastery in the whole of England he did not embellish either with buildings or ornaments, or books or estates'. Of Leominster's Breton and Cornish cults, most originated with Athelstan.

St Germanus, patron of St German's cathedral, was a major Athelstan cult adopted at Leominster. His feasts appear on four occasions in the Nero Calendar. One, on 30 September, is a scribal error, where *Hieronimus*, St Jerome, had been taken for Germanus. Of two of the other feasts, 27 May is represented in more than half the Anglo-Saxon calendars, whilst 31 July features in virtually all but the earliest. The fourth feast, 3 November appears in but four other calendars. Germanus is also in both the Leominster litanies. Overall, these are a clear mark of Athelstan's impact on the minster's litany in the early 10th century. The feast of St Neot, a Glastonbury monk who became a hermit on Bodmin moor, is celebrated in the Calendar, and only two others, on 31 January.[104]

The feast of Petroc, Cornwall's 6th-century patron saint, was celebrated in ten Anglo-Saxon calendars on 4 June, due no doubt to Athelstan's Cornish expedition. In the Nero Aii Calendar his feast is, uniquely, recorded on 23 May. Petroc is also invoked in the longer litany. Given such other unique dates in Nero as for St Helen and St Wilfrid, this possibly represents a similar, earlier and otherwise unrecorded tradition. St Indract is described in an Irish martyrology of c800 as meeting his death at Glastonbury. Either side of the altar in Glastonbury old church were shrines to Indract and Patrick. They are found together in the Galba longer litany. Indracht is found in only one other, without Patrick. The minster's cult was possibly stimulated by a *Life*, written after 970. In the other 45 Anglo-Saxon litanies, Iwi appears in but one, Branwalader in two, Neot in three, and Petroc in four.[105]

In Nero Aii is a poem addressed as a tribute to Athelstan, celebrating one of his greatest achievements, the submission of the Welsh and Scots kings near Penrith in 927 — the justification for his claim to be king of all Britain. The heart of the poem is:

> 'Letter direct your steps
> ...
> England (now) made whole:
> King Athelstan lives
> glorious through his deeds.'

Another, poorer, copy is found in a Durham Cathedral gospel book, where he is celebrated as benefactor of St Cuthbert's shrine. In Durham's *Liber Vitae* especial honour was reserved for Athelstan, whose gifts included a missal, two gospel books embellished with gold and silver, two silver cups with covers, and 96lbs of silver. To Exeter he was equally liberal. However, the southern March was as much a centre of his activity as the north-east or south-west.[106]

Athelstan was brought up by his aunt, Aethelfleda, Lady of the Mercians, and his claim to the throne was first recognised by the Mercian assembly, c924. His forceful Welsh policy brought many benefits to his lands west of the Severn. At Hereford the Welsh princes submitted to him c927. They acknowledged Athelstan's sovereignty, accepted the Wye as the boundary between English and Welsh, and paid an annual tribute of gold and silver, and 'handed over by the count', according to William of Malmesbury, '25,000 oxen'. The names of the rulers of Gwent, Dyfed, Brycheiniog, Morgannwg and Gwynedd, found on charters attributed to Athelstan, witness the tight control he exercised over Wales. It should therefore hardly surprise us that the prayer book demonstrates his imprint, as firm on the cults at Leominster as at Chester-le-Street, Exeter and elsewhere.[107]

At Leominster evidence of Athelstan's patronage lies in the minster's relic collection. Leominster held relics in common with other houses, to which they had been granted by Athelstan: relics of Bartholomew, Germanus and Lucius to Exeter, Glastonbury and Malmesbury; of Winwaloe, Breton abbot, to Glastonbury; of Branwalader, bishop of Dol, to Amesbury and Wilton; and 'the vestments of St Mary' and 'the Lord's manger' to Exeter, which also received, according to its relic list, both 'the Lord's altar' and 'the Mount of Olives whence He ascended into heaven', which, in the Leominster list, have been transformed into 'the altar whence He ascended into heaven'. It is therefore reasonable to assume that Leominster also obtained such relics from Athelstan.[108]

4 The Nun-Minster

By the early 11th century, the Leominster prayer book shows, Haemma's abbey had become a nunnery, served by prebendaries in the dual role of priests for the nunnery and for the minster's wide *parochia*. There is no firm evidence of the circumstances under which Haemma's abbey at Leominster was transformed into a nunnery. It has been suggested that this took place under the aegis of the nuns of Shaftesbury, in 1086 one of the largest and wealthiest nunneries in the country, founded by King Alfred, who appointed his daughter as abbess c888, and endowed it with 'estates of land and every kind of wealth'. The suggested link between the two houses is based on the evidence of Leland's somewhat unreliable informant, Thomas Hackluyt of Eaton, and on Leominster's possession of two of Shaftesbury's most prized relics, those of Edward 'king and martyr' and Aelfgyfe. Edward was slain at Corfe by certain zealous thegns of his half-brother, and buried without royal honours at Wareham in 978. Miracles occurring, his body was translated to the nunnery at Shaftesbury. Aelfgyfe, or Elgiva, first wife of the West Saxon king, Edmund (921–46), was buried there c944. Her cult was firmly established by the 970s, when many miracles were worked at her tomb.[109]

'The body of *Elvene*', Aelfgyfe, and 'the body of St Edward king and martyr' appear in Leominster's 1286 relic list (Table 6, nos 17 & 18). A 'certain large bone of St *Alfgive*, the queen' and considerable relics of Edward, recorded in the 1190 Reading list, will have been acquired from Leominster. However, the relics of Edward were far from a rarity; they appear in 13 other relic lists, besides that of Reading. Those of Aelfgyfe are in the Exeter and Durham relic lists, which also included those of Edward. However, it is notable that Aelfgyfe's feast on 18 May does not appear in Leominster's late Anglo-Saxon calendar, although it does appear in eight others. Her evocation in the longer litany is a later addition. It seems improbable that, if Leominster was refounded as a nunnery and daughter house of Shaftesbury, Aelfgyfe's feast would not have been written into the calendar and have appeared amongst the house's principal feasts.[110]

Leominster remained in high regard at the end of the 10th century and in the early decades of the 11th. In his will, probably before 994, Wulfgeat of Donnington, Salop, left half a pound of pence each to the cathedral and St Guthlac's, Hereford; four full-grown bullocks each to the monasteries or *cenobia* at Leominster and Wenlock; two bullocks to Penkridge and Tong; and one bullock each to Bromyard and Clifton-upon-Teme. More significantly, a short obituary for Earl Leofric of Mercia, in John of Worcester's *Chronicle* for 1057, refers not only to the earl's foundation of Coventry Abbey but also to 'his enrichment with valuable ornaments' of the *cenobium* of Leominster, Wenlock, and St John the Baptist and St Werburgh at Chester, and the church of St Mary's, Stow, 'gift of lands' to the monastery at Worcester and additions to the buildings, etc of Evesham Abbey. The inclusion of Leominster in the list is significant, as Herefordshire lay outside Leofric's earldom. Its spiritual power was evidently undiminished, for it was the prestige of a monastery that attracted gifts from the powerful.[111]

Catastrophe struck the nunnery soon after its enrichment. Harold Godwinson's brother, Swein, was created an earl in 1043, his responsibilities including the security of the southern March. This was no light matter. In 1039 Gruffudd ap Llywelyn, king of Gwynedd and Powys, had defeated and killed Leofric's brother, Edwin, earl of Mercia, at Rhyd-y-Groes near Welshpool, thus establishing his reputation amongst his people as the 'terror of the borders, portentous and invincible, against whom reprisals were of little avail'. In 1046 Swein and King Gruffudd allied to attack Gruffydd ap Rhydderch, king of Deheubarth (south-west Wales, with Brecon). On his return Swein, flushed with success and accompanied by his hostages, 'ordered (Eadgifu) abbess of Leominster to be brought to him and kept her as long as it suited him, and then he let her go home'.[112]

Such abduction, whilst untoward, was anything but unique in the late Anglo-Saxon era. King Edgar, champion of the monastic reformers, had a pronounced weakness for novices. He was smitten by Wulfthryth, a young girl at Wilton who was to become abbess, rearing their daughter, Edith, in her minster. The authors of the *Regularis Concordia* sought a solution to this thorny problem by recognising Edgar's queen as 'protector and fearless guardian of the community of nuns', a role assumed also by her successors. In 901 King Edward the Elder's cousin seized Wimborne and one of its nuns. In 1015 Edmund Ironside abducted a high-born widow from Malmesbury Abbey.[113]

Two Worcester sources throw light on Swein's motives. For John of Worcester, his intentions were fundamentally honourable, suggesting that Swein left England for Denmark 'because he was not permitted to marry Eadgifu'. Hemming, on the other hand, smarting from Swein's seizure of some of the church of Worcester's Shropshire lands, wrote that Swein was so addicted to vain glory and pride that he claimed that Canute, not Godwin, was his father. He avers that Eadgifu was carried off by force and kept by Swein 'as his wife' for a year. His claim, that she was only finally released as a result of pressure from an archbishop of Canterbury and bishop of Worcester, is difficult to accept. Swein was, however, a man of ungovernable passions, who shortly afterwards murdered his cousin, Beorn. Eadmer tells us in his *Historia Novorum* that Eadgifu bore a son called Hakon, who in 1052, with another of Godwin's grandsons, was handed over as hostage to Duke William of Normandy. Swein, seeking expiation for his murder of Beorn, went on pilgrimage, barefoot, from Flanders to Jerusalem but on his return died in Lycia, 'from severity of the cold'.[114]

Eadgifu lived to a ripe old age, for at the time Domesday Book was written she was residing at the site now dignified with the name Fencote Abbey (Figs 4.1 a&b). Although there is no contemporary evidence that the nunnery was dissolved on account of Eadgifu's fall, Domesday records that 'she, herself, held' the Leominster sub-manor of Fencote, near Hatfield, with one hide of land, 'before 1066'. This strongly suggests that Edith, Edward the Confessor's queen, who inherited the position of 'protector and fearless guardian' of the nuns, had made provision for the abbess after her return c1047 to live, in retirement, at Fencote, which is described as the abbess's personal property. For her to hold Fencote thus would have been quite inconsistent with her continuing role as head of a monastic community. Even in Anglo-Saxon England, where nuns were permitted some indulgence in terms of minor private possessions, all conventual land was held in common. Fencote had been part of the minster estates prior to Eadgifu's abduction in 1046. It reverted to the royal manor of Leominster after her death. Pope Nicholas's Taxation shows Fencote assessed, with Buckland, at 720 acres c1291 (see Table 10). It is also referred to on a number of occasions in the Leominster Cartulary and Coningsby's 14th-century *Register*.

Fig 4.1a & b Fencote today

Domesday Book also records that Leominster was at farm for £60 'besides the sustenance of the nuns. If (properly) valued it would be worth £120.' R.V. Leonard, and others following him, suggests this implies that the community continued in existence until 1086, and that the £60 difference between farm and valuation is accounted by the nuns' 'sustenance'.

However, in his 1125 foundation charter, Henry I announces, 'know you, that three abbeys were formerly destroyed in the kingdom of England, their sins requiring it, that is to say Reading, Cholsey and Leominster, which a lay hand has long possessed, and has alienated and divided their lands and possessions'. However, Domesday Book records not only that the abbess held Fencote in 1086 but that she had held it 'before 1066', and that there were still 'nuns' at Leominster. It is difficult to believe that the £60 refers to the amount granted for 'sustenance of the nuns', rather than a revaluation of the terms on which it had been farmed for some years.[115]

This being the case, we must assume one of three things. The first is extraordinary, that Henry I was prepared to compromise, by mendacity, his royal foundation at Reading where his body would rest in front of the high altar, assured of the perpetual prayers of the community; or there were further 'sins', at Leominster, after Domesday, of which we have no knowledge; or Henry I was singularly ill informed about the minster church. But he had visited Leominster in the summer of 1121, and his principal agent there, Richard de Capella, had been keeper of his seal and master of his scriptorium for fourteen years prior to his consecration as bishop of Hereford in 1121. In 1123 Capella carried out a searching enquiry for historical evidence as to the spiritualities of the minster. It was well after both these events, in 1125, that Henry I issued his foundation charter.[116]

As protector, Queen Edith would have provided not only for the abbess, but also for her nuns; hence the Domesday reference to the nuns' 'sustenance' from the farm of Edith's manor of Leominster. The Latin term used by the Domesday scribe is *victus*, more precisely translated as food or victuals. With a diminishing number of nuns from 1046, it is difficult to believe that their 'sustenance', or 'supplies' could have cost £60. What the Domesday scribe calls 'provisions' was evidently something similar to the small pensions awarded to the religious after the Dissolution, but paid in kind, not in cash.[117]

The difference between the £60 farm of the estate and the county's valuation of £120 in 1086 can be explained by the necessities of local politics. Centuries earlier, Bede, in a letter to Bishop Egbert, drew attention to the military implications of large tracts of land being granted to the Church rather than to thegns, who had the ability to protect it. The truth of his words became evident for Herefordshire during the years when Gruffudd ap Llywelyn was king of Powys and Gwynedd, 1039–63. Swein had diverted his attention to Deheubarth, but after his departure Gruffudd turned, with great success, against Herefordshire.

In 1052 he defeated Earl Ralph the Timid, Swein's successor, and his combined Anglo-Saxon and Norman forces. As the Anglo-Saxon Chronicle carefully explains, the battle took place 'very near Leominster'. Three years later, when Gruffudd attacked Hereford, the English fled. He burned down the town, killed the priests in the newly-built minster, 'stripped it of its holy objects, treasures, robes and everything', and then it also was set ablaze. After Ralph's death in 1057, Herefordshire was added to Harold's Wessex earldom to provide a unified command for the defence of western England against the Welsh. Gruffudd, whose 'immense spoils, innumerable victories and treasures of gold, silver, gems and purple' earned him the name of 'shield and defender of the Britons', died in 1063. This gave Harold his opportunity to carry the battle into Welsh territory. Given their size, the Leominster lands would, for both Ralph and Harold, have been a significant, and legitimate, resource for the defence of their county.[118]

Further significant evidence came to light in 1950. When the console was detached from the organ, a channel had to be cut from its original to its new position in the south aisle. An obliquely cut trench revealed 'about sixteen skeletons', 'all buried with their heads to the east which interested us at the time very much and from which we concluded that they were in all probability nuns'. Dr Thompson identified them all as female, and under the age of 40. No further documentary evidence is available. Another possible pre-Conquest survival of the minster is an Ionic or Green Man capital, evidently removed from the priory after 1123 (Plate 18).[119]

5 Royally Endowed. The Domesday Book Evidence

Domesday Book describes the great manor of Leominster in a long, and somewhat confusing, entry. In 1066, when Edward the Confessor's queen, Edith, held the manor, the demesne, consisting of 16 'members', was assessed at 80 hides (Table 3.1). In 1086 a quarter of that demesne, 20 hides, had been detached and was in the hands of major Norman landowners (Table 3.2). A further group, of 28 holdings, some 35 hides, was also detached by 1086. 'These lands', we are told, 'lay in Leominster before 1066', at which time 'their customary dues were paid to Leominster'. The names of the Anglo-Saxon tenants and the rents they paid are carefully listed. Here the past tense is used, and there is no mention of rent in 1086, confirming that these lands had been alienated. The names of their new Norman lords are given (Table 3.3). The Domesday scribes drew attention to two further estates, 'which had belonged to the manor of Leominster before 1066', but were now in the hands of King William. At Much Marcle 17 hides had been held by Earl, later King, Harold; and at Stanford Regis 4 hides by his sister, Queen Edith (Table 3.4). The total hideage of Leominster manor prior to 1066 was thus 135¼ hides, but that is not all. Embedded in the text for the county are three other manors which had belonged to Queen Edith but were now in the hands of Roger de Mortimer: Leinthall, Shobdon and Orleton, each at 4 hides (Table 3.5). Their geographical position, and the fact that Leinthall was one of the 16 Leominster 'members', suggests strongly that these also were 'detached'. In this case, the assessment for the full manor in 1066 should be raised to 147¼ hides.

The Norman lords of the detached lands listed in Tables 3.2, 3.3 and 3.5 formed a very powerful group. Roger de Lacy, largest of the lay tenants in Herefordshire and Gloucestershire and political heir of William fitz Osbern, the earl of Hereford who died in 1071, held 10 of these hides. With their castles at Weobley and Ludlow, the de Lacys were the dominant family of the region until the death of Walter II in 1241. Their successors were the Mortimers of Wigmore. Walter de Scohies, with 6 of these hides, held the castlery of Caerleon. Urse d'Abitot, sheriff of Worcester, the plunderer of Worcester cathedral lands, held 5 Leominster hides, at Edwyn Ralph and Butterley. Ralph de Tosny, brother-in-law of William fitz Osbern, 4½ hides, was lord of a great fief in Norfolk, Hereford, Worcester and Shropshire, which included Clifford castle. William fitz Norman, 2 hides, forester of Herefordshire, had Kilpeck with its castle as the caput of his lordship. Osbern fitz Richard held Wapley, though even the Domesday commissioners qualified his claim to hold it by the king's gift, 'as he states'. Whatever the nature of their claims, all these men held a considerable stake in the defence of the county.[120]

Wigmore, the site of Ralph de Mortimer's castle, commanded the Teme valley to the north and, with it, the line of the Roman road between Hereford/Kenchester and Wroxeter. Aymestrey, Leinthall and Shobdon controlled the highlands south of Wigmore, to the bounds of Kingsland. Orleton lay to the east of Leinthall. All these lands had passed into the hands of Mortimer. Herein lie the origins of the great marcher family that eventually became earls of March. Wigmore Castle, and the compact group of manors about it at Aymestrey, Shobdon, the two Leinthalls, Orleton and Brimfield, thus sheltered Leominster from attack from the north. The close relationship between the Mortimers of Wigmore and the priors of Leominster becomes, as will be shown, one of the recurrent themes in the history of the monastery and its borough. Osbern fitz Richard was lord of Richards Castle, with its garrison of 23 men. This lay to the east of Wigmore, controlling the principal route between Leominster and Ludlow. Richards Castle and Wigmore were supplemented by the Lacy castles of Weobley to the south-west and Ludlow to the north. Behind this formidable defence network, the rich agricultural lands, not only of the manor of Leominster but of the whole county, could be fully developed. Only on one occasion was there a major Welsh break-through, after Owain Glyn Dwr's victory at Pilleth in 1402. Leominster's detached lands were but a small price to pay for the security and development potential thus assured.

Analysis of Domesday Book provides the first detailed evidence as to the extent of the lands that Merewalh had granted to Edfrith more than four centuries earlier. In 1066 it amounted to virtually 150 hides, valued at £192 5s 5d. This 'gigantic' Domesday manor of Leominster F.W. Maitland compared with the large and valuable Gloucestershire manors of Berkeley and Tewkesbury, worth respectively £170 and £100 in the Confessor's time. The heart of the lordship extended almost 12 miles north to south, from Wigmore and Leinthall to Sarnesfield and Hope-under-Dinmore, and some 18 miles east to west, from Edwyn Ralph to Wapley. As will be seen, as late as 1123 lordship and *parochia* were in places practically coterminous.[121]

As the events of the first half of the 11th century suggest, an endowment of over 100 hides for Edfrith's church, even at the time of Merewalh's conversion, seems to represent generosity to the point of extravagance. In a society where military resources available to the Crown were based on land, as Bede recognised, this would lead to the

3.1 Demesne Lands in the time of King Edward the Confessor: 16 'members' held by Queen Edith

Lustone	Luston
Iarpol	Yarpole
Elmodestreu	Aymestrey
Brumefelde	Brimfield
Estune	Ashton (-in-Eye)
Stoctune	Stockton
Stoca	Stoke (Prior)
Mersetone	Marston (Stannett)
Uptone	Upton (Court?)
Hope	(Miles) Hope
Bretlege	Brierley
Ivintune	Ivington
Cerlestreu	Cholstrey
Lentehale	Leinthall
Gedeven	Edwyn (Ralph)
Fernelau	Farlow (Salop)

Total: 80 hides, £120

3.2 'Of the 80 hides of this manor', 20 hides were held by major Norman lords:

Land		Hides	Value in 1086 £ s d	Lord in 1086
Gedevan	Edwyn (Ralph)	3		Urse d'Abitot
Humbre	Humber	3½		Roger de Lacy
Brochemt	Brockmanton	1½		" " "
Elmodestreu	Aymestrey	1		Ralph de Mortimer
Letehale	Leinthall	8		" " "
Lege	Lye	½		Wm fitz Norman
Ettone	Eyton	1		" " "
Subtotal			12 11 0	
	?	1½?	1 5 0	Leofwine Latimer
Total		20	13 16 0	

Grand Total, 1086 (3.1-3.2): 60 hides, £106 4s

Table 3 Domesday Book: The Manor of Leominster

3.3 Subinfeudated Lands: ‘These lands lay in Leominster before 1066’

	Land	Hides	Value		Lord	
			1066	1086	1066	1086
Hetfelde	Hatfield	5	£4	£5	Leofled	Hugh Donkey
Wapletone	Wapley	2		£1	O f Richard	Osbern fitz Richard
Buterlei	Butterley	1		£2	Ketel	Urse d’Abitot
Fencote	Fencote	1			Abbess	Abbess
Hantone	Hampton (Wafre)	½	£2	£1 10s	Browning	Roger de Lacy
Hantone	Hampton (Richard)	2	£1	£2	Edwy	“ “ “
Sarnesfelde	Sarnesfield	1½		£1	Saeric	“ “ “
Gadrehope	Gattertop	1		£1 10s	Alwin	“ “ “
Wighemore	Wigmore	½			Alfward	Ralph de Mortimer
Bromefelde	Brimfield	3v		7s 6d	Ernsy	“ “ “
Forne	Ford	1 + 1v)			Alfward	Ralph de Tosny
Bradefelde	Broadfield	1)	£2 15s	£3 15s	“	“ “ “
Sarnesfelde	Sarnesfield	½)			“	“ “ “
Eton	Eaton	1½	£2	£3	Leofnoth	“ “ “
Riseberie	Risbury	2	£1	£3	Edwin	William de Scohies
Wavertune	Wharton	1	£1	£1	Wulfward	“ “ “
Newentone	Newton	½		Waste	Browning	“ “ “
Dilge	Dilwyn	1	5s	£1	Aelmer	“ “ “
Hetfelde	Hatfield	½	5s 5d	8s	“	“ “ “
Bradeford	Broadward	½	£1	£1 10s	Leofnoth	Wm fitz Norman
Hantone	Hampton (Mapenore?)	1	£1	£1	Edric	Drogo fitz Ponz
Hamenes	Hamnish	1	£1	£1 3s 4d	Ernsy	“ “ “
Miceltune	Middleton	1½	£1	10s	Aelfric	Durand the Sheriff
Dilge	Dilwyn (Sollers?)	2	£1	£2	Ravenkel	Ilbert
Lutelei	Luntley	2	£2	£1 10s	“	“
Alac	Knoakes Court	1	10s	10s	Alfward	Gruffydd the Boy
Unidentified		½	Waste	15s		“ “ “
Iarpole	Yarpole	1v	Waste	3s	Aelfric	Leofwin Latimer
Total		33 +5v*	£21 15 5	£36 11 10		

v, virgate; *= 34¼ hides but Domesday Book total ‘32 hides’ *Domesday Book*, F & C Thorn, 1.11-37

3.4 ‘Before 1066 two manors belonged to this manor’:

Merchelai	(Much) Marcle	17	£30	£30	Harold	King William
Stanford	Stanford (Regis)	4	£5	£5	Queen Edith	“ “
Total		21	£35	£35		

Total, 1066 (3.1+3.3+3.4): 135¼ hides, £176 15s 5d

Thorn, 1.7, 1.9

3.5 Leominster? Manors held by Queen Edith, 1066

Lintehal	Leinthall	4	£2 10s	£5	Queen Edith	Ralph de Mortimer
Scepedune	Shobdon	4	£6	£7	Queen Edith	“ “ “
Alretune	Orleton	4	£7	£5	“ “	“ “ “
Total		12	£15 10s	£17		

Grand Total, 1066 (3.1+3.3+3.4+3.5): 147¼ hides, £192 5s 5d

Thorn, 9.7, 10, 19

Table 3 Domesday Book: The Manor of Leominster

dramatic depletion of the thegn land required for defence. However, the ability of Merewalh, as ruler of the Western Hecani, the folk west of the Severn, to hand over most of the rich lowlands of north central Herefordshire to the Church supports the belief that his relations with the Welsh were good. When they deteriorated his successors were faced with a problem that ultimately led to alienation. Evidence from southern England shows similar liberality in the same era: at Gloucester, Malmesbury and Barking where estates of some 300 hides had been granted. Eafe's lands about her minster in Thanet were some 80 hides, but at Wenlock her daughter, Mildburg, if we accept her *Testament*, received at least 220.[122]

After the Alfredian foundations of Wilton and Shaftesbury, the valuation of the Leominster lands at £176 15s 5d prior to post-Conquest detachments compares favourably with those of other Anglo-Saxon nunneries. Given the true extent of its pre-Conquest estates, this is hardly surprising (Table 4).[123] However, due to its remote situation west of the Severn, it has rarely received due consideration.

The compact character, extent and central situation of Leominster manor are all tokens of its antiquity. By contrast, the cathedral's holdings within the county were dispersed. Only a small number formed compact groups, and these were relatively small: about Hereford and the minsters at Bromyard and Ledbury; the four manors of Preston-on-Wye, Tyberton, Madley and Eaton Bishop; and three abutting the Forest at Walford, Ross and Upton Bishop. The remainder, Wormsley, Canon Pyon, Ullingswick, Woolhope, Brockhampton and How Caple, were widely scattered. Such dispersal does not betoken a single early grant, as at Leominster. In the matter of the royal estates, the policy of Merewalh's sons was very different from that of their father. Like Bede, they were concerned about the necessity to retain adequate thegn land.

Domesday tells us that Edith's 80 hides of demesne were divided into 16 'members'. These are all named, and fit well into the pattern of the priory's demesne estates, as described in Coningsby's *Register*, based on the 14th-century court rolls. They show the Leominster lordship divided, for administrative purposes, into four *herneys*, a term derived from the Old English *herness*, 'obedience, or district obedient to a single jurisdiction'. It was used to describe the lands of two ancient minster churches, Berkeley and Bromfield, in the neighbouring counties of Gloucester and Salop. 'The currency of this term in the 12th century is good evidence that what can only be described as a manorial court had been a well-established institution before the Conquest ... the preservation of the Old English term (after the Conquest) is remarkable testimony to the strength of the Old English

Nunnery	**£**	**s**	**d**	**Founded**	**Founder**
Wilton	234	15	0	ref 871	Alfred?
Shaftesbury	234	5	0	by 893	Alfred
Leominster	176	15	5	?	?
Barking	162	19	8	ref 870	Edgar
Romsey	136	8	0	c907	Edward the Elder
Winchester[1]	65	0	0	c900	Alfred
Amesbury[2]	54	15	0	c980	Queen Aethelthryth
Wherwell	52	4	0	c985	Queen Aethelthryth

ref reformed; [1] 'manor of Itchin held by Hugh fitz Baldric in 1086'; [2] 'depredations of certain magnates' recorded in Domesday Book

Table 4. Late Anglo-Saxon Nunneries: Some Domesday Valuations (Adapted from D.Knowles The Monastic Order in England, 940-1216 *(1963) 702-3)*

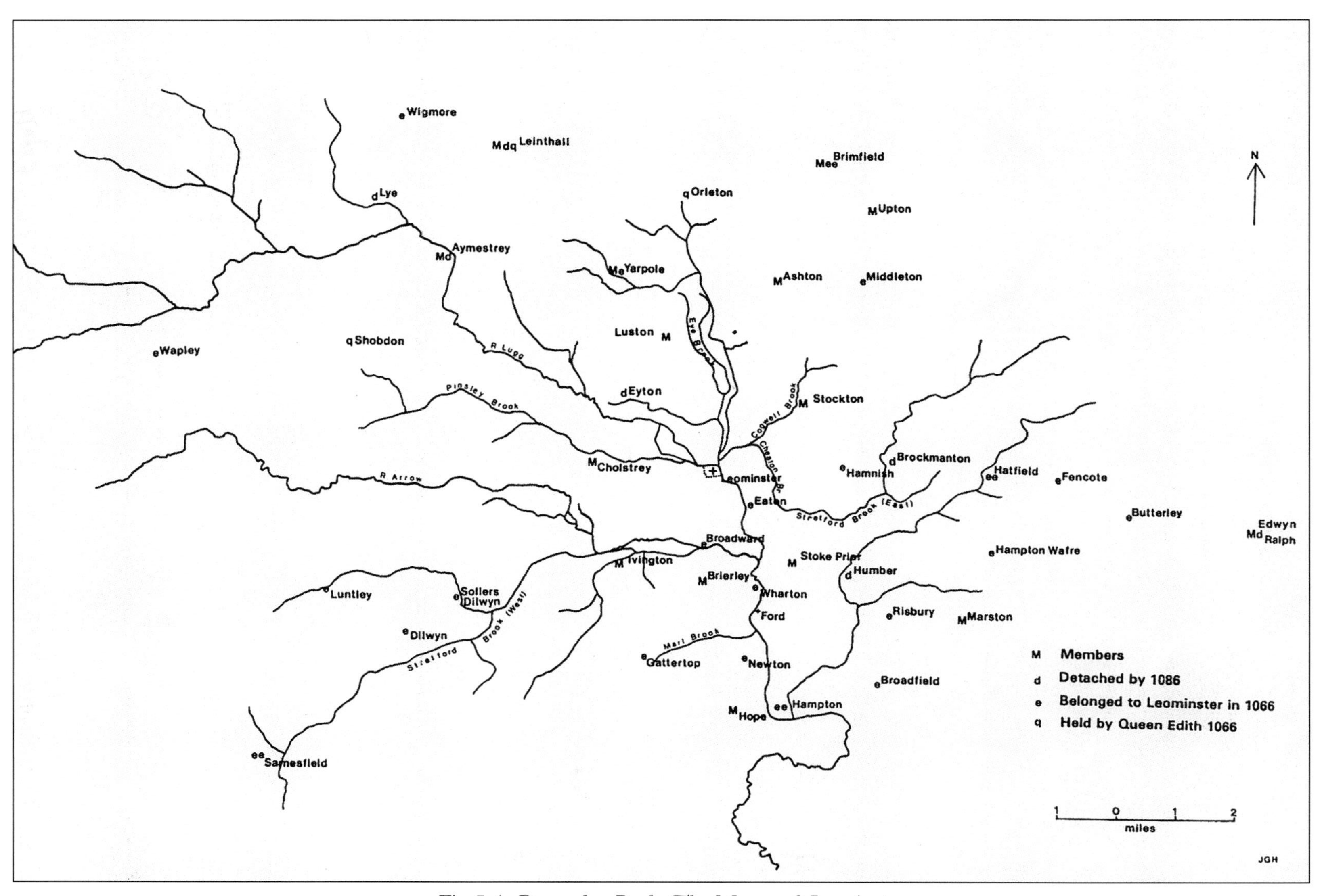

Fig 5.1 Domesday Book: The Manor of Leominster

traditions underlying the institution.' What we have here is an administrative framework inherited by the priory from its Anglo-Saxon predecessor, the minster church. However, at Leominster, there was not merely one *herneys*, as at Berkeley and Bromfield, but four.[124]

Their location reflected the cross-shaped drainage pattern of the area. North to south this was formed by the Ridgemoor brook which flowed into the Lugg and Kenwater just north of the precinct, and the Lugg which then flowed due south until it had to skirt Dinmore Hill, the southern boundary of the lordship. The west-east axis was formed on the west by the Lugg and Pinsley, and on the east by the Whyle brook, which became the Stretford and then the Cheaton brook. Thus in the north-west there was Luston *herneys*, with Stockton *herneys* east of the Ridgemoor brook, and Stoke (Prior) *herneys* to the south, across the Stretford-Cheaton brooks. The fourth *herneys*, Ivington, lay to the south of Luston and the wedge of royal land between Lugg and Kenwater, about Kingsland. To the east the Lugg separated it from Stoke (Prior). There is a strong relationship between the geographical bounds of this great lordship and those of the Leominster *parochia*, even as late as 1123. As Kemp explains, the '*parochia* had been more extensive at an earlier date'. Indeed, this is hardly surprising, for both will have originated in Merewalh's grant to Edfrith of c660 (Fig 5.1).[125]

All but three of the sixteen members named in Domesday Book can be placed in one of the four *herneys*:

Luston	**Stockton**	**Stoke (Prior)**	**Ivington**
Luston	Brimfield	Stoke	Ivington
Yarpole	Ashton (-in-Eye)	Marston (Stannett)	Cholstrey
Aymestrey	Stockton		Brierley
	Upton (Court?)		
	(Miles) Hope		

Whether Upton is Upper (Court) or Lower is not clear, but it certainly was not Nun Upton, which belonged to the nuns of Limebrook, a mile south of Lingen. Of the remaining members Leinthall, the 8-hide holding of Ralph I de Mortimer, will have looked to Luston, whilst Edwyn (Ralph) with Butterley, the 4-hide estate of Urse d'Abitot, will have formed part of the *herneys* of Stoke (Prior). Stockton, apparently, had to attempt to cope with distant Farlow, now a detached part of Herefordshire, north of Cleobury Mortimer in Shropshire (Fig 5.2, 6.3).

Almost a century ago, Maitland suggested that the great Domesday manor of Leominster with its 'neat symmetrical arrangement — 80 hides, 16 members, 8 reeves, 8 radknights, 16 beadles — very probably had a Welsh (British) basis'. The symmetry is not quite what he thought, for there were 16 mills, but only 15 beadles and 15 reeves in the time of Edward the Confessor. Glanville Jones has identified the 13th-century *Book of Iorwerth* as a model of territorial organisation for the interpretation of early settlement history which, 'though theoretical, was not completely divorced from reality'. On the Welsh March, and elsewhere, 'there was much less discontinuity in the use of landed resources than hitherto believed'.

In this model, fourfold divisions play a fundamental part, four holdings giving one vill and four vills making up a multiple estate. Elsewhere, Jones put forward the thesis that almost everywhere along the March a striking continuity could be demonstrated in the administrative arrangements of settlements between prehistoric and medieval times; a continuity which appeared to be more closely associated with the iron-age hillforts than with the relatively few Roman villas found on the Welsh March. 'Nowhere, perhaps', he said, 'is this more striking than at the hillfort at Ivington near Leominster in Herefordshire' which, in the pre-Conquest era, had become a *herneys* of the

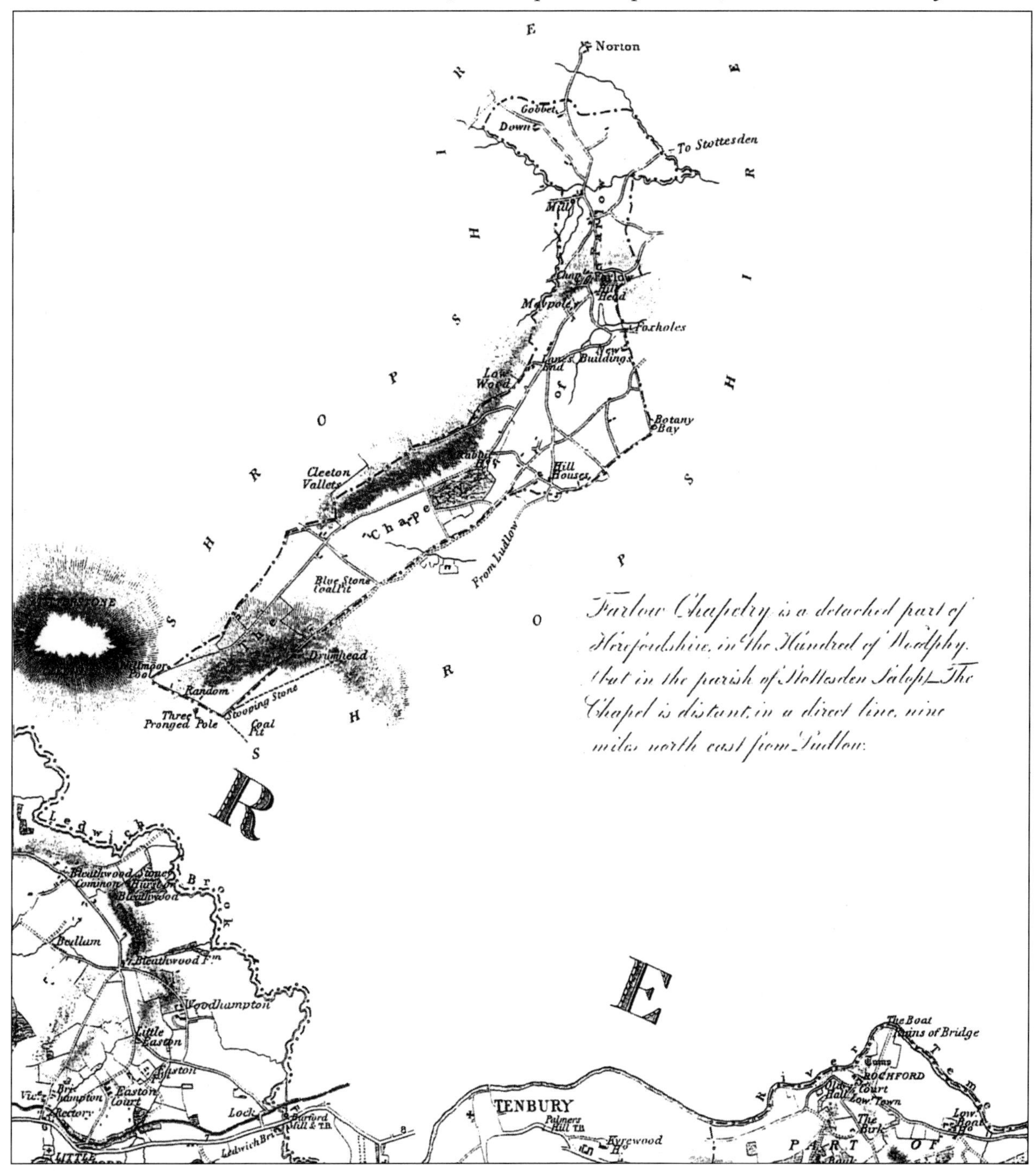

Fig 5.2 'Farlow detached part of the county of Hereford', Bryant's Herefordshire *1839*

vast manor of Leominster. Haslam has posited a similar relationship for other early settlements in Wiltshire. In Herefordshire Jones also found a link between the shareland of the Welsh law books and the Welsh hide on the one hand, and the Domesday carucate on the other.[126]

The fourfold division described above does not invalidate, but elaborates Jones's theory, for each *herneys* had a major multivallate hillfort situated on its segment of the upland periphery: Croft Ambrey, 38 acres, in Luston; the Bache, 10½ acres, in Stockton; Risbury, 28 acres, in Stoke Prior; and Ivington, 48 acres, already mentioned. If the hillforts were the predecessors of the *burys* as estate centres, the major question remains, how and when were the four territorial units brought together? How long had Leominster existed as a 'gigantic manor' prior to its gift by Merewalh to Edfrith as the endowment of his minster?

Plate 1 Galba Axiv f20r, Leominster's unique copy of the Adiutor Laborantium ('Helper of those who labour'), attributed to St Columba. BL© *see p31-2*

Adiutor laborantium,	*Helper of those who toil,*	*gubernator fidelium,*	*Governor of the faithful,*
bonorum rector omnium,	*Ruler of all the good,*	*hostis inpoenitentium,*	*Enemy of the impenitent,*
custos ad pro pugnab(c?)ulum	*Custodian of the ramparts*	*iudex cunctorum iudic(i)um,*	*Judge of all judges,*
defensorque credentium,	*Defender of the believers,*	*Castigator errantium,*	*Chastiser of those who sin,*
exaltatu(o?)r humilium,	*Exalter of the lowly,*	*Casta uita uiuentium,*	*Pure life of the living,*
fractor superbientium,	*Breaker of the proud,*	*Lumen et pater/luminum,*	*Light and father of all lights*

2

a

b

3

4

5

c

d

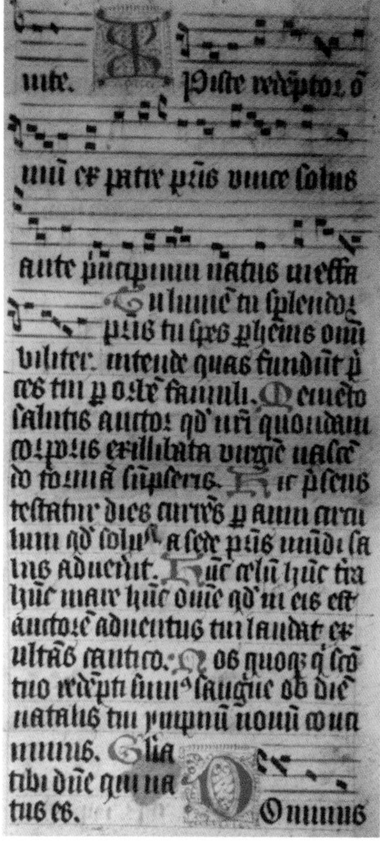

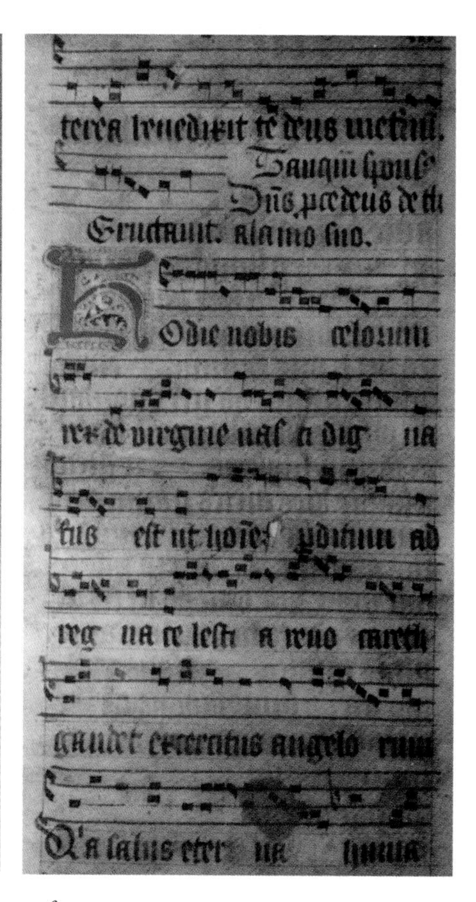

a *b* *c*

Plate 3a-c Leominster parochial breviary (pp237-40) (HRO 567/2/1/68)
a) Vigil of Nativity, 24 December: Salvator mundi Domine, Qui nos salvasti hodie, In hac nocte nos protege, Et salva omni tempore. Adesto nunc propitius: 'Lord, Saviour of the world, Who has redeemed us today, Protect us in this night, And save us at any time. Propitiously help us now'
b) Nativity, 25 December: Christe, Redemptor omnium, ex Patre, Patris unice, solus ante principium natus ineffabiliter: 'Jesus, the Father's only Son, whose death for all redemption won, before the worlds, of God most high, begotten all ineffably ...'
c) Hodie nobis coelorum rex de virgine nasci dignatus est: 'Today the King of heaven has for us deigned to be born of a Virgin'

Opposite: Plate 2a-d Leominster parochial missal (pp237-40)
a) the blessing of holy water, for which a vessel of water, salt on a plate, and a towel to wipe the priest's fingers would be prepared (p238) (HRO 567/2/3/1);
b) the blessing of bread to be given to the people on Sundays and a blessing with the chalice over the people on principal and double feasts (HRO 567/2/3/1);
c) & d) Hereford Use: the Proper of the Saints celebrating feast days in October (the numbers adjacent to the texts indicate the references to the saints in the red entries): 1) St Luke, 18th; 2) St Frideswide, 19th; 3) 11,000 virgins; 4) St Romanus, 23rd; 5) Translation of St Thomas (of Hereford), 25th (HRO 567/2/3/3)

Plate 4 Sumer is icumen in, *Harley MS 978 f11v BL©. English text black; Latin, sacred, text red. Boxed text: instructions for performance as a round. Pes, parts for lower voices, on bottom two lines.* *(see pp141-6)*

6 Refoundation: Mother and Daughter

The Foundation of Reading Abbey

Late on the night of 25 November 1120 Henry I's only legitimate son, the 17-year-old prince William, embarked on the *White Ship* at Barfleur in Normandy for his return to England. The king had set sail just before twilight but the prince's crew, 'immoderately filled with wine, exclaimed that those now ahead must be left astern'. The *White Ship* 'flew swifter than the arrow' but the carelessness of the intoxicated crew drove her onto a rock. The sole survivor was a butcher from Rouen. All others, including prince William, two of Henry's other children and many members of his household, including the earl of Chester, were lost. On hearing the news Henry 'fell unconscious to the ground ... never to smile again'. Six months later he founded the abbey of Reading, 'for the salvation of my own soul, those of King William (the Conqueror) my father, King William (Rufus), my brother, William, my son ... and all my ancestors and successors'. This he planned as his burial place where 100 monks would chant masses for the repose of his soul, in perpetuity. Henry I died in Normandy but was buried in his abbey, before the high altar, at a ceremony attended by King Stephen, his successor, in January 1136, yet two and a half centuries later Reading's monks had well nigh forgotten their founder. In 1398 Richard II only renewed the monks' rights and privileges on condition that they repaired Henry's tomb, and his effigy upon it, within twelve months.[127]

Welsh affairs brought Henry I to the Marches in 1121. After the death of its prince, Owain ap Cadwgan in 1116, Powys had been split up under the rule of his brothers who, as soon as they heard of the earl of Chester's death in the *White Ship*, descended on his county. Henry responded by moving 'a mighty host against the men of Powys as soon as summer came and it was easy to find and follow paths'. At Whitsuntide he held court at Westminster. In mid June a day's journey west took him to Reading where, on 18th, he laid the foundation stone of the abbey. Shortly afterwards he was in Hereford with Ranulf, his chancellor, the archbishop of Rouen and Richard de Capella, the newly-appointed bishop of the diocese.[128]

Henry I's route from Hereford into Shropshire lay through Leominster, still the centre of the vast royal manor described in such detail in Domesday Book. There can be little doubt that this was the occasion when Henry decided to refound its ancient minster as a cell of Reading, possibly inspired by the relics that were no doubt shown to him by the minster priests during his visit (see Table 6). His foundation charter explains the circumstances under which Leominster was granted to Reading: 'know that three abbeys were formerly destroyed in the kingdom of England, their sins requiring it, that is to say, Reading, Cholsey and Leominster which a lay hand has long possessed and has alienated and divided their lands and possessions. But I, by the advice of bishops and others of the faithful ... have built a new monastery at Reading in honour of the Mother of God and ever Virgin Mary, and of the blessed John the Evangelist and to that monastery I have given Leominster and Cholsey with all things belonging to them.' At only one of these three churches, Cholsey, a very late Anglo-Saxon foundation, is there any architectural evidence of the Anglo-Saxon forerunner: the quoins on one of the arches of the central tower have good long-and-short work (Fig 6.1).[129]

Fig 6.1 Cholsey Church today, with crossing tower

Like his father, William I, Henry I had been deeply attracted by the grandeur and ceremony of the liturgy at the great reformed Benedictine monastery of Cluny in Burgundy, in particular its lavish use of all the arts, especially music, architecture and sculpture, which accompanied it. His sister, Adeliza, countess of Blois, had become a Cluniac nun and her son, Henry of Blois, King Stephen's brother, was educated at Cluny. Henry himself made unparalleled contributions towards the building of Cluny III, underwriting the completion of the great nave and, in 1131, providing an annual grant of £100 to meet running costs. Two decades after his death Abbot Peter the Venerable of Cluny paid tribute to Henry in his *Mandatory Epistle*:

> Among all the kings of the Latin West, who for the last three hundred years have testified their affection for the church of Cluny ... Henry, king of the English and duke of Normandy, has surpassed all others in his gifts and has shown more than an ordinary share of love and attachment to (Cluny). It was he who perfected that grand basilica, commenced under the auspices and donations of Alfonso, king of Spain, exceeding all other known churches in the Christian world in its construction and beauty.[130]

Cluny, at 520ft, was the longest Christian church of its day. So inspired, Henry built Reading also on a grand scale. It was only 50ft short of the 500ft of the contemporary cathedral at Canterbury, whilst its Norman priory at Leominster, although only a cell, was merely some 10ft shorter than

Fig 6.2 Cholsey Barn prior to May 1815

Hereford's Romanesque cathedral. Even Reading's barns were on a grand scale. Cholsey barn, demolished in 1815, was the largest in Europe, 303ft in length and 51ft in height (Fig 6.2). Its nearest English rival, Beaulieu abbey's barn at St Leonard's, was a mere 224ft. The size of Leominster's barn is unknown but, when 'fired by a comet' in 1594, it burned for fifteen days.[131]

The vast sanctuary at Cluny assaulted the senses. Here liturgy and art came together. The series of eight capitals on the piers of the ambulatory expressed 'the cosmography and system of the Christian church in an allusive and symbolic (sculptural) statement of the quaternities'; these included the four Seasons, the four Cardinal and the Theological Virtues, the four symbolic Trees and Rivers of Paradise, together with figures representing the eight Tones of Plainchant. The vast church, completed by Henry's patronage, was eventually dedicated by Pope Innocent II in 1130. On arrival the pilgrim was confronted by a central portal 40ft wide and 62ft high, dominated by a tympanum bearing Christ in Majesty.[132]

Henry's motives in refounding Reading and Leominster were not unalloyed. Having visited both in 1121, he was well aware of their strategic importance. At Reading the Great West Road divided, one section going via Oxford to Gloucester and Hereford, the other taking a more southerly route to Bristol and Bath and crossed by the major road from the midlands via Oxford to Winchester and Southampton. As William of Malmesbury points out, 'Henry built his monastery at Reading between the rivers Kennet and Thames in a spot calculated for the reception of almost all who might have occasion to travel to the more popular cities of England. There he placed Cluniac monks who at this day (1125) are a noble pattern of holiness and an example of unwearied and delightful hospitality. Here may be seen what is peculiar to this place; for guests, arriving every hour, consume more than the inmates themselves.'[133]

Leominster also occupied a nodal position, although of regional rather than national significance. It was almost equidistant between the great royal castle at Hereford and that of the de Lacys at Ludlow on the strategic route along the Marches from Chepstow, Monmouth and Hereford to Shrewsbury and Chester. This was crossed by a major east-west route, later the London-Aberystwyth road, coming from Pershore and Worcester through Bromyard, which bifurcated at Leominster. The more northerly route followed the Lugg valley by way of Presteigne into central Wales, whilst the more southerly, the present-day A44, followed the valley of the Arrow to enter Wales by way of Kington and Radnor. Both monasteries thus provided excellent staging posts for the king, his household and officials on their constant peregrinations. All the English monarchs from Henry I to Edward I used Leominster Priory, as of right, on their journeys through the Welsh Marches. Henry III was a particularly frequent visitor. The abbey at Reading was even used as a meeting place of parliament on a number of occasions. As will be seen in Chapters 11 and 15, such royal visitations imposed an extraordinary burden on monastic finances.[134]

Henry I's brief campaign in 1121 to reassert his authority over the men of Powys ended in triumph. Powys acknowledged his authority and gave him a tribute of 10,000 head of cattle. During the campaign, however, he experienced a sharp reminder of his mortality. A few Welsh archers in a wild, wooded valley, ambushed his force. One discharged an arrow at random amongst the English. It struck Henry I about the heart. 'The king had a great fright exactly as though the arrow had gone through him' but, on account of the corselet and armour he was wearing, it recoiled. Conscious of the death of his brother, William Rufus, found dead in the New Forest with an arrow in his breast, Henry feared it had been fired from his own ranks. He moved apace with the building of Reading abbey.[135]

At Henry I's request Abbot Pons of Cluny sent his prior, Peter, and seven of his monks to serve the new monastery at Reading, where they were joined by a number of others from Lewes Priory, the premier Cluniac house of the realm. The royal foundation ceremony took place on Henry's way to Wales, on 18 June 1121. On his return from Powys Henry sought to ensure that work on the abbey proceeded with all expedition. In April 1123 Prior Peter, his mission evidently completed, was permitted to return to his duties at Cluny. As his successor, and first abbot, Henry chose Hugh of Amiens, a Cluniac monk who had already shown outstanding ability as prior of Limoges, c1115–20, and then of Lewes, 1120–3. He became one of the foremost churchmen of his age. After seven years' service at Reading he was elected archbishop of Rouen. Reading is first referred to as an abbey in a bull of June 1123 that gave papal protection and confirmation of its possessions, including Leominster. As priories, all Cluny's daughter houses acknowledged their obedience and subjection to the abbot of Cluny, but as Reading now had its own abbot, it was no longer subject. Nevertheless, it retained the Cluniac Use, that is the Cluniac form of the Roman rite. Henry's formal foundation charter was issued in 1125. Papal confirmation came in April.[136]

Leominster Priory

Despite its size and grandeur Henry I's monastery at Leominster remained a dependency, a cell, of Reading abbey for over four centuries. It was thus a priory, not an abbey. The superior was usually termed dean or prior, occasionally proctor or *custos*. This was one means of formally emphasising that his appointment, and its termination, was at the will of the abbot of Reading. This was to lead to conflict with the bishops of Hereford right up to the Dissolution. To ensure Leominster's dependency, both prior and monks remained members of the Reading community, and the customary conventual complement of twelve monks was never exceeded; on occasions it fell as low as six. In Henry I's words, the monks were 'to tarry there, to pray for us and our said progenitors from time to time' and 'to entertain the poor, travellers and strangers'. The priory's purpose, other than the service of God, the singing of masses for the repose of the souls of Henry, his ancestors and successors, and the provision of hospitality and alms, was to sustain its mother house by financial support. Such payments represented, on average, about two-thirds of the priory's annual income. In 1291, out of temporalities totalling £303 3s, £240 (80%) went to Reading; in 1536 the comparable figures were £660 16s 8d and £438 4s 8d (66%).[137]

Copies of Henry I's foundation charter are to be found in two of Reading Abbey's surviving general cartularies, BL Egerton 3031 and BL Harley 1708. It is also in the Leominster Priory Cartulary, BL Cotton MS Domitian Aiii. The charter defines the three principal sources of the abbey's and priory's revenues: their estates; the profits of justice from its borough and hundred courts; and finally their spiritualities, the income of dependent churches etc, chapels, churchyards, offerings and tithes, a source that it defended rigorously.[138]

Temporalities

Details of some of the priory's temporalities, its estates, the 'appendages, woods, fields and pastures, meadows and waters, with their mills and fisheries' of Henry's charter, can be found in Domesday

Book. From 1086 these remained, unchanged, in royal hands until granted by Henry to Reading. The Domesday survey makes it clear that they represented but some half of the lands that had belonged to the pre-Conquest church of Leominster. By 1086 there were but 60 hides, valued at £60 as opposed to 135¼ hides worth £176 15s 5d in the manor of Leominster in the time of Edward the Confessor (see Table 3.4 & Fig 5.1).[139]

Soon after his appointment in 1123, Abbot Hugh assumed control of the priory's estates. These continued to be administered in their four ancient *herneys*. This is evident from Hugh's charter of 1127 granting Ailward a hide of land in (Miles) Hope in the *ministerium* of Stockton, another in Lucton within the Luston *ministerium* and ten acres within the Leominster *ministerium*. For these Ailward 'made full service as a radknight', that is one who road on escort duty, and with messages, as the vital link between Leominster and Reading, and paid 10s each year at the feast of SS Peter and Paul (29 June), the patron saints of both minster and priory. This is the earliest reference to the priory's affairs in the Leominster Cartulary.[140]

Ministerium, the Norman-French word meaning bailiwick, was applied initially, but the priory's records soon reverted to the ancient term, *herneys*. Thus in 1334 the halimote, or manorial, rolls refer to the 'west *herneys*', a term which recurs in the court rolls, but in 1350 to the *herneys* of Ivington. Ivington has always been closely associated with Leominster and 'west *herneys*' or *westharnes* was sometimes used in a more restricted sense relating to the Grange as the priory's home farm. In 1349 we have 'Stocton *cum harness*', and in 1350 'Luston hernes with the hamlets' and later the '*hernes* of Stoke (Prior), with its members and appurtenances'. Each was administered from its own *bury*, that is court or sub-manor. The four *burys* can still be seen on the current 1:25,000 OS maps. At Ivington the stonework of its medieval gateway remains, and Pevsner maintains that the upper half-timbered chamber is also of pre-Reformation date. At Stockton there is evidence of the medieval fishponds, mill and dovecote. For the regular meeting of the prior's court at the four *burys* the Old English term, *halimote*, was retained. It was still meeting at Stockton, under the Halimote Tree, in 1794. All the evidence indicates that Leominster's Benedictine monks were maintaining an administrative framework established early in the Anglo-Saxon era.[141]

Secondly, there were the profits of justice from the abbot's courts. Henry I's charter had granted 'all jurisdiction over assaults, thefts, murders, effusions of blood and infractions of the peace as much as belonged to the royal power' within the hundred, later the liberty, of Leominster. This required the men of a number of surrounding lay manors to attend the Leominster courts 'in accordance with previous practice'. 'If they refuse the Crown will compel them.' The abbot thus had jurisdiction not only over his own men but those of some neighbouring lords. In addition he was granted 'every immunity, power, quittance and liberty that the king had power to confer'. At the time this implied the exclusion of the king's officers from the abbot's liberties of both Reading and Leominster but, with the rapid development of royal justice under Henry II, it was to mean, in practice, that the king's judges met at Leominster in special session with the prior or his representative taking the chair, the profits etc going to the abbot. The king's coroner, however, had, as late as 1409, 'to beg licence to sit in the town'. This he was granted, but 'only on condition he proclaimed this licence'.[142]

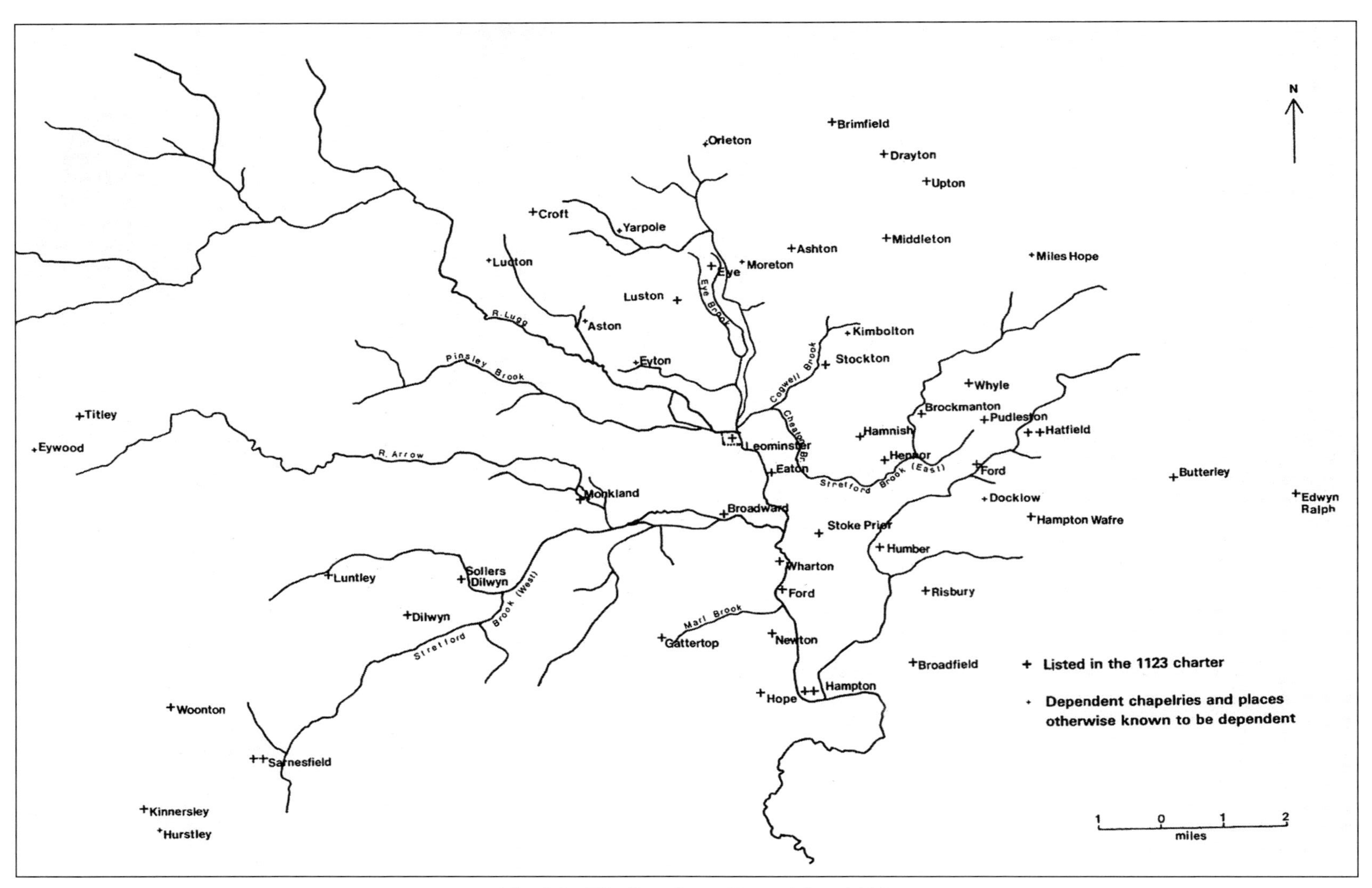

Fig 6.3 The Leominster Parochia, *1123*

The *Parochia* and Spiritualities

Much more important than the profits of justices were the spiritualities, payments due to the priory as the successor of the minster as mother church, 'the tithes, offerings and (dues from) the cemeteries' referred to in the foundation charter. Such dues continued to be paid to the mother church when lesser churches were founded within its *parochia*, its wide area of pastoral responsibility. Given the turmoil of the years prior to and after the Norman Conquest, it is not surprising that, as with the Leominster lands, many of these spiritualities had been lost. In 1123, acting no doubt on royal instruction, Bishop Richard de Capella came to Leominster and called a jury of 'ancient and trustworthy men' to vouch, in his presence, for those places owing obedience, and thus financial dues, to the newly-founded priory, as successor of the ancient minster. These Capella listed in a charter, formally confirming their obedience to the abbot of Reading. This identified 39 places, 43 if the double settlements are included (Fig 6.3 & Table 5).[143]

For John Blair Leominster's *parochia* was 'one of the biggest mother parishes known in England'. Kemp has a map of the *parochia* c1200, but in 1066 it was considerably more extensive on the west, for Titley, Woonton, Sarnesfield and Kinnersley were all included in Capella's 1123 charter.[144] Hurstley was not listed in the charter, but other evidence shows it had been part of the *parochia*. Certainly, Merewalh's grant of an extensive lordship to Edfrith's minster will have carried with it responsibility for the spiritual wellbeing of its folk. This will have passed to the monastic church founded under Haemma. Yet there are considerable divergences between the places listed by the Domesday scribes as within the Leominster lordship and those

5.1 Places named in the 1123 Charter:

Ashton-in-Eye, *Essetuna*	Humber, *Humbra*
Brimfield, *Brumesfelda*	Kinnersley, *Kinardeslega*
Broadfield, *Bradesfelda*	Knoakes Court, *Ach*
Broadward, *Bradeford*	Luntley, *Luntelega*
Brockmanton, *Brocmanetuna*	Luston, *Lustona*
Butterley, *Buterlega*	Middleton, *Michlatuna*
Croft, *Croftona*	Miles Hope, *Hopa*
Dilwyn, *Diliga prima et secunda*	Monkland, *Leena*
Drayton, *Dreituna*	Newton, *Niwetuna*
Eaton, *Eatuna*	Pudleston, *Putlesduna*
Edwyn Ralph, *Gedesfenna*	Risbury, *Risebiria*
Eye, *Eya*	Sarnesfield, both,
Ford, *Forda*	*utraque Sernesfelda*
Ford-in-Pudleston, *Forda*	Stocton, *Stockton*
Gattertop, *Gatredehopa*	Stoke Prior, *Stokes*
Hamnish, *Hamenesce*	Titley, *Titelega*
Hampton, both, *utraque Hamtona*	Upton (Court?), *Uptuna*
Hampton (Wafre?), *Heentuna*	Wharton, *Wavertuna*
Hatfield, both, *utraque Hethfeld*	Whyle, *Wihale*
Hennor, *Henoura*	Woonton, *Winnetuna*

BL Cotton MS Domitian Aiii f59v

5.2 Places not named in the 1123 Charter:

Independent Chapelries	Others
Docklow	Eywood
Eyton with Lucton	Hurstley
Kimbolton	
Orleton	
Yarpole	

Table 5 The Leominster Parochia *as listed in Bishop Capella's Charter of 1123*

listed as within the *parochia* in 1123. There are hints that the members of Capella's inquest were subjected to pressure from interested lay lords, for the bishop judiciously terminated his charter, with the qualification that the jurors had abstained from giving evidence about very many, *plurimus*, places which of old were part of Leominster's *parochia* 'because they were too antiquated'. This sounds a convenient let-out clause, not merely for the members of the inquest, but also for the bishop.

A number of these places, omitted on grounds of 'antiquity', can be identified. As already noted, Wigmore, Aymestrey, Leinthall, Orleton and Shobdon all formed part of Ralph I de Mortimer's new castlery or lordship of Wigmore. Lye, also detached, was held by William fitz Norman, and *Wapletone* (Wapley) by Osbern fitz Richard (see Tables 3.2, 3.3 & 3.5).[145] These lands now belonged to that powerful group of Norman lords, including Ralph I de Mortimer, who held such a considerable stake in the defence of the county, men quite unprepared to countenance any compromise over their parochial rights. Thus, in 1066 the Leominster *parochia* had extended, as Fig 6.3 shows, some 21 miles east to west, from Edwyn Ralph to Eywood, beyond Titley; and some 12 miles north to south, from Brimfield to Hope-under-Dinmore.

The 1123 charter was not merely an attempt to re-establish the spiritual authority of Edfrith's minster church after a period of almost 80 years' turmoil. It was a means of securing for Henry I's newly-founded abbey at Reading the considerable revenues due from the Leominster *parochia*. Abbot Hugh I ensured that Capella's charter was confirmed by Archbishop William of Canterbury. These rights the abbots of Reading defended in the courts with great vigour over more than four centuries. Their actions were not confined to lay lords. Between 1127 and 1130 Abbot Hugh I successfully pleaded to Archbishop William of Corbeil for the removal of clerks whom Peter, archdeacon of Hereford, and his ministers had intruded into his chapels at Ford and Hampton Mapenore without his knowledge or consent. The relations between the abbots and priors and the churches and chapels of the *parochia* have been the subject of detailed examination by Kemp.[146]

The Leominster Cartulary

For subsequent evidence of the priory's temporalities and spiritualities, one has to turn to the Leominster Cartulary, BL Domitian Aiii. A list of its most important charters was published in the *Monasticon*, together with an index of the principal place-names, both being identified by the original folio numbers. The Latin texts, with summaries, of the more significant Leominster charters were published by Kemp in the *Reading Abbey Cartularies* in the Camden Society series. Copies of some of the Leominster charters will also be found in the Egerton and Harley cartularies, and Vespasian Exxv, as well as BL Additional Roll 19617 and MS 6693, pp119–263.[147] The Domitian Cartulary was kept at Leominster. In a number of charters it is recorded that the original was kept at Reading; conversely, in a number of Reading cartularies, certain charters relating to the priory are described as being kept at Leominster.[148] The Leominster Cartulary is in three sections. The first, ff38r-132v, was written after 1257; the second, ff 133r-175v, after 1305; and the last, ff179r-244v, in the 15th century.

The first sequence commences with the royal foundation charter and is followed by other royal, papal, papal legates', archiepiscopal and episcopal charters, the most numerous being those of the bishops of Hereford, which commence with Richard de Capella, 1121–7, and end with

Ralph de Maidstone, 1234–9. There follow charters of nobles with strong local interests, including Roger fitz Miles, earl of Hereford, d1155, Waleran, count of Melun and earl of Worcester, d1166, William (d1211) and Reginald de Braose (d1228), with Walter (I or II?) de Clifford, Hugh of Kilpeck, and Stephen, John and Walter Devereux. The Leominster Cartulary makes it clear that there were very few benefactors among such laymen. Grants to the priory were slight in value and from the humble. The sequence ends with two major groups of charters. Firstly, there are grants of local freeholders, small amounts of money, lands or rents, together with quitclaims, sales and exchanges, most of which cannot be satisfactorily dated. The second group consists of grants and leases made by nine of the first twelve abbots of Reading, from Hugh (1123–30) to Richard of Chichester (1328–62). The transactions recorded in both groups relate to free tenants, for virtually every charter referring to land also refers to a fixed rent. There is no mention of the services or customs associated with servile tenure.

The second sequence provides some 120 charters recording grants of land, mostly in the 13th century, rarely more than a few acres, and of rents, rarely more than a few shillings. The third sequence opens with copies of two very large grants of land to the conventual Lady Chapel, of November 1331 and April 1350. Otherwise grants of both lands and rents are, as in the second, small. The last 26 charters are in a markedly inferior hand.

The Leominster Cartulary thus differs dramatically from our other major documentary source relating to the management of the priory's lands, the Coningsby *Register*. This was drawn from the 14th-century halimote rolls of the four *herneys*. By contrast, the concern here is with the terms of servile, to the exclusion of free, tenure. To provide a balanced, overall picture of both the freemen and customaries living and working in the lordship is therefore difficult.

The Monastic Community

There is a marked contrast between the prior's apparently lowly status as a mere *custos* or keeper and the extensive powers with which he was vested as the abbot's deputy. He sat in judgment in his own courts, free of shire and hundred courts. In the exercise of this justice he had both his own courthouse and gaol. For much of the medieval period his court met in the Great, or Frere (Brothers') Chamber above the Priory Gate, halfway down Church Street. The gaol lay to the south side of the street (see Fig 11.5). The abbot's temporal jurisdiction extended further. The prior thus had full responsibility for the management of the extensive estates. He had two bailiffs, one for the borough, the other for the liberty of Leominster, that is the abbot's lands outside the borough. In addition, he was responsible for the spiritual as well as physical wellbeing of the monastic community. Given such a range of experience, it is hardly surprising that of some 33 known priors of Leominster at least seven rose to abbatial status. Two were elected abbots of other Benedictine houses: Prior Robert to Crowland in 1175, and Prior Walter to St Mary's, Shrewsbury, in 1221. The latter had his personal seal, not as prior but as papal judge delegate. It was inscribed EXALTABITUR. QUI. SE. HUMILIAT., 'He who humbleth himself shall be exalted'. It portrays, under a crescent and a star, a man's head in profile, looking to the right (Plate 19a). In the National Archives, this is attached to a charter, giving his judgement that Bordesley Abbey, in lieu of their tithes in Bearley, *Burl'*, in Warwickshire, should pay '10s a year, less 2d,' to Chatillon Abbey. Five others succeeded to the abbacy of the mother house: Adam de Lathbury in 1226; three in succession in the mid 14th century, Henry of Appleford, c1342–61, William of Dumbleton 1361–9 and John of Sutton 1369–78; and Thomas Worcester in 1519.[149]

Evidence for the early years of the monastic community at Leominster is slight. Annals, composed probably at Leominster, record that 'the strict observance of the (Cluniac) order' commenced in 1139. However, a body of monks was there considerably earlier, operating as a grange of Reading, for a charter of Robert de Bethune, bishop of Hereford 1131–48, concerning spiritual dues from Broadfield parish, about a mile north of Bodenham, records an agreement between 'the monks of Leominster and Miles the constable'. This can be dated 1131x37, as one of the witnesses, Godfrey, abbot of Winchcombe, died on 6 March 1137. A later phrase in the charter refers to 'the monks of the *parochia* of Leominster'. They were thus serving the spiritual needs of the area, formerly the responsibility of the ancient minster church, as well as defending Reading's financial interests in that *parochia*.

The 1127 charter granted to Ailward is evidence that Reading monks were already fulfilling a more secular role, administering the priory's extensive estates. Thus Hugh, first abbot, was able to be specific about the lands at Miles Hope, near the county boundary with Salop, and at Lucton and Ivington, which amounted to two hides plus ten acres. Of a similar date is Hugh's charter defending Reading's interest in its chapels at Ford and Hampton. A party of Reading monks had thus been despatched, very soon after Hugh's election in 1123, to act as custodians of the abbey's landed and other interests at Leominster and also to initiate plans for the construction of the priory church.[150]

7 The Romanesque Monastic Church

Almost square in shape, for most visitors Leominster Priory is very confusing. It can be understood only in terms of its long history. In the Middle Ages what appeared to be structurally one building was, functionally, two — a monastic church and a parochial church. As a result of the dissolution of the greater monasteries in 1539, only the parochial church, in the nave, remains. Henry VIII's commissioners ordered the demolition of the monastic church — the eastern end, transepts and crossing, together with the easternmost bay of the north aisle, with its processional door that the monks had used for entry into their choir — and all but one of the conventual buildings. The site became a quarry for building materials.

It was not unusual to retain part of a former monastery for parochial use. Similar examples, where the nave was retained, can be seen locally, at Chepstow, Usk, Deerhurst and Shrewsbury. At Pershore and Little Malvern, on the other hand, the parishioners gave up their nave to move into the monastic church to the east. Given the history of their ownership with the prior and his monks, it is hardly surprising that the people of the borough of Leominster elected to retain their parish church in preference to the monastic. Some towns were loath to lose any part of their ancient abbeys. In order to retain the whole building, the Tewkesbury burgesses paid the king £453, the value of the lead on the roof at 5d a foot and of bell metal at 2½d per lb; but at Great Malvern, where the roof had already been stripped of its lead and the bells sold, the parishioners paid only £20. At Crowland merely the north aisle was retained in use as the parish church. Possessed of a very large parish church, Leominster's responsibilities in terms of upkeep would have been considerable. The decision to allow the monastic church to go is therefore understandable, but it has left us with this strange, initially very puzzling, square edifice. It has been suggested that 'nowhere is the development of the non-monastic nave so marked as at Leominster', possibly a reflection of the size of the Saxon minster's *parochia*.[151]

Construction of the Romanesque priory began, as usual at the east end, c1125. To minimise disruption to services, the ancient minster may well have been retained until the monastic church was complete. The building of the nave and aisles, the parochial church, was to prove a more complex matter. The cloister, to the north, had conventual buildings on three sides. Of these the stone-built section of the so-called 'Priory House', now a Youth Hostel, is all that remains.

The *Opus Dei*

The prime purpose of the monastic church was the performance of the *Opus Dei*. Nothing, said St Benedict, was to be set before the work of God. This was amply reflected in the design of Benedictine churches. The High Altar, enhanced by a wooden or stone reredos, sculpted, painted and gilded, dominated the whole church. At the east end a number of steps, the *gradus presbyterium*, led to the sanctuary where a further step or steps gave access to the altar. The presbytery was

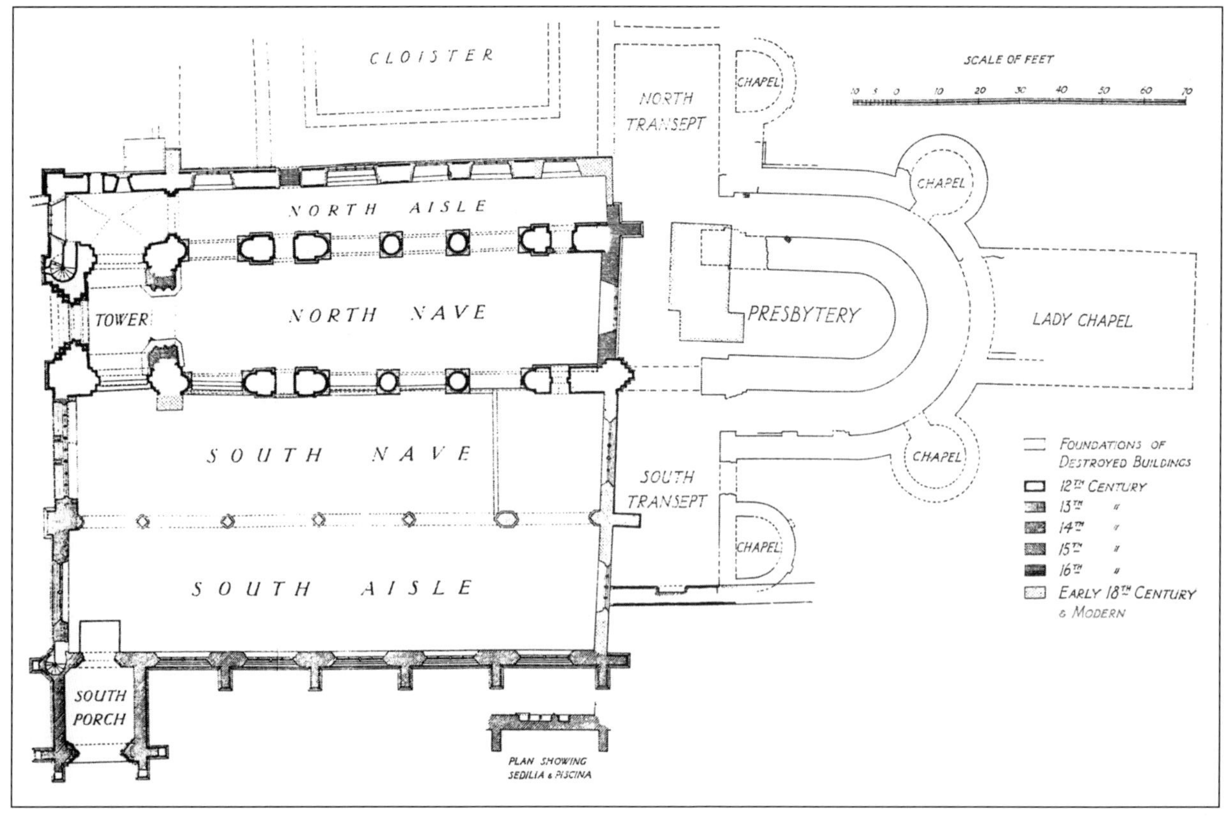

Fig 7.1 Leominster Priory, showing excavated monastic and parochial churches

devoid of other features, except those essential to its service: three seats, *sedilia*, placed on the south or 'epistle' side of the altar, for the celebrant and his two assistants, a deacon and sub-deacon; the credence from which the bread and wine were taken; and the piscina for the ablutions of the priest's hands, chalice and paten. Such simplicity of design enhanced the commanding presence of the altar.

To the west lay the monastic choir, occupying most of the crossing and one bay of the nave. The monks' wooden choir stalls would have followed the normal pattern, forming an enclosed space, facing each other on the north and south of the crossing. The prior and sub-prior's stalls were on the south and north of the stalls returning against the east face of the stone screen of the pulpitum. Excavations in 1853 revealed the narrowness of the priory's transepts and thus of the crossing, some 20ft east to west, as compared to some 35ft at Great Malvern and Tewkesbury. The monks' stalls could not take up the full 20ft of the crossing, for there had to be access from the night stairs in the north transept, and passage across the choir to the south transept. Leominster's monastic choir was therefore remarkably constrained, providing room for only some twelve choir stalls. This underlined the abbots of Reading's determination that their priory should remain a dependent cell, a policy that, in the late 13th century, was the cause of sharp conflict with bishops Cantilupe and Swinfield (Fig 7.1).

Here in the choir the community celebrated the Divine Office, the canonical prayers at fixed hours of the day and night, described by St Benedict in chapters 8 to 19 of his *Rule*. 'As the prophet saith: "Seven times in the day I have given praise to thee". We shall observe this sacred number of seven if, at the times of Lauds, Prime, Terce, Sext, None, Vespers and Compline we fulfil the duties of our service ... the same prophet said of the Night Office (Nocturns): "At midnight I arose to give thee praise." At these times, therefore, let us sing the praises of our Creator for the judgement of His justice.' The year was divided into winter and summer, each with twelve hours of day and night. The monks rose at the eighth hour of the night, in deep winter about 2am, and processed from their dormitory, at Leominster on the north side of the church, down the night stairs into the choir for Nocturns, now known as Matins. Lauds came with daybreak, the Day Offices ending with Compline, literally 'the completed hour'.

The pulpitum, a substantial screen, closed the monastic choir off from the parish church. It presented a front to the west, broken only by a central entrance, permitting monastic processions access from the nave. At all other times this entrance was secured by lock and key. Particularly fine stone pulpita at Canterbury and York are decorated with statues of the English kings, arranged in elaborate niches. Today the precise site of the Leominster pulpitum can be established from the position of the stone stairway that gave access to its loft, used for readings at certain festivals (Fig 7.2). This can be seen on the south side of the easternmost pillar of the south arcade. Blocked after the Dissolution, it was re-opened by George Gilbert Scott in 1862, when a string of ten plain black beads, the decade of a rosary, was found. The pulpitum was probably of wood, like those at Hexham and Carlisle, for there is no evidence of its removal on the inner face of the two easternmost piers of the nave arcades.[152]

Fig 7.2 Pulpitum stairs from the south

Despite the independence granted by Henry I's 1125 charter, Reading and thus Leominster retained, at least in the early days, the full Cluniac observance. This took the form of an 'increase in the number of psalms and prayers recited daily, together with an ever-growing elaboration of ceremonies in the performance of the liturgy', and 'extreme attention to regularity and uniformity in the performance of all corporate duties'. Its 'regular, tireless, all but ceaseless service ...' used 'every means of chant, of ceremony and of ornament available to render that service more solemn and more splendid'.[153] For the public the high point came with processions on principal feasts and Sundays, when the monks left their choir for other parts of the church.

The Asperges procession, on Sundays, was especially popular. After the blessing of the holy water and before High Mass, the monks asperged, or sprinkled, each of the altars in their own church, and then processed in two ranks through the easternmost of the two north aisle doors into the cloister. They were led by the holy water bearer, followed by the bearer of the processional Cross between two candle-bearers, the thurifer with censer and acolytes with lighted candles, and then the celebrant, with his deacon and sub-deacon walking in front. The procession, with the prior at the rear, moved around the claustral buildings, sprinkling and blessing each before entering through the west portal. Moving down the nave of the parochial church, the procession would halt at the Great Rood. The prior, moving between the two ranks, joined the hebdomedary at the head of the procession for the singing of the collect, the asperging of the parochial altar, the altar *ad crucem*, and the saying of the bidding prayer for the church, the king and queen and all benefactors. At some larger houses special markings in the nave indicated the precise position where each member of the procession should stand. Prayers completed, the community passed through the gates on either side of the rood screen and at the centre of the pulpitum for the celebration of High Mass in its own choir. Some of Leominster's early 11th-century Asperges prayers are preserved in the Nero/Galba prayer book, and prayers for the blessing of salt and water can be seen in some of the folios of Leominster parochial missal (Plate 2a).[154]

The impression such ceremonies made on the laity was profound: eyes, ears and nose were assaulted. The splendour of the architecture and sculpture, the richness of the vestments, the use of light and darkness, were intensified by the glories of medieval plainsong resounding through the building, and the sight and smell of the swinging censer. During such processions, as with the great festivals, the laity could feel a deep, for many an overwhelming, sense of awe and participation in the ceremonies performed. Nevertheless, relations between monks and laity were to be eroded, not only by familiarity but more especially by the prior's financial and other demands. The history of the priory church was punctuated by a series of bitter conflicts.

A Pilgrimage Church

The only parts of the monks' church to survive the Dissolution are the lower courses of the south wall of the south transept, with its early-14th-century tomb recess ornamented with ballflower, and the southeast pier of the crossing (Figs 7.3 and 7.4). Nevertheless, its plan was recovered by excavation in 1853. The young Edward Augustus Freeman, later Regius Professor of Modern History at Oxford and author of the great six-volume *History of the Norman Conquest* (1867–9), who had led a visit of the newly-formed Cambrian Archaeological Society to the priory in 1851, developed a considerable interest in its unusual plan. The arrival of the Shrewsbury and Hereford Railway Company's navvies in December 1852, to build an embankment in the meadows a few hundred yards to the east, offered the opportunity to excavate. In a small trial dig some 5ft of soil was removed from the workhouse garden, revealing what was described as 'a cell or covered tomb'.

Freeman now intervened, persuading the workhouse's Board of Guardians to grant the Society permission to negotiate with the railway company for the excavation of the foundations of presbytery, crossing and transepts of the priory church, which were on the Guardians' land. In return for the right to use the soil so excavated for its railway embankment, the company provided the labour force.[155]

The majority of greater English churches in the early 12th century terminated with the high altar in a rectangular east end. As at Hereford, some had a central apse projecting slightly. Chapels and chancels were also square-ended in the earliest Cistercian churches. Such a plan precluded procession behind the altar. At Hereford and Abbey Dore ambulatories were added in the early 13th century, but both remained rectangular at the east end.[156]

At Leominster, in marked contrast, the excavations revealed that the eastern end had been periapsidal, its sanctuary ending in a large apse, resembling that at Reading.[157] Around this the aisles continued as a processional way or ambulatory, behind the high altar. The outer wall of the ambulatory was pierced by arches, giving access to two circular chapels on the south-east and north-east. At the east end would have been another circular chapel, but in 1853 only the vestiges of a large rectangular Lady Chapel were found. The excavations also revealed an apsidal chapel on the south transept, which would have been paired with another on the north. Leominster's east end thus reflected that of its mother church, except that, to emphasise its more prestigious role, Reading had two chapels on each transept.

Fig 7.3 South-east pier of the Romanesque crossing. showing the base for the springing of the arch

The Poor Law Guardians succumbed to pressure from Bishop Hampden, the Lord Lieutenant and other gentry, as well as the Archaeological Institute, the Cambrian Archaeological Society and the Oxford Architectural Society, all prompted by Freeman, to leave the excavations open. Further excavations in 1932, apparently unrecorded, showed, as Freeman had speculated, that the rectangular eastern Lady Chapel had indeed supplanted a circular chapel at the extreme east end, like the other two. They also confirmed that the northern transept had an apsidal chapel similar to that found in the south transept in 1853 (Fig 7.4).[158]

The periapsidal plan was first adopted c918 at Tours, where St

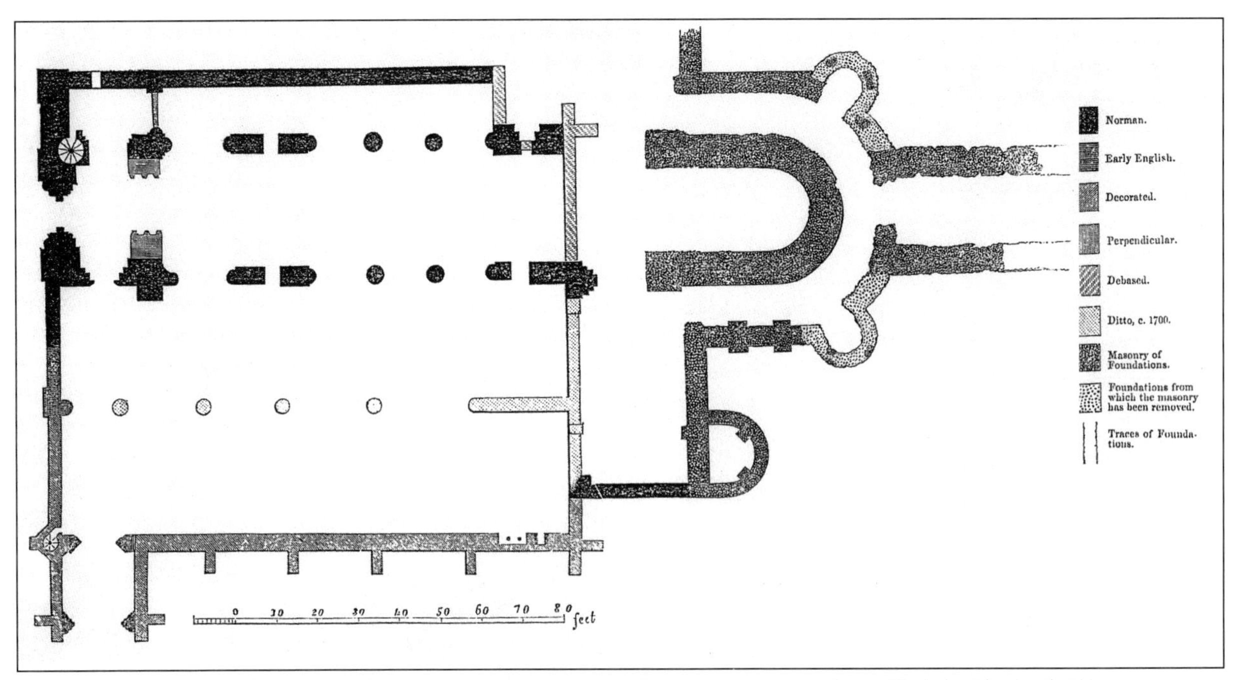

Fig 7.4 Leominster Priory: results of the 1853 excavations. (Roberts JBAA *27 (1871))*

Martin's tomb was sited behind the high altar at the head of the apse. The ambulatory thus provided access for pilgrims. This plan was subsequently adopted by the principal churches on the pilgrimage routes to the shrine of St James at Santiago, each of which had a major shrine: St Martial at Limoges, where the first abbot of Reading, Hugh of Amiens, had been prior c1115–20; Ste Foi at Conques (Fig 7.5a); and St Sernin at Toulouse. All have five periapsidal chapels except Conques, which had three. At Cluny this plan was taken to the extreme. There were not only five chapels about the great apse, but also two pairs of transepts, with two chapels on each of the four arms.[159]

In England the adoption of the periapsidal plan by a number of cathedral and major monastic churches was linked to the 10th-century renaissance of the cults of Anglo-Saxon saints, in which King Athelstan played such an important part. It was boosted by the publication of a range of saints' *Lives*. St Augustine's Abbey, Canterbury, took the lead, providing an architectural model for others, including Reading. Begun about 1073 by Abbot Scotland, the eastern arm, crossing, transepts and first two bays of the nave were completed before his death in 1087. The eastern arm consisted of choir, with ambulatory, three radiating chapels and a crypt beneath, whilst the transepts each had their own apsidal chapel. The ambulatory facilitated the passage of numerous pilgrims. Above the high altar, in a reliquary on a shelf, were the relics of King Aethelbert with 'books sent by Pope Gregory to St Augustine', the missionary of the English and first archbishop, whose relics lay in the easternmost chapel. Around the ambulatory were spaced the shrines of Augustine's ten successors as archbishop, with those of St Mildred and Abbot Hadrian in the north-eastern and south-eastern chapels. At Reading 'pilgrimage was an essential function of the new church from the start', but the abbey lacked relics, as its predecessor, the Saxon minster church, had been utterly destroyed by the Danes. This problem was soon remedied by Henry I and his family, and by the plundering, by division, of Leominster's remarkable collection.[160]

Figs 7.5 (a) Conques amd (b) Fontevrault: three periapsidal and two transeptal chapels

After the death of her husband, the Holy Roman Emperor Henry V, Henry I's daughter Matilda, who on her father's death was to contest the throne with Stephen, returned to England in 1126. She brought with her the arm of St James the Great, which she had appropriated from the Imperial Chapel at Aachen. This prestigious relic, enclosed in a gold shrine, Henry I presented to Reading Abbey. The renown of its miraculous healing powers attracted more pilgrims than to any other shrine in England — until the canonisation of Thomas Becket in 1173. Indeed Henry II held the arm in such awe that, on two particularly stressful occasions, he had it brought to him to secure its blessing. Not surprisingly, some 327 English medieval churches were dedicated to the apostle James.[161]

The family made other grants to Reading. William X, duke of Aquitaine, no doubt persuaded by his daughter, Eleanor, Henry I's queen, gave a statue of the Child Jesus, which came to be known as 'the Child of Grace' on account of its miraculous powers. Even in the late 15th century it had its own chapel and the cult was still strong. The regard in which Henry I's second son, John, held the abbey and its relics stands in marked contrast to that of his elder brother, Richard the Lionheart, who, anxious to finance his crusade, made off with the golden reliquary that protected the hand. John was so inspired by the hand that he gave Reading its second great treasure, part of the skull of the apostle Philip. In this way the royal family, by ensuring a great concourse of pilgrims, created a suitable setting for Henry I's burial place. His tomb, with its life-size statue, was in front of the high altar, which dominated the whole abbey church.[162]

Leominster's Relics

Relics of the saints were held in awe, whether of martyrs who died for their faith, or of confessors whose witness was expressed through their lives. The working of miracles, during life or after death, proved sanctity. The saints were revered as a bridge between Heaven and Earth. At Tours an inscription on St Martin's tomb explains that, although his 'soul is in the hands of God ... he is fully here, present and made plain in miracles of every kind'. Through the supernatural presence, the saints were eagerly sought as patrons to act as intercessors for the living with the Divinity. They were called upon in cases of social need, during wars, plague, fire, famine, shipwreck, swearing of oaths etc. When the city of Worcester was on fire, the shrine of St Oswald was carried into the town. A house hastily given to the saint by its owner was miraculously preserved, whilst its neighbour, not so insured, was consumed. When a great plague, destroying young and old, raged in the city, the monks, singing litanies and imploring mercy, carried the reliquary around the walls. The pestilence departed immediately. Even the water in which the saint's bones had been washed had miraculous powers. As the miracles of St Thomas of Hereford show, an incredible variety of individual needs was also met: the blind received sight, the lame walked, the dumb were granted speech, the mad were returned to sanity, even the hanged were restored to life. All were living proof of Thomas's sanctity. In William of Malmesbury's *Life* of St Wulstan of Worcester, more than 100 miracles, most carefully checked and recorded, are described. To the monastic community, relics were important as a means of displaying the antiquity and prestige of individual houses.[163]

Although none of Leominster's relics could rival the hand of St James or the skull of St Philip, the archaeological evidence shows that, like Reading Abbey, the priory was designed as a pilgrimage church. Its ambulatory and chapels were no empty replication of its mother house but, as at Reading and elsewhere, were built to facilitate the passage of pilgrims anxious for a glimpse of its treasures. The monks anticipated the throng of pilgrims that, as in the heyday of the Anglo-Saxon minster, visited the relics and participated in the feast days of its calendar — and their flow of offerings. Once the priory's eastern arm was completed the large crowds, bearing their lighted tapers to place before the shrine and reliquaries, could be shepherded around the ambulatory by a small number of monks.

1. Of Bethlehem, where the Lord was born.
2. Of the Lord's manger.
3. Of the incense and myrrh which the magi offered to the Lord.
4. Of the stone of Jordan.
5. Of Gethsemani, where He supped.
6. Of the Lord's palm.
7. Of the Lord's tree (cross).
8. Of the cross of Dismas and Gesmas (the two thieves).
9. Of the sponge which was offered to the Lord as He hung on the cross.
10. Of the linen cloth in which the body of the Lord was wrapped.
11. Of the incense with which the Lord's sepulchre was perfumed.
12. Of the altar whence He ascended into heaven.
13. Of the vestments of Saint Mary.
14. Of Saint Mary's mantle (*pallium*).
15. Of Saint Mary's coffin.
16. The body of Saint Thomas, Abbot of the same Church.
17. The body of Saint Edward, King and Martyr.
18. The body of Elvene.
19. The body of Ethelmod, King and Martyr.
20. Of the relics of Bartholomew,
21. … Germanus,
22. … Lucius,
23. … Modestus.
24. Of the vestments of John's nephew.
25. Of the relics of Julianus and Aaron
26. … Salvius the martyr,
27. … Exaudi, (and)
28. Of the relics of three whose bodies are contained in one sepulchre, (namely) Cola, Eleranus and Colman.
29. Of the relics of Saint Peter.
30. Of the sepulchre of Peter and Paul.
31. One tooth of Luke the Evangelist.
32. Of the relics of Margaret, of Primitivus.
33. Of Paul the Confessor, who led a serpent through the desert
34. Of the relics of Branwallator,
35. … of Benedict the Bishop (of Wearmouth and Jarrow), his son,
36. … of Milburga,
37. … of Edburga the Virgin,
38. … of Cisa, Bishop and Anchorite.
39. Of Moses' rod.
40. Of Cecilia's vestments.
41. Of the relics of Paul,
42. … of Martin.
43. One bone of Winwalloc.
44. One stone with which Stephen was stoned.
45. Of the relics of Huna the priest, Etheldritha's chaplain.
46. Of John's sepulchre.
47. Of the relics of Eleutherius, *primicerius* (martyred with St Denis at Paris).
48. Of the relics of several martyrs, confessors and virgins, whose names are not written here.
49. Of the earth where the bodies of Patercius (Patrick), Colunchille (Columba of Iona) and Brigid,
50. … Finnanus, Cirianus (Kieran of Clonmacnoise or Saighir), Fetinus (Fechinus), Colledius the Bishop, Commanus, Ultimus (Ultanus) (all Irish saints)

Reg Swinfield 124-5

Table 6: 'The Relics kept in the Church of Leominster from Time Immemorial'

Bishop Swinfield (1283–1317), like Robert de Bethune, was inspired by the wealth of Leominster's relics. In 1286 he commanded one of his scribes to copy the list of more than 60 relics, held at Leominster 'since time immemorial'. The scribe evidently had difficulty reading this list, but he showed little interest, or initiative, in his task. Misspellings are frequent, and there is at least one, serious, omission. Making no sense of the initial entry, he transcribed the unusual name of Leominster's first abbot, Haemma, as Thomas (16). Numerically, Leominster's wealth lay in its relics of Anglo-Saxon saints such as Mildburg of Wenlock (36), Eadburg, granddaughter of King Alfred (37), and Edward of East Anglia, king and martyr (17). Other relics included those of the Irish saints Patrick, Colum Cille and Brigid (49), whose relics were found together by St Malachy at Downpatrick in 1185, and Finan and Kieran (50); and the Bretons, Branwalader (34) and Winwaloe (43) (Table 6).[164]

Reading has two relic lists. The first, of 1190, is in the early Reading cartulary, BL Egerton 3031, which also provides full details of the books in the libraries of both abbey and priory. It identifies 242 relics. Not a few had been plundered from its daughter house, presumably shortly after it became a cell. As a number of these relics are also found in the 1286 Leominster list, this was apparently a matter of division. Plundering, and frequently theft, of relics was a common occurrence in the Middle Ages. The most famous occasion was the theft of the bones of St Benedict from Montecassino by the monks of Fleury, now St Benoît sur Loire. It has been suggested that not a few of Athelstan's relics were acquired in this way. Both the Reading 1190 and the Leominster 1286 list include relics of the Leominster saints Haemma and Aethelmod (19), and of Edward, king and martyr, his grandmother, Queen Aelfgyfe (18), Mildburg (36), Eadburg (37) and Branwalader, as well as others of Welsh, Irish or Celtic origin. The second Reading list was drawn up at the abbey's dissolution in 1539. Although only 23 items are named, a full list, we are told, 'wolde occupie iij schetes of paper to make particularly'. However, the 23 relics do include the arms of David and Edward, king and martyr, as well as 'a chawbone of saynt Ethelmod'.[165]

The most important of Leominster's relics related to the Holy Family (1–15). The collection also included relics of St Peter (29); the sepulchre of Peter and Paul (30); a tooth of St Luke the Evangelist (31); St Margaret (32); St 'Paul the Confessor', the hermit of Thebes, died c347, 'who led a serpent through the desert' (33) and for whom two lions dug a grave; and a stone with which Stephen was martyred (44) (see Table 6).[166]

Robert de Bethune, most saintly of Hereford's bishops, aptly expressed the view of contemporaries. Of Leominster's treasures he declared forthrightly: 'We know and have learned by undoubted proofs that this church is loved of God for in it are contained relics of the saints in greater and more precious in quantity than we can find words to express'. Even allowing for a certain hyperbole, these words convey vividly the wonder of an undoubted connoisseur at a collection which, according to the lights of his day, was quite awesome, far outshining that of his own cathedral, which had been utterly despoiled when the Welsh stole all its relics, vestments and treasures in 1055. As John Blair points out, Leominster had 'three Anglo-Saxon saints (Edfrith, Aethelmod and Haemma) which is most unusual for a non-cathedral site before the (10th-century) Benedictine Reform.'[167]

Having underlined the quality of Leominster's relics, Bishop Robert went on, as part of the dedication of the church, to ordain and decree that forever 'in that church' and 'throughout its *paro-*

chia a festival be solemnly observed every 10 October (the festival of the Kentish priest, Paulinus, who converted King Edwin of Northumbria and became first bishop of York) in honour of all the saints whose relics are contained there'. Such feasts were introduced at many religious houses in the 12th century. William of Malmesbury describes a similar occasion at Worcester cathedral, which he visited between 1113 and 1124, where a special shrine had been made for all the church's relics by St Oswald, bishop 961–92. In the late 11th century Bishop Wulstan created an even more magnificent shrine, which included the relics of Oswald himself. The octave of the saint's translation, reburial, was then adopted as Worcester's feast of the relics.[168]

At Leominster only four of the many insular saints commemorated in the Anglo-Saxon minster's calendar were accorded the distinction of a principal feast in the post-Conquest era. These were Aethelmod on 9 January, David on 1 March, Edward, king and martyr, on 18 March, and Edfrith on 26 October. Leominster never had Edfrith's relics, but of the remaining three only Edward (2) and Aethelmod (4) are found in Swinfield's copy of the list of relics. The most serious of Swinfield's scribe's mistakes was the omission of St David.

The cult of St David was formally recognised in 1120 by Pope Calixtus II, who proclaimed that two pilgrimages to St David's cathedral were equivalent to a pilgrimage to Rome. Subsequently Bishop Iorwerth, Gervase, of St David's (1215–29) granted an indulgence of 21 days to pilgrims visiting David's shrine at Leominster on his feast day, as did Bishop Dionysus of Elphin. Bishop Cadwgan of Bangor (1215–35) also granted an indulgence to pilgrims to the shrine, but of merely 13 days. David's feast, on 1 March, is celebrated in the Nero Aii Calendar, and he is invoked in both the Galba Axiv litanies. Reading claimed a 'rib and bone of St David' in its 1190 relic list. This must have been amongst those plundered from Leominster, for David's 'arm' is specifically referred to in both Gervase and Cadwgan's indulgences. There can therefore be no doubt that some of David's relics remained at Leominster, notwithstanding their absence in the Swinfield relic list. This was a claim that even David's own cathedral could not make, for his alleged body was only 'discovered' outside the cathedral south door in 1275.[169]

Despite the wide-ranging evidence of the priory's 'awesome collection of relics', we have knowledge of only one other shrine at Leominster, that of Edward, king and martyr. In 1534 it was reported that Sub-Prior John Reading had embezzled many valuable objects from the priory. These included the parcel-gilt front of St Edward's shrine. There are thus records of two shrines in the priory. Given his principal feast, there would certainly have been a third, for St Aethelmod. The semi-circular chapels of the transepts and ambulatory will have housed these, and other, shrines. That of King Edward was probably above the high altar.[170]

The 1190 Reading relic list refers to *Sci hemme primi abbis leonis monasterii*, and the Swinfield copy of the Leominster list reads *Corpus sancti Thome, abbatis eusdem ecclesie*. This is the *Haemma Abb(atis)* found in Calendar Nero Aii. Given this recognition of Haemma as 'first abbot' in 1190, it may be that initially the Benedictine abbot and convent of Reading were reluctant to accept as fundamental the role in the origins of the minster, now their priory church, of Edfrith, a Northumbrian priest and monk of St Columba. The people of the Leominster *parochia*, however, held on tenaciously to the memory of Edfrith, their missionary and the founder of their church. As pilgrims, their voice was decisive. In 1290 the abbot of Reading accepted the transfer of Leominster's great autumn fair to the festival of St Edfrith on 26 October. By the early 14th century such was the interest in the saint that Bishop Orleton caused one of his clerics to copy that section of the text of Much Wenlock's *Life of St Milburga* which described Merewalh's conversion. This Orleton now entitled *The Legend of St Etfrid, Priest of Leominster*. In 1346 Bishop Trillek borrowed Wenlock's copy of the *Life* — probably for a similar purpose. By 1433 the list of principal feasts included that of St Edfrith, on 26 October, but not of St Haemma, on 25 May.[171]

The 1853 excavations that revealed the periapsidal ending of the monastic church also provided evidence of the layout of the crossing piers, one of which, on the south-west, remains virtually intact, up to the springing of its lost arch (Fig 7.4). Part can be seen protruding from the exterior of the present east wall. At Tewkesbury the crossing piers still carry a magnificent Romanesque tower. At Leominster, however, the failure to strengthen the western crossing piers above arcade level indicates that a central tower may never have been constructed. More important, as Fig 7.1 shows, the presbytery, transepts and crossing do not align with the nave, demonstrating clearly that there was a dramatic change in design between the completion of the former and the commencement of work on the latter.

8 The Parish Church

For almost half a millennium the minster church had tended the spiritual life of the lay folk of its *parochia*. This would have been achieved by services at Leominster, possibly in St Andrew's church at the Poplands, the establishment of rural chapels and a peripatetic ministry. For Benedictine monks and Augustinian canons the nave of their conventual churches, a bay west of the pulpitum, frequently served as a parish church. It has been estimated that the nave, or at least one of the aisles, was parochial in the churches of some 119 Benedictine monasteries and 37 Augustinian priories. This was the means adopted by the abbot of Reading to fulfil his responsibilities to the laity of Leominster's *parochia*. Chaplains were provided to conduct services in the chapels in its more distant areas.[172]

Such joint use frequently led to conflict between monks and parishioners, even to the building of separate parish churches. Some, as at Southwark, St Albans and Romsey, flanked the monastery; others, as at Westminster, Glastonbury, Abingdon, Cirencester, Evesham and Bodmin, were free-standing within the monastic precinct; yet others were built outside the precinct. Similar conflicts arose at Leominster, where the parochial church remained a part of the conventual building. Subsequently it was enlarged, in two stages, to accommodate the borough's growing population. First a spacious south nave, consecrated in 1239, was constructed on the site of the Romanesque south aisle; then the existing Decorated south aisle was added, c1320. Nevertheless conflict between the two parties became so intense in the second half of the 13th century that in the autumn of 1282 Archbishop Peckham put forward a compromise solution, the building of the Forbury chapel. This did not solve the problem.[173]

The original building sequence at Leominster, first the monastic and then the parochial church in the nave, is clear, but the date of completion of the two parts is not. The only documentary evidence relating to the parish church is the visit of Bishop Robert de Bethune, after June 1131, to consecrate the altar of the Holy Cross, *ad crucem*, and another, dedicated to SS Mary Magdalene, Margaret and Katherine. Bethune's subsequent charter refers to the use of the parish church, not the monastic church to the east, for the first altar he consecrated was the parochial altar. As its name, *ad crucem*, indicates, this was situated at the rood screen, which stretched across nave and both aisles immediately west of the pulpitum. Doors or gates on either side, usually kept locked to ensure privacy and seclusion for the community, permitted the Sunday procession to return to the monastic church to the east.

Over this screen, dominating the church, a strong wooden beam carried the Great Rood, Christ Crucified with the Virgin on the left and St John on the right, proclaiming the fundamental message of the church, Christ as Saviour. At Pershore, where the abbey was dedicated to the Virgin and St Eadburg, the parochial church was sometimes referred to as the church of the Holy Cross from such a rood.[174] To all visiting the altar *ad crucem* on the church's festivals Bethune granted remission of seven days' penance, but to those visiting the altar of SS Mary Magdalene, Margaret and Katherine merely three days'.[175] The status of the altar of the Holy Cross is further confirmed by the fact that the vicar who served it received annually from his parishioners twelve sheaves of corn from each virgate of arable. Even after the vicar's corn tithes were commuted to an annual payment of half a mark, 6s 8d, c1190, his vicarage continued to be described as '*ad crucem*', and a petition from prior and sub-prior to Bishop Trefnant in 1397 refers, unambiguously, to the altar of SS Mary Magdalene, Margaret and Katherine as 'within the parish church'. Indulgences were the most powerful means at Bethune's disposal to promote reverence for the two new parochial altars. His visit thus marks the initiation of services in the parish church.[176]

The precise date of Bethune's visit is not known but, as the see had been vacant between 1127 and 1131, the parishioners may well have been without a parochial altar for some years. It is unlikely that consecration took place after Henry I's death in December 1135, when 'the kingdom was convulsed'. Stephen was scarce crowned before revolt broke out in Wales, and by May 1138 Hereford castle suffered the first of two sieges. During the second, a year later, the cathedral itself was used as a vantage point for the attack on the royal castle. Eventually even Bethune had to flee, to Shobdon. By the time of his visit not only had the monastic church of presbytery, crossing and transepts been completed, but construction of the parochial nave was far enough advanced to permit the altars *ad crucem* and to SS Mary Magdalene, Margaret and Katherine to be used for services.[177]

The Nave Architecture

Whereas the priory's eastern arm conformed to the well-defined pilgrimage church type, its nave was a complex structure, the work of a number of different periods and hands. Its design is both unique and enigmatic. As noted, the architectural nave does not align with the presbytery and high altar. In particular its north arcade is considerably out of line with that of the presbytery. Thus, the present north nave is noticeably wider at its east end than at the west, for its north and south arcades are not quite on the same alignment. How can such a dramatic change in the original plan as the 1853 excavations revealed at the crossing be explained? Is it related to the remarkable narrowness of the crossing already noted? Was the change of plan between Stage 1, the

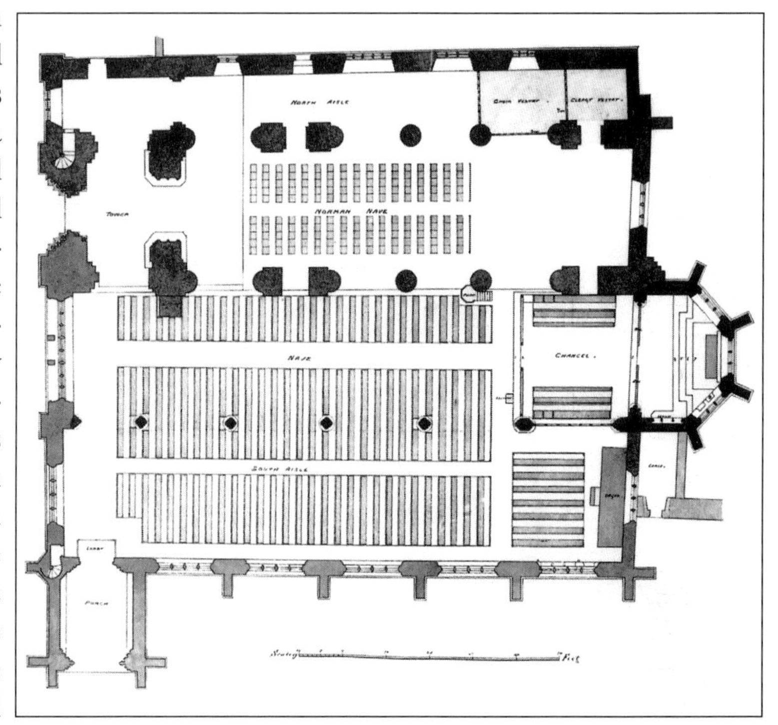

Fig 8.1 George Gilbert Scott's plan showing the misalignment of the north wall of the north aisle and proposed eastern apse. © *RIBA*

monastic, and Stage 2, the parochial church, in part due to pressure for economy, once the abbot recognised the need to keep the maximum complement of monks to twelve? The suggestion in Chapter 7, that the ancient minster church was retained for parochial use whilst the east end was being constructed, together with Sir George Gilbert Scott's belief that the foundations of part of the priory's north aisle wall belonged to its Saxon predecessor, could offer the explanation.[178]

The problems raised by this apparent failure to articulate the parochial nave with the monastic presbytery were lost in speculation about the unique arcade design of the nave, begun during the Cambrian Archaeological Association's 1851 visit. Freeman was intrigued by the unusual bays. Heavy circular piers characterised the large Romanesque churches of the Severn valley and beyond, as at the Benedictine abbeys at Shrewsbury, Great Malvern, Tewksbury and Gloucester, and at Hereford cathedral. At Leominster, however, as Freeman explained, instead of heavy circular piers there is 'a flat projection in which a tall and narrow round-headed arch is set'. Unmoulded and uncarved, these arches came to be described as forming 'solid bays' (Figs 8.2a&b, Plates 9a&b).

Fig 8.2a&b Nave arcade from the south: a) today, with one solid bay and b) probable original intention with pair of solid bays (Roberts JBAA *27 (1871))*

Nevertheless the architect was well aware of the local use of heavy circular piers, for on either side of these solid bays he attached semi-circular piers in the Severn valley style, with scalloped capitals (Figs 8.4 & 8.5). The abaci were moulded or enriched with trilobe and billet designs. 'The cause of this singularity', Freeman continued, 'I do not understand at all and I do not remember to have seen anything like it elsewhere.'[179] The mystery was heightened by the fact that, for the central bays, conventional circular piers of the Severn valley type had apparently been employed (Fig 8.2a).

Some 20 years after the Cambrians' visit the British Archaeological Association came to Leominster. According to their Secretary, Edward Roberts, 'much discussion took place on its many peculiarities and the difficulties it offered to the student in respect of the unusual details of (nave) construction and irregular features in the subsidiary arrangements. Several views were expressed, but no one seemed satisfied with either his own or others' attempted solution of its riddles.' All agreed that 'it is full of strangeness and beauties that demand careful research and study, greater than have yet been given to it'. When Roberts returned to Leominster, he found the answer to the problem posed by the circular piers of the central bay. The clumsily matched vertical joints in their columns and the wall above showed that all four central piers were the result of subsequent modification, probably representing a wide-ranging plan to remodel all the solid bays to conform to the pattern of the circular piers found in the other great Benedictine monasteries of the area (Figs 8.4 & 8.5).[180]

Fig 8.3 Remaining solid bay of Romanesque south arcade from the north

Yet Roberts was unable to give a satisfactory answer as to the original intention of the architect in providing the unusual solid bays. Several suggestions have been mooted. For Sir Alfred Clapham, writing in 1933, 'the purpose of the (original) solid bays was presumably to carry very broad transverse arches, perhaps in connection with a barrel vault (over the nave)'; but elsewhere he admitted, 'no attempt was ever made to erect a barrel vault over the main spans' of the nave in England.[181] If the flat projections had in fact been continued as transverse arches across the Leominster nave, they would have had to span some 22 feet.

More recently, a very different explanation has been put forward. Jean Bony and George Zarnecki have suggested that the nave arcade, with its solid bays, was originally intended to carry three domes. This is not as fanciful as it sounds. In Aquitaine such domed churches were very popular in the early 12th century. They took two forms, the cruciform and those with domes-in-line. The finest example of the former is the great pilgrimage church of St Front at Périgueux, completed just after 1120, where the five domes formed a cross, as at St Mark's, Venice; but the usual design was to have a number of domes in line, covering the nave and crossing, as at Angoulème cathedral and, further north, at Fontevrault in Anjou.[182]

At Périgueux, as at St Mark's, the cruciform structure provided an effective counter-balance to the powerful outward thrust of the domes. At Angoulème and Fontevrault, where north and south aisles were abandoned, the extraordinary thrust of their domes in line was countered, internally, by very stout wall piers with pairs of attached columns to carry the transverse arches between the domes (Fig 8.7). These were incorporated into strong outer walls with matching external buttresses. Fontevrault and Leominster were similar in a number of respects. Both had eastern arms of the pilgrimage church type, at both a radical change in the overall plan was adopted before the nave was constructed and, ultimately, they had similar west fronts. Accepting the suggestion that the original intention was to use domes-in-line to roof the nave, the critical difference is that at Leominster it was to be attempted whilst retaining the traditional English aisled plan. Possibly the abbot would not permit the aisles to be abandoned?

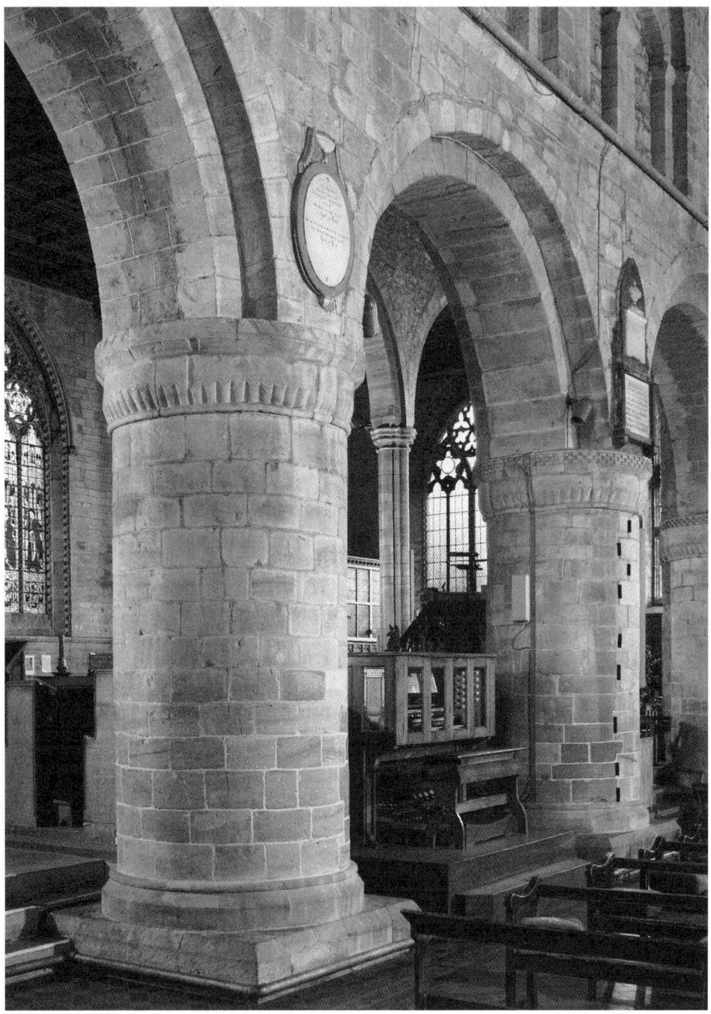

Fig 8.4 (top) Capital of modified pier
Fig 8.5 (bottom) Modified solid bay of Romanesque south arcade from the north

Fig 8.6 Fontevrault: longitudional section of presbytery, crossing and first bay of nave, showing domes etc.

Fig 8.7 Fontevrault: nave looking east during reconstruction showing massive support for domes

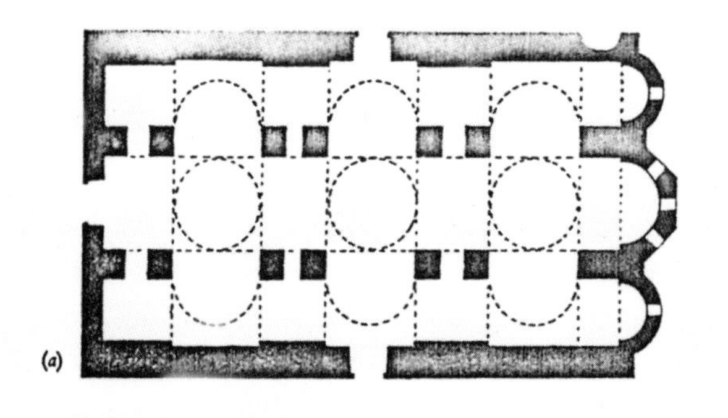

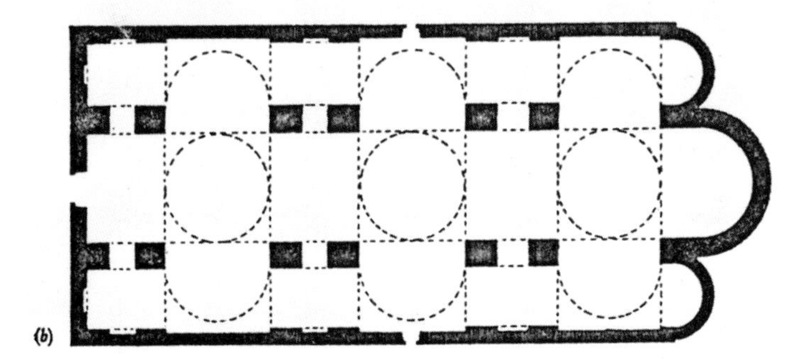

Fig 8.8a&b Plans of St Lazare, Larnaca (top) and St Barnabas, Famagusta, Cyprus

Whatever the case, this would have fatally weakened his building, for even these massive bays, pierced by narrow arches, could not of themselves have adequately countered the outward thrust of the three intended domes.[183]

It would not be surprising if Fontevrault had been the inspiration. The counts of Anjou and Maine were neighbours of the dukes of Normandy. Relations between them, though often far from cordial, were nevertheless close. In 1119 Henry I's heir, William, had married Matilda, daughter of Count Fulk. After Prince William was drowned in 1121, Matilda returned to Anjou and took the veil at Fontevrault, where she later became abbess. This explains Henry I's strong emotional attachment to Fontevrault, which was reflected in his financial provision for the abbey. In 1129 he made an 'inviolable' annual grant of £100 (Rouennais) and some £33 (English), doubling the latter in 1131. His annual grant to Cluny for maintenance, made on its consecration in 1131, was £100 (English).[184]

J.T. Smith, writing in 1963, fully accepted Bony and Zarnecki's suggestion, that Leominster's solid bays were built to support three domes, but believed the model came from Cyprus. There several churches, such as St Barnabas at Famagusta, the annex church attached to the ruined basilica of St Epiphanius at Salamis, and St Lazare at Larnaca, are aisled and have three domes. These are carried on solid bays with tall, narrow round-headed arches similar to those at Leominster (Figs 8.8a&b). According to Smith, Leominster's original plan was for a nave of at least three domed bays with transverse arches between them, the arches being supported on the massive piers. The purpose of the tall and narrow round-headed arches within the solid bays, he proposed, was to give access to the aisles. Why, Smith asked, was such an adventurous plan abandoned — a failure of nerve, fears about the stability of the intended nave, or inaccurate setting out of the foundations due to unfamiliarity with the structure envisaged? Certainly Leominster's plan provides a number of examples of such inaccuracy (see Fig 7.1). Both dome hypotheses have been criticised, but satisfactory alternatives have yet to be developed.[185]

Whatever the original intention for Leominster's nave, there were certainly other major changes of plan. The triforium consists of eight arches on the north, but nine on the south, each containing a pair of inferior arches, but the distribution of these arches bears no relationship either to the arcade below or the clerestory above. The clerestory, however, does relate to the arcade, for each bay consists of a pair of blind arches, one on either side of a window of similar design, and centred on the arcade below.

The nave retains another outstanding feature. On the triforium of the sixth, seventh and eighth bays of the south arcade are considerable remains of a wall-painting scheme of the second half of the 12th century. As William of Malmesbury explained, 'we think it is not enough ... unless the walls glisten with various coloured paintings and throw the reflection of the sun's rays upon the ceiling'. Some of these wall-paintings were very simple, as in the Cistercian houses. At Fountains, by the south transept, white lines are painted on the wall plaster, simulating ashlar work. At Leominster the patterns are complex, and much of the design is now difficult to make out. There is a single design on the side piers of the triforium arches, but two on the wider central pier. The diamond-shaped design appearing on the left side of the central pier (Plate 10a) is repeated on the right-hand side pier in Plate 10b. On the right hand of the central pier is an intricate pattern, with a repeating design of six half circles; on the left pier a bold triangular design. According to the Royal Commission, the two minor arches were originally open, in which case the patterns will have stood out more clearly. The infilling, no doubt, was to give additional stability to the nave. In the 12th-century work of the parish church, some 14 different masons' marks can be found.[186]

9 The West Front: Portal and Capitals

Two West Fronts?

Leominster's west front, exterior and interior, provides a splendid display of Romanesque sculpture. The exhibition of *English Romanesque Art, 1066–1200* at the Hayward Gallery in 1984 brought together its many strands, emphasising the close interrelationship of all the arts at that time. It also drew popular attention to what has come to be called the Herefordshire School of Romanesque Sculpture. It is curious that this child of an age so alien to our own has become so popular. This is due to its vigour and immediacy, but especially to the very remoteness of the world it inhabited.

Leominster Priory has been described as 'one of the most puzzling of all English Romanesque monuments'. This comment applies as much to the west front as to the construction of the nave. The west portal is not round-headed, Romanesque, but slightly pointed, anticipating the Gothic

Fig 9.1 Leominster west front showing pointed portal with early Romanesque capitals, and billet moulding as on abacus of nave pier (see Fig 9.7b)

(Fig 9.1). So are the north and south arches supporting the tower (Plate 13). On the other hand, its capitals are of the heavy convex, or cushion, type characteristic of the early Romanesque. This problem was addressed by Sir Alfred Clapham in 1934, who points out that the west tower, 'though of the twelfth century, is an addition to the original design. An alteration in alignment in the north arch of the west tower' shows that this 'did not form part of the original design'. Nevertheless he recognised that architecture and sculpture were in conflict: the carving on the west door was of an earlier date than the pointed arch in which it was placed. Seeking to explain how early capitals were to be found on a later façade, Clapham suggested 'it is possible that the west doorway on which this carving occurs was built before the tower was contemplated and that the tower itself was an addition with the reconstruction of the (pointed) north and south arches supporting it'.[187]

Zarnecki accepted that the tower was added in the second half of the 12th century, and that the decoration of the west doorway and window above 'belong to the original design of the west front and were executed about the middle of the century', c1150. But the pointed shape of the doorway was not introduced into England until c1170. The only explanation of this paradox is that the capitals, both on the façade and on the inside of the west door, are re-used pieces from an earlier, Romanesque, west front. This is confirmed by close inspection of the joints, such as where the triangular cavity between two capitals has had to be cemented up to replace the original lug (see Fig 9.6). The implication is that the Leominster sculpture is earlier than has generally been accepted.

Fig 9.2 West end. South nave

Early use of pointed arches was never as decoration, but always in relationship to vaulting, as with the rib-vaulted aisles at Kirkstall of the early 1160s and the reconstruction of Fountains' nave, completed c1170. Indeed, at both these sites the round-headed arch was retained for the non-structural western portals. Round-headed arches were still employed structurally for the nave at Margam Abbey, finished c1170. A date of 1150 for the pointed arch of the Leominster doorway, therefore, cannot be sustained. The south face of the late 12th-century west tower can be seen from the south nave (Fig 9.2). The original, western building line is marked by the wide buttress. To the west, at arcade level, is a pointed arch, lower and narrower than its Romanesque counterparts. The stringcourse above the Romanesque south arcade does not continue above the western, pointed arch, where the level is lower. Above, the open arch, now infilled, looked into the extension of the Romanesque south aisle. This is quite inconsistent with the existing west front belonging to the original design.[188]

The pointed arches are not the only indications of a post-1150 date for the west front. The simplicity of its design stands in marked contrast to those of other contemporary greater churches, and indeed to Reading itself which, as Baxter and Thurlby explain, was built when 'rich architectural decoration was the order of the day'.[189] A desire to enrich west façades developed prior to the mid 12th century. In some cases this became an inordinate love of decoration, expressed in an orgy of arcading. The Romanesque west front of Hereford cathedral, 1107–48, which collapsed in 1786, was a splendid example. It was embellished with interlaced arcades at six levels. The central portal was deeply recessed, with multiple arches and capitals, all decorated (Fig 9.3). Similarly rich arcading can still be seen at the west end of St Botolph's Priory, Colchester, Rochester cathedral and Castle Acre Priory, Norfolk, and there are impressive remnants on the southern side of the west façade at Malmesbury. Multiple arcading occurs on towers such as that at Tewkesbury, and within the chapter-houses of the Cluniacs at Much Wenlock and of the Augustinians at Bristol. This tradition did not die with the arrival of Gothic, as the multiple arcading added to Lincoln cathedral west front in 1240 was to show.

From the 1170s 'inordinate love of decoration so characteristic of later Anglo-Norman buildings' gave way to 'the reassertion of a certain simplicity, even barrenness, involving an apparent rejection of most ornamentation (and) a surprising retreat to an unrelieved flatness of ... the west wall as simply a plane'. Local examples are the west end of the parish churches of Ledbury and Bishops Cleeve. At Ledbury the late-12th-century west front was 'built outside the earlier front'. It is notable that both west portals retain the round-headed arch, yet a number of the capitals are transitional, approaching, to varying degrees, the typical concave bell, stiff-leaf and waterleaf capitals of the Early English style. At Leominster, however, the reverse is the case: the arch is transitional, but the capitals are of the convex, cushion type, characteristically early Romanesque.[190]

Fig 9.3 Hereford cathedral. Romanesque west front prior to collapse

Was Leominster the fount from which the Herefordshire School of Romanesque Sculpture sprang? Should it really be called the Leominster School? Such a suggestion has recently been rejected.[190] Yet Zarnecki, whose original analysis of the sculpture remains the substantive work, believed that 'Leominster was the transmitting centre'. The difficulty, however, was his belief that the sculpture on the west doorway and window was contemporary with the pointed door, and must have been of c1150, 'some ten years later than the work at Shobdon'. Zarnecki thus concluded that it was 'probably from the cloister, rather than the west end, that the style of the Southern School (and thus Reading) made its first appearance in Herefordshire'. Nevertheless, he conceded that some of the Shobdon motifs were 'obviously derived from Reading' (by way of Leominster), although absent from the (present) Leominster doorway. Moreover, he accepts that 'the sculptural decoration of Leominster was influenced by the mother house', and that the earliest part of the church, the east end, was built with assistance from Reading masons. Given Henry I's enthusiasm for and patronage of Cluny III, would he not have sought to ensure that the sanctuary at Reading, where he was to be buried, was also 'the head, centre, focus of all — the boldest, most interesting and beautiful part of the church'?[191] If Leominster was the inspiration for the Herefordshire School, this would have been due to the quality of the lost capitals of its sanctuary. Some of their motifs, Samson and the lion, for example, would surely have been reflected in the capitals of the original west façade?

As noted in the previous chapter, at the time of Robert de Bethune's visit to Leominster, 1131–5, construction was far enough advanced to permit the parochial altars *ad crucem* and to SS Mary Magdalene, Margaret and Katherine to be used for services; hence the grant of indulgences to those visiting the altars. This being the case, the original west doorway and sculpture would appear to predate the work at Shobdon. How otherwise can we explain the early Romanesque capitals in a doorway with a pointed arch?

The Sculptured Capitals, 1–14

The twelve Romanesque capitals of the outer and inner faces of the west tower of the priory are thus remnants of a more extensive programme. Leominster, as a royal foundation, like its mother house at Reading, would certainly have had sculptured capitals decorating the arcade of the ambulatory around the high altar, in recognition of their proximity to the altar, and to thrill pilgrims visiting the relics. The loss of all trace of these, and possibly others on the cloister arcades, means that the remaining capitals are all the more precious. The Reading capitals and their abaci, the square upper members, were sculpted from one piece of stone, an expensive option, but at Leominster they were sculpted from separate blocks and then cemented together. It is significant that the designs differ considerably, not only on the capitals but also on their abaci, reflecting a varied origin. The motifs of the capitals are described below, followed by those of the abaci.

Only fourteen decorated capitals remain, of which nos. 13 and 14, on the inside of the west window, are possibly later work. All surmount columns or shafts on the exterior and interior of the west front. Unlike the capitals which would have been on the free-standing ambulatory piers, they present two, not four, faces for decoration. On all eight capitals of the façade the design on one face is repeated on the other and, where appropriate, they are confronting. Thus, the two lions on capital 5 of the west portal stare bleakly at each other. The motifs on capitals 1–6 are

Fig 9.4 Window above west portal with capitals (7-8)

carved carefully to emphasise the convex shape of the capitals. On capitals 1–3 the subjects are depicted within interlaced foliage, recalling the plant scroll characteristic of early Northumbrian crosses. All but one of the motifs employed are to be found in other, frequently in many, works of the Herefordshire School. The description, from left to right, commences on the exterior, with the west door (1–6) (Fig 9.1) and the window above (7–8) (Fig 9.4) afterwards moving inside to the door arch (9–12) and finally to the window above (13–14), on each occasion moving from left to right (Plate 7).

West Portal North, 1–3

1. Birds. Often described as doves, but in respect of their attitude, beak and talons more like hawks, they are depicted in profile within interlaced foliage. The heads are held high, and the beaks are markedly curved. Only one of the wings, raised and slightly curved, is shown, whilst the tail stands out straight. The distinction between primary and secondary feathers is carefully detailed. Both feet can be seen, one on the ground, the other held high. On capital 8 are eight similar birds, but here the wings are raised in a scythe-like shape. This type of bird was one of the most popular motifs of the school. It is found in the foliage on the third shaft of the Shobdon chancel arch, on the Castle Frome and Eardisley fonts, the tympana at Brinsop and Fownhope, and the south doors at Rowlestone and at Kilpeck (Plate 7.1).

2. Reapers. Two men, stooping low, cut the interlace foliage. The bodies are in profile, but the heads are full face. They have moustaches, broad noses and the deep-set eyes characteristic of the school. They wear cone-shaped hats, and a one-piece garment with trousers, with long, convex stripes running vertically down the body. The figures on the Kilpeck south doorway, described by the Royal Commission as 'Welsh? warriors in peaked caps of Phrygian form, ribbed hauberk and long trews', have similar trousers, but with bands round their waists. Both forms are found on the Eardisley font and the second pier of the Shobdon chancel arch (Plate 7.2).

3. Serpents. A pair of confronted serpents within interlaced foliage, as in 1 and 2. They have the characteristic boldly-cut oval eye; the mouths are wide open, with the upper part much longer than the lower. One is covered with scales. The whole creates a picture of great malevolence.

Comparable serpents appear on the St George and dragon tympana at Brinsop and Ruardean, on the south portal at Kilpeck, and at Shobdon, on two capitals, where they are winged and knotted with two legs, as dragons (?), and on one of the shafts, winged but without legs (Plate 7.3).

West Portal South, 4–6

4. Foliage. Three rows of buds between opening leaves probably represent an attempt at a Corinthian form of capital. This is a unique subject for the Herefordshire School, and rare elsewhere in England at this time, but there is a fine free-standing example of a Corinthian column at Anselm's crypt in Canterbury cathedral. On the tower arch at Sompting, Sussex, is a pair of capitals which, as at Leominster, have three superimposed zones of narrow, upright leaves, but these are much more crudely executed (Plare 7.4).[192]

5. Lions. The most famous of all the Leominster capitals, this is possibly a reference to Edfrith's dream. The lions confront each other, bodies in profile but, as with the reapers, heads in full face. Their eyes are large and bulging, staring out bleakly; the ears erect and cat-like; their noses well-featured, with deep creases on either side, as with the masks on capital 9; and mouths open. Both have luxuriant manes, with curls at the end; long, heavy paws with well defined claws, not unlike the talons of the birds; and tails curled between the back legs and over the body. Four lions parade around the Shobdon font; the winged lion of St Mark on the Castle Frome font has the same stance and characteristics. The lions of the Leominster school have little in common with those in the Canterbury crypt, except for the tail curled between the back legs and erect cat-like ears. Only one has the luxuriant mane, ending in curls (Plate 7.5).

6. Palmettes. Variously described as 'scrolled conventional foliage', 'mirror foliage' and 'palmette', this motif has a very long history. In Greek architecture it was called *anthemion*, flower ornament. Here it ends in a triple leaf, virtually a fleur-de-lys. This common motif of Anglo-Saxon art is found throughout the works of the Herefordshire School. In all cases the strands are held tightly at their waist by bands. It is found on the right arch at Shobdon, the Kilpeck south door, at Rowlestone and Rock (Plate 7.6).

West Window, 7–8

7. Ring Motifs. There are four rings on each face, clasped by four masks similar to that on capital 11. The rings, which are beaded, thus appear to be issuing from the face of the masks. Each ring is inhabited by a bird in profile but, in contrast to those on capital 1, with a markedly curved wing. This design finds its boldest expression on the Shobdon chancel arch, where ten rows of such rings enclose birds, animals and pattern work. Other examples are on the Kilpeck south door, the Stottesdon font, and at Rowlestone and Brinsop (Plate 7.7).

8. Birds of Prey. These are similar to those of capital 1 but in a more dramatic pose. Evidently hawks, they are shown in profile, each attacking a smaller bird (a dove?). The hawk's head is down, pecking at the neck of the other bird while its talons hold it firmly by the back. The right-hand pair is very badly worn due to rain penetration from the lack of cover above, and the whole has been

Fig 9.5 Capitals 13 & 14 on inner face of west window a) capital on north, b) capital on south

crudely repaired with cement, now beginning to crumble and crack. The left-hand hawk, apart from its head, is well preserved. Its primary and secondary feathers, and those on the upper leg, are carefully sculpted. Between the pairs of birds what appears to be a bud emerges from four leaves. Similar birds appear on the Shobdon chancel arch, the Kilpeck south door, at Ribbesford, and at St Giles at Aston. The motif is very ancient, found far beyond Britain: at Sant' Ambrogio, Milan and even as a bas relief in the Armenian State History Museum, Yerevan (Plate 7.8).

West Portal, Inner Face, 9–12

(Plate 7.9-12 & Plate 14)

The four capitals on the inner face of the west door are related, but not identical, pairs. The outer capitals are formed of interlace strands, single on capital (9), and double on (10). There are similar strands on the Castle Frome font. There are jawless masks, with vine scrolls and bundles of grapes issuing forth on the capitals on the inner shafts, (11) and (12). The mask on (11) is of a human, his beard plaited in two strands. The mask on (12) has vine branches issuing from both its mouth and apertures in the head. The grape harvest here is more prolific. The mask is closely related to those which clasp the rings on capital 7.

West Window, Inner Face, 13–14 (Figs 9.5a&b)

The shafts on either side of the interior of the western window also carry capitals. These, but not their abaci or rings, are probably of later date than the series of twelve already considered. They are different, both in design and the stone used. The rings at the base of the capitals are however of the same stone as the twelve originals.

The Abaci (Fig 9.6)

Designs on the abaci of the fourteen capitals differ considerably. These were chamfered, cut away at a 45° angle, on their lower section, the upper

Fig 9.6 Abacai showing triangular cavities between the abaci cemented up, and disparity in pattern

and lower parts being decorated quite differently. In the process of reconstruction the abaci were treated in a rough-and-ready fashion.

On the west portal (1–6), the northernmost abacus, above the Birds (1), retains a lug on the left side of the chamfered section. Its purpose can be understood by comparing the left side of this capital with its neighbour, above the Reapers (2). As there is no lug on capital (2), the resultant triangular cavity between the two capitals has had to be cemented up (Fig 9.6). The same defects can be seen between the abaci of (2) and (3), and between (4) and (5), and (5) and (6). The lower, chamfered, and upper, unchamfered, sections of the six abaci are of varying designs.

A star design occurs on the upper sections of capitals 1 to 5, but whilst (1) and (2) have four points, (4) and (5) have both four and six points, and (3) has eight. The four-point star, or saltire, motif, is found on early 11th-century buildings in Normandy and was used, in abundance, to decorate the doorcase of the great rectangular keep at Chepstow, described as 'the earliest dateable secular stone building in Britain'; Turner now suggests c1081–93. Four- and eight-pointed stars, as well as billet moulding, were used on the west doorway of Ludlow castle's round chapel, but the capitals are of the later, scalloped, type, not the heavy cushion type of Leominster's west portal. As Coppack dates the chapel 'no earlier than the 1120s or 1130s', this also indicates a much earlier date than the mid 1150s for the decoration of the original façade of Leominster Priory.[193]

The chamfered sections of these five abaci bear a trilobed leaf within triangles, with beading between the triangles. The abacus of the Palmette capital (6) is quite different. The upper section is distinctly narrower, with a totally different design. The chamfered section has semi-florets, which occur elsewhere.

Abacus (7) also has a trilobe within triangles, and beading, but the leaf design is much fuller and the leaf points alternately upwards and downwards. A flower with eight deeply-carved petals can just be made out. Abacus (8) has semi-florets, similar to those on capital (6). The upper section has a continuous pattern of overlapping leaves pointing left. This abacus appears not to have been completed, preparing us for what we are to meet on the inside.

The abaci of the interior of the west portal and west window (9 to 12) introduces further patterns. (9) has full flowers, rather than the semi-florets of (6). The trilobe leaf design is not on the chamfer, as with abaci (1) to (5), but on the upper section. A decorated strip replaces abacus (10), with a semi-floret above. For (11) it is merely plain stone. Abacus (12) is outstanding. It has small, confronted volutes, as on the Rowlestone chancel arch. Confronted volutes are one of the distinctive motifs of the Romanesque churches about Dymock.[194] The upper part of the abacus has two serpents intertwined about a single horizontal strand, similar to that on the third shaft of Shobdon's chancel arch. Most surprising of all, on the left is Samson struggling with the lion, a miniature mirror-image of the Samson and the lion on the Stretton Sugwas tympanum (Plate 5).

Although ill-fitting, abaci (13) and (14) are both original work. The chamfered section of (13) has semi-florets which not only differ in design from those on capitals (6) and (8), but also point alternately up and down. Abacus (14) is unique. At the angle is an unusual head, with eyes, nose and mouth portrayed with utmost simplicity (Fig 9.5a&b). On either side are horizontal designs, unlike anything else at the west end.

Such a range of re-used capitals and abaci can have come only from the earlier west front. The three-lobed leaf within a triangle, the most frequently encountered abacus design of the west front, is found on the abacus of the easternmost capital of the north arcade, early work in the nave (Fig 9.7a). Billet moulding, as on the string course on the west front, is used on the abacus of the third pier of the south arcade (Fig 9.7b). As the piers approach the west end the abaci become plain (Fig 9.7c). Other

Fig 9.7 Abaci. a) Easternmost capital of north arcade, three-lobed leaf within a triangle; b) Third pier of south arcade, billet moulding; c) They become plain towards the west end

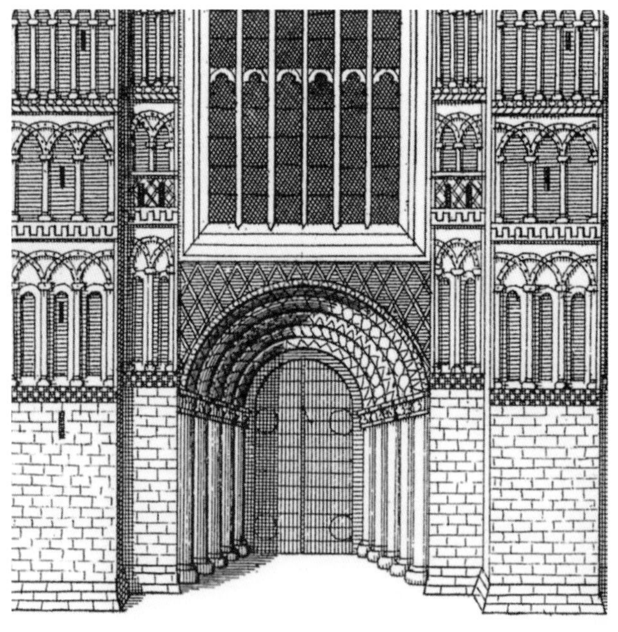

Fig 9.8 Detail from Fig 9.3 showing the 6 orders of the Romanesque west door at Hereford Cathedral

designs on the façade will, no doubt, have been found at the east end. The porch of Hereford cathedral's Romanesque façade had six orders, and five pairs of capitals (Fig 9.8). As the range of abacus designs at the west end of the priory is greater than would be required for such a porch, this suggests a wider use of decorated capitals. This should not surprise us.

The Tympana of the Herefordshire School

Zarnecki also points out that Leominster is 'the only surviving doorway of the School without a tympanum'. But he is referring to the present, later, portal. The figure of Christ in Majesty on the tympanum of the Cluny west portal had a powerful impact on western Christendom. It was destroyed during the French Revolution, but fragments have been discovered and a reconstruction made. Christ was within a vesica held by two angels standing on clouds. The vast size of the tympanum obliged the sculptor to include two further angels, attendant by Christ's feet, together with the symbols of the evangelists, John and Matthew at the top and Luke and Mark in the corners at the base.[195] This subject was too wide-ranging to be transferred satisfactorily onto smaller tympana. At Rochester cathedral the sculptor had great difficulty accommodating the Majesty held by two angels, together with

*Fig 9.9 Tympana: a) Shobdon, b) Hereford and c) Rowlestone (*TWNFC *(1984) 370, xv, xvii, xviii)*

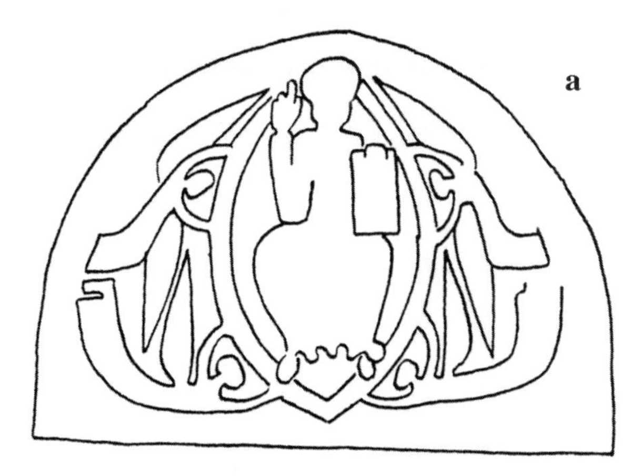

Fig 9.10 Tympana: a) Hereford, b) Shobdon and c) Rowlestone

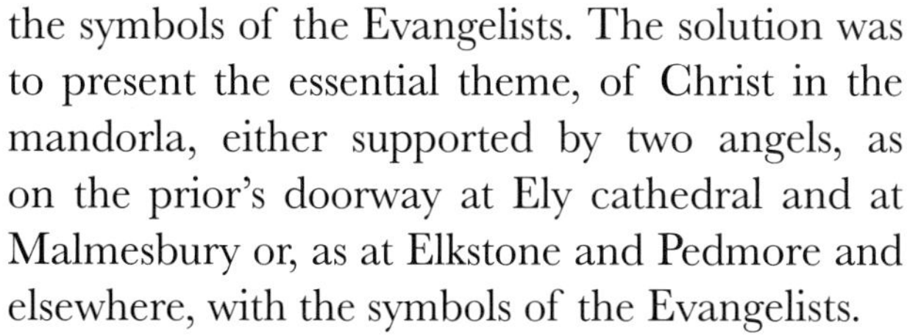

the symbols of the Evangelists. The solution was to present the essential theme, of Christ in the mandorla, either supported by two angels, as on the prior's doorway at Ely cathedral and at Malmesbury or, as at Elkstone and Pedmore and elsewhere, with the symbols of the Evangelists.

Christ in Majesty is the subject of three of the extant tympana of the Herefordshire School: at Shobdon, on the former south portal; at Rowlestone, on the south doorway; and on the tympana removed to St Giles' Hospital, Ledbury Road, Hereford (Figs 9.9a,b&c). In each case Christ is shown, as at Cluny, seated within a vesica, His left hand holding the Book, the right raised with two fingers in blessing. In the Herefordshire School the vesica is held by four, not two, angels. They do not stand on clouds, but fly in 'precipitous positions and a little as if they were tumblers in action'. At Shobdon and Hereford the legs of the angels almost touch. At Rowlestone, the last and weakest but by far the best preserved of the three, the legs and wings of all four angels are splayed upwards to accommodate them within the tympanum (Figs 9.10a,b&c). For English tympana, this portrayal is unique to the Herefordshire School. However, the four-angel Majesty is found in some Anglo-Saxon illuminated manuscripts. The best-known example is in the New Minster, Winchester, charter of 966, where King Edgar is shown offering his charter to Christ, seated on a rainbow within a vesica supported by four angels. Their stance, unlike those of the Herefordshire tympana, is remarkably successful. Four angels supporting the Glory is the form of the Ascension in the eastern church, as in the frescoes of the sanctuary of St Sophia, Ochrid, Macedonia, and at Panayia tou Arakou at Lagoudhera in the mountains north of Limassol (Fig 9.11).[196]

Hereford cathedral had no tympanum, but Christ in Majesty is the subject of two of the original capitals from the presbytery. These were no model for the Herefordshire School, for both hands are raised, there is no benediction, no book, and the figures are placed within arches resting on piers and capitals. If Leominster was 'the transmitting centre' for a range of other motifs, espe-

Fig 9.11 Lagoudhera, Cyprus. Byzantine Ascension with four angels, c1192

cially to nearby Shobdon, the possibility has to be considered that it was the source of this powerful image, with its four angels. Whether the inspiration was from Cluny, or from an Anglo-Saxon manuscript, may well remain unresolved.

Anglo-Saxon Influence

Whilst Reading was a major influence, it was but one. At Leominster, as Boase has pointed out, 'we are aware both of traditions and symbols forgotten or never known in the more cosmopolitan centres of the south'. The confronted birds of capital 1 are an ancient Christian symbol. They appear in a form similar to those at Leominster on the arms of a cross of c800 preserved at Cropthorne church, and on the arms of a cross-shaft of similar date at Acton Beauchamp, re-used as a lintel for

Fig 9.12a-d Anglo-Saxon birds. a&b): Cropthorne; c) Acton Beauchamp; d) St Oswald's, Gloucester (© Gloucester City Museum and Art Gallery)

the south door of the tower. The Cropthorne birds are 'the closest sculptural parallels' to those portrayed in the early 9th-century *Book of Cerne*, both being derived ultimately from Northumbrian works, such as the Jarrow, Ruthwell and Croft cross-shafts. A similar, but more accomplished, rendering of the bird motif was found during excavations at St Oswald's Priory, Gloucester, where on face B of cross-shaft 30/31 'a beautiful little bird perches on a tendril and a berry bunch and pecks one of the elongated berries'. The St Oswald's bird's posture is different, but it rests within a volute and is otherwise very similar to those at Leominster. This cross has been dated to the late 8th century. Cropthorne and Acton Beauchamp were but priest-minsters. St Oswald's, on the other hand, was a monastic church founded by Aethelred and Aethelfleda, rulers of the Mercians, and here the remains of four cross shafts have been discovered (Figs 9.12a,b,c). Given the mid-7th-century date of Leominster's foundation, one would anticipate that, when the new priory church was about to be constructed, there would have been similar, possibly greater, evidence of Anglo-Saxon sculpture. The Cropthorne birds and those on the Croft cross-shaft have been likened to those in the *Book of Cerne*, which provides analogues for prayers 19, 23, 24, 25, 31 and 68 in the Galba prayer book.[197]

Vine scroll was one of the most popular sculptural motifs of the Ancient World, whether inhabited, as with the labours of Hercules on a pilaster of the Severan basilica at Leptis Magna in Tripolitania, or uninhabited, as on the Monumental Arch of the Colonnaded Street at Palmyra, Syria. Vine scroll proved almost as popular with the sculptors of the early Northumbrian crosses, where it was used in less exotic form as plant scroll, often inhabited with birds and beasts. On one side of the Bewcastle cross, Cumbria, birds are portrayed both in profile and frontal, but at the related Ruthwell cross, Dumfries, all the birds are shown frontal. The cross-shaft from Croft-on-Tees, North Yorks, has a central stem with three pairs of scrolls. In the lowest a pair of birds, in profile, confront each other, both having one foot raised, as at Leominster. The left-hand bird has its wing up, the other

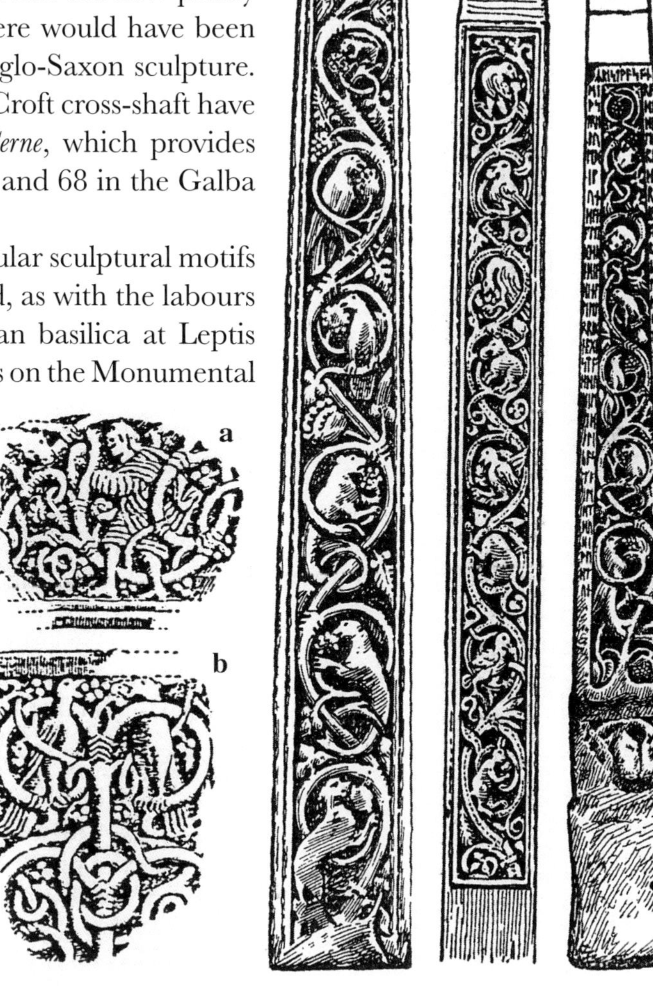

Fig 9.13 Northumbrian scroll. a&b) Jarrow, c) Bewcastle, d) Otley, e) Ruthwell

by its side. The raised foot is also prominent on the Aldburgh cross, North Yorks, on which a pair of birds are back to back in a volute, whilst Otley number 1 cross-shaft has single birds in profile in plant scroll. The earliest representation is probably on the architectural frieze at Jarrow, dated 'early 8th century'. This has a plant scroll inhabited by two birds, one on the left in profile, the other virtually frontal. Plant scroll on another panel from Jarrow is inhabited by a man and a beast. The man's drapery has ribbed folds, as on capital 2 at Leominster and other sculptures of the Herefordshire School. The Mercian birds developed from those on the Northumbrian crosses (Figs 9.13a-e).[198]

The Present West Front

What was the model for the present, that is the second, west front? Jean Bony was the first to draw attention to the close affinities between the west façade at Leominster and contemporary buildings in the county of Anjou, in particular to Fontevrault, where the nave was completed c1150 (Figs 9.14a&b and 9.15). Henry I's interest in that abbey has already been noted. The marriage of his widowed daughter, the Empress Matilda, to Geoffrey Count of Anjou preserved this link. On the death of Stephen in 1154 their son became king of England as Henry II (1154–89), but he chose to be buried at Fontevrault, not Reading. Here also were buried his queen, Eleanor of Aquitaine,

Fig 9.14a&b The west front at Leominster (left) and Fontevrault (right)

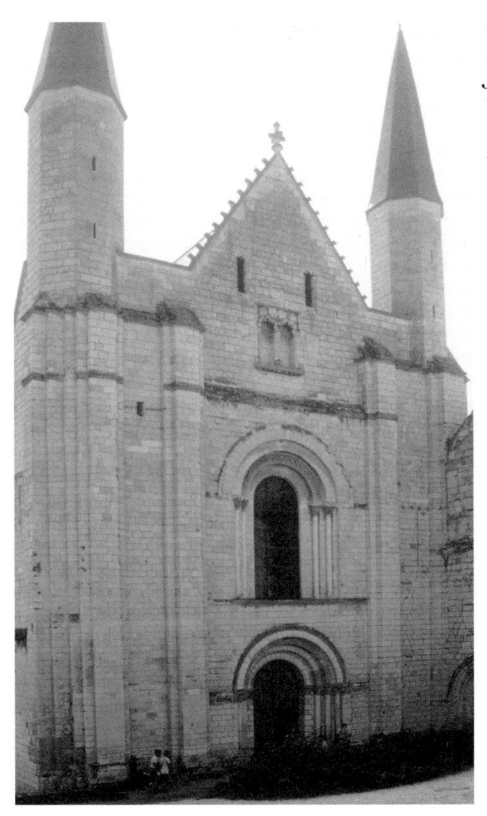

Fig 9.15 The west front at Fontevrault showing corner buttresses and turrets

their son, Richard I, the Lionheart, and his brother, King John's, widow, Isabella of Angoulème. Their tombs can still be seen.[199] Yet links with Reading were not forgotten. For the Angevins, especially Henry II, Reading served as the English counterpart of Fontevrault. In 1156 Henry's eldest son, who died in infancy, was buried here, at the feet of Henry I by the high altar. Another son, the illegitimate Reginald, earl of Cornwall, was also buried in the abbey, in 1175. Henry II thus had dual loyalties, to Fontevrault and to Reading, including its priory at Leominster.

Fontevrault's nave was completed c1150. Four years later Henry of Anjou was king. His first task was to re-establish royal authority. This brought him to the Welsh March, where Hugh Mortimer of Wigmore and Cleobury, who held the royal castle at Bridgnorth, refused to submit. Henry II led the assault on Hugh's castles. Given his reputation as a great builder, it may well have been at this time that he decided to intervene at Leominster, where the priory had suffered severely during the troubles of Stephen's reign. The west portal at Fontevrault has a round-headed arch, in contrast to the pointed arch of the doorway at Leominster; but if the relationship is one of mother and daughter, this should be anticipated. Certainly the pointed arch provides a date for the Leominster west front in Henry II's reign.[200]

Simplicity of design of the west front was a characteristic that, as already noted, emerged in the 1170s. In this respect the churches at Ledbury and Bishops Cleeve followed Leominster. Both were more than mere parish churches. Ledbury, for Pevsner the premier parish church of Herefordshire, had been an Anglo-Saxon minster, responsible for the spiritual well-being of what in the 12th century became its ten surrounding parishes. The monastery at Bishops Cleeve was the recipient c779 of a grant of land from King Offa of Mercia, but by 899 was in the hands of the bishops of Worcester, who built a major manor house there. Throughout the Middle Ages Ledbury and Bishops Cleeve remained major centres of episcopal administration. The Romanesque western windows of both churches were replaced in the Decorated period. Otherwise, despite the difference in size, the similarity of their west fronts to that of Fontevrault is quite startling.

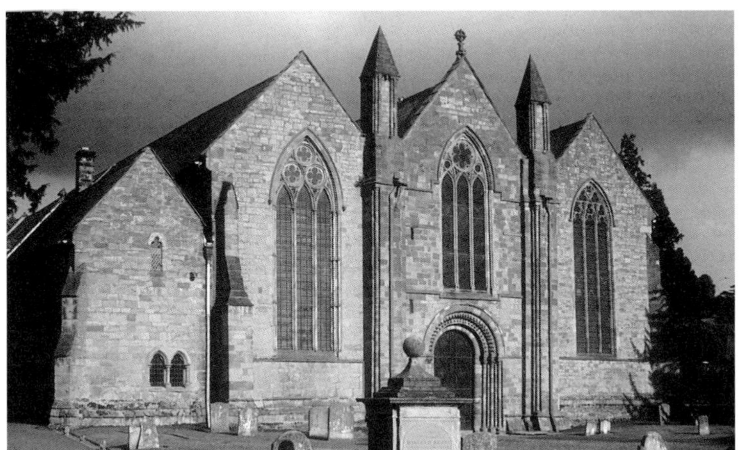

Fig 9.16 The west front at Ledbury

At the French abbey the central gable has octagonal corner buttresses that continue above the upper string course, to become turrets with conical pinnacles (Fig 9.15). At Ledbury and Bishops Cleeve the buttresses and turrets are square, but otherwise the layout is the same. At Ledbury the original façade is now dominated by the later, very much enlarged, aisles[202] (Figs 9.16 and 9.17).[201]

Fig 9.17 The west front at Bishops Cleeve

The probable explanation is that when the bishop of Hereford, either Gilbert or Robert Foliot, was reconstructing the west front of Ledbury's parish church, he was moved by the simplicity of that at Leominster. Ledbury in its turn was the model for the bishop of Worcester at Cleeve. The façades of Ledbury and Cleeve enable us to visualise Leominster's late-Romanesque west front. Now masked by the 15th-century tower, it would originally have terminated in a gable, with the buttresses on either side carried up to form a pair of turrets with shafted angles and pyramidal caps. This design is reflected in the early-14th-century octagonal turret built at the south-east end of the south aisle.

There are other reasons for believing that the west front was built during the reign of Henry II. The years of Stephen's reign, the great anarchy, 1135–54, were not propitious for church building in the Severn valley, one of the centres of military operations. Conflict over the succession between Stephen and Matilda led to open hostilities after Henry I's death in 1135. 'The kingdom', we are told, was 'convulsed; peace and justice vanished, with fierce and mad designs from the hearts of many'. Miles, constable of Gloucester, changed sides, joining Henry I's illegitimate son, Robert earl of Gloucester, in inviting Matilda to England. In 1139 Miles then turned on Stephen's garrison at Hereford. In his attempt to relieve the castle the king got only as far as Leominster. The burgesses, having learned how Miles, his antagonist, had pillaged and burned Worcester, and how its men, 'bound in couples like hounds, were carried away to a miserable captivity', temporised with Stephen, seeking to maintain their neutrality. 'Some, taking counsel, swore fealty while others refused, sending him this message: "although we will not swear, the king may, if he pleases, trust to the truth of our words".' As Stephen withdrew to Worcester, they apparently saved their borough from a similar onslaught. Matilda rewarded Miles with the earldom of Hereford.[202]

By granting indulgences of 40 days for those in mortal sin and 20 days for others, Gilbert Foliot, bishop of Hereford, sought early in Henry II's reign to provide financial support for the priory, where he said the monks had, by 'long and numerous troubles and misfortunes, scarce enough to sustain the divine service'. Further evidence of the travails suffered by the priory in Stephen's reign is found in a charter by which Roger earl of Hereford granted it the valuable manor of Broadward, with its wide meadows, in free alms for the health of his soul, and as reparation for 'the damage done to its men and possessions by the earl and his men during the time of war'.[203]

10 The Cloister and Conventual Buildings

Soon after 1123 the first monks arrived from Reading. They would have found the Anglo-Saxon precinct, defined by the Kenwater to the north, the Lugg to the east, with its great earthen bank and ditch, enclosing some 30 acres, to the south and west.[204] Shortly after the priory's foundation the abbot of Reading, with the assistance of Bishop Richard de Capella, established a small borough immediately to the west of this enclosure (see Chapter 16). The burgage plots on which some of the earliest houses were built ran back from what is now Drapers Lane eastward to the line of the old bank and ditch (see Fig 1.3). Such burgage plots are characteristic features of the medieval borough, long but narrow, with shops and houses on the street front and extensive rear gardens. The standard practice for the Benedictines, whose monasteries were mostly in towns, as at Reading and Gloucester, was to close the precinct to the secular world by walls, frequently of carefully dressed stone. At Leominster the 350 feet or so of the present wall running north from the Forbury chapel is on the line of its predecessor, the medieval precinct wall. It has yet to be established whether any part of the medieval wall remains. The cartographer who drew the first 25" OS of the town confidently described the south-west quadrant of wall as 'Priory Wall (Remains of)' in Gothic script. This was evidently rebuilt in brick when the road was built from Church Street, across the 'Monks' Dungeon' (site of) to the new Sorting Office, facing Corn Square, along the inside of that wall (Figs 10.1& 11.5).

Fig 10.1 Leominster: a remnant of the, as yet unsurveyed, precinct wall

Wherever possible the monks built their cloister to the south of the church, nestling between the south transept and nave, where the high walls of the buildings gave shelter from the cold north and easterly winds. Here maximum advantage could be taken of the warmth and light of the sun. Ultimately, however, the site of the cloister, and the conventual buildings surrounding it, was dictated by the water supply. At Reading, the Kennet and its small tributary, the Holy Brook,

Fig 10.2 Cloister area from the west tower showing the site of the Kenwater marked by trees, and top right the stone-built west range of Priory House

both ran to the south of the abbey, but at Leominster the Pinsley Brook, and thus the cloister, lay to the north. This supplied fresh water for cooking and brewing, and for the lavatorium outside the refectory where the brethren would wash their hands before and after meals. At St Peter's Abbey, Gloucester, where the cloister was also on the north, with water supplied by culverts from the Fullbrook, the abbey buildings, to the south, gave the monks peace from the hubbub of Westgate and the borough.[205]

The Pinsley brook was the *Onye* in 1250 and *Oney* on Saxton's county map of 1577. The river's name was probably derived from the Welsh *on* (ash trees), suggesting that an existing water supply had been tailored to serve the Anglo-Saxon minster. After the brook leaves Vicarage Street the straight line of its channel, taking it under the buildings on the north side of the cloister, indicates culverting. If Anglo-Saxon in origin, it would have been improved by the Benedictines in the early 12th century. At Reading the lie of the land also suggests major works to bring the waters of the Holy Brook to the abbey buildings (see Fig 11.2). Indeed some Benedictine monastic conduits were as long as 3 miles. The water was then distributed to the various offices, kitchen, lavatorium etc. At Leominster this was through lead pipes, for the Leominster Chamber Minutes of 1750 refer to 'the lead lately found in Priory Green', the site of the cloister, and a letter to be sent 'to the Countess of Coningsby (the lady of the manor) informing her the Council was seeking the opinion of Mr Harley or some other counsel'. Evidently at the Dissolution Henry VIII's agents, in their haste, had collected but then abandoned some of the lead water pipes. Given the relatively small quantity involved, it is unlikely that this lead was from the roof.[206]

The concept of the cloister, a rectangular plot with a covered walk along all four sides, with its garth, a garden, came down from the colonnades of the ancient world. At Leominster the only physical evidence of the cloister is on the outer face of the north wall of the priory, the 'shadow' of the arch, capital and shaft that carried the vaulting for one bay. At Reading in 1802 a sketch shows four such shadows, but here arches, decorated capitals and shafts remain (Figs 10.3a&b). During the 2005 excavations at Leominster, the line of the western cloister walk (A) was located in its expected position (Fig 10.4). Its width was 2.5m. The remains of mortar bedding for the paving, of which there was no trace, indicated the approximate height of the robbed out floor of the cloister,

Figs 10.3 (a) Leominster: cloister shadow on the north wall of the priory (b) Reading: 'Mrs Clements' Garden'

some 1.2m below the floor level of the north aisle of the priory church. To the right of the cloister walk were the *in situ* remains of the foundations of the western cloister arcade (B), and part of the cloister garth (C); to the left is the line of robbed-out foundations of building on the western side of the cloister (D) and interior of building (E). Steps, now infilled, are shown on Fig 7.1, leading from the north aisle to the cloister. The stairway that served the entrance, with its internal and external lintels, was rebuilt in the late Middle Ages (see Chapter 22). It will be noted that its position aligns with the centre of the western cloister wall walk. The relationship between this western, processional doorway and the cloister has now been hidden by the building of the priory toilets etc, served by a new doorway and stairs to the east of the medieval lintels mentioned above.[207]

Fig 10.4 Excavations photo showing: (A) line of the west cloister walk; (B) in situ *remains of the foundation of the western cloister arcade; (C) part of the cloister garth; (D) line of robbed-out foundations of a building on the west of the cloister; (E) interior of building (see also Fig 1.1)*

A top soil horizon containing 13th-century pottery was encountered within the area of the cloister garth. The most important medieval finds were the 539 fragments of glazed floor tiles, all in post-Dissolution contexts. The vast majority were cream and dark green in colour, presumably laid chequer board fashion around the cloister, but some have decorative designs. The tiles were probably produced locally, in the Deerfold/Lingen area (see Chapter 18). Other building materials included broken stone roof slates and lumps of tufa.

The position of the various buildings around the cloister was determined by the practical needs of the community. Their arrangement differed from one monastic order to another but all, except that of the Carthusians, were variations on the Benedictine plan, the most ancient and in many respects the most simple. Thus, although almost all the conventual buildings were swept away at the Dissolution, we can speak with confidence about their position and layout at Leominster.

The Eastern Range

The layout of a typical east range is illustrated at the Cistercian house of Cleeve, Somerset (Fig 10.5). Moving left to right, that is from the monastic church to the refectory, there is first the entrance to the library or strongroom, then the chapter-house entrance, with a window on either side. Next are the day stairs, serving the dormitory on the first floor, of which the small windows can clearly be seen; finally there is the entrance to the parlour. At Leominster the eastern range lay to the north of, and in alignment with, the north transept. It would have been, as usual, of two storeys. At ground floor level was the slype, a tunnel-like passage adjacent to the outer wall of the north transept, providing direct access to the monks' graveyard about the eastern end of the

Fig 10.5 Cleeve Abbey: east range, with dormitory at first floor

church. A fine, early Romanesque slype can be seen at Worcester cathedral. Due to its proximity to the transept, in many monasteries, as at Abbey Dore, the slype came to serve as a sacristy, for the reception of the altar vessels and vestments etc. Next would have been the principal building of the eastern range, the chapter-house, where, after Prime, the community came together. The prior took the chair, a raised seat at the east end, with his chief officers, the obedientiaries, at Leominster the sub-prior, precentor, almoner etc. The brethren sat on stone benches at either side. The meeting began with a reading, from a lectern in the centre, of a chapter from the Rule of St Benedict, with commentary or sermon. From this both meeting and building derived their names. Day-to-day business was then transacted and administrative matters discussed. Chapter ended with complaints and open confessions of faults, breaches of the Rule, by members of the community, for which correction would be received at the hands of the prior.

At Reading, with its 100 monks, as at other large monasteries, the chapter-house had of necessity to project eastwards, beyond the line of the eastern claustral range. At Leominster, with its complement of a mere twelve monks, there would have been no need for such an eastward extension. To emphasise the importance of the chapter-house, its doorway and the windows on either side, especially the capitals, were often subjects of rich sculptural decoration. As the capitals of Reading's cloister arcade were so decorated, it is reasonable to assume that those at Leominster received particular attention from the priory's own school of sculptors. Some fragments of chevron ornament, replicas of such on the priory's west portal, can be seen in the conservatory on the south side of the Grange. These may well have formed part of the chapter-house doorway (Fig 10.6 & compare Fig 9.1).

Figs 10.6 (a) Fragments from the chapterhouse doorway(?) showing chevron ornament (b) detail from the west portal

The parlour was usually next door. Conversation, forbidden within the cloister and claustral buildings, was conducted here when necessary. Outside the day stairs led to the dormitory, with the *calefactorium*, the warming room, beyond. In the early days only here and in the kitchens would a fire have been permitted, and

Figs 10.7 Valle Crucis: east range with dormitory over

admission was restricted to those engaged on the business of the house. For example, here notes made by the monks with a stylus on wax tablets could be erased, by the gentle application of heat, so the tablets could be used indefinitely. A sandstone foundation excavated close to the Priory House may have been associated with the warming room.[208]

Above chapter-house, parlour and calefactorium, was the dormitory or dorter. St Benedict advised 'let all sleep in one place ... let a candle burn constantly in the cell until morning ... let them sleep clothed and girded with belts or cords ... and thus always be ready, so that when the signal is given they rise without delay, and hasten each to forestall the other in going to the Work of God yet in all gravity and modesty. Let not the younger brethren have their beds by themselves, but amongst those of the seniors, and when they arise for the *Opus Dei* let them gently encourage one another because of the excuses of the drowsy.' We have therefore to imagine a long room with stone walls, low roof and beds down either side, as in the hospitals and public schools of the 19th century. Later in the Middle Ages the rule was tempered by the introduction of wooden partitions between the beds so that each monk could have his own cubicle. Some of the small windows from the priory's dormitory can be seen in the rockery of the conservatory on the south side of the Grange (Figs 10.8). As these are Romanesque, round-headed, they indicate that the eastern range of the cloister was completed not long after the church. They should be compared with the later dormitory windows *in situ* at Cleeve, Somerset, and Valle Crucis near Llangollen, which look, not east into the monastic graveyard, but west, over the cloister. Even though they are considerably later, at both monasteries they remained small, as at Leominster (Figs 10.7 and 10.8).[209]

Here the south wall of the dormitory would have been built against the north wall of the north transept so that the monks could descend, by means of the night stairs, into the transept

Figs 10.8 Leominster Priory: Romanesque windows in the outhouse of the Grange

Figs 10.9 Valle Crucis: gothic (cusped) dormitory windows and corbelling to carry pentice roof over cloister walk

Fig 10.10 Kirkham Abbey: entry to rere-dorter with alcove for a lantern to left

and the choir for the night office. The monastic timetable, *horarium*, varied according to the monastic year — winter, Holy Week and summer — but at all seasons the night stairs played a major part in the life of the monks, saving them from chilly night-time excursions, between 2am and 3am, into their north cloister. Where night stairs survive, as at Bristol cathedral and St Andrew's, Hexham, their deeply worn stone steps attest to their daily use by the community over some four centuries.

At the north end of the dormitory a door gave direct access to an adjacent *necessarium*, or rere-dorter, the monastic lavatory. Above the door a light would burn all night. One can still see, at Cleeve, the hook upon which the lantern hung, and at Kirkham, near York, the housing for the light by the door leading from dormitory to rere-dorter (Fig 10.10). Frequently described as a latrine, this was in appearance more like a modern water closet, lacking the ball-flush system. Cabinets with wooden seats were perched high above the culverted section of the Pinsley brook, which here served as the main drain (see Fig 1.3). The ratio of cabinets to members of the community was high; in many houses there was one for each monk.[210] Effective sanitation and attention to personal hygiene were recognised as important means of reducing health hazards for such an enclosed community. It has been suggested that the western section of the 'Priory House', now virtually rebuilt, may have been the *necessarium*.

However, it does not adjoin the northern end of the dormitory range, on the alignment indicated by the foundations of the transept, and thus the dormitory.

The North Range

This was dominated by the refectory or frater, a large room, usually parallel with the cloister walk. In Cistercian houses, however, it was at right angles. The prior and his obedientiaries sat at a high table at the east end, and the brethren at two tables in line with the longer walls. Above the high table would be a large crucifix or other suitable object. At Worcester the hacked remains of a great, sculpted and painted Christ in Majesty, surrounded by the symbols of the Evangelists, still looks down from the east end. Meals were taken in silence, whilst a member of the community read from a lectern. Outside, close to the entrance, was the lavatorium, where the monks would wash their hands and face on entering and leaving the refectory, and comb their beards first thing in the morning. Occasionally elaborately decorated, circular or polygonal roofed structures were built in the cloister garth, as at Durham and Wenlock, but most lavatoria were simple, long, shallow stone troughs with a series of brass taps, as can be seen at Gloucester and Worcester. Near at hand would be an aumbrey or recess with towels. The kitchen, frequently free-standing to reduce risk of fire, would be close by, normally to the west, near the *cellarium*, the storehouse, whence provisions would come. At Leominster fresh water from the Pinsley brook was supplied directly to kitchen and rere-dorter.

The West Range

This also was dominated by one structure, the *cellarium*, the point of contact between the cloister and the Outer Court. The demands of the Cluniac liturgy left little if any time for physical labour. Those who worked here, under the supervision of the cellarer, would be lay servants. The site of this western range was established during the 2005 excavations. Remains of part of a substantial cellared masonry building attached to this side of the cloister walk were found. Its walls and floor levels had been entirely removed by post-Dissolution robbing. Two phases of masonry were found in the eastern wall of the *cellarium*, the earlier consisting of substantial, but undated, trench built, mortared sandstone rubble. This was apparently truncated and partly robbed out during the late 14th or 15th century. It was replaced by a much narrower and shallower masonry foundation. This also was extensively robbed out after 1539.[211]

The cloister was much more than a covered means of communication between the different parts of the priory. It was pre-eminently a place for study. 'Idleness', said St Benedict, 'is the enemy of the soul. Therefore the brethren should be occupied at stated times in manual labour and at other fixed hours ... in sacred reading. In the days of Lent let them receive a book apiece from the library to read consecutively, straight through.' The procedure is described in a decree of Archbishop Lanfranc, c1070. 'Before the brethren go into Chapter the librarian ought to have all the books brought together into the chapter-house and laid out on a carpet.' Each monk was to bring his book with him and, as the librarian read out the record, 'let each brother when he hears his own name pronounced, return the book with which he had been entrusted; and let him who is conscious of not having read the book through ... fall down on his face, and pray for forgiveness. Then let the librarian hand to each another book for reading ... and put on record the names of the books and who receives them.' *The customs of Cluny*, of which there was a copy in Reading library, indicates that the annual return and lending of books took place in the chapter-house on the second day of Lent. Book titles and names of borrowers were entered into a register reserved for that purpose.[212]

The hours devoted to reading were spent in individual cubicles called carrels, of which splendid examples can be seen in the Gloucester cloister. At Leominster the north cloister will have received some sunshine in the summer, but in the winter, in the shadow of the priory church to the south, it would have been bleak. Despite the introduction, at a later date, of such small luxuries as screens and wainscotting to keep out the worst draughts, and the use of straw to cover the cold, flagged pavement, for some of the monks concentration must have been difficult. The Rule advised 'let one or two of the seniors be deputed to go round the monastery at the(se) hours ... and see there be no slothful brother giving himself to idleness or gossip and not applying himself to his reading, so that he is not only useless to himself but a distraction to others. If such a one be found (which God forbid) let him be corrected.' Here also took place the copying of books to be added to those available for study and the replacement of service books worn out by constant use.[213]

Two important buildings usually lay beyond the cloister: the infirmary and the quarters of the abbot or, as at Leominster, the prior. The former was usually in the peace and quiet to the east of the cloister and consisted of an open or arcaded hall with beds down each side and a chapel to the east, similar to most medieval hospitals. In all but the smallest houses it would have had its own kitchen and sometimes, as at Gloucester, where the ruins of the aisled hall still stand, it was within its own little cloister. The prior's lodgings would have been similar in most respects to the infirmary, with a hall in which he could offer hospitality to important guests, and a chapel. It would also have had at least one private chamber with its own toilet facilities, suggesting a site on or close to the Pinsley brook.

The 'Priory House'

The only conventual building to survive the Dissolution is the so-called Priory House. This may have served as the prior's own house, or the infirmary. Recorded by Brown and Wilson in 1979, it consists of three linked structures, built over the canalised Pinsley Brook (Fig 10.11). Engravings by Stukeley of 1722 and Price of c1795 provide valuable evidence as to its condition in the 18th century (Figs 10.12a-d). The external arches over the culvert, at both eastern and western ends, are shown by Price and are still visible today. There is access to the, now dried-up, culvert from a manhole in the ground floor of the central block. The second floor was added to the central and eastern ranges

Fig 10.11 Entry point of the culverted Pinsley brook under Priory House

Figs 10.12a-d Four views of Priory House
a) Stukeley from the north (b) Stukeley from the south
c) Price from the north d) Price from the south

Fig 10.13 Priory House: double lancet on the south wall with cusped head and hood-mould

Fig 10.14 Priory House: archway from the first-floor hall to a chapel, now painted white

c1837–41, after it became the Leominster Poor Law Institution. The principal accommodation in the Middle Ages was at first-floor level, with a hall in the centre and chapel at the eastern end. The western end has been almost completely rebuilt. It has been suggested that it served as the rere-dorter for the dormitory of the brethren but, as noted, its position does not allow entry from the west range. The 18th-century illustrations show triple lancets at the east end of the chapel, with two singles on its north and four at ground-floor level. The hall was lit by a single lancet and pair of lancets on its north, and two pairs of lancets on the south. By 1795 all the fenestration had been replaced, except for the two pairs of lancets in the hall[214] (Figs 10.12 and 10.13).

The mouldings and other architectural evidence, analysed by R.K. Morris, suggest two main building periods. The first, c1200–25, is the era of the lancets and was probably contemporary with the modification of the Romanesque north aisle, with its triple lancets at the west end. The moulded arch between hall and chapel is also of this period (Fig 10.14). Support for a date of c1225–30 comes from one of two mason's marks identified by Morris in the Priory House. This is a type of inverted R, which has been recorded at Reading Abbey and also at the Grandmontine priory at Craswall. The latter was founded, probably during his shrievalty of Herefordshire, 1216–23, by William II de Lacy, lord of Weobley, Ewyas and Meath, whose castle at Longtown lay only some five miles to the south of Craswall.[215]

The Priory House was modified in the early 14th century. The evidence lies in the hood mouldings of the cinquefoil-headed windows in the south wall of the hall, which Morris relates to the north transept windows of Dilwyn church. This date is confirmed by the plinth moulding of the buttress at the north-west corner of the chapel, similar to the decorated mouldings of the south aisle of Dilwyn church, c1320. Overall, this suggests conservation work at the east end and the upgrading of the hall with new fenestration.

For Stukeley, writing in 1724, this was the prior's lodge, but for Clapham in 1934 and Brown and Wilson in 1994 it was the infirmary. As yet there is no conclusive evidence. With internal dimensions of the upper hall some 42ft by 18ft, if the Priory House was built as an infirmary, it was on far too ambitious a scale for a community with a maximum of twelve prayer monks, whose numbers had dropped to six by 1276. It is hardly likely that they had increased after the Black Death of 1349, when the death toll at Reading justified the ordination of 30 monks five years under the canonical age of 25.[216]

By the end of the 12th century the growth and development of abbatial powers had led many abbots to withdraw from their community. The abbot was responsible for hospitality to visitors at home, and was of prelate status when abroad. He thus required accommodation appropriate to both. Whilst some residences were near the west end of the claustral range, 'especially' amongst the Benedictines, as at Canterbury cathedral, Durham, Winchester and Worcester, they were 'nearly always close to the conventual dormitory and rere-dorter'. The Leominster prior, apparently of lowly status, had to cope not only, as between 1216 and 1233, with frequent royal visits but also with the administration of a great estate. Lack of accommodation of a suitable nature in 1216 could well explain the construction of this building in the early 13th century. Had it been at the north-east, rather than the north-west, end of the precinct, the prior and his visitors would have been subjected to all the noise and bustle of the town and its industrial area of Broad Street and the Marsh not far away. Certainly by the late 13th century, probably earlier, the priors were already living in some style. In 1286 one prior enjoyed hunting and hawking in his woods. In 1347 another had peacocks and swans to embellish the grounds of his residence. The Leominster prior and sub-prior had a pleasance about the Pinsley, with herb garden, fishponds, swans and peacocks. The prior's residence would have been adjacent. If Priory House was used as the prior's lodge between the 13th century and the Dissolution its suitability for domestic occupation could explain why it was the only conventual building to be retained in 1539.[217]

Excavation of part of the western block in 1979 revealed a range of bones from animals, fish and birds, our first evidence of the dietary regime at Leominster. The 83 mammal bones included those of 15 pig, one sheep/goat, 29 possibly also sheep/goat and one cat. There were 24 eel, 101 herring, one cod, one haddock, 9 perch, 2 plaice/flounder, 9 salmon/trout bones, together with 14 from domestic fowl, 34 from immature fowl, 16 from geese, one from a song thrush and one from a jackdaw. The presence of herring, haddock and cod bones is notable, as all are salt-water fish. Dietary issues are discussed in the following chapter.[218]

11 Security, Hospitality and Diet

At the heart of the life of most Benedictine monasteries lay a contradiction, between the desire for withdrawal from the world in order to pursue a life of prayer and meditation, and the position of most major houses, in the heart of large towns. Monasteries therefore often became foci for trade. Some, like Leominster, had originated as minsters, with wide responsibilities for the spiritual welfare of their surrounding *parochia*. The response to the growth of towns at the gates was to build precinct walls, in an attempt to regain seclusion. This was of little avail when the church was shared with the parish. The Cistercian answer was to withdraw to newly-founded houses in 'the wilderness', far from the resort of man where, with the help of *conversi*, lay brethren, to work their estates, they hoped to regain true monastic seclusion. On such remote sites, they even went so far as to demolish any house outside their precinct wall.[219]

At Reading, and Leominster, this problem was aggravated by the special obligation of hospitality imposed by Henry I in his foundation charter. The siting of both houses on strategic routeways has been noted. Royal visits not only imposed severe financial strains, but at both abbey and priory they diverted the attention of the abbot and his senior officers from their primary duty, the *opus dei*. These visits, and at Leominster those of local dignitaries such as the Mortimers, with their entourage, horses and the like, introduced a lifestyle quite alien to the Rule, and will have had a profound impact on the diet as laid down by St Benedict. Between July 1216 and September 1237 Leominster Priory received at least six royal visits of one night's duration or more. The character of such occasions is reflected in Henry III's command to the bailiffs of Bridgnorth in November 1232, to 'cause two tuns of wine to be delivered to the priory' in readiness for his overnight sojourn there. Apart from the provision of such hospitality, considerable care was taken to keep the worlds of the monk and the laity apart.[220]

The Gatehouse

The only access to the priory was through the gatehouse, which projected outward from the precinct wall. The site of Leominster's gatehouse is confirmed by the position of the Forbury chapel, the chapel at the gates, which straddled the precinct wall. In the Middle Ages Church Street thus ended at the gatehouse.

The date of the gatehouse's construction is not known. According to F.G. Blacklock, writing in 1898, it was 'a fine Early English' structure. He gives no authority for his statement, and admits that 'no drawing or engraving of it is extant as far as the writer can discover'. In 1660 the gatehouse was leased at a rent of 2s pa, but in 1722 Stukeley reported that the 'fine gate-house' had been 'pulled down not long since'. Like its counterpart, the Compter Gate at Reading, it was a firm reminder of the secular authority of the abbots, as lords of Leominster. In its Upper Chamber, also known as the Frere or Brothers' Chamber, the prior sat in judgement as the abbot's deputy. Later he was to be joined there by the royal justices. On the Gate's outer face, symbolising the abbot's secular lordship and jurisdiction, were displayed the arms of Reading Abbey, azure three escallops or. A document of 1410 refers to it as the White Gate, suggesting a building material other than the local red sandstone of which the priory was built.[221]

Early gatehouses had only a central archway, large enough to accommodate fully laden carts. This is the type to which Reading's inner gate belonged. Most later gatehouses had in addition one or even two smaller flanking archways for pedestrians. The cobbled passage under the archway was usually vaulted and could be closed to the outer world by massive wooden gates provided with spy holes or grating to permit inspection of visitors, especially at night-time, before they were admitted. Locally monastic gatehouses can be seen at Great Malvern, Wigmore, Worcester's Edgar Tower and Tewkesbury. The porter, who was permanently stationed here, usually lived in a small lodge at the side of the passageway.

Custody of the gate was an important office, for here the monastery came into direct contact with the outside world, with all the hazards that involved. It was for this reason that most monasteries had but one public entrance. Benedict's *Rule* describes the porter's role. 'At the gate to the monastery let there be placed a wise old man, who knows how to give and receive an answer and whose ripeness of years suffers him not to wander. This porter ought to have his cell near the gate so that they who come may always find someone at hand to give them an answer. As soon as anyone shall knock or a poor man call to him, let him answer "Deo gratias" or bid God bless

Fig 11.1 Reconstruction bird's eye view of Reading Abbey

him and then, with all the gentleness of the fear of God, let him answer quickly in the fervour of charity. If the porter needs solace let him have with him one of the younger brethren.' In smaller monasteries the role of porter and guest master was combined, and the porter was invested with the distribution of alms. The earliest reference to such an officer for Leominster is in 1123–30, when Abbot Hugh granted a hide of land at Marston Stannet, a mile south-east of Priddleton, to Nigel the porter. This parallels the grant to Ailward the radknight in its reference to 'the service which he owes us'.[222]

Outer and Inner Courts

Leominster's 30-acre precinct was divided into two courts, a layout that can still be seen at Reading (Figs 11.1 and 11.2). Once the visitor had passed the scrutiny of the porter or his deputy, he entered the Outer Court, where the worlds of monk and layman met. At both Leominster and Reading it was, and still is, known as the Forbury. The Old English *Foreburg* usually meant 'outwork', but was here used in the sense of 'forecourt'. An entry in the Leominster Cartulary refers to the chapel built at Archbishop Peckham's command as being 'in *le Forbery*'. The assumption is that the term came, with the monks, from Reading where, as at Leominster, the Forbury remains an extensive open space in the town centre. At Reading it lay to the north and west, but at Leominster to the south and west of the precinct. When the monks shared their church with the parish, the lay cemetery would be found in this area. Here also, when the monks wearied of the tensions arising from sharing their

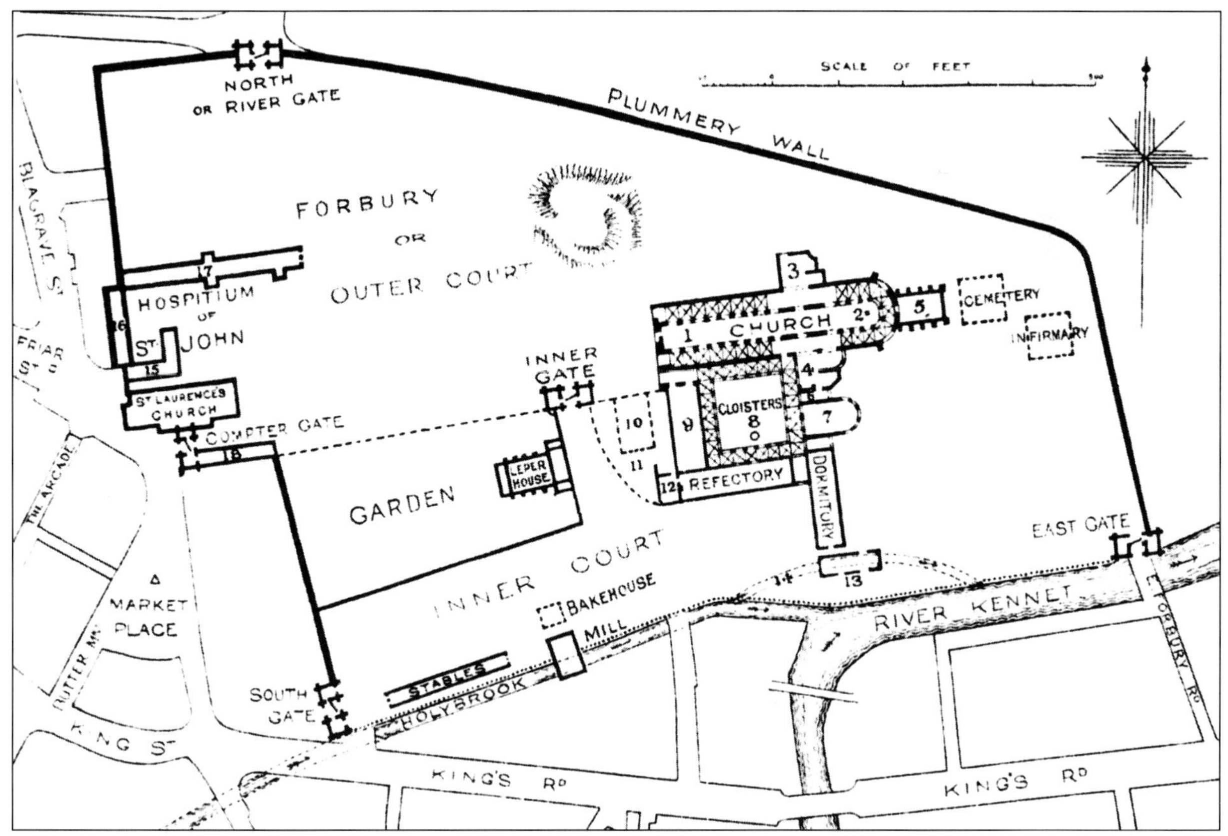

Fig 11.2 Plan of Reading Abbey

place of worship with the laity, they provided separate parish churches, as at Westminster, Ely and Evesham.[223]

At Leominster a pathway led from the gatehouse across the Outer Court to the west portal, and later the south porch, giving access to the parish church. A wall formed the boundary between the two courts. The line of the wall separating the Inner from the Outer Court is probably represented by the stone wall extending from the north-west angle of the church, which still forms part of the northern boundary of the graveyard. It then crosses the road known as The Priory to form the southern boundary of the National School, eventually linking up with the precinct wall, Even before the Dissolution in 1539 there may have been some residential development along this pathway, probably the vicarage and houses for the chantry priests. It now forms an eastern extension of Church Street. The Outer Court served as a home farm. Here were the great barn, granary, bakehouse and brewhouse, with the mill on the southern reaches of the Pinsley. These are discussed in the next chapter.

Figs 11.3a&b The Forbury at Reading (top) and Leominster

At Reading, and at other large Benedictine houses, an Inner Gate ensured seclusion for the cloister and its various offices within the Inner Court (Fig 11.2). Whether there was such an inner gate at Leominster is not clear. The appointment of a deputy gaoler in 1393 refers to the Inner Gate, but this could have been an alternative title for the Forbury Gate, to distinguish it from the town's gates or bars: the Lower Gatehouse in the South Street, Upper Gatehouse in the West Street and Eastern Gate in Etnam Street.

The Gaol

The earliest reference to the gaol is in 1231 when Henry III pardoned Reginald of Grendon, charged with the death of Stephen of Pudlestone. There will have been a monastic gaol at Leominster from the early 12th century, for Henry I's charter had granted the abbot of Reading 'all jurisdiction over assaults, thefts, murders, effusions of blood and infractions of the peace as much as belonged to the royal power'. As at many other monasteries, the gaol stood close to the priory's gatehouse — in stark

Fig 11.4 Reading: the Inner Gate

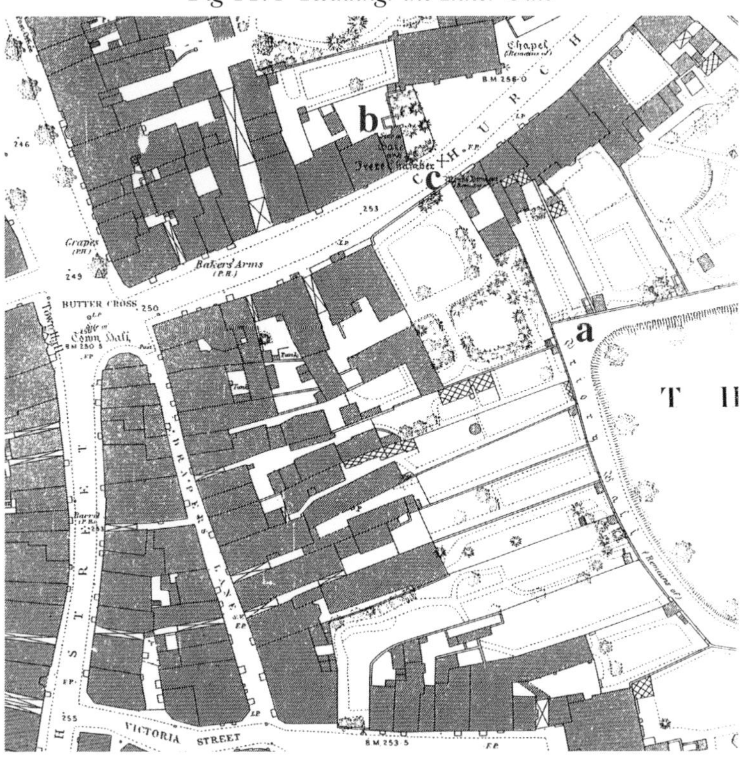

Fig 11.5 OS Plan showing a) 'Priory Wall, remains of'; b) 'Gate and Frere Chamber'; c) 'Monks Dungeon'

contrast to St Bernard's precepts on the quality of hospitality. Blacklock records in 1897 that the gaoler's lodge and abbot's prison were on 'the south side of the roadway, just within the gate'. 'The old Prison is now used as a warehouse, the iron rings and staples to which the prisoners were fastened were until recently still to be seen in the lower part of the walls of the interior.' Price, however, writing in 1795, refers to 'the site of the Dungeon' as being converted into a stable. The site of the 'Monks' Dungeon', together with that of their 'Gate and Frere Chamber', is marked on the 1:500 OS plan of 1885 (Fig 11.5). All traces of the prior's gaol were removed when the road was constructed from the south side of Church Street, opposite the Forbury chapel, to provide vehicular access to the rear of the post office. Nearby, a few courses of masonry can be seen, and in the middle, the bottom of a doorway. This may be all that remains of the front wall of the gaoler's lodge (Fig 11. 6).[224]

As for the inmates, the Patent rolls provide details of William de Bulleden, who was held in 1248 'for the death of a certain stranger'; Saer Mauveisin in 1275, 'for harbouring Henry his brother and Cuthbert Cokyn indicted of larceny in the late king's time'; and Richard Turnabuten Acton in 1282, 'for the death of Nicholas Red'. Evidently friends or relatives brought fresh evidence to the attention of Edward I in Ludlow that year as, on security being given, Richard was granted his freedom by the king who 'learns by inquisition taken by the sheriff that he is accused of the said out of hatred and not because he is guilty thereof'. Other prisoners, probably apprehended locally, were held for crimes committed in other parts. Thus in 1346 John de Leche of Stafford, accused of killing William de Draycote at Stafford, was imprisoned at Leominster.[225]

Fig 11.6 Vestiges of the gaoler's lodge at Leominster?

In 1293 William le Waleys, burgess of le Pole (Welshpool), outlawed for the death of John le Coytere of Leominster, was pardoned 'provided he surrendered to Leominster gaol within 40 days'. Such pardons were not infrequent. In 1400 the bailiffs of the borough were ordered to liberate David Smyth of Leominster, imprisoned because of 'evil words by him spoken, it is said, against the king's person, as the king has pardoned him every such misprision'. Other prisoners were released on the orders of the court. John Mylys, 'as appears by the record of Thomas Phylyp, coroner, in 1528', was pardoned for having killed Richard Shepard of Leominster as this was in self defence, but Philip Scarlet of Leominster, butcher, had to languish in the abbot's gaol eight and a half months before receiving his pardon 'for having on 14th October last killed Philip Dyer of Leominster, labourer, in self defence'.[226]

The practice of granting pardons to criminals was begun by Edward I, to raise troops for his wars in Gascony and Scotland. It has been calculated that in the last thirteen years of his reign he issued some 1,700 such pardons. Attempts to curb the practice in Edward III's reign met with limited success. Thus Robert de Servyngton (Sivington in Acton Beauchamp?), who had been committed to gaol 'for the death of Thomas le Burn of Lemynstre' and had successfully effected a brief escape, was granted a royal pardon in 1339, 'in consideration of his having gone beyond the seas in the king's company and staying there until now'. He had to find 'sufficient security to be of good behaviour from now and to come to the king, wherever he may be, when called upon so to do and to stay for one year at his wages'.[227]

Given the proximity of gate and gaol, it is not surprising to find that in 1393 John Luntley of Lucton was granted charge of the priory's inner gate and the deputy gaolership of the manor. He was to hold these offices 'for 99 years, if he lives so long', and be 'observing to the said abbot and convent of Redying and to the prior or priors of Leominster for the time being, in all lawful and honest commands'. His duties were defined as to keep safely the gaol, with the prisoners received there, and to hold safely anyone taken, attached or arrested, for whatever cause, and delivered to his custody. In return he was granted one robe of the sort of the serving men and an annual salary of 4s, with 'all small profits belonging and due to the said office'. For his victuals, he was to receive in the hall of the manor of Leominster the same as the serving men, *valettus*: every day 'two white loaves and a flagon of the best ale with a mess of meat or fish as shall be served to the others within

Plate 5 Samson and the lion, on abacus of capital (10) (see p91 & Plate 7.10)

Plate 6 14th-century south porch with 13th-century archway (see p150)

Plate 7 Romanesque capitals and abaci (pp86-92)
Capitals 1-6: West Portal (pp87-8)
North side: (1) Birds (2) Reapers (3) Serpents, all confronted in interlace foliage

South side: (4) Foliage (5) Lions (6) Palmettes

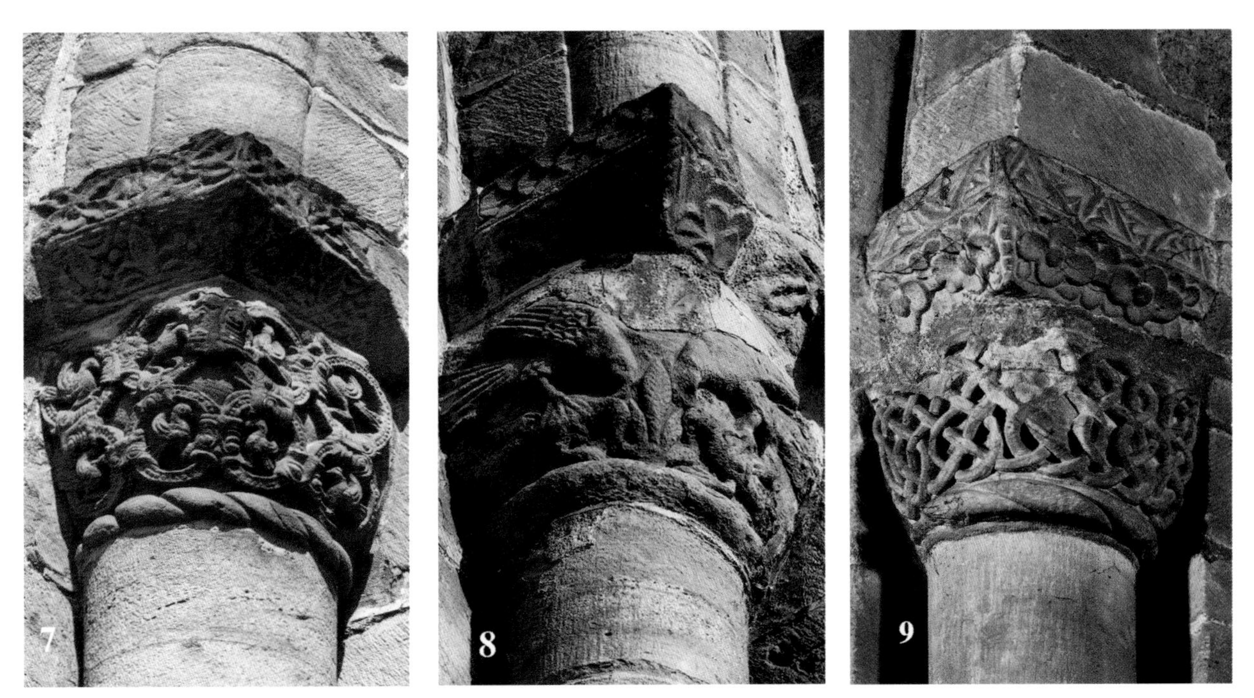

Capitals 7-8: West Window (pp88-9)
(7) Ring motif (8) Birds of Prey

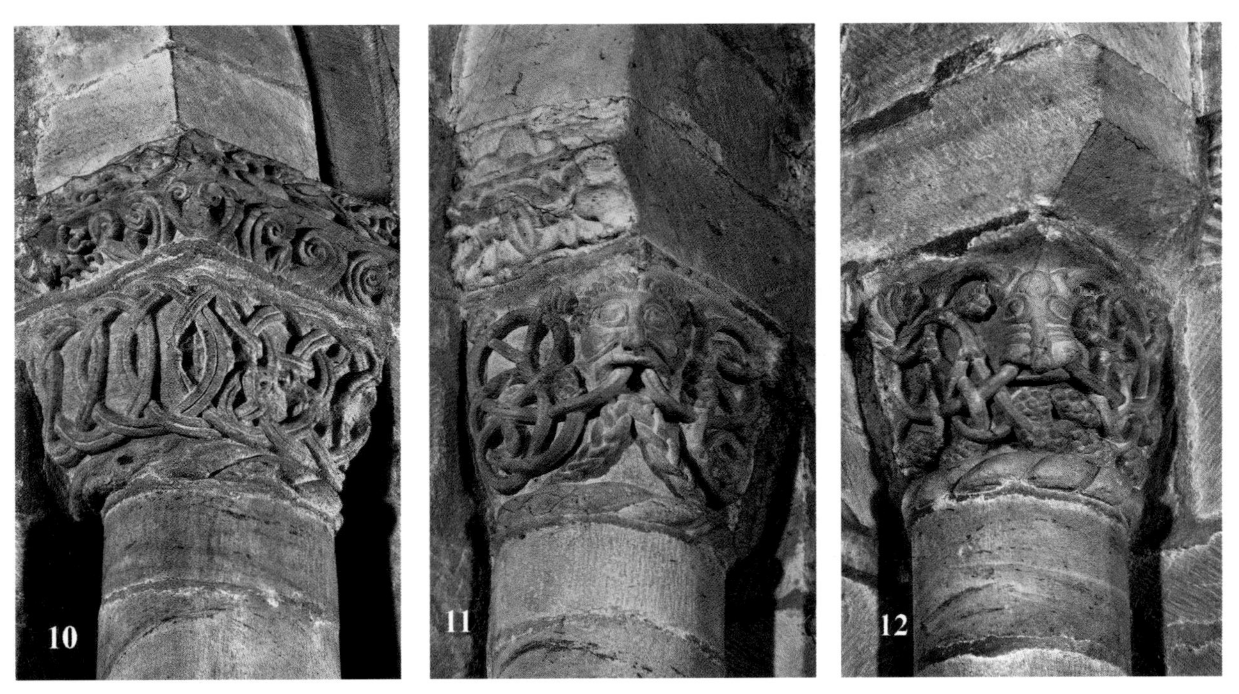

Capitals 9-12: West Portal, inner face (p89)
(9) Single interlace (10) Double interlace (11) Green man mask and interlace (12) Mask and vine branches

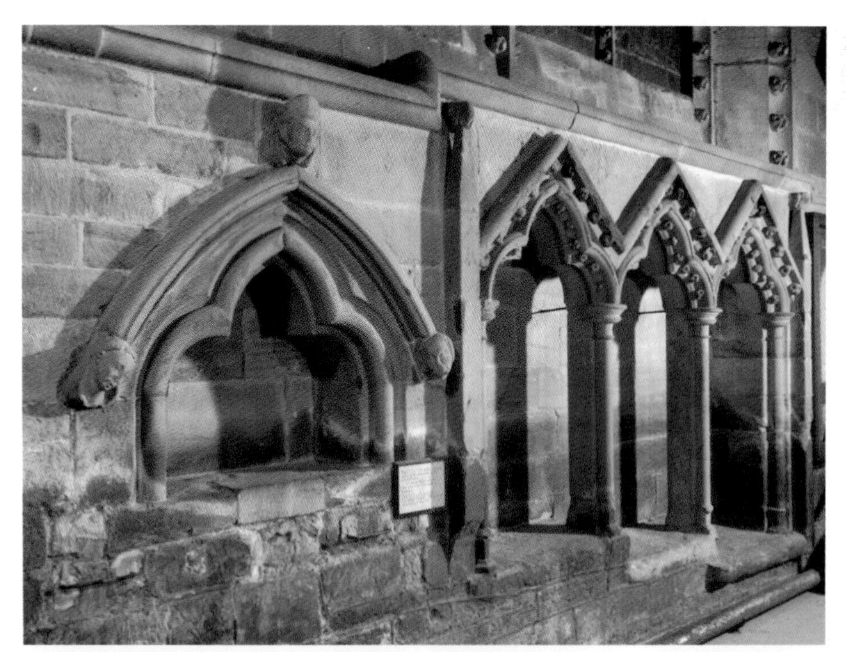

Plate 8 South Aisle: Sedilia with ballflower, piscina without

Plate 9a Romanesque north arcade from the south-west

Plate 9b Romanesque south arcade from the south-west

Plates 10a & b South arcade, showing Romanesque wall painting: a) triforium arch; b) detail of central pier

Plate 11a Wheel of Life, c1275;
11b David playing his harp

Plate 12 Exterior of parochial tower from north

Plate 13 West tower interior showing 15th-century strengthening arch on east to support the third stage

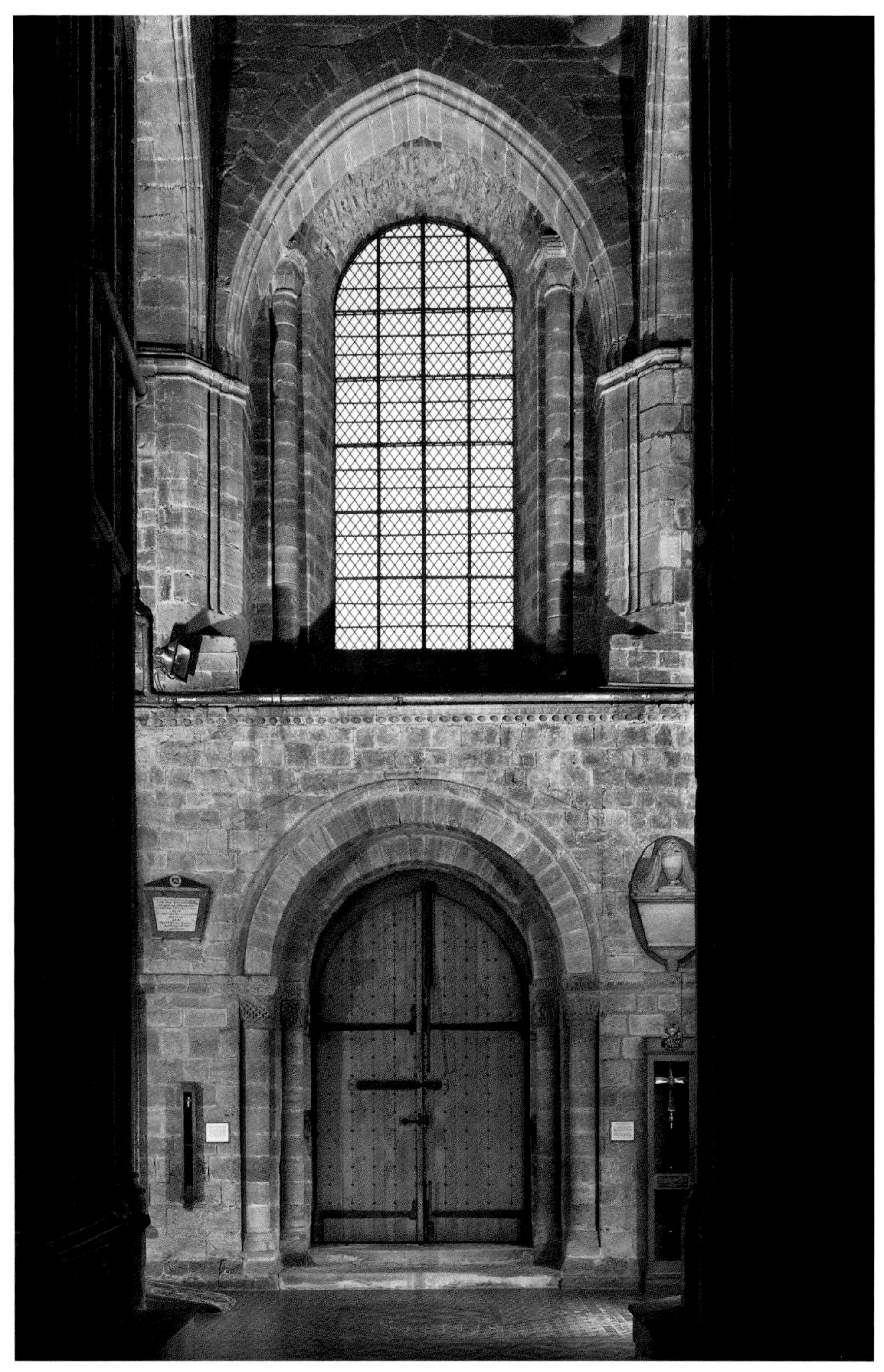

Plate 14 West tower interior showing west portal and window with Romanesque capitals 9-14 (see Plate 7 & Fig 9.5)

Plates 15a-c
Early 14th-century south aisle windows with ballflower ornament and details of window head, betraying Hereford and Gloucester links

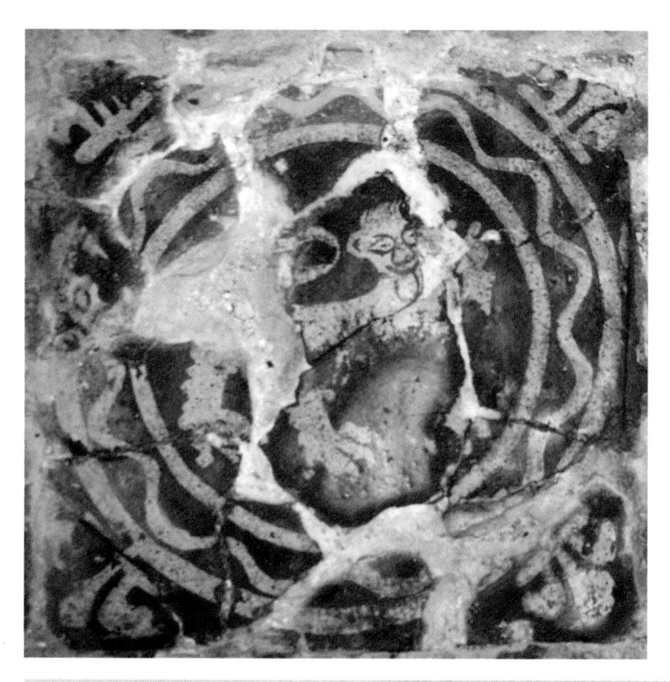

Plate 16 Leominster Priory: Tile (1) a lion passant (?) guardant, possibly a mirror image, reconstructed by George Gilbert Scott (see p192)

Plate 17 Gloucester and Leominster west windows: a) Watercolour of Gloucester Cathedral. Anon. © Gloucester City Museum & Art Gallery; b) Leominster Priory

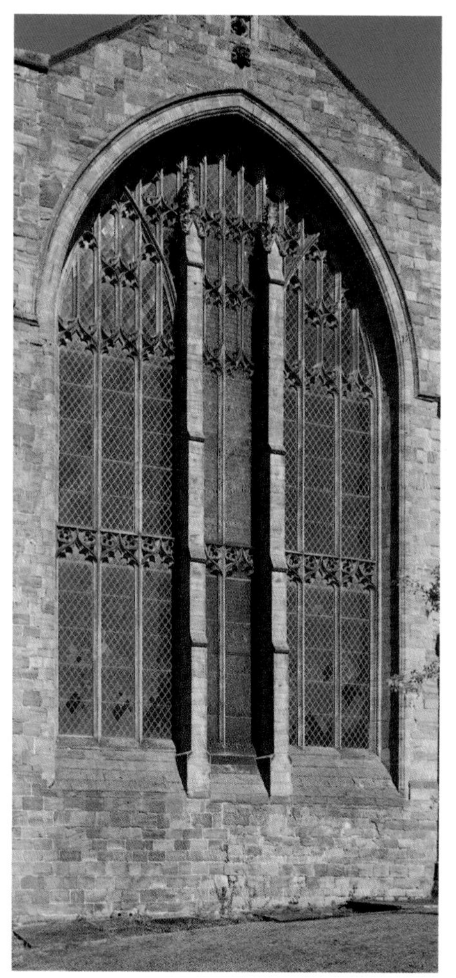

Plate 18 11th-century Ionic/ Green Man capital, probably taken from the minster on its reconstruction after 1123? (Courtesy Tony Reeve)

Plates 19a&b Two of three Leominster Seals: a) Prior Walter's Seal of 1220 attached to an indenture, TNA E329/186 © The National Archives; b) Leominster Borough Seal attached to parliamentary returns of liberty bailiff, TNA C2191 (see pp174-5)

the hall on those days'. If 'for any necessary cause John absents himself or through debility cannot personally execute the said office, he is to find at his own charge a fit and sufficient servant, for whom he will be answerable, during his absence'.[228]

The porter had a deputy. In 1410 abbot and convent 'granted to John Spycy the office of Under Porter ... for his life. By keeping which office and by overseeing and assigning the hay and provender of the stables for the guests', John was to receive 'every day one prykked loaf and a crowned loaf as well as a white loaf of the Hall bread, a pot of the best ale, one flagon of the second, and a pottle (*pocello*, half a gallon) of the second ale as often as it shall be drawn to be served there (in the servants' hall), as the custom is (and) ... every day half a mess (of meat or fish) according to the provision for the day'. For his costume he was to receive 'six yards of cloth of the boys' sort every year. If by illness, infirmity or negligence he do not execute his said office he is to find at his own charge another honest man to perform the said office. If he absent himself from keeping the said gate one whole natural day without licence, the above mentioned allowances shall be withheld.'[229]

Hospitality

Chapter 53 of Benedict's *Rule* treats of hospitality. 'Let all guests that come be received like Christ Himself, for He said "I was a stranger and ye took me in." Let especial solicitude be shown therefore in the reception of the poor and the pilgrims, because in them Christ is the more received.' Henry I's foundation charter defined more closely the obligations of hospitality. Well aware of the ways of the world, he insisted that at Reading and Leominster alms 'should be used for hospitality for the poor, pilgrims and guests', not for 'the abbot's lay kindred and others'.

The Almonry

Charity was dispersed to the poor, aged and infirm at the almonry, close by the Gate. Here, *The [Augustininan] Customs of Barnwell*, Cambs, tells us, the almoner 'ought to submit with calmness to the loud voiced importunity of the poor and help all petitioners as far as he is able ... remembering that they are made in the image of God and redeemed by the blood of Christ'. According to Blacklock, the almonry 'was on the south side of the present Church Street, within the priory gate'. However, an area north-west of the Forbury chapel, west of the National School, is still known as Almsbury. Price adds, 'the name of a meadow, now called *Almery Close*, designates the site of that conventual building'.[230]

In fulfilment of his abbey's obligations to provide relief for the poor and hospitality to pilgrims and guests, between 1189 and 1193 Abbot Hugh II replaced Reading's original almonry, built in the early 1130s by Abbot Ansger, with the Hospitium of St John, by the Compter Gate. The revenues of the adjacent St Laurence's church were diverted to the maintenance of thirteen poor men and women, and its south aisle became their chapel. Those from Leominster Priory's fulling mill were diverted for the benefit of Reading's pilgrims.[231] Additional support for Leominster's almonry came only after the end of John's reign, when Bishop Hugh de (Hampton) Mapenore (1216–19), a local man, granted Prior Walter a licence to appropriate Ford chapel for the benefit of the almonry in its work of hospitality and care of the poor; but Mapenore was careful to ensure also that prayers were said for the repose of his own soul, those of his parents and of Bishop Giles de Braose, his predecessor.[232] Ford chapel, which was but a small two-cell Romanesque structure, was rebuilt in 1851, on its old foundations. The ford across the Lugg, after which chapel and settlement were named, had by Leland's time, c1540, been replaced with a bridge.[233]

Subsequent entries in the priory's cartulary show that the country folk of Ford and its vicinity maintained an interest in the almonry. There are records of a range of small grants in free, pure and perpetual alms, in return for which the donors requested prayers for the repose of their own souls and those of other members of their family. William of Ford gave a piece of meadow and John Liulf one acre of meadow in 'Folkeia', later Volka or Volkey, the great stretch of meadow that extended virtually from the end of Etnam Street to Ford, at its most extensive at the confluence of Arrow and Lugg near Broadward. William son of Luke granted the (labour) services due from specified lands held by Matthew Urry, Walter Luke, William of Wiggeton, Henry of Humber and Stephen de Lane. In a second charter he granted the services due from Richard son of Gerald for a messuage and eight acres in Stoke (Prior). For 'the salvation of the souls of her parents, ancestors and successors' the widow Alitia, daughter of Peter de la Stone, granted the almonry two acres, and later a further acre. Hugh le Stane gave one acre, Robert of Wiggeton two and John *Medicus* 12 acres. Richard Lane's grant, 'to God and the almoner of Leominster', was carefully qualified, 'for the sustenance of the poor'.[234]

The priory's almoners continued in the market for land about Ford. Prices varied considerably. John St Lawrence, almoner, bought a messuage with 28½ acres in Ford and a further 14 acres for £2 plus 5s annual rent, presumably to cover the services due from the lands, but for a further messuage and only four acres he paid £1 3s and an annual rent of 1s. From Brother Reginald, almoner, Robert de Mapenore received £2 8s 7d for seven acres of arable in Hampton Mapenore (part of Hampton Court), and £3 and an annual rent of 5d for a further five acres in Hampton.[235]

Of the beneficiaries, the poor and infirm, there is no record. At the almonry, close to the Inner Gate, the daily dole, surplus food and clothing etc, was distributed. Frequently all that would be available were the 'broken meals', the leftovers from the tables of the monks, their guests and servants. Evidence from episcopal visitations of other monasteries shows that often the poor could not rely even on such 'broken meals', which on occasions the monks used to feed their packs of hounds. One expects that the priory had a small window especially designed for distribution of the dole, similar to that still visible at St Peter's, Gloucester (Fig 11.7). This is built into the wall of the former almonry, immediately to the west of the principal entrance, St Mary's Gate.[236]

Fig 11.7 Gloucester: 14 College Green showing dole window in the east wall

Hostelry

For honoured guests, nobles, knights, bishops, abbots and fellow monks travelling about on their business, there was a hostelry in the Outer Court. This usually had a hall open to the roof, with accommodation in one cross-wing and the services in the other. The guesthouses at the great Cistercian houses of Kirkstall and Fountains were situated between gatehouse and the cellar in the west range of the cloister, but that at the Augustinian priory of Thornholme, Lincs, was close to the main gate. According to *The Barnwell Customs*, by the hosteller's 'showing cheerful hospitality to guests the reputation of the monastery is increased, friendships are multiplied, animosities are blunted, God is honoured, charity increased and plenteous reward in Heaven promised'. Furthermore, he should have not merely 'facility of expression but also elegance of manner and a respectable upbringing. He ought neither to do or say anything but what sets monastic life in a creditable light.' At Leominster the nearby stable block to accommodate the mounts of visitors, and of prior and sub-prior, was also under the control of the guest master. By the 15th century standards of hospitality had apparently declined, as in 1408 the prior paid his hosteller only 2s per annum, the same as he paid his gardener — and the keepers of his own and his sub-prior's palfreys.[237]

The most taxing of guests was the king, with his retinue. A monastery of the size and with the wealth of Reading might welcome such visits, when the abbot could use the occasion to secure confirmation of his charters or the grant of new privileges. Reading Abbey even provided a meeting place for parliament, possibly in 1263, certainly in 1440, 1453 and 1466.[238] At Leominster royal visits were usually related to the threat or outbreak of hostilities in the Marches and Wales. Thus King John was there on 1 August 1216, Henry III on 25-26 September 1223, 21–22 August 1226, 21–22 May 1231, 11 December 1232 and 13 September 1233. Of Leominster's hostelry building there is no trace. Once the prior had established separate and substantial quarters for himself, this is where royalty would have been accommodated.[239]

Corrodians

Also in the Outer Court, near the gate, would have been the quarters of the corrodians. Corrodies were provisions made by monastic houses for accommodation, board and clothing in old age. They came in a number of forms, but were usually a type of annuity, granted in return for lands, rents or cash. Other corrodies were awarded to those who had served the house well. Occasionally wives, and even servants, were included in the terms of the contract. The recipient might even have food and fuel delivered to his home. For the priory this was a relatively easy way of raising money in times of adversity. Sometimes it provided an opportunity to acquire valuable lands. A corrody negotiated between 1143 and 1155 involved a three-part transaction. Roger, earl of Hereford, gave Adam of Middleton, presumably his servant, 'certain meadows', which Adam was to transfer to the priory in return for reception into the community and maintenance for life. Such meadowland was valued highly. In an age that knew nothing of sowing grass seed like corn, hay could be harvested only where it grew naturally, by rivers, streams and wet places. In consequence, winter provender for animals, especially horses, was limited and expensive.[240]

The corrody of John Redyng of Leominster in 1445 was more typical. He was 'to receive of us and our successors viz every day one white loaf, one prykked loaf, a mess of flesh and fish, the same with which the monks are served in their hall, and a gallon of conventual ale to hold for his life'. On the other hand, 'for the good services done us', in 1429 Walter Polter's corrody was only half the measure granted to John Redyng: 'every week, four white Hall loaves and three prykked loaves, three and a half messes of flesh or fish, according to the day, four flagons of the best ale and every year three yards of plain cloth of the serving men'.[241]

Other corrodies were granted at the instance of major patrons, such as the Mortimers. Above all the king, as patron, expected corrodies to be granted to his aged royal servants. Thus in 1318 Robert the Goldsmith of Ludlow, 'who had long served the crown', was sent by Edward II to the abbot of Reading to 'receive the allowance for a monk and a robe yearly and other necessities of life in the priory of Leominster'. In 1376 Peter de Cornewalle, Edward III's esquire, was sent to the abbot 'to take for life such maintenance in Leominster Priory as Robert the Goldsmith, deceased, had at the late king's command'. In 1384 Richard III requested the prior and convent of Leominster to admit Benedict of Hilton, 'being of great age and having no maintenance, and minister to him such sustenance as others heretofore had at the command of the king's forefathers'. Prior and convent were commanded to reply by the bearer of the king's letter, under the seal of their house, what they will do. The Crown also lodged royal sergeants and their horses at the priory on a regular basis. At least one bishop sent his manservant to be accommodated at the priory during his absence from Hereford. In 1525 the priory experienced what was virtually the death throes of the corrody system, when Henry VIII's daughter, Princess Mary, was sent to Ludlow as the figurative head of the Council of the Marches. Several of her servants finding themselves redundant and without a living, the prior was required to take a number of them 'unto your convenient finding'.[242]

At Leominster officers of the household appointed 'for life', such as Luntley, the porter in 1393, and Spycy, under-porter in 1410, were to receive food, drink and clothing after retirement, so long as they found 'at their own charge another honest man to carry out their duties'. John Mawne was of quite a different station altogether. 'For the service he has done us and what he shall hereafter do', he was granted maintenance in victuals and drink for his life 'in our manor of Leominster. He shall be served at dinner and supper as the fellow monks are, except only on flesh days, on which he shall be served as the other esquires are. If he be sick he shall have the same maintenance in his chamber within our manor and shall receive yearly during his life one robe of the suit of our esquires, four loads of fuel, a chamber which John Mason, chaplain, inhabited, and a stable in the angle next the stable pole for one horse to be kept, with hay only. Further, when he dwells in the town of Leominster or elsewhere without the bounds of the said manor, he shall receive two white (monks') loaves, one prykked loaf, one flagon and a half of best ale, one mess and a half of flesh or fish according to the day.'[243]

The quality and quantity of food, drink and clothing granted to corrodians and household servants were expressions of status. Three types of bread are mentioned. Luntley the porter received two white loaves of the (servants') hall, whereas Spycy, the under-porter, received a white loaf of the hall, one prykked loaf and a crowned loaf. The two latter were inferior, having a good measure of bran or even oats mixed with the wheat. Ale came in gallons, flagons and pottles, either as best, conventual, or second ale. As to meat or fish, Spycy received only half a mess each day, Luntley one mess and Mawne one and a half. A man's livery was the most evident expression of his status. Mawne, whose business on behalf of the priory frequently took him out and about in the town and to the priory's other estates, was clothed as an esquire, had his own chamber, and a stable and hay for his horse. Luntley, on the other hand, received a plain cloth robe of the serving men, and Spycy merely 'six yards of the cloth of the boys' sort'.

Monastic Diet

Corrodies also provide information on the monastic diet. Mawne's contract shows that, except during periods of fast, the Leominster monks were 'served at dinner and supper'. St Benedict devoted chapter 39 of his *Rule* to 'the measure of food'. 'We think it sufficient for the daily meal, whether at the sixth or ninth hour, that there be at the tables two dishes of cooked food, because of the variety of men's weaknesses: so that he who may not be able to eat of the one may make his meal of the other. Therefore let two cooked dishes suffice for the brethren; and if there be any fruit or young vegetables let a third dish be added ... but let all abstain from eating the flesh of four-footed animals, except the very weak and sick'. Why did St Benedict distinguish between the flesh of animals and birds? Like many of his contemporaries, he may have regarded the flesh of fowls, though more delicate, as less apt to stimulate the passions. On the other hand, it could have been that beasts were in a different category, having been created, as Genesis explains, on the day after the fish and fowl.

Meat was introduced into the monastic kitchens prior to the 12th century, originally to be eaten only in the company of guests, then in the infirmary, and later during periods of 'recreation' or as part of the numerous feasts enjoyed at many of the English Benedictine monasteries. All the food allowances to corrodians mentioned above refer to meat or flesh before fish. Nevertheless, evidence from elsewhere emphasises the predominance of fish in the monastic diet. At Canterbury the daily fish allowance was either one plaice, 2 soles, 4 herrings or 8 mackerel. At Westminster Abbey fish dinners totalled about 215 a year, almost two in three.[244]

The most interesting data comes from the kitchener's accounts of the Benedictine abbey at Selby. There 27 monks were resident in 1362 and 29 in 1496–7, over twice the full complement of a dozen at Leominster. The abbey had easy access by the Ouse and Humber to the North Sea. In 1416–17 the kitchener received 21 oxen, the carcasses of 51 cows, 25 bullocks and heifers, 21 calves, 86 pigs, 22 piglets, 395 sheep, 66 lambs, and 45 coneys from the abbey's warrens. As to fish, he accounted for 38,590 red (smoked) herrings and 1,440 white herrings, plus 1,200 red herrings for distribution to the poor on Maundy Thursday, 8 April, and 112 on All Saints Day, 2 November. Of salted fish there were 477, of dried 869, salmon 104½ and two sprints, including 16½ from the monastic fishery, 5 great eels, 1,221 small eels (5 great and 800 others from the abbot's fishery, 406 of the small eels from the Ouse dam), 4,519 pikes, pickerels, roach and perch, of which 3,600 roach and perch, the 8 large pike and 49 pickerels came from the lord's dam. Of fowl there were 27 swans and cygnets, 7 from the dam, 18 partridges and 2 pheasants from the warrens, 33 herons, of which 9 were a gift to the archbishop of York, 105 geese and ducks, 36 capons, 181 cocks and hens, 24 chickens, 731 pigeons, of which 287 were from the abbey's dovecotes, and 2,760 eggs.[245] What probably astonishes most in this list is not the quantity so much as the variety of food, especially of fish and fowl. However, the kitchener does not distinguish between supplies made to the monks' refectory and the abbot's residence, where the powerful and influential had to be appropriately entertained. At Leominster, apart from the king's household, members of the Mortimer family of Wigmore would have dominated the list of such dignitaries. On these occasions, meat and all manner of luxuries would have been served in great quantities, after which the poor at the gates would have fared well, if only briefly. Such feasting may go some way to account for the large numbers of oxen, bullocks, calves, pigs and lambs consumed at Selby, thus distorting, to some degree, the ratio between four-legged meat on the one hand and fish and fowl on the other.

There is a wide range of evidence as to the source of such supplies at Leominster: the three ponds between the Pinsley and Kenwater, and fisheries on the priory's millponds and dams, as well as the major rivers; the dovecotes, orchards and herb gardens of the four burys and elsewhere; honey renders from demesne tenants, amounting to £3 5s in 1086; hens and eggs also due from the customaries, as from the millers and others; geese from married villeins on all four *herneys*; the hunting of deer; and, for the special occasion possibly, swans, peacocks and probably also herons from the prior's pleasance. Such mention as there is of tithes includes corn, lambs, wool, geese, pigs and pigeons from Ivington, Brierley, Wharton, Stagbatch and Cholstrey, and bees and apples from Luston.[246]

In the Selby kitchener's accounts an important distinction is made between commodities purchased and those produced on the abbey's estates. This provides some indication of the degree to which the house was self-sufficient. In this respect there seems to be a considerable contrast between the Selby records and the account books between 1287/8 and 1324/5 of the Yorkshire Augustinian priory at Bolton bridge in Wharfedale. This owes more to location than dietary differences between the orders. At Bolton cows, pigs, sheep and, until 1304/5, oxen for consumption came largely from stock; thus expenditure on meat was low. It formed less than a third of the kitchen expenses before 1305; fish accounted for almost two-thirds, of which salt-water fish, with high transport costs, must have formed a considerable element, for the Wharfe at Bolton, unlike the Ouse at Selby, was not navigable. At Leominster, as far from the sea as any place in England, the costs of salt-water fish, even if dried or, like the red herrings, smoked, would have been even higher, but evidence from the borough records shows that such fish were available at the weekly market.[247]

This underscores the need to maximise local production. Meat production at Leominster, as compared to Selby and Bolton, was high. This applied equally to cows, bullocks, pigs and sheep, as will appear in Chapter 20. Domesday Book gives some impression of the quantity of fish being taken from local rivers as early as 1086. From Leominster's 16 mills alone 3,000 eels were taken annually. Renders of fish amounted to 17s. From the Ford, Broadfield and Sarnesfield's fisheries came 600 eels, whilst Broadward, granted to the priory in 1154x55 by Roger Earl of Hereford, provided a further 500, making a total of 4,100 eels. Bones found during the 2005 excavations indicated that fish was an important element in the monastic diet in the late 7th and early 8th centuries.[248]

12 Household, Stipendiaries and the Family of the Manor

St Benedict ordained that 'the monastery, if it be possible, ought to be so constructed that all things necessary such as water, a mill, a garden, a bakehouse and the various crafts may be contained within it so that there may be no need for the monks to go abroad for this is altogether inexpedient for their souls'. Most of the buildings linked to the administrative and workaday life of the priory were thus in the Outer Court of the Forbury. Much of the activity which sustained the monastery, especially the production of bread and beer, staples of the diet of both monks and their servants, was conducted in this area, south of the priory, which also served as the home farm. Here, in what the records refer to as the Grange, were all the buildings one associates with such a place: barns, stables, brewhouse, bakehouse, smithy, wain sheds, pig styes, stock yard, dovecotes, a mill and so forth. Of such buildings only the site of the Great Barn and Pinsley Mill are known. The others gradually fell into decay after the Dissolution. However, documentary sources of the priory, and evidence from other monastic sites, enable us to form a comprehensive picture of the activities that took place here. In the Outer Court laymen would be met aplenty and here, alone, were women permitted entry.[249]

3s 4d	**6d**
First Smith	Second Butler
Under Tyler[1]	Third Butler
	Second Baker
2s	Third Baker
Lieutenant or Deputy	Sub-dean's Servant
Clerk	Dean's Servant
Dean of the Chambers	Miller
Panterer	Maltman
Taylor or Groom of the Wardrobe	
Porter	**3½d**
	Laundress
1s 6d	Sexton's Boy
Second Smith	Scullion
	The Boy that washes the Monks' Vestments
1s	(Under Tyler)
Hostler	
Porter's Servant	
Butler or Manciple	**3d**
Baker	Lieutenant's Boy[1]
Keeper of the Dean's Palfrey	
Keeper of the Sub-dean's palfrey	
Gardener	
Huntsman	

[1]Clerical error; should read 3½d? HRO M31/9/1f5v

Table 7 Wages of the Family in the Priory of Leomister at the feast of the Nativity and Easter, paid by the hands of the Clerk in 1407/8

A Leominster manuscript, 'Wages of the Family of the Priory at Christmas 1407 and Easter 1408 as paid by the hands of the Clerk', lists 30 such servants with their occupations, all working within this Court (Table 7). There has been notable debate about the ratio of staff, those 'who kept the establishment working, such as esquires, grooms, cooks, bakers, brewers, barbers, porters, cleaners etc'. Using the survey of lesser monastic houses of 1536, Knowles arrived at a ratio of 1:1.1. As a cell of Reading, Leominster's complement of monks was never allowed to exceed twelve and is known to have fallen, even in the 13th century, as low as six. A lay household or *famuli* of 30, in the early 15th century, suggests a minimum ratio of servants to religious of 3:1.[250]

Details in the 1407/8 list enable us to identify the activities of the various members of the 'family' in the Outer Court. The production of adequate bread and ale for the needs of monks, servants, corrodians and guests, and for distribution as alms, was the primary concern. Each consumed daily at least one 2½lb loaf of bread, made from wheat or mixed grain. Large quantities of grain were also required for ale production. At Beaulieu Abbey and Bolton Priory, where total ale production was 50,000 gallons a year, the religious received a gallon of ale a day. At Leominster, where ale was usually measured either by the flagon or the pot, John Redyng was granted a daily gallon in 1445.[251]

The Great Barn, or Grange, dominated the Outer Court. It stood in the area near the fountain overlooking the cricket pitch. Both 'Tithe Barn' and the 'Ancient Doorway' leading to it are marked on the 1:500 OS plan of 1885 (Fig 12.1). Although built as a monastic barn, where grain harvested from the priory's demesne lands in the four *herneys* could be stored and winnowed, the term tithe barn continued in use long after the Dissolution. This was for good reason, as a rare entry relating to the payment of tithe in the 1381 halimote rolls for Fencote reminds us. Each harvest David the Welshman, like all other parishioners, had to carry his tithe corn, 'threshed and winnowed and at his own charge', to this great barn in the Grange at Leominster, some 6 miles from the three common fields of Fencote.[252] The title, the Grange, came to be applied to the whole of the southern part of the precinct. In June 1541, after the Dissolution, the Crown granted a local man, Philip Hoby, one of the gentlemen of the Privy Chamber, a lease of certain tithes of corn, flax and hemp within the limits of 'Westharneis, alias the Grange,' in the lordship of Leominster, together with a barn etc, 'parcel of the lands which belonged to Reading monastery'. So large was this 'great barne in Lemster' that, when it was 'fired by a comet' in 1594 the conflagration lasted fifteen days.[253]

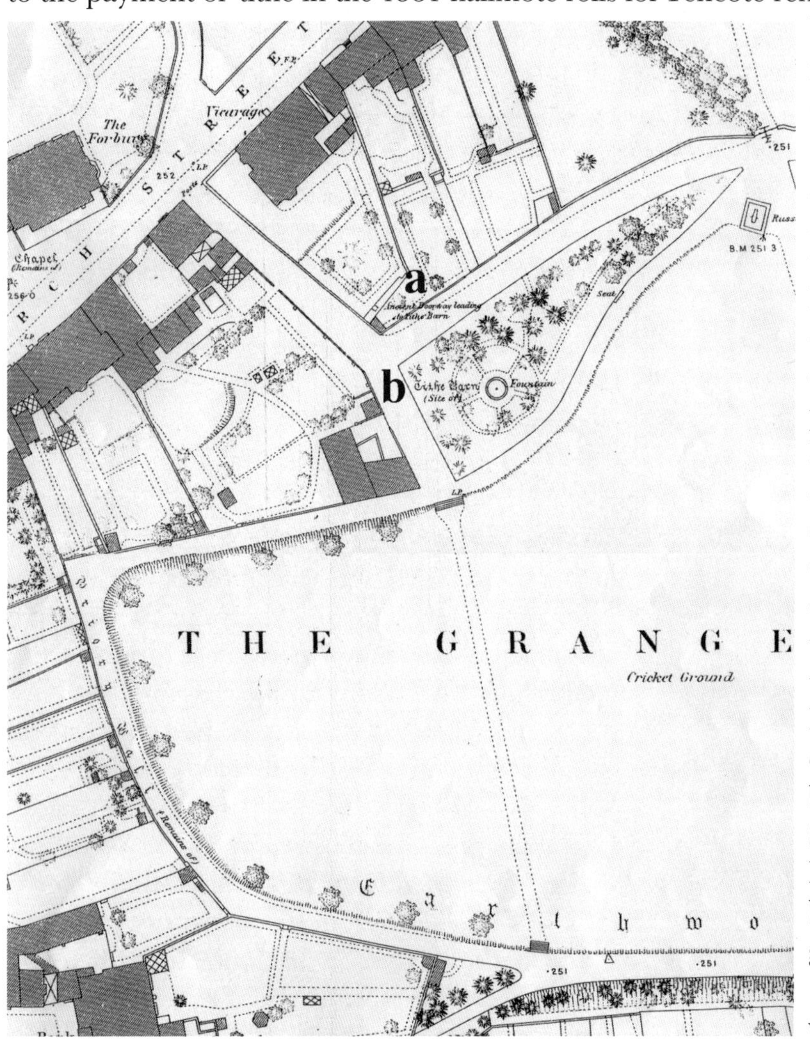

Fig 12.1 1:500 OS Map showing
a) 'Ancient doorway leading to Tithe Barn' and b) 'Site of Tithe Barn'

Where building stone was readily available, as at Leominster, almost all ecclesiastical tithe barns had walls and roof tiles of stone, and broken stone roof tiles were found within the cloister area during the 2005 excavations. Nevertheless, the framework had to be timber, whether cruck- or box-framed. In both cases, but especially the cruck frame, the timbers required were massive. Pershore Abbey's Leigh Court barn had eighteen cruck blades, each 34 to 40ft long. Evesham Abbey's Middle Littleton barn, of eleven raised base crucks and aisles, had a capacity of some 160,000 cubic feet. The extraordinary duration of Leominster barn's fire is explained in part by the timber frame and by the great length and width of the barn's timber roof. Reading Abbey built barns on a large scale. That at Cholsey was the largest in Europe, 303ft long and 51ft high. Yet Cholsey's estate was no match in size for that of Leominster. Today the largest barn in this area is at Frocester, thirteen bays long and measuring 186ft by 30ft, but the Benedictine barn at Abbotsbury, Dorset, one of the largest in the country, is 272ft long and 31ft wide.[254]

Monastic barns had wagon porches, placed centrally on either side. The height of their doorways, usually some 12 to 13ft, was adequate to admit wagons fully laden with sheaves, for unloading into bays on either side. In Herefordshire, where barley was rarely grown except on the sandy soils of the south, wheat, which thrived on the heavy loams, was usually accommodated on one side and oats, more tolerant of rain than barley, on the other. During late autumn and winter, groups of men with hand flails undertook the back-breaking task of threshing the grain on the stone-flagged floors of the bays and their wagon porches. For this hot, tiring and dusty work the threshers were kept well lubricated with beer, if of inferior quality. Here also, with porch doors open, the chaff was removed from the grain by winnowing. The straw was used as winter fodder or bedding for the animals.

Once threshed, the wheat and malt grain from the Great Barn was stored in the granary or garner, which also received grain from the burys. This was usually close to both bakehouse, *pistrinum*, and brewhouse, *bracinum*. To maintain its condition, grain had to be kept in a dry and airy place: if damp, it would go mouldy; if warm, it would germinate. There had also to be protection against attack by vermin — and theft. The usual answer was to store it in a free-standing structure built on stone piers, like the 13th-century cruck-framed granary close to Shaftesbury nunnery's manorial barn at Bradford-on-Avon, or on straddle stones, conical stones topped by circular or domical ones. The alternative was to accommodate the grain over an existing open-fronted building, such as the cart or wain shed, thus ensuring adequate ventilation. Birds could be kept at bay by nets. To hinder theft the grain was usually stored in timber hutches, not sacks that could be easily removed, and the door kept securely locked. There is no reference in the Leominster list of wages to a *granitarius*. Responsibility for the safekeeping, checking and recording of the grain was probably included in the duties of the panterer, master of the pantry, who supplied the bread to the monks' refectory, serving men's hall, guesthouse and almonry, for his salary, 2s per quarter, was one of the highest.

In the 1407/8 list of the quarterly wages of the 'family', the miller's wage was only 6d. Mills had been a prominent feature of the economy of the area even prior to the Norman Conquest. The sites of two Mercian mills have been excavated at Wellington quarry, just south of the priory's lands on Dinmore Hill. Another is referred to in the Staunton-on-Arrow charter of 958. In 1086 there were eight mills within the manor, worth £5 8s, and three more at Broadward, Risbury and Hampton Mapenore, lands lost by Leominster after the Norman Conquest. Such manorial mills are discussed in Chapter 19.[255]

Once the manor passed into the hands of Reading Abbey, the potential for the development of mills on the Lugg, Arrow and other watercourses was fully exploited. The Leominster fulling mill, the profits of which were appropriated for pilgrims visiting Reading, is an early example of the abbey's adoption of new technologies, in all probability direct from Cluny. By the Dissolution many of these mills were ruinous. Howton and Chaundlers Mill and Tanmyll, all near Leominster, were 'wholly in decay', 'fallen quite to the ground' and 'totally decayed'. But in 1567 the corn mills 'called Priorie mills or Vine mills' were still fully operational. This, the priory's principal mill, had always stood within the precinct, at its south-eastern corner, adjacent to where the town ditch, flowing down the outer side of the southern *vallum monasterii*, joined the Pinsley brook. For much of the 19th century its successor was known as the Etnam Street Mill, but in the 20th as the Pinsley Mill (Fig 1.3).[256]

Monastic bake- and malthouses were usually close to one another; at Fountains, excavated in 1888, they were under one roof, divided by a massive rubble wall. To minimise fire risk, they were vaulted with stone slates. The disastrous conflagration in 1288 that destroyed much of Pershore Abbey church, and 40 houses in the borough, originated in the bakehouse. There are many other examples of such fires. Given the paucity of information on bakehouses, it is unfortunate that the remains of the large guesthouse bakery at Kirkstall were 'needlessly destroyed by the civic authorities at the turn of the last century'. All that is known is that it had two ovens. The need for a reliable water supply gives some clue as to the site of Leominster's *pistrinum*. It would have had large brick ovens and a kneading trough, to produce white or hall, prykked and crowned loaves. At Worcester Priory four types of loaf were baked: white, ordinary, servants' and shield, the last probably baked, like oat cakes, on an iron griddle. At Leominster John Corbet, appointed baker for life in 1415, was to receive '1s a quarter, seven of his own white, hall, loaves and seven of his prykked loaves, together with seven flagons of the better ale from the offices of brewer each week, and a livery of six ells (7½ yards) of cloth of the sort of the serving men each year at the Nativity of Our Lord, if he executed his office in person, faithfully and honestly'. His two assistants were paid only 6d.[257]

With no local-grown barley, most of the priory's oats were used in brewing, but some went to the stables. At Selby, the brewer was assisted by two grooms in his malthouse and two more in his brewhouse. In 1407/8 Leominster's 'maltman', like the miller paid 6d, worked without assistance. At his malthouse, *toralium*, the oats were steeped in a vat or cistern of water for a few days and then spread over the stone-flagged floor where they could be moved about whilst germinating for a week and a half. For the final stage they were taken to the floor of the kiln to dry and then bagged for use as required. Beer, the second staple of the medieval diet, came from the brewhouse in a range of qualities. Servants' and corrodians' contracts specified the type and quantity they were to receive. The butler or manciple enjoyed the same 1s salary as the baker. His two assistants, like the baker's, received 6d. His office was originally related to the buttery, where drink was stored, but came to be extended to include the purchase of such provisions as were not available on the estate.[258]

The gardener's wages of 1s underline his considerable responsibilities, which included not only the kitchen or vegetable gardens but also the herb and physic gardens. His vegetables were the basic ingredients for potage, a staple of both monks and household staff. Greens, beans, peas, leeks, onions and garlic were required. His orchards produced apples, pears, plums, probably even cherries and medlars, and nut trees would also be found. Domesday Book shows local honey production was high; but salt, pepper, saffron, rice, cumin and figs had to be purchased. The gardener was also responsible for the rich meadows between Pinsley and Kenwater, the hay from which fed the palfreys of prior and sub-prior, and of honoured guests.[259]

In the 13th century the bishops of Hereford had extensive vineyards at their manors of Bishops Frome, Cradley and Ledbury, and by their palace at Whitbourne. In 1298 the 12-acre Ledbury vineyard yielded seven pipes of white wine, the equivalent of some 2,200 bottles, and one pipe of verjuice, a sharp vinegar for cooking. Place-name evidence shows that Leominster had vineyards on sheltered south-facing sites, south of the bury at Hope-under-Dinmore, and of Ivington bury and Park, and a third, on a south-east-facing slope, just to the north of Moor Abbey at Middleton. Climate change and cheap Gascon wine led to the demise of many ecclesiastical vineyards, although transport charges almost doubled the cost of imported as compared to home-produced wine. In 1398–9, the abbot of Selby's chamberlain paid £7 13s 4d at Hull for two pipes, casks, of red wine, each of 105 gallons, 'for the same lord's consumption'. The total wine bill for the year, including transport, was £36 19s. At Bolton in 1308/9 eight *dolia*, 2,016 gallons, were bought. In 1397 Henry Kyngeslone of Ludlow arrested a six-horse cart belonging to the priory taking wine, presumably a number of such pipes, and salted herrings to Leominster Priory. It is not known whether production continued in any of Herefordshire's medieval vineyards, but there was wine-making, on a small scale, in the 17th century.[260]

Lowliest of wage earners were those paid a mere 3½d a quarter. There is reference to an 'Under Tyler', but no tiler, and to a sexton's boy, but no sexton, to act as caretaker in the church, and as bell-ringer and grave-digger. The laundress, who would have had her own laundry, with running water, received no more than 'the boy that washes the monks' vestments'. The Selby accounts portray the hierarchy of laundresses employed by a large Benedictine house: those who served the lord abbot received 10s a year; the sacrist and keeper of the fabric, 5s; the guest house 3s; the infirmary 2s; and the laundress of the refectory towels and linen 16d.[261] In the top echelons at Leominster, paid 2s a quarter like the porter and panterer, were the lieutenant, the deputy in charge of the household's salaried staff, who had his own 'boy' yet received no more than the clerk, the tailor or groom of the wardrobe, and dean of the chambers. Head and shoulders above all the other household staff, the smith, in charge of the forge, earned 3s 4d per quarter. Even his deputy received 1s 6d.

Prior and sub-prior lived in considerable style, befitting their role as administrators of a large landed estate, which by 1536 was providing the mother house with £438 4s 8d per annum, some two-thirds of the priory's annual income of £660 16s 8d. Each had his own servant and a keeper for his palfrey. Other staff no doubt, such as the tailor or groom of the wardrobe and the dean of the chambers, would have spent considerable time on their affairs. The gardener took care of the orchards and areas of grazing reserved for their palfreys, as well as the various gardens. Much of this land became a pleasant retreat for prior, sub-prior and their guests. In the 14th century such havens were fast becoming essential elements of display. The great bard, Iolo Goch, celebrated the pleasance at Sycharth, west of Oswestry, in his poem 'On the Court of Owain Glyn Dwr'.[262] Here were 'lawn for peacocks, heronry, orchard, vineyard, dovecote and fishponds stocked with pike and salmon'. On the prior's lands close to the banks of the Kenwater were fishponds, orchards, dovecote and a mill. In 1347 'certain sons of iniquity, inspired by nefarious daring and diabolical instinct', broke into the prior's enclosure, killing two of Prior John of Gloucester's peacocks and stealing two of his swans. No doubt the prior had herons as well. The Dissolution returns provide details of the garden of half an acre, two orchards — the Great of more than 8 acres and the Little of one acre — and beyond them, Over Mill. The fishponds, stews, served with running water, were in Pinsley Mead between the Pinsley and Kenwater. The greater fishpond, shown on Gallier's *Plan of Leominster* (1832) (Figs 1.3 and 16.6) and indicated on the lst edition of the 1:500 OS plan (1885), was virtually an acre, whilst the lesser was quarter of an acre. The area thereabouts retains the evocative name, Paradise.[263]

In the Outer Court, as well as the 'family' of the priory, were seven agricultural workers: an overseer, carter, swineherd, shepherd, stock-keeper, pindar and pindar's boy, who all worked on the home farm, the Grange. A second list of 1407/8 gives details of their wages, which contrast markedly with those of the family, as they did not receive bed, board and livery (Table 8). This second list also includes those who worked at the four burys and three other granges. At the Grange the steward, who was paid 10s per annum, was in overall control, yet the carter received 13s 4d, for the transport of produce from the burys was critical to the economy of the priory. In the cart house he would have an ox-drawn *plaustrum*, which could carry well over five quarters of wheat, much more than the horse-drawn cart or tumbril. Both were two wheeled, but the *plaustrum*'s wheels, usually clad in iron and costing almost three times those of a cart, were much sturdier. Also in the cart house would have been at least one tumbril, built of ash rather than oak. Both types of vehicle could be extended by ladders held in place by ropes attached to wooden pegs on either side.[264]

Horses and oxen were in the care of the stock-keeper, who earned a mere 6s 8d. In the piggery the swineherd, paid 10s, would feed his charges on cereal, general waste and dregs of malt from the brewing process. During the autumn he would fatten them on the stubble and, when the acorns were ripe, take them into the nearby pasture woodlands for some six weeks prior, for most, to slaughter. Other farm workers at the Grange were the shepherd, pindar and his boy, paid 8s, 5s and 2s respectively. Cowherds are identified as Ivington and Luston, but not at the Grange where the duties perhaps fell to the stock-keeper. The total bill for these farm workers was £3 1s 8d.

	Overseer/ Steward	Stock-keeper	Carter	Shepherd	Swineherd	Cowherd	Pindar	P's Boy	Park Keeper/ K of the Wood	?	Total £	s	d
The Grange	10s	6s 8d	13s 4d	8s	10s		5s	2s		6s 8d	3	1	8
Ivington				6s	5s	4s	5s	2s	20s	2s	2	4	0
Luston				6s	5s	4s	5s	2s		4s	1	6	0
Stockton				5s	6s		5s	2s				18	0
Stoke				6s			5s			2s		13	0
Hope				6s			5s		5s	2s		18	0
Hyde				6s						2s		8	0
More				0 this yr						2s		2	0
Total	10s	6s 8d	13s 4d	£2 3s	£1 6s	8s	£1 10s	8s	£1 5s	£1 0s 8d	£9	10s	8d

HRO M31/9/1 f5v

Table 8 Wages of the Farm Workers of the Manor and Burys etc, 1407/8

13 Library and Scribe

'A cloister without its library', it has been said, 'is like a castle without its armoury'. For Thomas a Kempis it was 'a kitchen without stewpans, a table without food, a river without fish or a well without water'. A monastery's books were a reflection of its spiritual life. Firm evidence as to the quality and range of the Reading and Leominster libraries is found in BL MS Egerton 3031, a Reading cartulary. Otherwise known as the Fingall cartulary, it was discovered in 1792 by a bricklayer, 'secreted in a very concealed and unknown corner' in the Earl of Fingall's Shinfield House, near Reading. The manuscript retains its original late-12th/early 13th-century binding of oak boards covered with white leather. Its lists of the books in the two libraries were written by the same hand between 1180 and 1191. The only other monastic library catalogues of such an early date are those of Rochester, Burton, Bury and Whitby.[265]

The cartulary lists Reading Abbey's most precious possessions: its relics, books and charters, in that order. Of the relics, only those at Reading are described, but there are two quite separate lists of books, Reading's on folios 8v-10v and Leominster's on 12v (Fig 13.1). This distinction, between the treatment of the books and the relics, is significant. Although housed on two separate sites, the books were considered parts of a single collection, that of St Mary of Reading, for the two sections are headed 'These books are kept in the church of Reading' and 'These books are held in the church of Leominster'. The relic collections, on the other hand, were regarded as quite separate, an important part of the identity of the individual houses — even though Reading's had been considerably enhanced by the removal or splitting of a number of Leominster's Anglo-Saxon and Celtic items.

Seventy-seven books are listed as at Leominster. For a mere cell of no more than a dozen monks, this compares not unfavourably with some 204 books at Reading, where the full complement was 100 monks, 261 at Bury St Edmunds and 241 at Rochester Cathedral, but only 86 at Whitby and 70 at Burton-on Trent in the same period. Most had been laboriously copied by hand in the cloister by members of the community, pre- as well as post-Conquest. The value of books was reflected in the strict regulations concerning loans: the insistence on pledges of at least equal value from outsiders, and the malediction commonly found on the first page: 'This is a book of St Mary of Reading. May whoever hides or alters it be anathema.' Even John Trillek, their own diocesan, had to give the monks of Wenlock his written bond in 1346 when he borrowed their *Life* of St Mildburg.[266] The most precious possession was the first item on the list, after *Hii libri habentur in Leonensi ecclesia*, an entire bible, *Biblioteca ex integro per ordinem* (Fig 13.1, lines 1 & 2). Of Reading's four copies, one, 'made by G. the cantor', was kept in the cloister. Leominster had two complete texts of the Evangelists as well as individual volumes of Matthew, Mark and John, two copies of Ecclesiastes and Solomon bound up together, two copies of the Apocalypse and commentaries on Joshua, Judges, Isaiah, Jeremiah and Leviticus, as well as the Evangelists.[267]

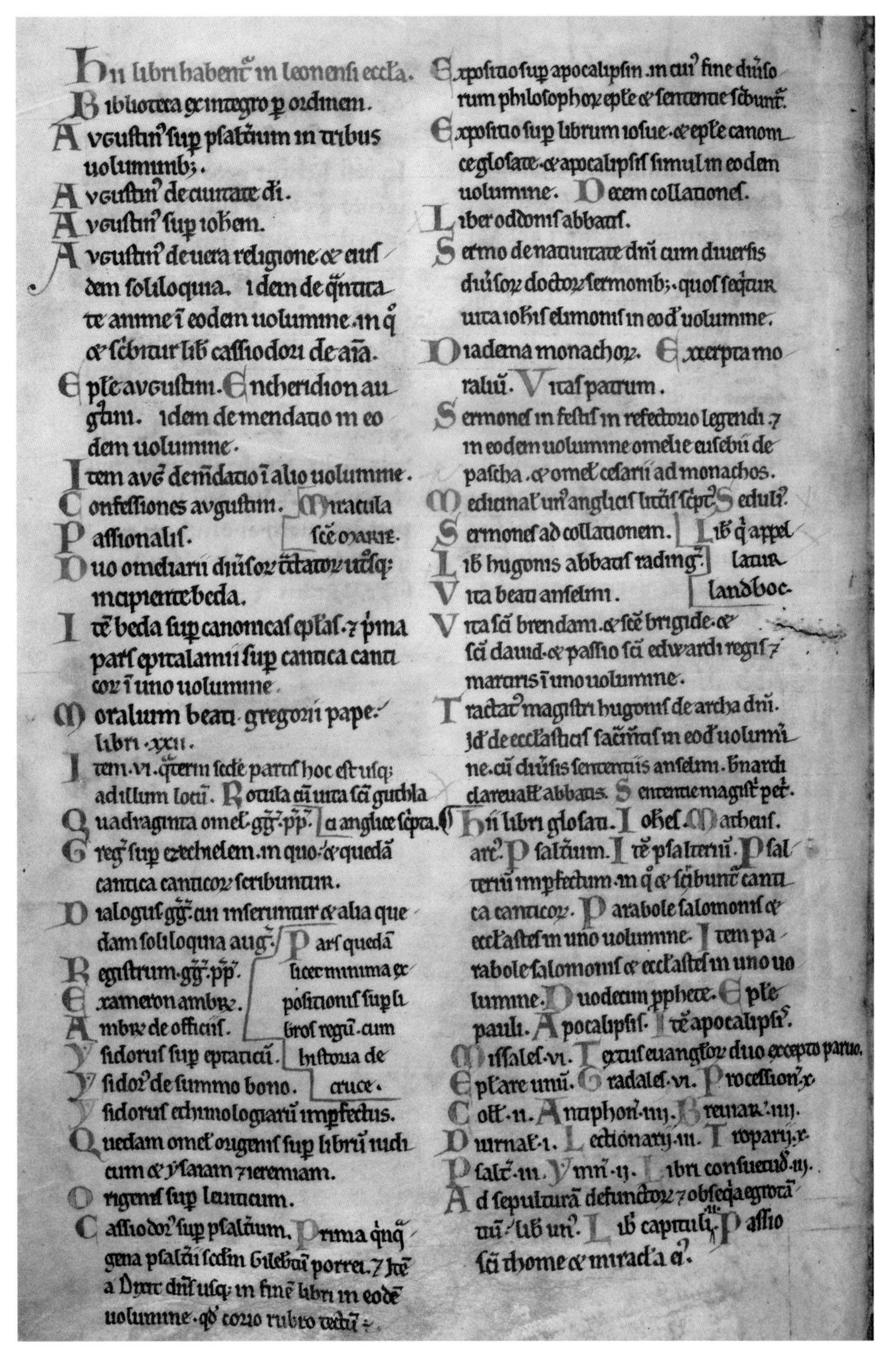

Hii libri habentur in leonensi ecclesia.
Bibliotheca ex integro per ordinem.
Augustinus super psalterium in tribus voluminibus.
Augustinus de civitate dei.
Augustinus super iohem.
Augustinus de vera religione et eiusdem soliloquia. idem de quantitate anime in eodem volumine. in quo et scribitur liber cassiodori de anima.
Epistole augustini. Encheridion augustini. idem de mendacio in eodem volumine.
Item aug. de mendacio in alio volumine.
Confessiones augustini. Miracula sce marie.
Passionalis.
Duo omeliarii diversorum tractatorum usque incipiente beda.
Item beda super canonicas epistolas. et prima pars epitalamii super cantica canticorum in uno volumine.
Moralium beati gregorii pape. libri xxii.
Item vi. quaterni secunde partis hoc est usque ad illum locum. Rotula cum vita sci guthlaci anglice scripta.
Quadraginta omelie gg. pp.
Greg. super ezechielem. in quo et quedam cantica canticorum scribuntur.
Dialogus gg. cui inseruntur et alia quedam soliloquia aug. Pars quedam licet minima expositionis super libros regum. cum historia de cruce.
Registrum gg. pp.
Exameron ambrosii.
Ambrosius de officiis.
Ysidorus super eptaticum.
Ysidorus de summo bono.
Ysidorus ethimologiarum imperfectus.
Quedam omelie origenis super librum iudicum et ysaiam et ieremiam.
Origenis super leviticum.
Cassiodorus super psalterium. Prima quinquagena psalterii secundum gilebertum porrei. et habent a Dixit dominus usque in finem libri in eodem volumine. quod corio rubeo tectum.

Expositio super apocalipsin. in cuius fine diversorum philosophorum epistole et sententie scribuntur.
Expositio super librum iosue. et epistole canonice glosate. et apocalipsis simul in eodem volumine. Decem collationes.
Liber oddonis abbatis.
Sermo de nativitate domini cum diversis diversorum doctorum sermonibus. quos sequitur vita iohis elimonis in eodem volumine.
Diadema monachorum. Excerpta moralium. Vitas patrum.
Sermones in festis in refectorio legendi. et in eodem volumine omelie eusebii de pascha. et omelie cesarii ad monachos.
Medicinale unum anglicis litteris scriptum. Sedulius.
Sermones ad collationem. Liber qui appellatur landboc.
Liber hugonis abbatis rading.
Vita beati anselmi.
Vita sci brendani. et sce brigide. et sci david. et passio sci edwardi regis et martyris in uno volumine.
Tractatus magistri hugonis de archa domini. Item de ecclesiasticis sacramentis in eodem volumine. cum diversis sententiis anselmi. bernardi clarevall. abbatis. Sententie magistri petri.
Hii libri glosati. Iohes. Matheus. Marcus. Psalterium. Item psalterium. Psalterium imperfectum. in quo et scribuntur cantica canticorum. Parabole salomonis et ecclesiastes in uno volumine. Item parabole salomonis et ecclesiastes in uno volumine. Duodecim prophete. Epistole pauli. Apocalipsis. Item apocalipsis.
Missales vi. Textus evangeliorum duo excepto parvo. Epistolare unum. Gradales vi. Processionales x. Coll. ii. Antiphonarii iiii. Breviarii iiii. Diurnale i. Lectionarii iii. Troparii x. Psalteria iii. Ymnarii ii. Libri consuetudinum ii. Ad sepulturam defunctorum et obsequia egrotantium liber unus. Liber capituli. Passio sci thome et miracula eius.

Fig 13.1 Leominster Priory Book List c1190, from the Fingall Cartulary, found by a bricklayer in 1792, secreted in Shinfield House near Reading (BL Egerton MS 3031 f12v)

Liturgical Books

The books fall into two main categories: service books, for use in the choir, and books for study in the cloister etc. Liturgical volumes formed about half of the collection at Leominster. There were various psalters, with texts of psalms and canticles. These were divided into eight parts, one for each day of the week, the last for use at evensong throughout the week. The psalms were the cornerstone of the medieval office, providing the basis for meditation. The demand for an ever-increasing number of saints' days led, however, to encroachments on the routine of the Psalter. Also listed are an Epistle-book, probably containing readings from the epistles for the whole year rather than only for the more important occasions and festivals, two hymnals, four antiphonals, the principal choir books giving the sections of the service sung in two parts, and six graduals giving the choral chants for the proper of the Mass. In the late 12th century the contents of such service books, and the Psalter, were being brought together in the breviary, of which the priory had four copies. The monks also possessed three lectionaries, containing lessons for Matins, and, although now going out of fashion, ten tropers giving short embellishments to the service. In addition there were two books of collects, with prayers for particular feasts, seasons, etc, and one diurnal, a small and therefore portable volume, containing all the day hours of the office except Matins.

Some service books were required on occasions other than the canonical hours. By the end of the 12th century it was increasingly the practice for brethren to take priests' orders. They would then have to celebrate Mass, usually at one of the side altars, daily before noon. There are six missals, suggesting that by 1191 probably a majority of the monks were in priests' orders. Even more numerous were the processionals, containing chants and prayers for liturgical processions. These were never large and had little or no ornament, for they had to be carried for long periods of time, as on Sundays and the principal feasts. Some included ingenious diagrams to indicate the places that members should take up on particular occasions, as at the Rood, each individual being indicated by a symbol of his office, such as a cross, thurifer, taper or reliquary. There were ten such processionals at Leominster. Its Anglo-Saxon prayer book, to which no reference is made in the library list, included prayers to be said in the various offices of the monastery during the Asperges ceremonies, as well as a copy of the famous processional hymn written by Ratpert of St Gall, who died in 884. One book in the library list, in addition to the missals, provided prayers for the priest visiting the sick or dying.[268]

Books for study in the cloister and elsewhere

The remaining books were primarily for personal study in the cloister, being loaned out on an annual basis; but the homilies, collections of discourses or sermons on the works of the Bible, were mostly for communal purposes, to be heard rather than read. Leominster's books included the Bible (2), Augustine on the Psalter, *super psalterium*, in three volumes (2), Gregory the Great's *Moralium* on Job in two volumes (13), and Bede on the *Canonical Epistles*, with the first part of *Epithalmium on Cantica Canticorum*, the Song of Solomon, in the same volume (12).

In Chapter 42 of his Rule St Benedict advised that 'when the brethren are taking their meals there should always be reading. Yet no one shall presume to take the book at haphazard and read; but let him who is to read throughout the week enter on his office on Sunday. Let the greatest silence be kept at table, so that no whispering, no voice, save the voice of the reader alone, be heard there ... lest occasion be given to the Evil One.' The reader was to receive a sop before he began, 'lest it be too hard for him to fast so long', but take his meal afterwards, with the cooks and servers. A volume in the Leominster lists recalls this practice: *Sermones in festis in refectorio legendi*, 'Sermons to be read in the refectory at festivals' (Fig 13.1, 2.6).[269] In the same volume were bound the sermons *de pascha*, 'On Easter', of Eusebius 'Gallicanus' and some of the short and homely 'Homilies', *omelie*, attributed to the first popular preacher whose works have come down to us, St Caesarius, archbishop of Arles, who died c542, but which are probably also the work of Eusebius 'Gallicanus'. Evidently these were also intended as mealtime reading. A later Reading list is more informative, giving titles of 22 volumes prescribed for reading in the refectory, over the annual cycle. These were kept in the dormitory, ready for use by the lector in the refectory.[270]

Reading in the refectory took place from a lectern, usually of stone, projecting high up on the south wall, access being gained by a stone staircase in the thickness of the wall. Examples can still be seen. There is one close to the abbey of SS Peter and Paul at Shrewsbury. Here the pulpit stands in isolation on the south side of the church, the claustral buildings having been demolished to build a new road in 1836. The pulpit is in the Benedictine refectory at St Werburgh's cathedral, Chester, but is surrounded by chattering tourists in what is now a cafeteria. At Beaulieu Abbey the Cistercians' refectory is now the parish church, but the pulpit, with its arcaded staircase, remains *in situ*.

There was also a daily reading preceding Compline, usually in the cloister or chapter-house. There Benedict suggested one of the monks should read from the *Lives* of the fathers, *Passionalis* (1.10), such as St John Cassian's *Conversations* with the saints of the Egyptian desert concerning the meaning of the monastic life, or other devout works. He advised against the Heptateuch or Books of Kings for these occasions, concerned that their historical content might excite the imagination rather than prepare the monks for night with sacred thoughts. 'It will not profit those of weak understanding to hear those parts of scripture at that hour'. Certain books are specially identified for such reading: at Leominster *Decem collationes*, 'Ten Collations' (2.2) and *Sermons at Collation* (2.8);[271] at Reading 'twenty-four *Collations* in one volume' and 'ten and fourteen *Collations*' in another.

Non-Liturgical Works

Of the non-liturgical books, more than half were patristics, works of the Latin Fathers, writers on church doctrine; but the earliest were the *Homilies* of Origen of Alexandria (c185–254). During the Severan persecution of 202, Origen was deprived of martyrdom at his father's side: 'the providence of Almighty God used his mother (who hid all his clothing) to defeat his ambitions for the benefit of mankind'. Thwarted in his ambition, Origen wrote to his father, 'Don't change your mind on our account'.[272] 'Not only Christian antiquity but the whole of the Middle Ages', it has been said, 'lived on in the treasures accumulated by Origen'.[273] Though his writings survive only in fragments, Leominster had his *Homilies* on Judges, Isaiah and Jeremiah (1.24), as well as *On Leviticus* (1.25). Many of his explanations of sacred texts took the form of *scholia*, critical notes written in the margins of ancient manuscripts. The Roman Cassiodorus, c485–580, was quite a different person. He served as minister to Theodoric the Ostrogoth, framing his edicts in traditional formulae, and wrote a *History of the Goths*. He retired in 540 to one of the two monasteries he had established, where he founded the tradition of monastic scholarship. The priory had copies of Cassiodorus's *De anima* (1.6), in which he sought to establish the spirituality of the soul, and his explanation of the Psalms, *Super psalterium* (1.26). Bound up with the latter was a gloss, marginal comment, on the *Psalter* by Gilbert de la Porrée, bishop of Chartres, who died in 1154 (1.26). Another copy, with his *Epistles of Paul on the Psalter*, was at Reading. St Bernard brought charges of unorthodoxy against de la Porrée.

The works of three of the four great Latin doctors dominate the Leominster list, for the basis of prayer was not only the reading of Holy Scripture, but also the major commentaries by the Fathers. St Augustine of Hippo was the most popular in virtually all monastic libraries. Leominster held ten of his works: his *Confessiones* (1.9), a pæan of praise to God for His grace and conversion; *De civitate dei*, 'Of the city of God' (1.4), the two cities, love of God and love of self; the *Enchiridion* (1.7), a systematic account of church doctrine based on commentaries on the Creed, the Lord's Prayer and Charity; his letters, *Epistole* (1.7), of which some 220 survive, in three volumes; the *Soliloquies* (1.6); *De quantitate anime* (1.6), on the progressive purification of the soul; two copies of *De mendatio* (1.7 & 8), in which he shows there is no justification for lying; *De vera religione*, 'on true religion' (1.6), an attack on Manichaeism and paganism; and the tract on John, *super Iohannem* (1.5). Added in the margin near the *Confessions* is *Miracula sancta Marie* (1.10a).

St Gregory the Great was represented by six volumes: his earliest work, *Moralium* (1.13), was concerned primarily with moral theology, as was his commentary *On Ezekiel* (1.16). Other commentaries were his *Quadraginta omelie*, 'Forty Sermons' (1.15), preached on gospel texts, and *Cantica Canticorum* (1.16). The *Register* (1.18) is a collection of almost 700 of Gregory's letters, whilst the subject of *The Dialogues* (1.17) is the lives and miracles of the Italian saints. By St Ambrose of Milan there was *de officiis ministrorum* (1.20), which provided the clergy with the earliest treatise on Christian morality, in plan following Cicero's *De officiis*, and copies of his *Hexameron* (1.19), commentaries on the six days of creation. There were three works by Isidore of Seville: *Ethimologiarum imperfectus*, etymologies (1.23), an encyclopedia of the knowledge of his time, which remained influential throughout the Middle Ages; *De summo bono* (1.22), which became a popular medieval manual of the Christian faith; and *Super eptaticum* (1.21) on the Heptateuch, emphasising its spiritual rather than its historical meaning. No works of St Jerome are recorded at Leominster. This is surprising, since he was, with Origen, the leading figure in the foundation of medieval spirituality. There were some ten of Jerome's works at Reading, so it is possible that one or two were on loan from Leominster for copying.

One of the two volumes from the Carolingian religious revival is identified merely as 'Sedulius' (2.7a, in margin). This was a name borne by two religious writers of the era, both believed to have been from Ireland where, in its local form, *Seadhal*, the name was popular. The only evidence for Sedulius 'senior' is a brief extract from his *Tract* or *Commentary* on Matthew. [274] Much more is known about Sedulius Scottus, a poet at the court of the Emperor Lothar I and his three sons, 843–69. He had an outstanding knowledge of rare, classical and patristic writers. His religious works include *Commentaries* on Matthew, with some 250 references to Origen, *Epistles* of Paul, and *Prefaces to the Gospels*.[275]

The second was the *Diadema monachorum*, the 'Diadem of Monks' (2.5) by Abbot Smaragdus of St Mihiel at Verdun, a pupil of Benedict of Aniane. With his major work, the *Commentary on the Rule of St Benedict*, c817, it brought together the teaching of Gregory the Great on contemplation with that of St Benedict in his *Rule*. Both books were a major influence, ensuring that the monastic tradition of the west remained Benedictine. More concise than the *Commentary*, the *Diadem* proved more popular with copyists. For Smaragdus, the shield against temptation was constant attention to and meditation on scripture; concentration on constant repetition of sacred passages established them firmly in the mind. Such passages, he believed, should first be read and remembered, and then reflected upon, thus to be retained in the soul. In this Smaragdus was following Origen, Isidore of Seville and Bede.

Smaragdus had a major impact on at least two of the three great Anglo-Saxon monastic reformers of the 10th century. St Dunstan carefully annotated a copy of his *Commentary*, and St Aethelwold had a copy by his side as he translated St Benedict's *Rule* into Anglo-Saxon.[276] We have extant copies of the *Commentary* and *Diadem* from three major centres of the monastic reform movement. A mid-10th-century copy of the *Commentary* emanated from the Glastonbury scriptorium, and an early-11th-century copy from Abingdon, whilst the *Diadem* was copied at Christ Church Cathedral, Canterbury, in the third quarter of the 10th century.[277] Given the popularity of Smaragdus' two works relating to the *Rule* in both pre- and post-Conquest periods, it is strange that, although there was a copy of the *Diadem* at Leominster, neither of his major works was in the Reading library. Nevertheless the *Commentary* was evidently held in high regard there for, on his elevation to Cluny in 1199, Abbot Hugh II took with him what one assumes was his personal copy, effectively as an abbot's handbook.

There were only some half dozen works of the 10th century onwards at Leominster. They included the *Collations* (Fig 13.1, 2.3) of Odo, abbot of Cluny, who died in 942, a great lover of the arts, especially music, who did much to deepen the spiritual life of the order, and a copy of *Theological Questions*, written by Hugh of Amiens (2.9) during his time as first abbot of Reading, 1123–30. The *Vita beati Anselmi*, the *Life* of Anselm (2.10), archbishop of Canterbury c1093–1109, whose conflict with both William Rufus and Henry I, the priory's founder, over the questions of lay investiture of churchmen had led to two periods of exile, was probably either the text or abridgement of the *Life* written by Eadmer, the Canterbury monk who was Anselm's personal chaplain and secretary from 1093 to the archbishop's death in 1109, during which time he was scarcely absent from his side. *De archa domini*, *Of Noah's Ark*, by another Hugh, who was abbot of St Victor, Paris, and died in 1141, contained extracts of works by Anselm himself and by St Bernard of Clairvaux, who died in 1153 (2.12).

The final entry in the Leominster list was the *Passion of St Thomas and his Miracles* (2.19), in a different though contemporary hand. Becket, who had dedicated the abbey church at Reading for Henry II in 1169, was murdered by four of the king's knights in the north-west transept of his own cathedral on 1 December 1170. His canonisation in 1173 came only a decade or so before the compilation of the two book lists. There was also a *Life and Miracles of St Thomas, Archbishop and Martyr* at Reading, for which slight respect appears to have been shown; it was bound up with the *Tripartite History* of Cassiodorus and Epiphanius, and the *Lives* of Saints David, Brendan, Brigid, Petroc and Cuthbert! Numerous *Lives* of Becket were written shortly after his martyrdom, at least six before 1176, with a *Life* in French the next year, and another in Icelandic by 1200. The titles, *Passion of St Thomas and his Miracles* at Leominster, and his *Life and Miracles* at Reading, suggest both may have been based on the *Passion* and *Miracles* by Benedict, a Canterbury monk, who was at the scene of the martyrdom, where he was wounded trying to protect Becket. He became prior of Peterborough in 1175 and abbot in 1177. An alternative source could be the *Miracles* by William, another Canterbury monk at the scene of the martyrdom, who, being subsequently connected with the administration of the shrine, had first-hand access to the pilgrims and their stories of miracles.[278]

Little more than a century after the Conquest, few of the ancient monastic libraries retained works in Anglo-Saxon, the Norman Benedictines having swept away much of the old order, linguistic and bibliographic as well as architectural. The Benedictine house at Burton-on-Trent, founded by Wulfric Sprot in 1002, preserved a remarkable nine volumes c1172. In Glastonbury's great library merely four such works remained by 1243, two being dismissed as 'old and useless'. Leominster's pre-Conquest volumes provide a vital and direct link with its Anglo-Saxon minster. *Medicinalis unus anglicis litteris scriptus* (2.7) may have been a *Leechdom*, a collection of medical diagnoses, prescriptions, recipes, charms — and prayers. There were others at Glastonbury and Rochester, but the earliest, largest and most famous was Bald's *Leechbook* from late 9th- or early 10th-century Winchester, which included prescriptions for a wide range of afflictions such as shingles, a mad dog's bite, for balding, headache, women's chatter, under- or over-virility etc, and for safety from the race of elves and goblins. Leominster's prayer book, Cotton Nero Aii and Galba Axiv, contains two 'medical recipes for restoring the body to health through prayer' derived from Bald's *Leechbook*.[279]

Another Saxon work in the Leominster library was the *Liber qui appellatur*, 'book called' *landboc* (2.8a, in margin) the only one so listed in the Corpus of English Benedictine library booklists. The *landboc*, or charter, was introduced into England by the Church in the late 7th century to secure their grants of land in perpetuity. The term came to apply also to a collection of such charters. Thus the Benedictines of Winchcombe entitled their cartulary *Landboc*. It opens with what purports to be the 811 foundation charter of Coenwulf, king of Mercia (796–821), and confirmatory privileges granted by Pope Leo III that year and by Paschal in 818, but the charters that follow are of the late 12th century. The monks were using the Anglo-Saxon term *landboc* in an attempt to bolster their house's claims to antiquity.[280] This was not the case at Leominster. Given the amplitude and prestige of Henry I's foundation charter, the abbots of Reading and their priors at Leominster had no need for recourse to Leominster's Anglo-Saxon charters. Thus the *landboc* was given no prominence; indeed the scribe added the title, apologetically, in the margin. We must assume, therefore, that this was a collection of charters from the priory's predecessor, the Saxon minster. The early date of Merewalh's grant, and the compact nature of the minster's estates, suggests that Leominster's *landboc* was a counterpart to Mildburg's *Testament*, those early charters in which, as the *Life* tells us, Much Wenlock's 'ancient privileges were carefully inscribed'.[281]

Neither the Reading nor the Leominster collection could lay any claim to general literature, philosophy, grammar, logic or the classics, for such works only began to appear during the 13th and 14th centuries as monastic libraries grew rapidly. Books on history, quite numerous at Reading, were non-existent at Leominster — not even a copy of *The History of the Church* by Eusebius, died c342, bishop of Caesarea, the 'father of church history'. His was the only account of the critical early period, from Christ to Constantine. Bede's *Ecclesiastical History*, many of his commentaries and other books were held at Reading, but Leominster had merely his commentary *On the Canonical Epistles* (1.12) and *Duo omeliarii*, two homilies (1.11). For history the priory had to rely on such fragments as appeared in saints' *Lives*, but these were few. They included the *Life* of John the Almoner, *Elimonis*, (2.4), the patriarch of Alexandria, who died c616 and was famed for his distribution of 80,000 pieces of gold and silver to local hospitals and monasteries.

Lives and Cults of Guthlac, David, Edward, king and martyr, Brendan, Brigid and Petroc

The most significant *Lives* in the two libraries, however, relate to Leominster's pre-Conquest cults, for they provide further valuable links with the Anglo-Saxon minster, and underwrite the continuity of its religious life, even if only in terms of a small community of minster priests, between the convent's dissolution in 1046 and the arrival of the first Reading monks in the 12th century. The *Life* of St Guthlac (c673–714) is in a roll, in Anglo-Saxon: *Rotula cum vita sancti Guthlaci anglice scripta* (Fig 13.1, 1.14). Guthlac was born in the Welsh March and spent fifteen years of his early life there, fighting the Welsh. He then withdrew to become a monk at Repton, eventually seeking the hermit's life on an island in the Fens at Crowland. As his death approached Eadburg, abbess of Repton, sent him a shroud and a leaden coffin in which he was buried by his sister and four disciples who lived close by. His cult developed rapidly after his body was found in the tomb, incorrupt. The Leominster *Life* was probably a vernacular version, based on the famous *Vita* by Felix, c720. [282] Invocations to St Guthlac are found in both the Leominster Anglo-Saxon litanies. In the longer he is placed firmly with local saints, immediately preceding Leominster's own three saints, Aethelmod, Edfrith and Haemma (see Fig 3.2). Links between Leominster and Crowland were probably re-established as a consequence of the foundation of Ramsey Abbey, Hunts, by St Oswald of Worcester.[283]

At Reading the *Lives* of David, Brendan, Brigid, Petroc and Cuthbert are bound up in one volume. All except Cuthbert enjoyed pre-Conquest cults at Leominster. Similarly at Leominster the *Lives* of David, Brendan and Brigid were in one volume, with the *Passion* of Edward, king and martyr (2.11). David's was a major cult at Leominster in both the pre- and post-Conquest eras, as evidenced by his feast on 1 March in the Calendar, its continuance as a principal feast into the late medieval period, and the presence of his shrine, referred to in the Welsh episcopal indulgences. This shows that only part of David's relics, the 'rib and bone' of the 1190 relic list, was removed to Reading, and explains the copy of David's *Life* in both libraries.[284]

A collect for the undated feast of Brigid, whose relics were claimed by Reading, is included in the Leominster Anglo-Saxon prayer book, and there are invocations to Brendan in both litanies. He is found in only two others, one of Breton origin. Neither of these saints is identified precisely, but Brigid is celebrated in the Nero Calendar on 1 February, the feast of Brigid of Kildare. There were two Irish saints called Brendan. The feast, on 29 November, of the 'chief of the prophets of Ireland', Brendan, abbot of Birr, who died in 573, a disciple and friend of Columba whom he saved from excommunication at an Irish synod is, however, not found in any Anglo-Saxon Calendar. The more famous was Brendan, abbot of Clonfert, the so-called Navigator, who died in 575 and achieved wide popularity from a medieval romance of his voyage to a mythical island in the Atlantic. His feast, on 16 May, though not recognised at Leominster, occurs in Calendar 16 of Table 2, of Evesham Abbey, 1064–1170, suggesting that his cult may have been introduced from Worcestershire.[285]

Although there is no reference to a *Life* of Petroc in the Leominster library, there is firm evidence of the observance of his cult at the pre-Conquest minster, for his feast was included in its Calendar, uniquely, on 23 May. Elsewhere, it was celebrated on 4 June and 21 May. Further, other than Leominster's longer litany, Petroc is invoked in but four of the 46 Anglo-Saxon litanies.[286]

The relics of Edward, king and martyr, were also venerated at both priory and abbey. At Leominster he was held in particularly high regard. *Corpus Edward, regis et martiris* appears second in its relic list, after 'the body of St Thomas (Haemma), first abbot of this church'. There are also fragmentary prayers to Edward in the Nero/Galba prayer book. At Reading reference to 'Edward the Martyre (h)is arme' was included in both relic lists. Yet the abbey had no counterpart to Leominster's *Passion of St Edward, King and Martyr*.[287]

One Leominster book, not recorded in the Egerton library list, is now at the Bodleian as University College MS d.6. It bears the inscription, 'This is the book of dom. Henry Bray, sub-prior of Leominster'. Printed in Paris, 1510, it consists of three religious tracts. The first, *Speculum spiritualium*, is by John Wotton. The other two are by Richard Rolle, c1306–49, hermit and mystic of Hampole, Yorks, where he also served as spiritual guide to the nuns of a nearby Cistercian convent. Rolle was one of the first religious writers to use the vernacular as well as Latin.[288]

Of the 204 works listed at Reading in 1180–91 some 45 have survived. Of Leominster's volumes only four can be traced: two in the Bodleian, Laud Misc. 79, *Expositio super Apocalipsin* (Fig 13.1, 2.1), and Bodley 125, Odo of Cluny's *Collations* (2.3), in which the Reading monk, William de Wicumbe, listed the books he had copied during his three years at Leominster; and two in the British Library, BL Harley 1246, *Duo omeliarii diversorum* (1.11), and MS Royal 8Exviii, *Diadema monachorum* (2.5).[289]

The Leominster *Annals*

The surviving 12th-century Leominster copy of Smaragdus' *Diadem* is of particular interest, as a brief series of *Annals*, spanning the years 1066–1189, was written in the back of this volume, ff 94r-96v (Fig 13.2). These were edited in 1879 as *The Reading Annals*, but no such title appears in the text. As the only copy of the *Diadem* in the c1191 library lists was at Leominster, this suggests that what we have here is not the Reading, but the *Leominster Annals*. This can be confirmed by analysis of their text. Of the 19 entries prior to 1121, all but one, a reference to King Siward of Norway's visit to England, are in the Annals of the neighbouring Benedictine house of Tewkesbury, refounded by Robert fitz Hamo in 1102, the earlier entries of which were apparently based on a lost original.[290]

Although abbreviated sharply, all these Tewkesbury entries were otherwise copied verbatim. Furthermore, the subject matter of a number of the entries is related very specifically to the Severn valley: the death of Bishop Wulstan in 1095, the city of Worcester consumed by fire in 1113, a local earthquake in 1119, and even the death of Robert fitz Hamo in 1107. Only in 1121 do these annals spring to an independent life, with four Reading entries: foundation, 1121; Hugh, first abbot, 1123; Anscher, second abbot, 1130; and Henry I's burial at Reading, 1135. Such entries do not conflict with the conclusion that these annals were written at Leominster, for in 1139 we are informed that 'this year Abbot Edward (1136–c1154) sent Prior Joseph to Leominster to commence the strict observance of the (Cluniac) order' (Fig 13.2, highlighted section). This is followed by an entry for 1142, alluding to the Empress Matilda's escape from Oxford. Afterwards there is a 36-year gap, broken only by entries for solar eclipses in 1178 and 1180. The final entry is an appropriate termination for Leominster annals, recording 'the death of the glorious King Henry, son of the Empress'.

A Leominster Collection of *Saints' Lives*?

It has also been suggested that a three-volume collection of *Saints' Lives* of a mid to late 12th-century date formed part of Leominster's library. Two of the volumes, with entries from 30 November to 21 June and from 29 June to 16 September, are now in Lincoln Cathedral library, MSS 149 and 150. The third, spanning the period 17 September to 1 December, followed by *Lives* in no particular order, is in Gloucester Cathedral library, Medieval MS 1. Ker concluded that this collection of *Lives*

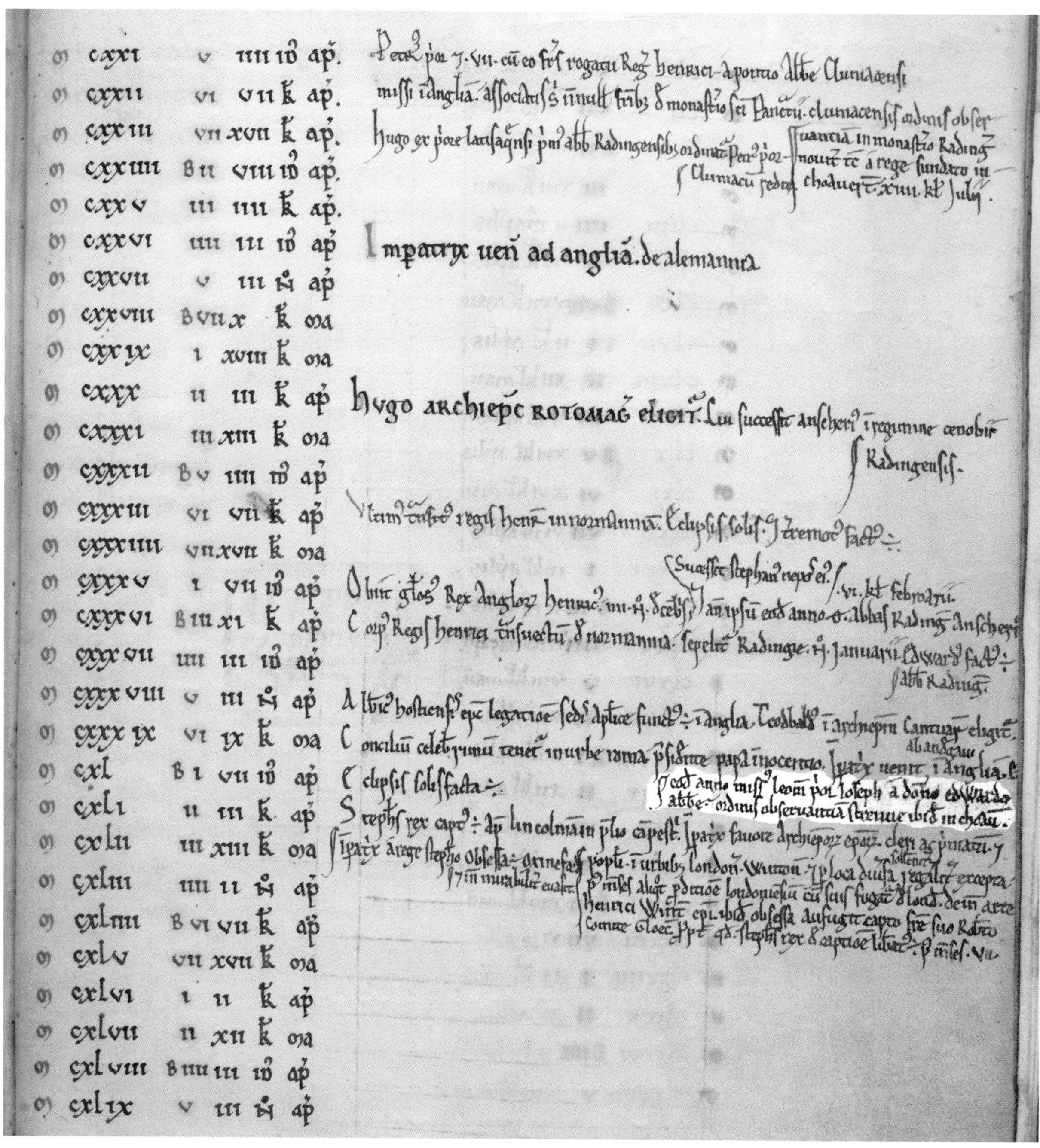

Fig 13.2 The Leominster Annals (BL MS Royal 8Exviii f95)

had belonged to Reading's cell at Leominster for two main reasons. Firstly, there were three entries showing an interest in St James and another in St Hugh, abbot of Cluny 1024–1109. Secondly, he noted that the one Gloucester volume was the gift to the cathedral of Fulk Walwyn of Hellens, Much Marcle, which lies halfway between Leominster and Gloucester. In the Gloucester volume is the short lectionary version of the *Life* of St Mildburg, referred to in Chapter 1, as well as a *Life* of St David, but relics of both were to be found at the abbey as well as the priory. More significant is the absence of Leominster's own saints, Edfrith, Haemma, and Aethelmod, and of the other special cults observed there. Almost all the saints recorded in the three volumes were widely recognised. Yet even with these, there are significant differences. For example, the Leominster Calendar celebrated the feast of St Justus, not on 18 October but 10 November. Their contents thus show that these volumes did not have a Leominster origin.[291]

The Reading/Leominster Seal

Just as the library books held at both abbey and priory were considered a single collection, belonging to St Mary of Reading, so was the abbey seal designed to express the two parts of one body. A fine Reading seal, held at Hereford Cathedral, was used to make the obverse and reverse wax copies. The obverse (Fig 13.3a) has three canopies, with ogee arches ornamented with tracery, crockets and pinnacles. In the larger, central canopy is the Virgin, crowned and seated on the throne with the Child on Her left knee and an orb in Her right hand. On Her right is St James, in a canopy, wearing the pilgrim's cap. His staff is in his right hand, and his wallet hangs from his waist. On the Virgin's left, in another canopy, is John the Evangelist, standing on his symbol, the eagle. In his left hand he holds a scroll inscribed IN PRINCIPIO (John I:1). In his right is the palm branch that the angel gave to Mary when he announced her forthcoming death. This, at Mary's request, John carried before the bier at her funeral. Left and right of the canopies, on the plinth and the background, is curling foliage. The inscription around the seal reads in Latin, S' COE ECCE COVETVAL' RADYNG' FVDATE I HONORE / SCE MARIE ET APOSTL'OR IOH'IS ET IACOBI: 'Seal of the conventual church of Reading founded in honour of St Mary and the apostles John and James'. Around the obverse edge is ANNO: MILLENO/TRICETENO: FABRICAT, 'Made the year one thousand one hundred and thirty-one'.

Fig 13.3a Reading/Leomnister seal: obverse

The reverse (Fig 13.3b) also has three canopies, similarly decorated. In the centre is Henry I, crowned and seated on the throne, in his left hand the model of a church and in his right a sceptre fleury. On his right is St Peter, standing holding his key in his left hand and a book in his right. On the king's left is St Paul, with the sword in his left and a book in his right hand. The inscription around the reverse reads in Latin, ENS. REX.HENRICUS^VMME:DEITAT': AMICVS / ^ ECUR'. DEGIT ENTV: DOM': ISTE: P'GIT: 'King Henry, being a friend of the supreme deity, lived in security; / this man completed the possessions of the house'. Inside the reverse edge is SIGNV: BIS: DENO: B'Q'RTO: CONSOCIAT': 'The seal was manufactured and adopted in 1328.' Although Reading Abbey is named, but Leominster is not, the seal is nevertheless a remarkable symbol of the two houses. Mary, James and John, on the obverse, were the patrons of the abbey; Peter and Paul, on either side of Henry I on the reverse, were those of Leominster Priory.[292]

Fig 13.3b Reading/Leomnister seal: reverse

14 *Sumer is icumen in*

The earliest surviving canon, a six-part composition, was a Reading Abbey work. *Sumer is icumen in* has been described not only as 'one of the most endearing and remarkable pieces of medieval polyphony' but also as the 'most famous of medieval (musical) compositions'. It is known as the *Sumer* Canon or Reading Rota, sometimes by its Latin text, *Perspice Christicola*, 'Pay heed, Christian'. The melody is sung by four voices, with two voices adding an ostinato pes, here the lower parts (Plate 4). The *Sumer* Canon is found in an early section of BL Harley 978, f11v, which is devoted to musical compositions, both monodic and polyphonic, of love and adventure: goliardic songs, and a varied collection of other materials, including a medicinal section and the *lais*, love lyrics, of Marie de France.[293]

The date of the *Sumer* Canon has been the subject of debate over many years, but recent work on the palaeography and content of Harley 978 has provided a secure dating. The Harley manuscript includes a monastic calendar on f15v, which gives details of feasts for January and February, similar to those of the calendar in the Reading cartulary, BL Vespasian Ev. The Canon is on the first gathering of the folios, the calendar on the second. The similarity in the handwriting of the calendar and of the instructions, explaining how the *Sumer* Canon should be sung, suggests that canon and calendar 'are not far apart in their dates'. Indeed the whole of BL Harley 978, we are told, was drawn up 'in no more than a few years'. An obit in the calendar indicates the Canon was compiled after the death, recorded in the abbey annals for 1261, of the Reading monk, John of Forn'. *The Song of the Barons*, ff107-14, celebrating de Montfort's victory at Lewes, May 1264, establishes the terminal date, for it would not have been included after his defeat, and death, at Evesham in August the following year. With relatively firm dates for the opening and middle sections, it appears that Harley 978, including its famous canon, was completed within a reasonably short period, 1261–5.[294]

Fig 14.1 *Ord'.li. W.de Wint'*

At the end, on ff160v-161, is 'A list of contents of the book of William de Winton' (Fig 14.1 and 14.2), its heading, *Ord'.li. W.de Wint'*, an abbreviation for *Ordo libri Willelmi de Wintonia*. The book itself is 'now lost', but the list gives details of seven groups of music. The first line reads *Spiritus et alme. R. de Burg*. As Burgate was not dignified with the title abbot, the Canon must have been composed prior to his election to that office in 1269. The rest of the contents, often quite wildly misinterpreted, is ably handled by Christopher Hohler.[295] They include a reference to a missing section attributed to William of Wicumbe.

The chronology is important, for it helps us to understand the roles of two Reading monks, William de Wicumbe and William de Winton (Winchester), in the production of the Rota. Both spent some years at Leominster Priory, Wicumbe prior to and Winton subsequent to the production of the *Sumer* Canon. Wicumbe's spell at the priory can be dated with confidence as c1245–9,

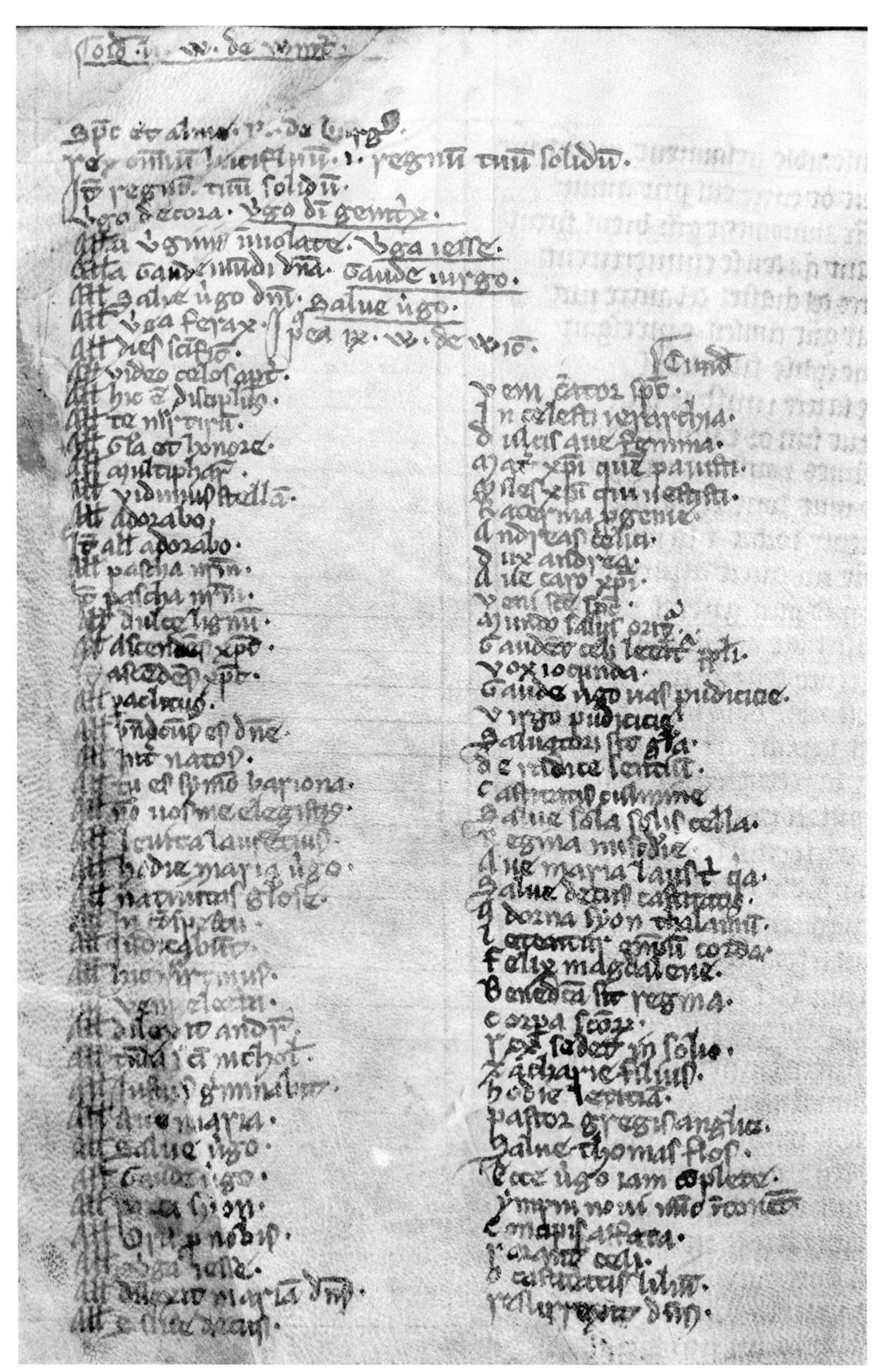

Fig 14.2 A list of the Contents of the Book of William de Winton (BL Harley MS 978 ff160v)

after which he returned to Reading. Winton was there by 1276, and was sub-prior by 1282. Both, therefore, were at Reading during the critical period, 1261–5.[296]

P(ost)ea R. W. de Wic.(umbe), 'Thereafter Responsories of W. de Wicumbe'. There is agreement between some of the titles in this list and those of music found on binding fragments known as 'The Worcester Fragments', now Bodleian MSS Rawlinson C400 and Lat. Liturg. b.19.[297] Furthermore, the backs of the Rawlinson fragments were used to record corn rents from the Reading manors of Blewbury and Hendred. This combination of evidence led Nicky Losseff to rename these Bodleian manuscripts as Reading, not Worcester, fragments. Luther Dittmer created a false trail when he read W. de Wic. as William of Winchcombe, a man who was known to be a prebend of St Andrew's, Worcester. He was unable to explain how a prebend of Worcester could at the same time have been a monk at Leominster.[298]

Fig 14.3 P(ost)ea R. W. de Wic.(umbe)

William of Wicumbe

It was some ten to fifteen years prior to the completion of this lost repertory at Reading, that Wicumbe had spent his four years at Leominster Priory. There he copied, excerpted and corrected sixteen books in the library. This we learn from a list, now only partly legible, at the end of a copy of Odo of Cluny's *Collations* (Fig 13.1, 2.3), the Leominster volume that, as already noted, is now in the Bodleian Library as MS Bodley 125. Wicumbe's stylus entries, on ff98v-99r, are headed, 'These are the labours of brother W. de Wicb.'. There follows his list of sixteen volumes, apparently composed for his personal satisfaction, for it was written in dry point, legible only if crayoned over. The period over which Wicumbe's 'labours' were completed can be established by his reference to the encouragement he received from 'Th.(omas), then dean'. The only dean (prior) of Leominster so named in the 13th century held office from 1226 until his death, recorded in the 13th-century Reading annals, in 1245. Wicumbe's four-year stint will thus have ended by 1249.[299]

Wicumbe had for the most part to copy service books needing to be replaced after heavy use in the choir. He produced a psalter, a customary giving directions regarding services and ceremonial, and a compotus in verse, giving the rules for the calculation of Easter, the rising of the moon and other matters for the ordering of the monastic calendar. Other works included a troper and processional, bound together as a workbook for himself as precentor, and a service book for the Mass of the Virgin. More to his taste was the copying of *De spiritu et anima*, supposedly by Augustine, into the back of a bible given to Reading library by its sacrist, Alured of Dover. This Wicumbe describes as a 'most useful book', a commendation he withheld from Isidore of Seville's *Synonyms*, which he also had to copy.

Little of this work was to his liking. At the express wish of J. de Abingdon, precentor, and R. de Worcester, sub-prior, he had to correct and amalgamate, according to the Reading Use, a collectar, which included prayers, chapters, responses and benedictions for the celebrant's use. Wisely, he confined his complaint to the back of Odo's *Collations*. He copied a small diurnal, a service book containing the day hours, 'with a most compendious calendar', *cum Kalendario compendiosissime*, which he had to abbreviate. Wicumbe extracted the 'marrow' from three volumes of Jerome and Augustine's *Epistles*. Another task was to produce potted versions of Gregory the Great's *Dialogues, Register, Forty sermons, Homilies on Ezekiel* and *The Evangelists*, all listed in the Leominster and Reading library lists.

It has been suggested that Wicumbe regarded his work at Leominster as 'some form of penal servitude'. His tone is frequently truculent, but he was to prove to be a man of wide musical interests, and a gifted composer. His list is the only evidence we have to illustrate book production, and the kind and quantity of work that scribes would have been carrying out in the Leominster cloister, a constant and important feature in the life of the priory. It also indicates what could be achieved in four years by an able, if recalcitrant, scribe.[300]

From Wicumbe's asides one gets some savour of the petty squabbles and rivalries inevitable in such a small and enclosed community. There was trouble over parchment, which was made from sheep- or calfskin and went through an elaborate and tedious process before it was suitable for use in the scriptorium. First soaked in water and lime, it was then stretched on special frames and carefully scraped. After all unevenness had been removed with pumice, it was then chalked to make it white. It is not surprising, therefore, to find one book written on the spare leaves of another, as in the case of *De spiritu et anima*, within or at the end of Alured's Bible. To complete a work, Wicumbe may have appropriated somebody else's parchment, as he notes carefully that his *Book of Lives* was written 'on parchment received from the precentor', and that the *Mass of the Virgin*, probably a polyphonic cycle, including such different categories of chant as *Alleluias*, sequences and the Ordinary, was produced 'on his own parchment'. Another work was stopped by 'malicious tongues'. Nevertheless one is left with the impression of four years of solid achievement, and one is grateful for the brief glimpse Wicumbe affords of life in Leominster's 13th-century cloister, and of the way the priory's library was built up and its service books maintained.

Our view of the composition of the *Sumer* Canon is greatly aided by the list Wicumbe wrote with his stylus at the end of Bodley 125: this shows that his skills were decidedly more than those of a mere copyist. All Benedictine monks were obliged to read music in order to participate in the daily offices, but Wicumbe was on occasions able to indulge his real love, for musical composition, a skill to be displayed fully after his return to Reading. In a great compotus, *compotum optimum*, he provided 'a certain treatise on music'. He refers to copying two rolls of polyphony, one three-part the other two. Such rolls of polyphonic music are otherwise unknown for this period. William was responsible for 'the notation of the chant' for the *Life of St Margaret*, written by fellow monk, Hugh de Wycombe. Here, in his list, he uses *imposuit*, 'he bestowed', rather than his customary *scripsit*, 'he copied'. His inability to further indulge his interest in composition was no doubt the principal reason for his impatience with the mundane copying tasks on which he had to spend most of his time. The 'malicious tongues' that stopped one of his works may have been a reaction to his flexibility in composition, unwelcome in the conservative milieu of Leominster at that time. If so, it would have changed, radically, after William de Winton's appointment as sub-prior at Leominster in 1282.[301]

On his return to the more liberal Reading, Wicumbe's skills no doubt flourished in the company of Burgate, de Winton and others. The subsequent period is notable for the highly developed musical culture at the abbey, which resulted in the lost repertory listed at the end of Harley 978.[302]

William de Winton

William is linked to the *Sumer* Canon through the contents of his book, listed at the end of BL Harley 978. That he was a man of wide interests is indicated by the contents of another of his books, which he gave to Reading Abbey, Bodley MS 848. This includes treatises not only on theology but also on arithmetic, geometry and astronomy. The texts for *Sumer is icumen in* are in both English and Latin. The English text is now accepted as primary, as there is no Latin text for the *pes*. The canon was, therefore, in origin a secular work. The sacred Latin text commencing *Perspice Christicola* was added to render the rota suitable for inclusion in the Harley manuscript. Furthermore, this is no 'Summer' Canon, as it is sometimes called. In the Middle Ages *Sumer* of the title began at Hocktide, the second Monday and Tuesday after Easter. The English text is that of a spring song, a celebration of spring, the season of the cuckoo's return, when the young man's fancy turns to love.[303]

> Summer has arrived, loudly sing 'cuckoo'. The seed grows and the meadow blooms and now the trees put forth shoots. The ewe bleats after the lamb, the cow lows after the calf. The bullock leaps, the buck farts, merrily sing 'cuckoo'. Cuckoo, cuckoo! You sing well, cuckoo, never stop now.

A recent study by Wulstan gives a very different, earthy, picture of William de Winton, drawing out the double entendre of the hunting theme. This is supported by the charges brought against him by Bishop, later Saint Thomas, Cantilupe in January 1282. The hunting theme is bluntly stated:

> ... Bulluc sterteth, bucke verteth,
> murie sing cuc-cu. Cuc-cu, cuc-cu,
> Wel singes thu cuc-cu, ne swik thu naver nu.

The medieval English *cuckewold* was an adaptation from the French, drawn from cuckoo, the bird that lays its eggs in another's nest. In 16th-century England the cuckoo was 'the cuckold's quirester'. Even for Plautus, writing his plays c200 BC, refers to a wronged man as a cuckoo. Wulstan sees William de Winton viewing himself as 'a rutting buck in pursuit of the doe'. 'The cuckoo's song as the harbinger of spring is double-edged, and the striking phrase about 'the buck farting' is, for Wulstan, 'a triumphant snook cocked at some unfortunate husband, a startled buck the taking of whose deer he celebrates as a merry lay'. As for the hunting theme, the pair of horns remains the symbol of the cuckold. Certainly, Winton's conduct whilst sub-prior at Leominster suggests that this interpretation of the text of *Sumer is icumen in* is in no way extravagant.[304]

Burgate completed the trio mentioned in Harley 978, for the list of contents at the end indicates he was composer of the Gloria trope, *Spiritus et alme*, the first piece of the missing repertory at the end of the manuscript. It was he who despatched Winton to Leominster, where he was a member of the community at the time of Cantilupe's 1276 visitation. By January 1282 Winton was sub-prior. Cantilupe, receiving allegations of Winton's gross incontinence with a canoness at the Augustinian priory of Limebrook, amongst others, summoned the sub-prior to appear before him to answer the charges. On his failure to appear, Winton's proctor gave an undertaking that he would attend the next law day, under penalty of a 13s 4d fine. Again Winton failed to appear.

Excommunicated by Cantilupe, he sidestepped the sentence by demanding the protection of the Canterbury archiepiscopal court on the grounds of an appeal to Rome.[305] By May Abbot Burgate had recalled Winton and his prior, Kington, to Reading. He then appointed Winton one of his five official advisers on the administration of the bankrupt abbey (see chapter 15).

There has been considerable speculation of the musical origins of the *Sumer* Canon. Dittmer believed that several Harley *Alleluia* settings came close to matching compositions in the 'Worcester' fragments. Attention has also been drawn to a passage in Giraldus Cambrensis's *Description of Wales* (1194). The Welsh, he tells us, 'do not sing in unison like the people of other countries but in many different parts in a company of singers, which one meets with frequently in Wales, you will hear as many different parts and voices as there are performers who at length unite, with organic melody, in one consonance and the soft sweetness of B flat'. A Bury St Edmunds chronicler also makes reference to a 'Westcuntre' music style, wherein intervals of major and minor thirds are much used. It has even been suggested that the evidence shows that 'the (Harley) type of *Alleluia* came from Leominster/Worcester, was represented also at Reading and is associated with William de Wicumbe, who was, if not the actual composer, at least actively associated with the compositions in question'. However, the 'links between Reading and Worcester now appear slim — if not non-existent', as Losseff points out.[306]

To understand the remarkable developments in polyphony at Reading, it has to be placed in a wider context, especially the literary items with which the music is found. These include *lais* of Marie de France, in which 'the love is always between persons of an exalted social status, often adulterous (a young wife closely guarded by a jealous old husband)' and 'not platonic, the physical union being discreetly alluded to as the ultimate goal'. They also include poems of the Goliards, 'educated jesters, buffoons and authors of loose or satirical Latin verse', and for the 19th century 'ribald clerks'. 'In very old French verse' are 'fabulous stories of love and strange adventures called *hais*, which were sung to the harp, as it appears in one of the tales'. This gives us a brief but valuable insight into the cultural milieu of William de Wicumbe and his associates at Reading. For John Harper, 'there is a possibility that the Latin text, *Perspice Christicola*, for Easter, could have been sung in the Priory', presumably during William de Winton's sub-priorate.[307]

15 Parish and Convent in the 13th Century

On the priory's foundation the spiritual responsibilities, which had rested with the minster priests and their predecessors for some four and a half centuries, passed to the abbot of Reading. The building of the new parish church, as the nave of the priory, has been described, but what of the clergy who served that church and its chapels? On the fate of the last minster priests the records are silent, apart from the reference to Ailwin, described as a 'canon' in a grant of Abbot Roger (1158–65). News of a conflict between the prior and the vicar of Leominster reached Bishop William de Vere (1186–98) during the vacancy of the vicarage. The former vicar, who had previously held the parochial altar with the chapelry of Hope-under-Dinmore, had received annually twelve sheaves from each virgate cultivated by his parishioners. These were due to him as scriftcorn, that is churchscot, payment to support spiritual care. The prior, however, representing the abbot as patron, claimed that, in the collection of these sheaves, tithes due to the vicar had been lost.

To resolve the matter, de Vere agreed that both tithes and scriftcorn would be paid direct to the monks, who would then grant the incoming vicar, Walter of Stockton, the cash equivalent, 6s 8d, in lieu of his scriftcorn. Walter was also to receive 1d 'and no more' for each Requiem Mass; reasonable dues for burials; payment for saying trentals, that is 30 such Masses for the repose of the souls of the dead, and for hearing confessions during Lent; pennies for marriages 'offered on the book at the priory door'; and all bread and ale offered by the faithful of Leominster and Hope-under-Dinmore. 'On account of the scattered nature of the parishes', Walter was to be assisted by three chaplains, who were to receive no more than 1d for each Mass said, together with the bread and ale offered by the faithful. Otherwise vicar and chaplains were to be fed at the monks' table. Such payments for Requiem Masses, trentals, confessions etc were to be the subject of virulent attacks by the Lollards, in particular by a local man, Walter le Brut, who gained considerable support amongst the abbot's manorial tenants (see p197). In all matters spiritual, authority in relation to the vicarage was to rest with the bishop.[308]

The difficulties were not resolved to the abbot's satisfaction. Maintaining that the parishioners were still failing to pay their tithes, he obtained papal condemnation of their actions. This de Vere commanded Walter and his chaplains to enforce, implying that they had been the cause of the problem. The truth, in all probability, was that many parishioners were confused as to the distinction between the two dues. However, it may well have been, as de Vere mentioned, that the burgesses of Leominster took the lead in this matter. Certainly, as incoming vicar, Walter of Stockton was in a weak bargaining position vis-à-vis the abbot in establishing the cash equivalent of his scriftcorn. A charter of Bishop Hugh Foliot c1230 notes that the vicar was to receive £2 per annum from the abbot of Reading's income from Leominster in addition to the 6s 8d granted c1186.[309]

The vicar's responsibilities were indeed wide-ranging, extending from the chapel at Hope-under-Dinmore in the south, through Leominster to further chapelries at Kimbolton, Lucton, Eye,

Fig 15.1 St James's church at Kimbolton, predominantly 13th century, from the Priory tower

Yarpole, Middleton-on-the-Hill, close to the county boundary, and Brimfield, with Ford (on the Lugg) being added c1217, and Stoke Prior and Docklow by 1291. Evidence of 12th-century work remains in some of these chapels. The most impressive is at Middleton, with its abundant zigzag decoration and billet moulding, both reminiscent of that on the west front of the priory. Kimbolton chancel probably dates from the first half of the 12th century. The nave was rebuilt later in the century. At Docklow, chancel and nave were rebuilt in 1880, but the early parts of their north and south walls may also be 12th century, and some reset stone fragments suggest Brimfield was built, at least in part, in the same period. In the 13th century towers were added at Docklow, Middleton, Brimfield and Kimbolton, where a south transept was also built at this time (Fig 15.1). Elsewhere evidence is lacking. Brimfield was rebuilt in 1834; Lucton in 1850; Ford in 1851 and Stoke Prior in 1863. Hope was drastically restored in 1879.[310]

Leominster: The new parochial south nave, south porch and north aisle windows

Where the nave served as a parish church in Benedictine abbeys and Augustinian priories, joint use almost always led to acrimony between convent and parish. Probably the most common causes of dispute were the clash of services and the ringing of bells. The outcome in many places was the building of a separate parish church within the Outer Court. Indeed, at Evesham and Bury St Edmunds two such churches were constructed. Less common was the decision to build onto the monastic church, as at Sherborne, where in the 15th century a parish church of six bays was attached to the west end of the abbey.

At Leominster the parish church was enlarged in the first half of the 13th and again in the 14th century. The expansion of the borough's street plan is described in the next chapter. At Leominster the replacement of the priory's Romanesque south aisle with a much larger, Early-English structure, now the south nave, is firm evidence of urban growth. It was also a powerful expression

Fig 15.2a&b Leominster Priory: details of corbels

of growing civic pride. A broad pilaster buttress to the south of the present great perpendicular window, built to harmonise with those of the Norman west front, confirms that the new south nave was similar in height to that we see today. Its pitched roof was designed to retain clerestory lighting for the monastic nave to its north. The carved corbels projecting at clerestory level from the north nave are of 15th-century date (Figs 15.2a&b). On the exterior of the west wall, a vertical break in the masonry is clearly visible under the great west window, showing that the base of the old west wall was incorporated in the new work (Fig 15.3). The new south aisle will have given an impressive sense of space, for it was almost 2ft wider than the Romanesque nave, and more than twice the width of the Romanesque south aisle. Whereas previously the view from the west had been marked by a change in floor levels and obstructed by the tower-

Fig 15.3 The break in masonry in the west wall indicates the width of the original Romanesque south asile

Fig 15.4 Dorchester Abbey, also an ancient minster church, showing parochial extension to canons' south aisle

Fig 15.5 Reset Early English capitals of the South porch

Fig 15.6 Bell-cote

arches, now the parishioners could enjoy the full view down all six bays. This was not the only such south aisle extension of a monastic church. Further examples can be seen at Blyth Priory, where the south aisle of c1290 is the width of the adjacent transept, and at Dorchester Abbey, Oxon (Fig 15.4).[311]

Today visual evidence of this Early-English south nave is slight. When a south aisle was added in the 1320s, the southern, external, wall of the new south nave was replaced by an arcade, and its piscina moved to serve the new south aisle altar (see Plate 8). The east end of the south nave was formed by the western wall of the monastic south transept, which was demolished at the Dissolution and has now been replaced with more recent work. The only major work of the early 13th century still visible is the parochial south porch. This was an important part of the rebuilding programme, because it meant that from 1239 the parishioners no longer had to share the Norman west portal with the monks. In the 1320s its Early-English stiff leaf capitals and shafts were incorporated into a second south porch, to serve the new south aisle (Plate 6). A similar parochial south porch was added at Blyth. A Sanctus bell-cote was constructed at the south-west angle of the new building. This bell was rung only at the elevation of the elements during the Mass. In the 1320s the bell-cote was moved to its present position above the new south-west pilaster (Fig 15.6).

The south nave was consecrated by Bishop Ralph Maidstone in 1239. During the 19th-century restorations a cross was found, painted within a circle under what is now the 15th-century west window. In heraldic terms, this was a cross formée, the arms widening from the centre. It was one of twelve crosses symbolising the apostles as the pillars of the church, painted on the interior and exterior when Bishop Maidstone reconsecrated the church on completion of the new south nave. As the plasterwork was in very poor condition, a tracing of the cross was taken and a copy painted on the precise spot.[312]

Fig 15.7 North aisle. Three-light windows with transoms at the east end

Further alterations were made, to provide more light for the early-12th-century north aisle. Three sets of lancets set into gables were built towards the eastern end of the aisle. Each originally consisted of five pointed and graduated lights, but after the Dissolution the two easternmost were rebuilt as three-light windows, with transoms added to give extra strength (Fig 15.7). These two, and the original third window, are shown on a sketch made by Freeman in the early 1850s (Fig 15.8). Later two new windows of the modified type were added, one at the east and

Fig 15.8 W.H. Freeman's sketch c1853. Two replacement and original third window

the other at the west end, whilst the original five-light window was completely restored (Fig 15.9). At the west end of the north aisle, below the Romanesque round window, a triplet of lancets was inserted, to provide further light (Fig 15.10). Despite the construction of the new south nave, both north aisle and 12th-century nave were evidently retained for full parochial use, as such a dramatic increase in the amount of light entering the northern part of the church would not have been a priority for the monks, who used the area west of the pulpitum but briefly, during their weekly processions.

When Thomas Cantilupe arrived for an episcopal visitation in 1275, the parishioners formally complained that they were not permitted free access to their church at every hour of the day and night. This led to a major confrontation between the bishop and Abbot Robert Burgate. Evidence given at this time confirms that the parish had paid for the early-13th-century building programme, and that the bells had been provided for parochial use. These bells, not to be confused with the Sanctus bell, became a further cause of dispute between monks and parishioners.

Fig 15.9 North aisle. Restored five-lancet window

The Wheel of Life

On the north wall of the priory's western bay is a large painting, dated c1275, of the Wheel of Life, depicting the six Ages of Man (Plate 11a). Although the wall painting was intended for a lay audience, this was a concept with which the monks had long been familiar. St Augustine had formulated the relationship between the six days of creation, the six ages of the world, that is from creation to the sixth era, which opened with the preaching of Jesus, and the six ages of man: infancy, childhood, adolescence, physical prime, maturity and old age. Isidore of Seville followed Augustine's six-fold division in Book XI, 'On Man and Monsters', in his encyclopaedic *Etymologies*, of which there was a copy in the priory's library list of c1180–91 (Fig 13.1, 1.23). At Leominster, however, there are not six but ten Ages of Man. Such a tenfold division probably originated in the Wheel of Fortune, as found in Boethius' 6th-century *Consolation of Philosophy*.[313]

Fig 15.10 North aisle. 13th-century triplet of lancets

The wall painting was discovered during the 1860s restoration of the Romanesque church, when whitewash was removed from the north wall, during which process much of the original painting was lost. George Gilbert Scott's intervention, at a late stage, saved what was left. Much of that has now deteriorated even further. To flesh out what remains we are dependent on the detailed examination and report made by G. McN. Rushforth and C.T. Praetorius after a visit early in the 20th century, at which time this area was being used as a coal cellar. From similar details in the Wheel of Life in Robert de Lisle's Psalter, Rushforth and Praetorius were able to identify the subjects of five of the Leominster medallions, together with that in the centre.[314]

The wheel is some 7ft in diameter. The ten medallions, depicting the Ten Ages, are connected by spokes to a central medallion. Around the rim vestiges of texts, in Lombardic script, relate to the subjects of some of the medallions. In the de Lisle Psalter these inscriptions encircle the individual medallions. Most legible parts of the priory inscriptions correspond to those in the Psalter, the only significant difference being the text of Early Manhood, which Rushforth reads as *Iam non visus specie sed vita letatur*, 'no longer does comeliness of appearance (or visage) please me'. This urged the parishioners to look beyond the vanities and transitoriness of worldly life.

With help from the de Lisle Psalter, Rushforth and Praetorius completed a number of the Leominster texts. The central medallion depicts the head of God, or Christ, against a red background, with the text, 'I see all, at once; I govern the whole by My plan'. At 7 o'clock is the first Age, Infancy (1): a woman holding her child, with the text: 'I am gentle and humble; I live on pure milk'. According to Rushforth and Praetorius she is in bed, but the recent cleaning may have revealed that, as in the de Lisle Psalter, she is sitting, with the child on her lap. Moving clockwise, there are (2) Boyhood, (3) Youth and (4) Early Manhood, all defaced. At the top is (5) Maturity, which Rushforth describes as a king enthroned, with the text: 'I am a king. I rule the world; the whole world is mine.' (6) Decline, is defaced. (7) Decrepitude: an old, blind and bowed man with a stick, has a child to his right. For Rushforth the old man's left hand did not rest on the boy's shoulder but was raised as if addressing or threatening him. (8) is defaced. The two last medallions, with (1), are the most detailed: (9) the Last Rites, with a standing figure on the left, another in the centre, and possibly the dying person on the right; and (10) Burial, a standing figure (the priest, with the coffin below?).

The background to the Wheel is painted with rectangular masonry. Both the blocks and their delicate scrolls of foliage are outlined in maroon. At the bottom, on the left, is the seated figure of David, crowned, wearing a flowing cloak and pointed footwear, and playing a harp. For Rushforth this has 'eleven strings if not more' (Plate 11b). Praetorius shows two other figures clearly visible above. The only other English wall painting depicting a Wheel of Life is nearby, at Kempley church. Attributed to the 15th-century, it also is on the north wall, has ten medallions, and what appears to be God or Christ in the central medallion. A possible third representation, in the north aisle of the nave of St Albans Cathedral, is almost completely erased, and identification remains doubtful.[315]

Financial Problems, 1245–c1289

First evidence of the acute financial crisis that plagued Reading and Leominster for 45 years, or more, came in 1245. As patron, Henry III intervened, requesting the abbot's knights, freemen and other tenants to give a subsidy to help the abbey meet its debts. As this evoked little response, he issued a further letter, regretting their reluctance and repeating his request.[316] The reasons for debt were twofold. Lavish and uncontrolled expenditure had continued, despite the ordinance of a church council at Oxford in 1221, that all obedientiaries should submit quarterly or half-yearly accounts. At Reading even annual accounts were not submitted, and in this respect the abbey was far from unique. The cellarer, sacristan, precentor and other obedientiaries all received earmarked income from specific sources, which they were free to use as they saw fit. Control, in so far as it existed, was dependent on the abbot's strength of will.[317]

Hospitality, above all that due to the abbey's patron, the king, was the other principal cause of debt. On a major national routeway, and with a splendid environment, Reading was especially vulnerable. Henry II held court there at both Whitsun, 1175 and Easter, 1177. It was a favourite resting place of Henry III, who stayed their with his entourage on several occasions. John stayed at Leominster in August 1216, shortly before his death. His son, Henry III rested at the priory on a number of occasions during his wars with the Welsh, in 1223, 1226, 1232 and 1233.[318] Such visits, whilst they could lead to gifts and the granting of favours such as charters for markets and fairs, imposed enormous burdens. A visit by Edward I to Peterborough cost the abbey £487 out if its annual income of £620.[319]

Little, if anything, was done to resolve these problems. In 1253 Henry III renewed his requests to the abbot's freemen and tenants to provide a reasonable aid to enable the abbey to pay off its manifold debts. Reading's indebtedness was not unusual. Amongst the Benedictines Canterbury Cathedral Priory owed £2,500 in 1255, despite the vast offerings at the shrine of Thomas Becket, and Peterborough and Gloucester some £2,000 each. The king sought to restrain Reading's creditors, both the Sienese merchants, Hugh and John Bonaventura, and members of the English Jewry.[320] With the election of Robert Burgate as abbot in July 1269, matters deteriorated even further. Reading and Leominster were afflicted not only by debt but also by serious breakdowns in monastic discipline.

Edward I came to the throne late in 1272. Unlike his father, as royal patron he was not prepared to let matters drift. Having repeated his father's requests to the abbot's men, he informed the Sienese merchants on 5 February 1275 that the abbey should be allowed two years to repay moneys outstanding. On 23 February he ordered that all servants and horses, with their keepers, lodged by the Crown and others at Reading and Leominster should be removed until abbey and priory were relieved of debt. In December Edward appointed Roland de Herleye, knight, as custodian of Leominster Priory. Herleye was to apply all income to the discharge of debt, except such sums as were required to find the prior and monks in food and clothing and, in accordance with Henry I's charter, to provide poor mendicants with alms. The phrase, 'by view of the abbot and prior of Reading', was added to the royal command as a face-saver for Abbot Burgate. The cause of all the problems was financial maladministration at Reading, not Leominster, for even in 1291 the priory was remitting £240, almost 80% of its a total income of £303 3s, to the mother house. Despite the measures he had introduced to re-establish solvency, Edward I stayed overnight at Leominster on 8 December 1283. In 1285 he appointed one of his royal clerks, John de Bruges, to the custody of the priory.[321]

Archbishop Peckham also intervened, twice, in attempts to solve Reading's debt problems. In 1281 he proposed the establishment of a central treasury, supervised by three treasurers who would control all income, and that the finances of abbot, obedientiaries and community at large should be combined. By 1284, however, cash was so short that even the dispersal of monks to Leominster and other houses was contemplated. The bishop of Salisbury, during a visitation later that year, recommended the appointment of five 'advisers' to the abbot. These were evidently chosen by Burgate, for the two Leominster recalcitrants, John de Kington and William de Winton, were included. Despite the combined efforts of archbishop and bishop, the abbey's debts only escalated. In March 1286 Edward I finally appointed Ralph de Broughton, royal clerk, as custodian of abbey and priory, with all goods and revenues pertaining.

At Leominster, despite the king's injunctions and the presence of a royal clerk, the prior had been contracting short-term loans from a member of the Hereford Jewry, probably Aaron son of Elias le Blund. In April 1287, with the authority of Edward I's Exchequer of the Jews at Westminster, the creditor was foreclosing on the priory's cattle. The king intervened personally, ordering the sheriff of Herefordshire to return the cattle and take no further action on the debts incurred by the prior. By 1289 Broughton claimed he had restored Reading to solvency. However, when Nicholas Whaplode was elected abbot in 1305, he discovered debts exceeding £1,200. Whaplode introduced fundamental economies, including a scrupulous examination of all accounts, the reduction in the number of servants to 37, and of refections (special pittances, extra dishes, and feast days, paid for by the various obedientiaries for the community) to ten. Debt remained a problem, for in 1364, in order to 'act prudently and moderate his expenses', Abbot William Dumbleton returned for a year to Leominster, where he had been prior.[322]

Episcopal Visitations 1276, 1283 and 1286

During the 12th century the Benedictines had been almost entirely free from external control. This problem was addressed by Pope Innocent III at the Fourth Lateran Council of 1215, by restoring episcopal responsibility for discipline in almost all monastic houses. However, only from the mid 13th century did episcopal visitation become common, and full records were rarely included in the bishop's registers.[323] It is thus fortunate indeed that the first register for Hereford diocese is that of Thomas Cantilupe, 1275–82, who included extended details of his visitation of Leominster Priory in 1276. The prior, Stephen Watton, had ordered that the church door be closed against the parishioners during celebration of the offices and at night-time. This is a reference to the door of the south porch, *quondam portam versus ecclesiam parochialem*, the Romanesque west portal being reserved for the monks. Watton claimed that, with no structural division other than the pulpitum between the monastic and parochial churches, the clamour of the laity interfered with the monastic offices. The parishioners naturally appealed to their bishop, who responded by a formal visitation, only six months after his consecration.

Cantilupe arrived at Leominster early in January 1277. On the first day he devoted himself to an examination of parochial affairs. The next day, the 11th, he visited the priory, accompanied by a clerical entourage totalling 36, mostly members of his household. They included his Official, Master Luke de Brée, also acting dean and treasurer of the cathedral, and Master Adam de Fileby, canon of the cathedral and of St Martin's, London, who frequently acted as the bishop's proctor. Three local vicars, Adam of Leominster, Herbert of Shobdon and Thomas of Aymestry, were also present, as were numerous chaplains, deacons, sub-deacons and others. The visitation opened in the chapter-house with a sermon by the bishop, propounding the Word of God. Cantilupe then examined the prior, Stephen de Watton, and sub-prior, Robert de Fikeldene; Master Gilbert de Heywood, one of his clerks, examined brothers William de Winton, the owner of the book whose contents are listed at the end of BL Harley 978 (see Fig 14.1), who was to become sub-prior by 1282, Jordan de Multone and Richard de Winton; whilst de Brée examined John de Tudyntone, suggesting a total of merely six monks, half the normal complement.[324]

At the end of March Cantilupe wrote his formal letter, *comperta*, to prior and convent, detailing those matters needing correction. First was the problem of the door. 'Although', he explained, 'your church should be common to all the faithful, especially the parishioners, at every hour, we found the door closed both in summer and in winter'. As a result, many evils had ensued and many more were likely to do so in the future. He provided four examples. 'The pure Body of Christ cannot be perpetually reserved in a place anything but sacred and perchance dirty and unworthy or without that reverence which so great a mystery requires to the no small scandal of the clergy and contrary to Christian religion'. 'Likewise the sacrament ... cannot be given to the dying at all hours.' 'Persons fleeing to the church for sanctuary have to endure repulse at times of urgent necessity.' Finally the parochial clergy 'are unable to say their offices and the parishioners cannot pray and pour forth their petitions to the Most High for their sins. Unable to do so, growing weary with standing, they return home and their devotions grow cold. Thus the church is often defrauded of its dues and the cure of souls is neglected.'

Cantilupe then turned to the matter of the bells. 'In every parish in the kingdom it is customary for bells to be rung at certain hours to stir the devotion so that the parishioners may attend services and seek pardon for their misdoings and hear the Divine Offices. We cannot but be surprised that the bells which were provided at the cost of the parishioners, for their use, are never rung nor allowed to be rung from which they do not pay what is due to their Creator.' We know that the Sanctus or sacring bell was in its cote on the west front, but not where the parochial bells were housed. They could not have been hung with the monastic bells in a central tower. However there would have been ample space at the west end of the Romanesque nave, as they would have been much smaller in the 13th century than those we know today. Otherwise a small wooden tower may have served.[325]

There were other serious shortcomings. On Sundays and feast days, the monks engaged in worldly affairs, a pernicious example that the laity followed. The rents and possessions granted by their founder, King Henry I, and others, for the daily distribution of alms to the poor and indigent, were cut short. The priory's responsibility to provide alms, despite the firm economies imposed elsewhere, were underlined in Edward I's letter of 1275, appointing Roland de Herleye as custodian of the priory. Cantilupe concluded his letter, 'we cannot connive or wink at these things which we beg and exhort you to correct by Trinity Sunday', 8 June that year. He then warned the community, 'Show yourselves zealous and careful, that you may receive a fitting reward from the Giver of all good things at the Day of Judgment'.[326]

With Abbot Burgate, who regarded Thomas's efforts as an encroachment on the liberties of his abbey, such words fell on stony ground. In May Cantilupe was obliged to adjourn once more his planned second visitation, for Burgate had gained the ear of Edward I. In August Cantilupe wrote to the king, requesting him not to countenance any further attempts at delay, and on 13th again ordered Prior Watton to give the parishioners that freedom of access to their church which he had repeatedly enjoined. Eleven days later, this having had no effect, Cantilupe told Watton either to remove the offending doors by the Sunday after the feast of the Exaltation of the Cross, 14 September, or face a £20 penalty for disobedience. Watton remained obdurate. The monks offered stout resistance, but the bishop was successful in having the doors forcibly removed from its hinges — but not for long.[327]

Cantilupe's challenge to the abbot's authority was formidable, for he had selected his ground well. The bishop was acting with due propriety in responding to the appeal of his flock. At Leominster, as at Reading, the burgesses had little love either for their lord, the abbot, or for his prior. Personal names, such as that of Thomas de Radyng, with John Cokyng Leominster's first Members of Parliament, demonstrate the firm family links between the two towns; thus the people of Leominster will have been fully conscious of the privileges the townsmen of Reading had wrung from the abbot in 1254. Relations between townsmen and abbot at Reading had deteriorated to such an extent by 1253 that a number of burgesses were slain. The abbot claimed that the burgesses lay in wait, day and night, for his bailiffs, assaulting them in the execution of their duties. In 1254 the burgesses secured a confirmation from the royal courts that Reading should have its own governing body, guild merchant, with all its appurtenances. This decision Henry III ratified in 1266. At Leominster, by contrast, the burgesses felt a deep affront to their civic pride by their exclusion from the church in which they had invested so handsomely some 35 years earlier.[328]

Cantilupe, a student first at Oxford and then at Paris, had been appointed a papal chaplain at the age of seventeen. He then studied law at Orleans and canon law at Paris, where his tutor was the Franciscan John Peckham, later archbishop of Canterbury. Twice chancellor of the university of Oxford, Cantilupe subsequently served as chancellor of the realm. Elected bishop of Hereford in 1275, he was not loath to stress the dignity of his office. A true lawyer, he defended 'every right of his church however insignificant with a vigour excessive — even by medieval standards'. The Leominster burgesses had found a firm champion. As late as September 1279, despite the matters raised at the visitation, relations between Cantilupe and Prior Stephen de Watton were, at least on the surface, reasonable, for Cantilupe found no difficulty in writing to Stephen, asking him to give hospitality to his valet, William de Neville, whilst he was out of the diocese.[329]

Cantilupe now became embroiled in conflict with Archbishop Peckham over a complex legal issue concerning the administration of a will. As this eventually led to his withdrawal to France, from July 1280 to October 1281 his legal battle with the abbot of Reading had to be conducted through his diocesan officers, in particular Robert de Gloucester, alias le Wyse, who was responsible for the bishop's coercive juridsiction. By May 1281 Abbot Burgate had transferred Stephen de Watton from Leominster to Reading's dependency on the Isle of May in the Firth of Forth. This was apparently linked to Burgate's efforts to sell May to the Scots. Following the appointment of English priors, King Alexander III had become alarmed at the danger of espionage. Burgate wanted money, and after Alexander's death he came to an agreement with William Fraser, bishop of St Andrews, now guardian of the Scots realm. To the scandal of many churchmen and the majority of Reading's monks, Burgate sold May to Fraser for £1,000.[330]

The conflict now moved to new, and for Cantilupe very unsure, ground, a challenge to the abbot of Reading's right to transfer monks, including prior and sub-prior, to and from his cell of

Leominster. Stephen's successor at Leominster was John de Kington; his sub-prior none other than William de Winton. When John refused to present himself for episcopal institution, as contrary to the privileges of the abbot of Reading, he was excommunicated by Cantilupe's Official, Robert de Gloucester. In July 1281 Edward I intervened, requesting Cantilupe not to molest the monk sent by the abbot to take custody of what the royal letter refers to as the 'manor', not the priory, of Leominster — evidently a repetition of the telling term that Burgate had used in his complaint to the king. Cantilupe replied, assuring Edward he had been misinformed, but as an appeal had been made against the execution, he would stay any further action until Christmas. Despite a personal letter from Cantilupe, Burgate refused to remove the prior, in the bishop's terminology 'the monk who is the cause of this dispute'. The appeal to Canterbury and Rome inhibited Cantilupe from any further action.[331]

In January 1282 Cantilupe believed he had a trump card. *Sumer is icumen in* had proved to be more than mere romantic yearning. William de Winton, Kington's sub-prior, was ordered to appear before the bishop to answer charges of 'incontinence with Agnes de Avenbury, an Augustinian canoness of Limebrook, and certain other women', the cause of widespread scandal. Despite the passage of some 20 years, the old buck was apparently still in pursuit of his does. Indeed, some three years earlier Cantilupe had made a formal visitation of Limebrook Priory. In his report to the prioress and nuns he found it necessary to refer to 'the frailty of your sex', by which they 'were more exposed to the snares of the devil. You should keep yourselves with all restraint and close the gates of your senses less an entrance be open to the evil spirit ... the flame of evil desires or at least fickle imagination'. They should occupy themselves in prayer, thus 'when temptation comes you fall not into sin. You must repress your bodily senses, remembering that between you and the world a great gulf is fixed.' Finally, he gave a firm warning. Especial care must be taken in the choice of confessors. They must be men of exemplary character, such as the Grey Friars of Hereford. No others should be admitted, 'save with our special licence'. After excommunication by Cantilupe, Winton, with Burgate's assistance, evaded sentence by an appeal to Rome. By May, however, his authority at Leominster assured, Burgate had brought both Winton and Kington back to Reading. Events were to show that the new prior, John Gerard, was no improvement.[332]

On 7 February a final confrontation had taken place between Archbishop Peckham and Cantilupe in the great hall of Lambeth Palace. Peckham castigated Cantilupe as a wolf in sheep's clothing, as of deranged intellect and an utterer of blasphemous mendacities. He then had a document read out. Whether this was a formal sentence or merely a threat of excommunication was a matter of great confusion, even at the time. Thomas died at Montefiascone on 25 August, on the last leg of his journey to conduct his own defence at Rome.[333]

The problem of the priory's closed door was apparently resolved by Peckham's intervention. Six weeks after Cantilupe's death he arrived at Hereford for an archiepiscopal visitation of his diocese, which was without a bishop until Swinfield's accession in March 1283. Peckham was in Leominster on 3 December, when he familiarised himself with the details of the conflict between monks and parishioners. In January he wrote from the episcopal palace at Sugwas, ordering the restoration of the doors, but commanding that the prior and convent should build a chapel at the gates of the precinct dedicated to the glorious martyr, Thomas of Canterbury, where the sacrament should be reserved and sanctuary could be sought.[334] When completed, the Forbury chapel was but a humble structure, some 60 by 28 feet, lit at the east end by a simple triple lancet window with three plain lancets on the south, a west door and a further lancet at the west end (Fig 15.11). The timber roof had to be replaced in the early 16th century. The existing roof is of five scissor trusses on hammer beams. Evidently the original bell-cote had also to be replaced, for the small timber structure shown on the RCHM photograph was dated 1729.[335]The building of even this simple structure was completed only in the early 15th century, for the monks embarked on it with the utmost reluctance. The parishioners were not impressed by their new chapel, even when completed — but it was some 40 years before they could take effective action.

Cantilupe's death did not end the dispute with the abbot of Reading. The matter of the bishop of Hereford's jurisdiction at Leominster was taken up again by his familiar and successor, Richard Swinfield, 1283-1317, who was devoted to Cantilupe. Untiringly, throughout his episcopate, he worked for Cantilupe's canonisation, which came three years after Swinfield's death. Within a month of his consecration, on 6 April, 1283 Swinfield carried out the first of two visitations of Leominster Priory. Like Cantilupe, he was accompanied by an impressive retinue, which included four members of the cathedral chapter, one of whom was later elected bishop of London, the abbot of Wigmore and the rectors of Eastnor and Colwall, as well as Adam, vicar of Leominster, who had attended Cantilupe seven years before. Swinfield himself, sitting in the chapter-house, examined John Gerard, the prior, Thomas de Wakyntone, the almoner, and brothers Nicholas de Byflet and Robert de Burley; Master Roger de Sevenake, a canon who was to be elected cathedral treasurer in 1295, examined brothers Maurice de Henle and Elmirus, whilst Robert de Gloucester, the chancellor, examined brothers Pain, Robert de Winchesburne and Richard de Winton. There were now nine monks, as compared to the six in 1276. The bishop's register carries no details of the findings, but these emerged in 1286 when the prior's failure to address them led to Swinfield's second visitation.[336] In the meantime at Reading in May 1285 Swinfield had to retract the most important of the claims which he and Cantilupe had made regarding Leominster Priory. He was obliged to confirm the right of the abbot and convent to move monks to and from their priory at Leominster according to the terms of Bishop Hugh Foliot's charter, itself a reiteration of Bishop Hugh de Mapenore's charter of 1217x1218.[337]

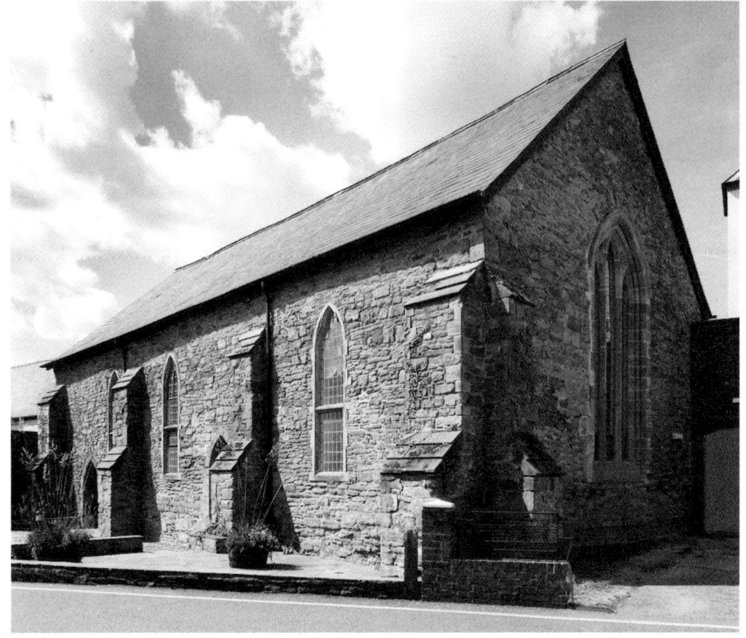

Fig 15.11 The late 13th-century Forbury chapel of St Thomas the martyr, a chapel at the gates

Swinfield was in no way deterred in his efforts to restore discipline at Leominster. At his second visitation, in December 1286, he deplored the fact that the number of monks still fell short of the lawful complement. He itemised five occasions on which fines, now totalling £150, had been incurred for neglect of episcopal injunctions. Six months later, 'weary of his life due to the great scandals which the clergy and people of his diocese suffer' on account of the behaviour of the prior and his monks, he wrote one letter to Burgate and another to his prior and convent. The letter to Burgate was forthright about John Gerard, the man he had selected to be prior, whose pernicious example gave rise to so many scandals. Not only did he forsake the religious life, 'hunting, hawking and hallooing in the woods' with shady characters, he also 'entertained vile and disreputable persons, of both sexes, as table companions, wasting the goods and possessions of his house'. But far worse was his 'extravagant and gross incontinence with many women including two daughters of one family'.[338]

Fig 15.12a Forbury chapel: a detail of 16th-century hammer beam roof

Turning to more general matters, Swinfield reports that the solemn contracts itemised at the last visitation remained disregarded and that failings in the monastic life were numerous. The Divine Offices were inadequately performed, the customary alms-giving and hospitality, enjoined by the foundation charter, had largely been set aside. Furthermore, the parishioners were unable to gain free access to their church, for the door was yet closed. This had evidently been the case for almost four years, as it had been reported at the first visitation that only minimal work had been undertaken on Archbishop Peckham's resolution of the vexed issue of the locked door, the building of the chapel at the gates.

Pleasures of the chase were not restricted to Leominster. Close at hand the abbot of Gloucester had eight sporting dogs and four greyhounds. At Peterborough and Chester the abbots had sporting rights. The Whitby monks hunted on the moors with bows and arrows, the Lanercost Augustinians had their own pack of eight hounds and a deer-leap. At Dunstable the prior went ferreting on the downs. Even the Cistercians had to be ordered not to keep sporting dogs or falcons. For Leominster, however, with hunting as so much else, the problem lay at Reading, where Peckham had also forbidden the monks to hunt or to keep hawks. This prohibition, one imagines, had no more impact on Burgate than Peckham's orders to build a chapel at the gates at Leominster. Indeed, the abbots of Reading still had their own huntsman in the early 14th century, and the chase was not their sole indulgence.[339]

The way Burgate conducted his abbacy explains much of Reading's financial troubles. He even used the abbey's gold chalice and certain precious books, including three bibles, as pledges for repayment of money. The monks, indignant at his general mismanagement, as well as the sale of their cell on the isle of May, forced Burgate to resign in October 1290.[340] Yet, as noticed, financial problems existed during Nicholas Whaplode's abbacy, 1305–28, and as late as 1361.

Fig 15.12b Forbury chapel, detail of carved head on the hammer beam roof

Collection of Ecclesiastical Taxation

Bells and the transfer of monks were not the only causes of conflict between the bishops of Hereford and abbots of Reading. Throughout the medieval period, conflict continued over the claims by Reading that its priors at Leominster were exempt from the liability of acting as collectors of clerical taxation within the diocese. On this, as on the transfer of monks, Reading's claims were based on the confirmation by Bishop Hugh de (Hampton) Mapenore in 1217x18 of 'the power to appoint and remove monks deputed to the keepership of the priory'. This Mapenore had conveniently linked to what he described as the abbey's 'ancient and established control of monastic affairs at Leominster'. It has been pointed out that, in thus allowing the abbot to appoint and depose the priors at will, Mapenore went well beyond the terms of the confirmation of the abbey's rights as made by his predecessors. This was not the only matter in which Bishop Hugh, a member of a local family, had been generous to the priory.[341]

Mapenore's charter was included not only in the Leominster Cartulary, but in all other extant Reading cartularies, and Abbot Simon wasted no time in obtaining confirmation of the charter, first in 1217x18 from Cardinal Guala, the papal legate in England, and then from Pope Honorius III himself, in July 1219. That he should have gone to such expense is a fair measure of the value he attributed to Mapenore's grant. When in 1285, two years after his first visitation of Leominster, Swinfield rested at Reading, a convenient place on his journey between Hereford and London, he had no option but to confirm the contents of Hugh's charter.[342]

The collection of clerical taxation and tenths was a burdensome, and often costly, task. An East Anglian prior commented pithily that this was 'a shrewd labour, a great cost and a shrewd jeopardy'. With Leominster the only major monastery in the diocese, there were few other clergy competent to assume such responsibilities. A number of Hereford's bishops were successful in persuading some of the priors of Leominster to act as collectors of ecclesiastical taxation within the diocese. Others attempting to do so later were pulled up sharply by the abbots of Reading and, on occasions, even by the Crown, prompted by the abbots. Although Bishop Hugh Foliot had confirmed the Mapenore charter soon after his consecration, he acted jointly with Prior Thomas of Leominster in handing over the receipts of the ecclesiastical fortieth that had been imposed on the clergy and collected in the diocese in 1233. In 1268, immediately prior to Richard Burgate's elevation as abbot, the priors of Leominster and Wenlock acted as joint collectors of the fortieth, and Prior Walter de Maders served as collector of the tenth for Hereford archdeaconry in 1292.[343]

There were no further calls on the priors until 1347, when Trillek testily dismissed the abbot's claim, that Prior John Bray could be removed 'at will', as a mere 'assertion'. A royal writ obliged him to withdraw his commission to Prior Robert of Gloucester to act as collector. In 1384 Bishop Gilbert, 'striving with all his might to impose upon the monks of Leominster the burden of collecting a moiety of the tenth recently granted to the king', was firmly reminded by the Crown that, although Reading monks were 'deputed to celebrate the Divine Office and pray for the king and his progenitors at Leominster, they are removable at will by the abbot, as appears by a composition made between Bishop (Mapenore) and the then abbot of Reading and confirmed by Pope Honorius III'. In consequence, Gilbert was obliged to appoint the rector of Byford and the vicar of All Saints, Hereford, to act in Bray's place. In July 1384 Gilbert did not get his way, when he nominated Bray and his sub-prior, Thomas Chaucombe, as collectors of the subsidy that year. His failure is surprising, for some three and a half months later he took up his appointment as Richard II's treasurer, and thus had as powerful a claim on the Crown as the abbot of Reading.[344]

16 The Monastic Borough

As with the minsters at Capella's episcopal boroughs of Ledbury and Bromyard, Leominster became the primary trading centre for its *parochia*.[345] Unlike at Tewkesbury, Domesday Book provides no evidence of permanent urban settlement at Leominster in 1086, but there can be little doubt that informal trading will have grown up at the gates of the minster from its early days as a mother church. For centuries before the Conquest, the minster would have been the economic focus for the whole of its *parochia*, extending from Orleton and Brimfield in the north to Dinmore Hill in the south, from Titley and Kinnersley in the west to Butterley and Edwyn Ralph, near Bromyard, in the east (see Fig 6.3). On Sundays church attendance will have been combined with all manner of marketing activity. On the great festivals of Easter, Whitsun and Christmas, at the feasts of the patrons, Peter and Paul, on 29 June, and founder, St Edfrith, on 26 October, and to a lesser degree on Sundays throughout the year, the country folk would buy and sell at the precinct's south-west corner. Here, at the *Corncepyng*, as it continued to be called throughout the Middle Ages, the two principal roads of the district met. In 1189 Richard I confirmed Leominster's fair, held on the feast of its patrons, SS Peter and Paul, and the three days following.

Leominster throws new light on the 'Ledbury model' as a conceptual framework for the origins, growth and decline of the other Herefordshire market towns, first enunciated in 1982 and reiterated in 1997 and 2005.[346] Leominster, like Ledbury and Bromyard, was the child of the church. The minster served not only as the spiritual but also as the economic centre of its *parochia*. However, its foundation, in the mid 7th century, was much earlier. More important, it was a royal, not merely an episcopal foundation. This was reflected in the size of its *parochia*, 'one of the largest in England'.

Although the foundation of all three boroughs was the work of Richard de Capella, again Leominster was the earliest foundation. This relationship is reflected in the similarity of the ground plan of Leominster and Ledbury. There is a further distinction. At Leominster evidence for the stages in the subsequent growth is not as clear as at Ledbury, where documentary evidence dates New Street, the final stage in its growth, as 1186. Thus the five principal stages of its development were completed within the remarkably short time of 60 years. It may well have been the same at Leominster, but although the records of the *custos* of the Lady Chapel are very rich, few can be dated. With the advent of the Black Death in 1349, all three boroughs witnessed a catastrophic population decline, and suffered marked contraction, with radical decay on the periphery, but a concentration of numbers at the centre. Leominster, in marked contrast to the two other boroughs, provides evidence of a remarkable economic revival in the 15th century. This is discussed in Chapter 22.

In the late Anglo-Saxon era, church and king had come together to oppose the evil of Lord's Day trading, but Leominster's market continued to be held on Sundays until 1218. In that year the

Council of Regency, under the direction of the papal legate, representing the pope as Henry III's guardian, commanded that the market should thenceforth be held on Thursdays. The economic impact was immediate, as was the reaction of Abbot Simon of Reading, who in 1219 persuaded the Council of Regency to move Leominster's market once more, this time to a Saturday. The bishop of Hereford's market at Ledbury, however, remained on a Sunday right through to the 15th century.[347]

Bishop Richard de Capella was Henry I's agent not only in establishing the extent of the Leominster *parochia*, but also in founding the borough of Leominster — immediately to the west of the precinct. Soon after, acting on his own account, he established three other boroughs, also at the gates of ancient minster churches, at his episcopal manors of Ledbury, Bromyard and Ross. Few were better qualified for this role. Capella, who had served Henry since 1107 as keeper of the royal seal, as master of the scriptorium had been responsible for the preparation and validation of all royal charters. During his early years in office a spate of charters, granting markets and fairs to cathedrals and monasteries, had passed through his hands. Thus he fully appreciated how the great ecclesiastical landowners were tapping the country's rising agricultural production and expanding trade. Three months after his election he persuaded Henry to grant him a fair at Hereford on the feast of St Aethelbert and two days following, with 'as good customs as any fair in England'. What Capella obtained was in reality royal confirmation of a fair, like that at Leominster, held 'since time out of mind'. Co-operation was extended. On Richard's advice, and at the royal command, a bridge was built across the Wye. Its purpose was not merely strategic, for trade was improved not by new roads but by new bridges.

The first reference to a borough at Leominster is in the grant by Abbot Roger (1158–65) of 42 acres of land outside the *burgum*, borough, of Leominster. A grant of Abbot Joseph (1173–86) makes it clear that the land within the borough was held subject to *legem bretolii*, the laws of Breteuil, a small town on the troubled southern border of Normandy. That Leominster was granted these laws and customs, not those of Reading, is further evidence of Bishop Capella's role in its foundation, for Breteuil had been the stronghold of William fitz Osbern, first earl of Hereford and one of the Conqueror's closest confidants. He had given its laws to Hereford, which he controlled jointly with the bishop, whence they were granted by various marcher lords to their new boroughs in the Marches and Wales. These included the de Lacy strongholds of Ludlow and Weobley. Later the de Lacys were to grant the Breteuil customs to the boroughs they founded in their great Irish lordship of Meath. As such seigneurial borough charters began to appear only in the late 12th century, we have to look to Henry II's charter to Pembroke, William Marshal's to Haverford and the de Lacys for Drogheda, Trim and Kells to gain some impression of the Breteuil laws and customs as granted to Leominster.[348]

These laid down that, 'If any man live in the town for a year and a day without challenge from any place, whether he be free or serf, he shall remain my freeman ever thereafter. ... I grant my burgesses that they and their heirs shall hold their burgages with their appurtenances for 12d to be paid yearly in lieu of all services.' At Kells c1210, as elsewhere, it was 'lawful for the burgesses to give, sell or mortgage their houses and burgages, saving the right of the lord (to his annual rent)'. One charter includes the interesting additional clause, 'without removal of their houses'. Although rent was 'according to size', 1s for a full burgage, 6d for a half-burgage etc, in virtually all cases tenure of a fraction of a burgage plot, however small, carried with it the same privileges in law as a whole burgage.[349]

Long and narrow, the burgage plot maximised the number of tenancies along the road frontage yet provided spacious land to the rear. The burgage, which characterised all medieval boroughs, conferred specific rights, privileges and liabilities in law. Rural tenure was servile and, even if his holdings were fully free, the villein suffered restrictions; but urban tenure gave freedom, not only from service on the land, so that a burgess could devote his time and energy to a craft or trade, but also to move, marry and devise his worldly goods as he pleased. Given such rights, the confines of a new borough had to be clearly distinguished from the manor out of which it had been carved. The borough became the manor denzein, the area within, whilst the rump of the manor or lordship became the foreign, the area without.

Topography

The topography of the new borough was determined by the bank and ditch that defined the minster's precinct to the south and west and the two strategic route ways that intersected at the Iron Cross: the north-south route spanning the Marches from Chester through Shrewsbury and Leominster to Hereford and Chepstow; the east-west, later the London-Aberystwyth road, now the A44, from Worcester and Bromyard to Leominster, then following the Arrow valley into Wales.

The clues to Leominster's physical evolution as a borough come, not from documents or archaeology, but from analysis of three distinct elements in the town plan, whose interrelationship is anything but random. First are the streets, and their mutual association into a street system; second, the individual plots of land called burgages which, with the streets, made up street-units or blocks, each with its own distinctive character; and finally the interrelationship of these street-units.[350]

The primary element, as at Bromyard, Ledbury and Ross, was a new, wedge-shaped, market-place, *altus vicus*. High Street formed its western, Drapers Lane its eastern, and Corn Street its southern limits. It was thus linked with the earlier and less rigidly defined market area, *le Corncepyng*, which by the 16th century had become Corn Market, but in the 19th century, with the advent of drapers and solicitors, assumed the grander title of Corn Square. Burgage plots were then pegged out, following the conventional form. Shops and houses were built on the street fronts, with extensive rear gardens. The length remained fairly uniform, at just over 200 feet. Unless defined in a charter, the original breadth is difficult to assess, because of side alleys to provide rear access and subsequent fragmentation and consolidation of plots. Normally, burgages were available to anyone who could pay the lord, here the abbot of Reading, the fixed annual rent of 12d. At Leominster the earliest extant details of the precise borough bounds are as late as Mary Tudor's charter incorporating the borough in 1554.[351]

The authority for establishing the **Market Place** was apparently Capella's, as Henry I's agent, but Leominster's topography suggests that the surveyor came from Reading, for the market areas of the abbot's two boroughs are remarkably similar. Both are wedge-shaped along a north-south axis, with burgage series to the south, east and west. There are further parallels: in each case the eastern series backs onto the monastic precinct and the principal access to the precinct is at the northern, that is the narrow, end of the market-place. In both towns market encroachment began quickly, and ambitious secondary market development was entitled Broad Street. At Leominster it was

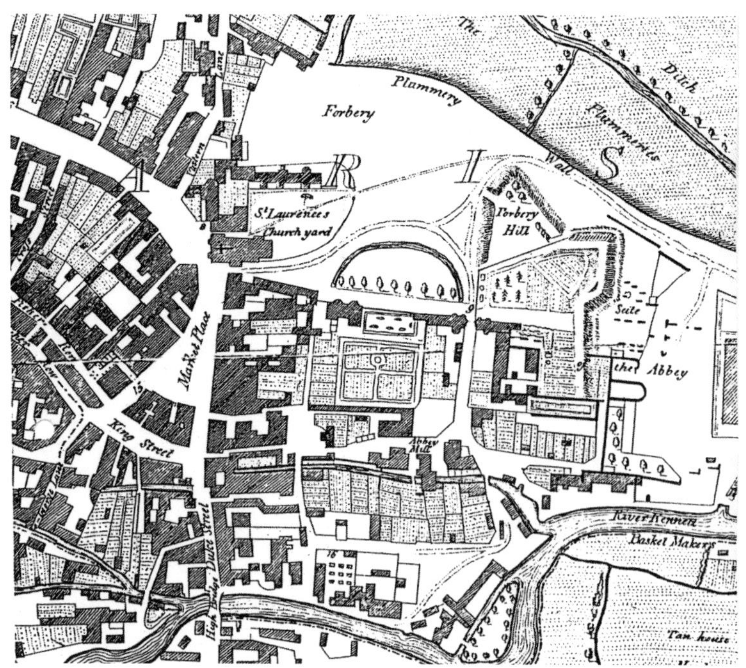

Fig 16.1 Reading market place area, from C. Coates' 1802 plan showing the extended market development curving away westwards

Fig 16.2 Plan of Leominster showing Capella's original wedge-shaped Market Place, Altus Vicus, *between the High Street and Drapers lane, filled with encroachment and narrow alleys, together with the northern extension of the market in the aptly named Broad Street*

a northward extension, at Reading a westward arch stemming from the broader, southern end of the wedge, King Street (Figs 16.1–16.3).[352]

Altus vicus, the Market Place, had three burgage series: on the east, reaching the bank and ditch of the monastic precinct, and to the west and the south. Over the years the market-place itself was subject to encroachment, a process that took place in almost all our market towns. The market booths and trestles, whether through policy or the laxity of bailiffs, gradually became permanent features. As a result, at Leominster narrow alleys are the only links between High Street and Drapers Lane (Fig 16.2). Their names, Ironmongers and Corvisers or Cordwainers Lane, of the shoemakers or other leather workers, Drapers Lane and the Butchery, now Victoria Street, recall the particular locations of the various specialist trades within the borough. By the later Middle Ages these were organised into nine Occupations or Trade Guilds: Butchers, Bakers, Weavers, Taylors, Mercers, Walkers (fullers) and Dyers, Tanners, Glovers and Shoemakers. In the retention of its medieval market encroachment, Leominster has been particularly fortunate. The only other major example in the locality are the market rows at Ludlow: Middle, Butchers', Shoemakers', Lockyers' and Barons' Row.

It is difficult to determine which was the second stage in the evolution of Leominster's town plan, West Street or what is now Broad Street. Sharing the name, *altus vicus*, **Broad**

Fig 16.3 Aerial photo (99-MB-0237). Altus Vicus, *centre left, between High Street and Drapers Lane showing narrow alleys, and the boundary of the monastic precinct above*

Street was regarded as an extension of the market-place. The wedge was abandoned. Modelled on Ludlow's large and highly successful, rectangular, east-west market, it was highly ambitious, some 400ft long and 60ft wide, extending from the north end of High Street as far as New Street (Fig 16.5a &b). Its original termination at New Street is apparently confirmed by the borough's ward structure. Broad Street, from the Butter Cross, where it is met by Church Street and Burgess Lane, formed the Cross and Pinsley ward, including New and Vicarage Streets. The area between the Pinsley and the Kenwater was known as Upper Marsh; Bridge Street, between Kenwater and the Lugg as Middle Marsh, and north of the Lugg as Lower Marsh. Broad Street thus linked the market areas and the infant industrial suburb known as the Marsh, based on the plentiful supply of water from the Pinsley, Kenwater and Lugg rivers (Figs 16.6 and 16.7). There were burgages in the Marsh prior to

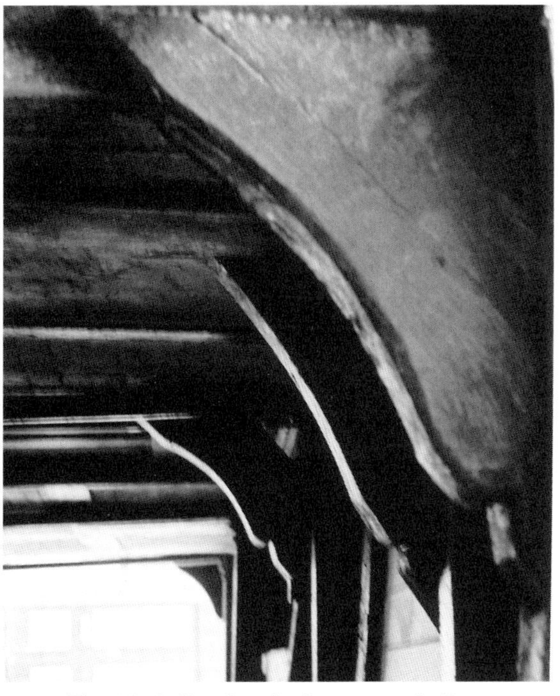

Fig 16.4 Brackets in Ironmonger's Row, part of the market encrochment in Leominster

Fig 16.5 a) Aerial photos of Leominster's northern market extension, Broad Street. Above centre left to top right. The Forbury chapel is shown near the bottom of the photo above, to the left of centre (99-MB-0237)
b) Aerial photo looking south along Broad Street to old Market Place (99-MB-0235)

1193, by which time the abbot of Reading's fulling mill was in operation. West Street, on the other hand, represented development of the major route from Wales. It gave direct access to the heart, the broader end, of the new market-place. Here the outline of many of the original burgage plots is still evident on both sides of the road.

The lst edition 1:500 OS plan shows that the burgage plots on **West** and **Burgess Streets** commenced beyond the end of the western series of both High and Broad Street (Figs 16.7a&b). They therefore represent later development. West and New Streets, established before 1249, were confined by a defensive ditch on the west. Access to West Street, one of the four principal routes into the town, was through Bargates, outside which an extramural market area was to develop. Here also, in the late 15th century, a suburb was established. Of this all signs have been erased by

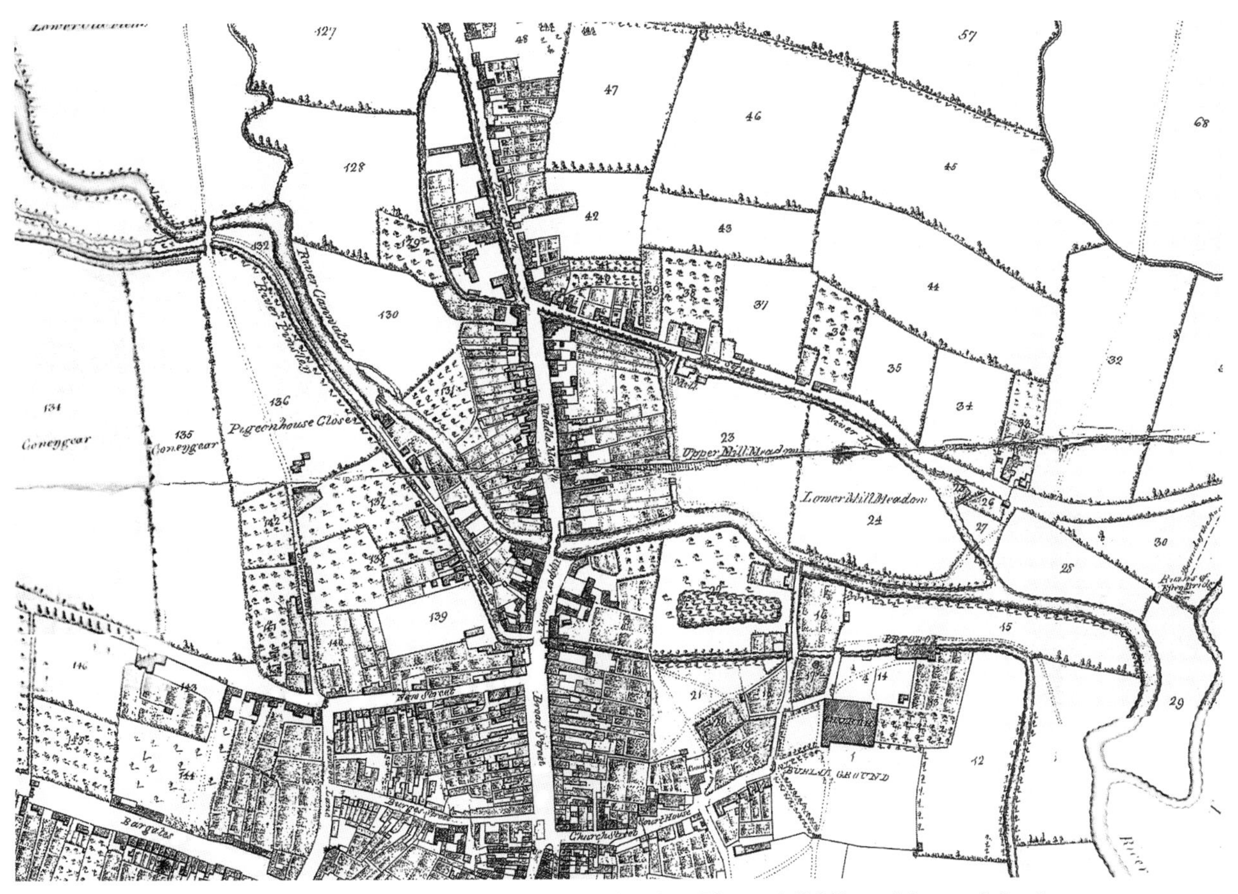

Fig 16.6 Gallier's 25" Plan (1832) showing Upper, Middle and Lower Marsh

Fig 16.7a&b Plan of West, Burgess and New Streets (left) and aerial photograph (99-MB-0231) looking west from over the monastic precinct with West Street on the left, Burgess Street in the centre and New Street on the right

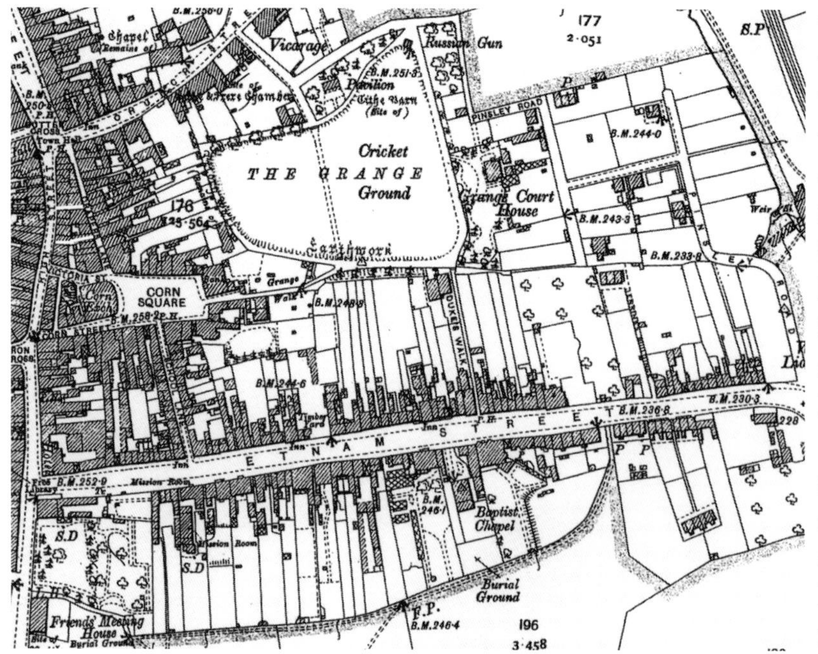

Fig 16.8 Plan of Etnam Street

the creation of the ring road. In these streets livestock continued to be sold at the annual fairs and weekly markets until the 19th century: pigs and sheep in Broad Street; cattle in West and Dishley Streets and Rainbow Lane; and horses in the town end of Etnam Street and in Turnbull Street, now South Street, between the Iron Cross and Etnam Street.[353]

Etnam Street, *vicus orientalis*, East Street in medieval records, was the last major piece of town planning (Fig 16.8). In many respects this was even more ambitious in its plan than Broad Street; almost as broad, it was twice as long. To accommodate a burgage series on the north side, the old line of the east/west route beyond Corn Square, of which Grange Walk is a vestige, was moved some 200ft to the south. At the Iron Cross this had originally followed a straight line from West Street, across the *Corncepyng* and Grange Walk, immediately south of the stream that ran along the southern bank of the minster precinct to the site of the Pinsley mill. This new street-line had in fact been determined by the early decision to lay out the burgage series to the south of the market-place. Vestiges of the original plots extending south from Corn Street can be seen on the lst edition OS 25" plan. Archaeological confirmation of this southern series of burgage plots comes from a watching brief undertaken at 3–5 Etnam Street, where evidence was found of the tails of some of the burgage plots, which had fronted onto Corn Square. In the later Middle Ages this early layout was lost as the result of the construction of School Street. However, at its eastern end, the Etnam Street development faltered, as the plan shows. The medieval burgage plots that can still be seen on parts of South Street and New Street probably represent the final stage in the growth of medieval Leominster, as did New Street at Ledbury, constructed by 1186.[354]

Common of pasture was frequently granted to burgesses, usually in a specified area. At Leominster and Reading there are references to the Portmanmore, that is the townsman's or citizen's more. The prior's burgesses had rights of pasture in some 24 acres in Leominster and Luston. They also had rights at Broadward Common and the Midsummer and Lammas Meadows. Communal action taken by the burgesses is first recorded in the time of Abbot Elias (1200–13), when he granted them 'all the pasture of the Broad, *Brade*, between Leominster and Eaton and the commons of Stodhurdesmore from Haspelee' as far as Hapelthorneleg", at an annual rent of 1 bezant. The gold bezant was of greater value, but the silver coin, more likely here, was worth between 1s and a florin, 2s. The first occasion on which the borough bailiff and seal are mentioned is in an agreement with Matthew de Gamage in 1244–5, granting the men of Leominster perpetual rights of ingress to and grazing for their cattle and flocks on Gamage Leasow, between the road leading to Eaton bridge and Walter de Mapenor's land next to the Broad, from 24 June to 25 March. For this they were to pay 6d per annum at the Nativity of St John, 24 June, 'by the hand of one of the bailiffs who for the time held office'. Not all animals could be put out to such pasture. At Corbridge, swine 'fed and living continuously within the burgages' were 'quit of pannage, but all others, fed in field (on the stubble) or in the wood, shall pay' — an interesting reflection on town life.[355]

The borough seal, affixed to this agreement with Matthew de Gamage, represented the legal identity of the community. Described as 'typically 13th-century in its iconography', it bears the legend 'COMMUNE LEOMINISTRIE' around the edge, with the 'N' of the last word in reverse. In the centre the figure of St Peter, barefooted and wearing a long cloak, holds the key in his right hand and the book in his left. At the head of the seal is a cross (Plate 19b).[356]

The Economy

The dynamic behind borough foundation was financial. Each burgage plot gave the abbot of Reading an annual income of 1s. There are no extant borough rentals for Leominster but at Ledbury, for example, the 78 burgages on the Homend produced an annual revenue of some £3. Tolls and stallage from the fairs and markets, with the profits of justice, that is fines levied at the borough courts, were further sources of income and thus jealously guarded.[357]

The great ecclesiastical landowners were well aware, not only of the financial potential of borough development, but also of the importance of stimulating trade within their boroughs. Thus Henry I's foundation charter granted that the abbot and convent 'and their men' be 'quit of tolls, customs and exactions in all markets and fairs whatsoever in England and Wales' and 'by land and water in ways and fields, in passing over bridges and through seaports throughout the whole of England'. No 'person small or great may exact anything, by way of due, custom or violence from the men, lands and possessions of Reading (Abbey); neither for riding nor expeditions nor building of bridges nor castles, nor carriage of transport by land or water nor other works, tributes or gifts'.[358]

The most significant of these rights was freedom from tolls for navigation, on the Thames for the abbot's men of Reading, on the Severn for the men of Leominster. Indeed, the value of the Thames trade was such that the abbots built their own wharves on the banks of the Kennet, immediately south of the abbey. Such rights were frequently challenged by interested parties, including royal officers. In March 1228 Abbot Adam of Lathbury, previously prior of Leominster, used the occasion of one of Henry III's many visits to Reading Abbey to draw the king's attention to a claim for £52 by the royal bailiff at Windsor for tolls unpaid by the abbot's men. The king upheld Adam's rights. In 1235 Lathbury turned his attention to the Severn, obliging the reeves of Worcester to confirm, by charter before the royal justices, the privileges of the men of Leominster: free entry and exit into their city, however and whenever they came; freedom to buy and sell all manner of merchandise; of access to their place beneath the Booth Hall; and from all tolls, stallage and portage whatsoever.[359]

The Leominster Cartulary includes an important clause, significantly omitted from the Reading copy, that these rights applied to all merchandise 'excepting leather, fresh hides, unfinished wool, wool thread and cloth', a powerful reminder of Leominster's staples. In 1407 Abbot Richard obliged Gloucester's civic leaders to record for posterity similar privileges which his men of Leominster enjoyed within that city. A firm hand had also to be taken with the men of Bristol. A royal writ ordered, 'as we have heretofore commanded others to permit the abbot, his monks and men to be quit of tolls, exactions and customs for all things within your bailiwick do not molest or disturb them ... and if any distress be made release them without delay or signify the cause to us why you obey not our mandate to you directed'. These rights, first granted in the early 12th century, were in 1554 incorporated into Queen Mary's charter for the borough of Leominster.[360]

Reference in the Worcester charter of 1235 to 'cloth, wool thread, unfinished wool and leather', indicates Leominster's principal economic interests, the processing of wool and leather. This is confirmed by the names of seven of the nine later 'Occupations' or Guilds. The primary processes, fulling, dyeing and tanning, were concentrated in the Marsh, which offered an abundant supply of water from Lugg and Kenwater. Traditionally fulling had been carried out by either walking or beating by hand the cloth in water. The cloth was thus compressed, giving it greater durability and resilience to weather. The use of fuller's earth, fuller's herb, soapwort, and stale urine removed impurities and oil. The fulling mill revolutionised this process. Like the corn mill, it was operated by means of a revolving drum attached to a water wheel. Two wooden hammers were raised and dropped alternately onto the cloth, in a great trough of water. In an era 'when water had become as decisive a factor as coal was to become in the 19th century', Leominster had a considerable advantage.[361]

Fig 16.9 The tannery before its removal to Queenswood Country Park, south of Leominster

The earliest English reference to fulling mills is in 1185, on the lands of the Knights Templars. The abbots' fulling mill at Leominster was in operation by 1193. It will have had exclusive rights for fulling within his liberty. Personal-name evidence confirms the continuing importance of fulling to the urban economy. Thus in 1281 Henry *Full(onis)* and William *le Folour* were involved in litigation in the Court of Common Pleas at Westminster. Both were men of substance, William with property in the town and Henry at Luston and Ivington. The name of another member of the group, John Tanhous, recalls Leominster's other primary trade. The town's last tannery, in the Marsh, beside the Pinsley Brook in Vicarage Street, was removed and erected as Tourist Information Centre, offices and toilets at Queenswood Country Park in the 1980s (Fig. 16.9). The textile and leather finishing trades, such as the Drapers and Corvisers, were located about the market-place.[362]

During the 13th century wool came to dominate Leominster's trade. English wool exports peaked at the end of the 13th and beginning of the 14th century. The Cistercian monasteries took the lead in wool production, as a price list of c1270 shows. Douai merchants paid the highest price, £50 Parisian per 364-lb sack, for wool from Margam, Tintern and Neath. By 1305 Amiens and St Omer merchants were operating in Leominster, but the prices they paid are not known. In 1311–21 the wool of Abbey Dore and Tintern commanded the highest price, £18 13s 4d sterling per sack. In 1337, however, the accounts of William de la Pole, the largest English wool exporter, show that, although he bought the relatively small quantity of 22 sacks in Herefordshire, as compared to 205 from Lindsay, 113 from Yorkshire, and 50 from the Cotswolds, the Herefordshire wool commanded the highest price. At £7 16s a sack it was 24% higher than its nearest rivals, the wool of Shropshire and the Cotswolds.[363]

Even in the late 12th century there is evidence of Leominster men seeking their fortunes far from home. A Dublin rental of that date includes amongst its 78 Welsh and marcher locative surnames *Hugo de Lemenester, Willielmus pistor de Limenistre* and *Radulfus de Limenistre*. Roger and Walter *de Leministre* appear in the register of St Thomas' Abbey, Dublin. John of Leominster was one of the principal burgesses of the royal borough and fortress of Carmarthen. In 1257 he had to advise Henry III that many of his townsmen 'are so destroyed and impoverished that they have abandoned the town'.[364]

Borough Government

The functions of borough government, through its courts of frankpledge or courts leet, were fourfold: firstly, the maintenance of law and order in matters delegated by the hundred court, or the subject of borough bye-laws, administered through six wards, the sub-divisions of the borough, each with its own constable. In the 1291–2 Iter rolls, when Isabel de Lindebrok sought refuge in St Andrew's church, acknowledging herself a thief and abjuring the kingdom, her chattels, valued at 3s, were forfeited to the court leet. Additionally, because these events happened during the day and the town had not taken her, the borough was in the mercy, power, of the abbot. The second function was the regulation of trade, especially weights and measures. By 1276 the sale of grain had to be by the London, not the heaped, quarter. This is confirmed in the 1291–2 Iter rolls, when it was alleged that 'the burgesses of the borough, when they buy corn, will have two heaps to every quarter, else they will not buy, to the prejudice of the country'. Twelve capital burgesses, when required to appear before the court, 'could not deny but that they bought as aforesaid against the king's command'. They were detained in custody and afterwards paid a fine of 5 marks, £3 6s 8d. for themselves and their fellow burgesses. Later, an ordinance of Edward II gave the mayor and bailiffs the right to examine measures every six months and apply their seal. The third function was the upkeep of Leominster's lanes and ten bridges. Their final responsibility was for sanitation, including street cleaning and water supply.[365]

Parliamentary Representation

Leominster was one of the five Herefordshire boroughs to return members to the Commons in 1295. For Bromyard and Ross this was the sole occasion. Weobley had members in seven parliaments between 1295 and 1306, but Hereford and Leominster were represented throughout the medieval period.

Material on borough politics becomes available after 1295, when Leominster returned Thomas de Radyng and John de Cokyng as its first two members. A John de Redynges sat in the Commons with William I Salesbury, 'merchant', in 1340. The Redynges family does not otherwise appear to have played a part in borough politics. However, in 1331 and 1334 a Hugh de Radynges was the recipient of the licence to found the conventual Lady Chapel (see Table 9).

Philip and Mary's charter of May 1554 describes the government of the medieval borough as invested 'since time immemorial' in a bailiff and 24 co-opted burgesses, the bailiff being elected by and from the 24. This is confirmed by the returns of members elected from 1422. For the most part such returns bear the names, not of all 24, but of twelve or so, in effect capital burgesses, who acted as electors (Fig 16.10). This system, one must assume, also operated in the 14th century. The elections were held in the borough's Guildhall, but the most powerful player was the abbot's bailiff of the liberty, who acted as returning officer.[366]

Certain families stand out in the lists of members elected to Parliament in the 14th and early 15th centuries. The lay subsidy rolls for 1341 name 32 taxpayers in the borough, paying a total of £4 10s 4d. The returns of members for the 14th century confirm the dominant position of the Salesbury family within the borough's ruling oligarchy. William I, who contributed 13s 4d, 15%, to the 1341 lay subsidy, served in twelve of the thirteen parliaments between 1332 and 1348. He was succeeded by William II, evidently his eldest son, who represented the borough in five of the eleven parliaments for which there are returns in the period 1362–77. In 1384 William II was nominated a county commissioner to collect the royal levy, of one-tenth on boroughs and one-fifteenth in the countryside. John I, possibly his younger brother, served in Parliament with William II in 1363 and 1366. His father-in-law, Thomas Orleton, had represented Leominster in March 1330 and, with John's father, William I, in 1337 and Philip Romayn in 1348. Thomas Salesbury, probably another of William II's brothers, served with William in 1373 and 1384.

The Romayn family, although allies of the Salesburys, could not match their Commons record. Philip le Romayn, who paid 5s towards the 1341 lay subsidy, had business interests in wool, for he served as a collector of wool in 1342. A John Romayn had represented Leominster in the Commons as early as 1306. First elected as William I Salesbury's partner in 1332, Philip served in seven parliaments between that date and 1348, when his fellow member was no longer Salesbury, but Thomas Orleton. Altogether five Romayns, two Johns, a John Junior, Philip and William, appeared in the Leominster parliamentary returns between 1306 and 1397.

Initially parliamentary attendance was brief: 21 days in 1330, 11 in March 1336, and 24 in 1361. Later in the century, sessions were much longer: 82 days in 1376, 88 in 1382, and 65 in 1402. As Members received expenses of 2s per day, it will have been business commitments at home rather than financial constraints that persuaded some of the urban hierarchy not to stand. John II was the last of the Salesburys to sit in the Commons. Having served in three consecutive parliaments, of 1413, 1414 and 1417, he was supplanted by a member of the Hood family. John's ambitions however were apparently local. After serving three years as deputy, he was bailiff 1426–30. Like William II he was also a county commissioner for the collection of tenths and fifteenths, in 1416, 1429 and 1430. With John II we find a member of a burgher family aspiring to gentility, for Bishop Mascall's Register of 1412 describes him as *armiger*, esquire. Richard, son of Hugh de Wynnesley, successfully combined activity in both local and national politics. Abbot's attorney and then bailiff of the liberty, 1422–42, he also represented Leominster in the Commons in 1422, 1427, 1432 and 1442. On one occasion, as bailiff and therefore returning officer, he even returned himself as Member of Parliament.[367]

Members of the urban oligarchy were major patrons of the parish church, both in terms of the foundation of its Lady Chapel and the training of its clergy. John I Salesbury and Richard Lorymer, Member of Parliament on five occasions between 1358 and 1381, were of the small group that applied to the Crown in 1397 for licence to alienate lands for the foundation of a parochial Lady Chapel. John I also provided 5 marks, £3 6s 8d, annually for John Staunton, deacon, to prepare for the priesthood, 1410–12, whilst John II Romayn gave similar support to Walter Brown in 1412.[368]

The nature of urban society was changing. No longer did 'town air make free'. In the 14th century Coningsby's *Register* records a half-burgage 'held in villeinage', and 'two burgages in Leominster' on the same terms. The days when burgage tenure conferred free status on outsiders had passed. In the mid 13th century there are records of the prior levying fines on those seeking freedom of the borough, which gave the right to trade in the market free of toll. Prior John of Gloucester (c1340–7) and his successors brought a series of actions in the borough court against those claiming such freedom through marriage to the daughter of a burgess. In 1342 John of Salesbury, who had married the daughter of Thomas Orleton, was obliged to pay 5s for freedom of the borough. Despite the devastating population decline caused by the Black Death in 1349, Henry Bell, son-in-law of John Nele, burgess, had to pay twice that sum, 10s. For William Pulton in 1351 and John Seward in the 1370s, the fine was 6s 8d. About the same time, before his daughter, Margaret, could marry a burgess, William Wall, villein of Stagbatch, had to pay *merchet* of £2 for the prior's licence.[369]

The rise of the Bradfords, a family whose origins lay outside the borough, at Broadward, was marked by the election in 1377 of John, son of Giles Bradford, to the Commons, where his fellow member was William II Salesbury. In 1385 and 1391 John was elected again. In 1383, he was under-bailiff of the borough. William II Salesbury, Henry Hoker and William Tanner junior stood as his sureties, in £20, that he would 'well and truly serve the abbot of Reading, executing all summonses, attachments, distresses and executions, faithfully accounting for the profits extracted out to him and paying the same when required'. John II Bradford restricted his political activity to the borough, where he was bailiff in 1423, 1425 and, following John II Salesbury, from 1430 to 1432. The distinctions between urban and rural society were being broken down. Members of the urban oligarchy were investing in land. Thus in January 1351 John I Salesbury, 'free burgess', who represented the borough in Parliament in 1363 and 1366, and John atte Walle, native, by licence made exchange of divers acres of free land which they had purchased, to consolidate their holdings, with a view to eventual enclosure. In 1392 we find such exchanges in the common fields being made by John Romayn and William II Salesbury.[370]

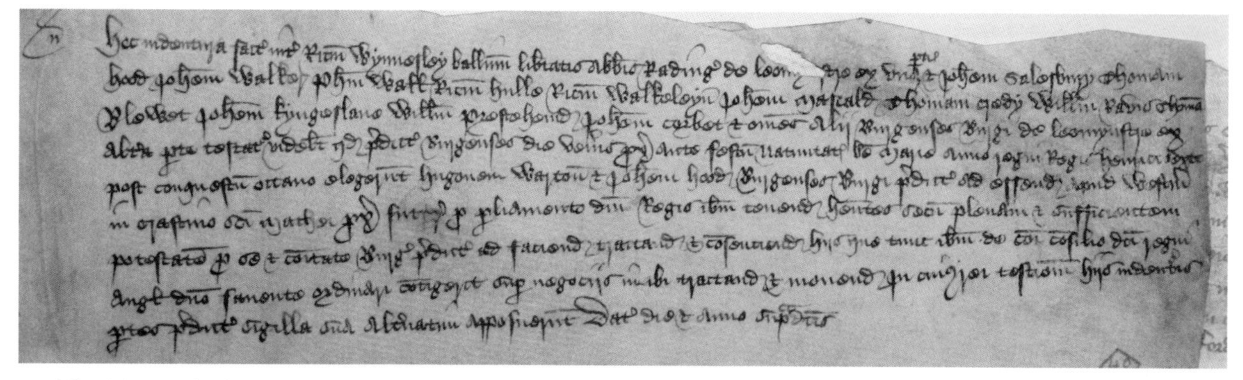

Fig 16.10 An indenture made between Richard Wynnesley, bailiff of the liberty of the abbot of Reading at Leominster on the one part and John Salesbury, Thomas Hood, John Walker, Philip Wall, Richard Hulle, Richard Wakelyn, John Mascall, Thomas Credy, William Davis, Thomas Blewet, John Kyngesland, Wm Prestehemed (Presteigne), John Corbet and other bugesses of the borough of Leominster on the other part testifies (to the election in the Guildhall of Hugh Wharton and John Hood in September 1429). (NA C/14/1/(Pt 1) 40)

Blount records that the Bradford mansion was in the South End of the town. It may have stood on the site of Dutton House, built in 1604 and later the residence of Thomas Coningsby, but Philip Bradford, 'frankeleyn', retained the house at Broadward. His will of 1458 gives some impression of the style that characterised the burial of Leominster's notable citizens in their parochial church. He left 2s to the altar of St Paul in the conventual church and 1s to the altar of the Holy Trinity in the parochial church, with 6s 8d to John Vir to pray for the swift passage of his soul through purgatory. His body, which was to be buried in the parochial chapel of St Anne, was to be 'covered on the day of my burial with black, woollen cloth', and was to be accompanied by 'six paupers clothed in 12 ells of black woollen cloth and carrying six wax candles by my body'.[371]

The Liberty of Leominster

Henry I's 1125 foundation charter granted the abbot of Reading 'all jurisdiction over assaults, thefts, murders, effusions of blood and infractions of the peace as much as belonged to the royal power ... in the manor of Reading and its dependencies', thus creating the liberty of Leominster, to the exclusion of the Crown's law officers. The men of certain neighbouring manors were to attend these courts according to the custom of former times. If they refused the king would 'compel them to appear, perform their duty and receive their fines'.

In Henry III's reign the royal justices were commanded to deliver the gaols, try all prisoners, of liberties as well as of counties, seeking thus to prevent the growth of private jurisdictions. At Leominster a compromise was reached, whereby the royal justices met not only at the county town, Hereford, but also at the courthouse of the liberty of Leominster, where the prior, representing the abbot, took the chair, and the profits of justice went to the abbot. As early as 1198–9 the justices for the shires of Gloucester, Hereford and Worcester held their sessions at Hereford on 9–12 September before moving on to Leominster. In 1221 the sessions were held on 21–3 July at Hereford, 26th at Leominster and 1 August at Worcester.[372]

The royal coroner, however, was allowed within the abbot's liberty only after 'begging licence to sit in the town' and after publicly proclaiming this licence at the opening of proceedings. However, this may not have been to the exclusion of local election, for the right of election of coroners at Reading was retained by the abbots well into the 15th century. Details of the pleas of the Crown for the liberty of Leominster held before the coroners, Philip Marescall and Richard de Stockton, two local men, for the session 20 November 1291 to 19 November 1292, provide much information on both liberty and borough. From such sessions the abbot derived considerable profit. When Nicholas Biffard was hanged, the abbot was adjudged his tenement, valued at £2 10s. Later, the prior of Great Malvern successfully claimed that Biffard's tenement was the property of the abbot of Westminster, and the abbot of Reading was obliged to 'render back the said tenement'.[373]

Deodands, objects that had caused death and were therefore forfeit to the abbot, were another fruitful source of revenue. When John son of Richard the physician was killed by a cart full of pease, due to the violence of the wind, the cart and pease were valued at 8s as a deodand. William Langton, driving a wagon with four oxen and a horse was killed by the same; deodand was valued at 31s. Richard Gaddy, felling an oak in Sarnesfield wood, was hurt and died after eight days; the value of the oak was valued at 3s 6d. John de Risbury fell from a stack of straw in Eton, broke his neck and died; value of stack, 12d. The court also took cognisance of purprestures, illegal enclosures or encroachments. Thus, when Richard de Longebroke was found guilty of making a pier upon the Lugg next the bridge of Eton, 40ft long and 8ft broad, and John de Forde of the like, upon the Lugg next Ford bridge, 8ft by 40ft, 'to the damage of the county', the bailiff of the liberty was to amend whatever is prejudicial to the county 'at the charge of Richard and John'.[374]

The foundation of Leominster borough created two distinct areas: the borough or denzein, the area within, and the hundred or liberty, the area without. Each had its own court, and a lay bailiff, appointed by and acting for the abbot. Frequently they acted jointly as the 'lord's bailiffs of Leominster', but the major role remained with the bailiff of the liberty. The 1291–2 coroner's rolls provide the earliest reference to such a bailiff, John Danehurst. Appointment was normally for life. Thus Richard Wigmore, appointed in 1407, held office until 1426–7.[375]

A copy of a bond for the bailiff of the liberty in 1335 defines his responsibilities. Henry Sutton, constituted in the office by will of the abbot of Reading, was to 'keep well the said bailiwick and indemnify and save harmless the said abbot against anyone whatsoever'. He had to levy the profits of his bailiwick and pay them to the keepers. 'To satisfy all damages that may happen' by his defect or negligence, he had to bind himself and his heirs that all his lands and tenements might be distrained by the said abbot. In 1427–8 the bailiffs, working with prior and sub-prior, were obliged 'jointly and severally as stewards, bailiffs and attorneys of the abbot's manor of Leominster, to hold all hundred courts and halimotes there; to challenge and use in our name all our liberties, franchises and pleas before what judges soever, or in what courts or other places soever, and by whomsoever exhibited. To hear, determine as also to perform, exercise and use all those things for our honour and profit that rightfully belong to the business aforesaid within this liberty of Leominster.' The Leominster Cartulary gives a different version of the bailiffs' oath:

> The Oathe of the ij. Bayllys of Leomstr. And of the Lybertye of the same.
> Fyrst ye shall bere feyth and fidelite to N(icholas Whaplode, 1305-28) abbott of Redyng and to hys officers and kepars of the prioury or maneur of Leomstr, and to their successors next after your allegiance duryng the tyme ye shall occupye offyce vndre theym.
> Item ye shallbe no detractour, euyll speker, or hurter of them either in their name or goods nor

yet to be of counscill wt. eny other in suche purpose but apone knowlege to you therof ye shall wt. conuenyent hast disclose and shew yt vnto theym or to eny of theym.
Item ye shalbe no w'drawer or keper to your own vse eny exchete, ryght, or casueltie that by vertue of kyngs charter myght growe vnto them w'in your office duryng youre tyme in the same.
Item ye shall indifferently execute all maner attachements, leveys, and other precepts of the courts within the seyde borough and liberte without sparyng oon to hurt an other duryng your office so help you God and halydome and by thys booke.[376]

By the 14th century, as the rise of the Bradford family shows, divisions between borough and the countryside beyond were being broken down. In 1324 a powerful alliance of town and country interests presented a serious threat to the abbot's authority within the court of his liberty. Twenty-eight tenants of the liberty, whose names are listed, refused to make presentations in that court 'relating to the spilling of blood and various other trespasses'. The evidence comes, not from the Leominster, but from the Reading cartulary, BL Harley 1708. The reasons why the tenants took this stand are not evident, but the issue over which they contested the abbot's rights was ill-chosen. On this matter, Henry I's foundation charter was very clear, granting the abbot of Reading 'jurisdiction over all ... effusions of blood ... as belonged to the royal power'. 'For their contrariness in this and other matters', the tenants had to pay Abbot Nicholas of Whaplode (1305–28) £100.[377]

The members of this alliance named at the end of the list can be readily identified as members of the borough oligarchy. John Cokyng, the borough's first Member of Parliament, was joined by eight others who had represented the borough: John Melide in 1315 and 1325, Richard Lyulf in 1315 and 1330, William Bernard in 1326, William Pryll in 1330, Philip Gody in 1335, John de Reading in 1340, together with Philip Romayn, 1332–48, and William I Salesbury on twelve occasions, 1332–48. Identification of the remaining 19 members is more difficult. Two, Roger Porter and William, son of Ralph, who appear at the end of the list, may also have been burgesses. All but two of the others bear locative surnames, and are listed en bloc, before the borough members. Such locative names are found within the borough at this time, but the arrangement of the names suggests the intention of describing two groups, one urban and the other rural.

From the north-west came John of Eyton; from the north-east Thomas of Edvin, Roger of Brimfield, Ralph of Stockton, possibly a relative of Richard of Stockton who had served as coroner in 1291-2, and, less than a mile away, Richard of Pateshall; from the south-east John of Eaton, James of Ford, John of Humber, Richard of Hampton (Richard) and Walter of (Hampton) Mapenore; and from the south-west John of Wharton, Walter of Sarnesfield and William of Staunton (on Arrow). All were men of substance, for all acknowledged the agreement to pay Abbot Nicholas £100 with their seals. The distinction between the two groups may not have been as clear as it seems. Just as a number of the more affluent burgesses, such as the Salesburys and Romayns, had begun to buy up land in the foreign, so some of the more prominent families of the foreign, such as the Bradfords of Broadward, were developing a political interest in the borough. Most remarkable of all, however, is the way this group of Members, who had dominated parliamentary representation and therefore borough politics before 1324, was able to continue so to do despite their apparent defeat at the hands of the abbot. The political dominance of the Salesburys and Romayns lasted until the early years of the 15th century. Unfortunately, very few names of the bailiffs, the abbot's representatives, are known at this time.

17 External Threats

Wales and the Marcher Barons

The borough's economic growth was not achieved without major setbacks. In Wales both Henry I (1100–35) and Henry II (1154–89) had preferred a loyal ally to a restive vassal. Thus for most of the 12th century, other than the years of Stephen's rule, royal policy had kept campaigns in Wales to a minimum. With the reigns of John (1200–16) and Henry III (1216–72), this changed. Conflict between the Crown and the Welsh princes, between the Crown and the marcher lords, and even between marcher lords, was recurrent. Not only the priory's western lands, but even the borough itself was vulnerable to attack. Undefended by walls and easily accessible from Wales and the March, Leominster faced peril on a number of occasions. In 1208, in revolt against King John, William de Braose, lord of Abergavenny, Brecon, Builth, Radnor and Limerick, fled to the Marches. Using Walter de Lacy's stronghold of Weobley as their base, William's sons, William and Reginald, stormed and sacked the borough of Leominster, as an appendage of the royal foundation of Reading. Half the town was consumed by fire. Their brother, Giles, elected bishop of Hereford in 1200, fled the kingdom. Upon his return he joined the rebel barons and their ally, Llywelyn ap Iorwerth, the Great, in opposition to John. War with Llywelyn, which had opened in 1212, continued after John's death, until the Peace of Montgomery in 1223.[378] Bishop Hugh de Mapenore (1216–19) threatened to excommunicate 'those who molest the church of Leominster', and both bishop Gervase of St David's and Cadwgan of Bangor, whose dioceses bounded that of Hereford on the west, made similar threats to those 'taking away the priory's property and disturbing the monks' goods'. The sacking of Leominster by de Braose's two sons had a searing impact on the minds of the Reading monks. More than half a century later, a Reading annalist recalled the event in detail. According to Coates, he even attributed the attack to Bishop Giles de Braose.[379]

In 1231 hostilities were recommenced, and a royal prohibition on the sale of commodities to the Welsh was proclaimed. However this, like later attempts to place embargoes on such trade, will have proved futile.[380] Having failed to bring Llywelyn to battle, Henry III withdrew from Painscastle about Michaelmas, leaving his enemy free to harry the priory's lands in west Herefordshire. Prior Thomas, the Tewkesbury annals tell us, was forced to buy peace for 'a great quantity of money'. Only after the receipt of this ransom did Llywelyn write to his bailiffs of Maelienydd (northern Radnorshire), commanding them to protect and defend from all injury, molestation and damage the monks of Leominster, their property and possessions. Despite such vicissitudes, the construction in the 1230s of the new south nave in the parochial church is evidence of population growth and a buoyant economy.[381]

Urban Rivalries and the Mortimer Connection

With royal power often either distant or ineffective, the priors had to find a powerful local patron. The death in 1241 of Walter II de Lacy, lord of Weobley, Ludlow and Ewyas Lacy, and the division of his lands between his two daughters, whose husbands' principal interests lay far away, left a power vacuum in Herefordshire and south Shropshire. The priors of Leominster thus allied themselves to the growing power and extended family interests of Ralph II de Mortimer, d1246, who had married the dark-eyed Gwladus, one of the daughters of Llywelyn and widow of Reginald de Braose, whom her father publicly hanged on a tree on account of his affair with his wife.[382]

For the borough, wool had become the most lucrative business. The priory's wool may have been sold directly to foreign merchants, such as those of Amiens and St Omer, who were buying in Leominster by 1305. Nevertheless Thomas Tope, bailiff of the borough, and Philip Romayn were appointed county collectors of wool in 1342. From the early 13th century there is considerable evidence of the suspicion and ill will that existed between Leominster and its rival markets for central Wales, Hereford and Ludlow. The borough's own merchants were overshadowed, the Moniwords of Hereford being amongst the best documented wool merchants of the late 13th and early 14th century. The family held the bailiffship of the city eleven times between 1274 and 1320. Buying wool from the smaller, non-monastic, producers with whom it was not profitable for foreign merchants to deal directly, they received payment in advance from the traders of Lucca and Cahors, to whom they delivered wool at the great fairs such as Winchester and St Ives. With the capital received they purchased Flemish and other cloth to retail in their own county.[383]

A reference to Roger Mortimer's bailiff coming to Leominster market and despoiling Llywelyn ap Gruffydd, the Last's, merchants is of particular interest, for it identifies the cantrefs from which these Welsh traders had come: Elfael, which lay between Builth and Presteigne, as far as the Wye on the south; Builth, much of the land between the Wye and the Towi; Gwerthrynion, following the Wye to the north; and probably also the cantrefs of Maelienydd and Ceredigion (Cardigan) to the west.[384]

In 1230 the citizens of Hereford brought a suit in the royal courts against the abbot of Reading, alleging that moving Leominster's market in 1219 from Thursday to Saturday was to the damage of Hereford's Saturday market. The suit failed, but the men of Hereford's renewed charge in 1237 resulted in a royal mandate to the sheriff of Hereford, to announce publicly that henceforth Leominster's markets would be held on Fridays. This move, by forestalling the Hereford market, was to Leominster's advantage. Here, no doubt, we can see the hand of the abbot. A century later however, in 1335, Leominster's market day was changed to Tuesday.[385]

Annual fairs were much more important than the weekly markets, especially in terms of the trade in Welsh cattle. Leominster's annual prescriptive fair had been held on the feast of the priory's patrons, SS Peter and Paul, 29 June, and the three days following 'since time out of mind'. This fair had been formally recognised by Henry I at the borough's foundation in the early 1120s, and confirmed by Henry II in 1170 and Richard I in 1189. Hereford already had a spring fair, on the vigil, feast of St Aethelbert, 20 May, and three days following, when in 1227 Henry III granted the city a second, autumn, fair, on the feast of St Denys, 9 October, and two days following. Between 1264 and 1282 abbots Richard Reading and Robert Burgate made effective use of their abbey's close relations with the Crown to protect the Leominster fairs.[386]

Fair days were also the occasion when Jews or their agents were seen at Leominster and neighbouring towns. Jews had been resident at Hereford since 1179. About 1220, under the patronage of the sheriff, Walter II de Lacy, the city became the seat of operations of Hamo of Hereford, one of the wealthiest Jewish financiers of his day. Aaron le Blund, grandson of one of the leaders of London's Jewry, established himself in Hereford about 1265. Whereas Hamo had served the local baronage, Aaron's clientele was not so august. For success in the county, Aaron had to have a tacit agreement with Roger III de Mortimer, from 1266 sheriff and constable of Hereford castle, the Jewry's ultimate refuge in times of trouble. Furthermore, Mortimer was now active in the land market, eagerly seeking to acquire local estates that stood as security for Jewish loans. Failure to repay the Jewry led to foreclosure and Mortimer's acquisition of the lands of such local lords as John de Balun of Much Marcle and Henry de Pembridge.

Under Roger's patronage, Aaron was able to operate within what would otherwise have been the hostile environment of the prior of Leominster's bailiwick. There his clients would have been much smaller fry than the Balun and Pembridge families. Thus John Catche of Hinton and Roger Peytevyn of Marston (Stannett?), with his sons John and Roger borrowed £7 13s 4d. Repayment was to be 13s 4d at Easter 1273, and £4 6s 8d at the Leominster fair next following, 29 June. Interest was additional and varied, according to the credit worthiness of the client, between 1d and 2d per £1 per week, that is 22% to 43% per annum. In 1275 William *le Ffulur* of Leominster borrowed £5 from Aaron on the vigil of the feast of St Mary Magdalene, 22 July, to be repaid on the morrow of Michaelmas, 1275. Walter son of Philip le Marescall of Leominster owed Isaac son of Hagin of Weobley £10. Although Hagin's business was centred on Weobley, he operated from Hereford where his house was in Maliers Street. This street, and with it the site of Hereford's medieval Jewry, disappeared with the construction of the Maylord Shopping Centre.[387]

The breakdown of law and order after the outbreak of the Barons' Wars brought the antagonism between Hereford and Leominster to a head. In 1263 Worcester was sacked by the earl of Derby. In 1264 Gloucester was punished for submitting to the baronial forces by Prince Edward, who imprisoned its principal citizens and demanded a £1,000 ransom. His marriage to the heiress, Maud de Braose, in 1264 brought Roger III de Mortimer (1231?–82) the lordship of Radnor and lands in Brecon, and with them virtual command of the marcher barons. The growing cordiality between the Montfortians and Llywelyn ap Gruffydd, who had united the Welsh princes under his leadership as 'prince of Wales', quickly converted Roger into an ardent royalist. After the defeat of Henry III and Prince Edward at Lewes in 1264, the marchers retired to the west, where, as a part of a general exchange, they were ordered to return the captives they had taken at the battle of Northampton earlier in the year. As ransom for Adam le Despenser, William Devereux had already pledged some of his lands to Roger Mortimer by charter. William's request to Roger for the return of his charter met with the laconic reply, 'it is in the prior of Leominster's hands for safe-keeping'.[388]

In November 1264 Roger de Mortimer, with his son Ralph, Roger de Clifford of Tenbury, Hugh de Mortimer of Richard's Castle, and other marcher lords, came to Hereford (then under baronial control) 'with a great army with banners displayed and grievously assaulted it from the first hour of day till night'. Given the close relationship between the prior and the Mortimers of Wigmore, it is hardly surprising that Mortimer's army included 'many of the liberty of the prior of Leominster'. The next day they attacked Hereford again, 'casting fire on Bissopstrete (Bye Street), and burned all that suburb'.

The following May Simon de Montfort arrived in Hereford, with Henry III and Prince Edward as virtual captives in his entourage. For two months Hereford became the centre of his administration. The men of the town seized their opportunity and descended on Leominster, in the words of the prior, 'taking, carrying away and consuming the goods of the priory and its other manors and lands to the value of £2,000 and burning a great part of the town'.[389] Henry, still in de Montfort's hands at Hereford, commanded Prior Robert de Arcubus to return Devereux's charter. Robert had thus to choose between his local patron, Roger Mortimer, and the king. Warned by Henry to come 'without delay lest peril should arise to you through detention', he restored Devereux's charter in the royal presence. 'For the prior's indemnity' against Mortimer, the king 'promised to save him harmless touching the restitution'. Ironically, in November 1263 Prior Robert had been restored to office at Henry III's express request, with the reassurance to Abbot Richard II that 'this grace shall not be drawn into a precedent' for such intervention.[390]

On 28 May Prince Edward effected a spectacular escape from his gaolers at Hereford, riding like the wind, first to Wigmore and then Ludlow castle. There he met Roger Mortimer and Gilbert de Clare 'in parliament'. On 3 August de Montfort was defeated and killed at the battle of Evesham, after Roger de Mortimer, with inferior numbers, had seized control of the only bridge across which he could have retreated. De Montfort's head was sent by Roger as a gift to his wife at Wigmore. The citizens of Hereford were the first to make peace with Henry III, but at a price. The prior for his part brought immediate action in the royal courts, claiming £2,000 damages for the attack on Leominster. He named some 35 Hereford men, including members of the city's principal families, such as young Roger Moniword, elected city bailiff in 1296. The outcome is not known, but conflict between Leominster and Hereford continued — over the dates of their respective fairs.[391]

Three months after the victory at Evesham, with Mortimer and thus his client, the prior, high in favour, Henry III granted Leominster an autumn fair, on the vigil and feast of St Michael, 29 September, and the four days following. In 1277 Hereford complained once again to the courts, this time that Henry's grant was to the injury of the king's own fair, held at Hereford on St

Fig 17.1 The Buck brothers' engraving of Wigmore Castle, base of Roger Mortimer

Denis's day, 9 October, and two days following. The jurors returned that the abbot's Michaelmas fair should be 'wholly quashed'. This proved a Pyrrhic victory, for in 1282 Edward I, no doubt recalling his incarceration at Hereford and Mortimer's part in his escape, granted the abbot, 'at the instance of John Gerard, monk of Reading', then prior of Leominster, a new fair at Leominster, on the vigil and feast of SS Cosmas and Damian, 27 September, and four days following, thus anticipating Hereford's 9 October fair by two weeks! In addition, Edward I granted the priory a third, spring, fair, to be held at Leominster on the vigil and feast of SS Philip and James and three days following. Ultimately, in 1290, as a consequence of yet further legal action by Hereford, Leominster's autumn fair was changed to that most appropriate, if not economically advantageous, of all dates — the vigil and festival of St Edfrith, the minster's founder, 26 October, and the four days following.[392]

Leominster's trading interests clashed not only with Hereford. In the first half of the 14th century Ludlow merchants played a significant role in the wool trade, but in April 1349 they laid complaint before the king that 'a large confederacy of evil doers has formed a plot against them when they come out of the town to trade'. Many Ludlow men had been 'assaulted and maimed at Leominster and elsewhere in the county of Hereford. Whereby some have lost their limbs and some have been imprisoned until they made fine.' Furthermore, the confederacy had 'besieged the town of Ludlow for a long time, for which cause none dare come forth to make their profit'. In 1556 no Ludlow man was prepared to attend as a livestock trader at the Leominster market. Indeed fracas between the youth, if not the merchants, of Leominster and Ludlow continued well into the last century.[393]

Close relations between the prior of Leominster and the lords of Wigmore were maintained under Roger II's successors, his son Roger III (1282–1326) and grandson, Roger IV, first earl of March (1326–30). After Edward II took Roger Mortimer, father and son, prisoner and lodged them in the Tower in 1322, the prior of Leominster was alleged to have been in correspondence with, and to have succoured, servants of the two men.[394]

The staid nature of much of borough life was enlivened by displays of military prowess by local lords, knights and esquires in jousts and *behourds*, both essentially training matches. Jousts, horseback combat between two knights, who would charge each other with their lances at rest, were often held in market-places, where wooden stands were erected for the ladies and other gentle spectators. The lance was also the weapon used at the *behourd*, the sport of esquires training for knighthood. This was a mini-tournament, where esquires fought against each other in two teams. The site was usually the town fairground, or a local landowner's park. Both jousts and *behourds*, with their crowds of spectators, attracted traders and merchants.

Such was the ardour of combatants, and spectators that, as at football matches, things could go horribly wrong. On 4 April, 1280, Edward I commanded the sheriff of Hereford 'to go in person to the towns of Hereford and Leominster and to inhibit the burgesses wholly from making an assembly of jousts and bourds on Sunday next after mid-Lent, or upon any other day'. He added that if the burgesses did not obey he would 'so chastise them that others doing the like against the king's orders shall be struck with terror'. Edward justified his prohibition on the grounds of 'the many evils and manifest breaches of his peace which may easily arise from such assemblies'. Such a disaster occured eight years later, at a *behourd* held at Boston fair, where the two teams, one dressed as monks and the other as canons, lost self-control and a general riot ensued. This provided an opportunity for attacks on merchants and townsmen, with thefts from their booths.[395]

Edward's statement should not be taken merely at face value. There were probably political implications. In 1280 his dealings with Llywelyn remained at a delicate stage, but the king believed the treaty they had made at Conway three years previously could become permanent. Roger II de Mortimer was, after Edward's escape from Hereford, his close friend and subsequently one of the guardians of his children. Nevertheless, in 1279, Roger had held, at vast expense, a great Round Table attended by a hundred knights and their ladies at Kenilworth Castle, the home of the king's brother, Edmund, Duke of Lancaster, and his wife, Blanche of Navarre. Such occasions were extraordinarily costly, but were also powerful political statements. Furthermore, Roger was the son of Llywelyn's daughter, Gwladus, and had been Llywelyn's ally in 1258. Whatever the case, Edward was determined to prevent the sensitive relationship between the marcher lords and the Welsh getting out of control.[396]

Having sworn a truce with Roger II de Mortimer, the 'Lord of Snowdon' complained to him in 1276 that 'his men, clerks and laymen, went to the markets and fairs at Montgomery and Leominster with their merchandise, but more than 122 were detained, and one slain'. This, he warned, 'gave him grounds for abandoning the peace'. If he did so, it would be 'unwillingly'. Such wantonness and provocation by the marcher lords led to a mass rising of the Welsh lords at a time not of Llywelyn's choosing. Edward I seized this opportunity for a final settlement in 1282. From Herefordshire and adjacent parts of the March he called for 1,200 footmen. The prior of Leominster was not exempt; he had to provide 100 such men-at-arms for selection of the strongest 'to be conducted to the army of Wales'. In March 1283 there was a further demand, for 200 men from the prior's lands. On 11 December 1282 Edmund Mortimer, Llywelyn's kinsman, and the royal host came upon the prince and his foremost men at Cilmeri. Most were slain, including Llywelyn, whose head was sent to London to be displayed at the Tower. Next year it was joined by that of his brother, David.[397]

Edward I imposed his own solution on Wales. Llywelyn's principality was divided by the Statute of Wales into five counties, on English lines, to become an appanage of the English Crown. Edward's son, Edward 'of Caernarvon', was invested — at Lincoln — as the first English Prince of Wales in 1301. Snowdonia was secured by a ring of castles. One of Edward I's principal servants in north Wales, Hugh of Leominster, was paymaster of the knights and esquires attacking Caernarfon in 1283. Next year he was clerk of works at both Caernarfon and Harlech castles. In 1295, as chamberlain of north Wales, Hugh was handling sums of £1,100 over four months for the works at Caernarfon. For his retirement he chose his native county. In 1308 Queen Isabella required Bishop Swinfield to provide him with a prebend, in effect a corrody, at Hereford Cathedral, with a pension in the meantime. The dean and chapter stalled, but Hugh was eventually presented to the prebend of Church Withington by royal mandate, holding it till his death in 1327.[398] Like Hereford, Ludlow and Shrewsbury, Leominster prospered as a result of Edward I's conquest of Wales, its role being a major marketing centre for central Wales. Subsequently only one serious Welsh uprising threatened the priory and its lands, the revolt of Owain Glyn Dwr, 1400–13. However, as the marcher barons retained their lordships, Leominster continued to suffer during their conflicts with the Crown, and amongst themselves, until the 1536 Act of Union formally annexed the whole of Wales to England.[399]

18 Church and Priory in the 14th Century

The Decorated South Aisle

Archbishop Peckham's attempt to resolve the conflict between monks and parishioners, by ordering the construction of the Forbury chapel, failed utterly to take into account the self-esteem of the burgesses. In the 1320s they constructed a south aisle in the new Decorated style. The quality of its architecture proves this was more a splendid expression of civic pride than a mere attempt to accommodate the increased population. For Pevsner, it is 'a showpiece indeed'. Freeman went even further: it is 'a building of singular magnificence ... with its series of five magnificent windows (and their companion at the west end) of equal size (it is) one of the noblest examples in existence of that variety of Gothic architecture'. Both men were intrigued by the 'whole composition' of the six windows, five on the south and another on the west, with their 'jambs, mullions and tracery profusely loaded with ballflower' decoration. These globular flowers, with three petals enclosing a small ball, characterised local buildings of the period (Plates 15a-c).[400]

Decorated architecture, particularly the use of ballflower, became highly fashionable in the west of England during the early 14th century. The earliest surviving examples, the crossing-tower and chapter-house at Wells, c1280–1306, suggest that a Wells master mason may have brought ballflower to Hereford Cathedral, where they encrust the central tower, on window jambs and tracery, gables, panels, string courses, buttresses and pinnacles. From the cathedral the fashion spread out to Leominster, Ledbury, Madley and across the Severn to Gloucester, Tewkesbury, Worcester, Hailes, Pershore and Evesham. Further east ballflower is found on Prior Sutton's tomb in the Lady Chapel at Christ Church Cathedral, Oxford, and to the south on tomb canopies in the Lady Chapel of St Augustine's Abbey, now the cathedral, at Bristol. Leominster's burgesses were strongly influenced by work at Hereford, built under Bishop Swinfield's authority c1310–15, and the south aisle of what was then the Benedictine monastery, now the cathedral, at Gloucester, begun by Abbot Thokey in 1318.[401]

This is confirmed by R.K. Morris, who has made a detailed study of Decorated architecture in Hereford and north Gloucestershire. For him Leominster is 'the key work in demonstrating the connections' between the crossing tower of Hereford Cathedral and the south aisle at Gloucester. On grounds of stylistic development, accepting Gloucester's south aisle as the initial impulse, Morris suggests that the Leominster south aisle was probably begun shortly after 1320. At the head of the aisle windows is a single circle divided into six compartments, with alternating trefoils and quatrefoils pointing inwards. This design was developed from the five-star motif of alternating trefoils and quatrefoils at the head of the south aisle windows at Gloucester (Fig 18.1). Even the small roundel at the centre of the Gloucester design is replicated at Leominster (Plate 15). Below the circle, at the head of each of the pairs of trefoiled lights, is a pair of smaller roundels, enclosing a cinquefoil. These are derived from the upper stages of the central tower of Hereford Cathedral,

Fig 18.1 Gloucester Cathedral: south aisle window showing five-star motif

where each side has a pair of windows flanked by blind windows made up of two lights, headed by a cinquefoil within a roundel (Fig 18.2). This cinquefoil within a circle was also used at the head of the windows of the polygonal chancel at Marden, and of those of the north aisle at St Laurence's, Ludlow.[402]

The priory also followed Hereford Cathedral central tower and the Gloucester south aisle in its luxuriant display of ballflower. The outer frames of the exterior of all five windows are enriched with three rows of ballflowers, and the tracery between the pairs of lights is decorated with smaller ballflower ornament. There is more on the interior of the windows, and even the sedilia at the east end (Plate 8 & see back cover). It has been calculated that at Leominster there are 820 such ballflowers on each window, at Gloucester, where even the buttresses are encrusted with ballflower, some 1,400.

At Leominster the heads at the ends of the dripstones or hood moulds, which carry the water away from the windows, are of particular interest, but unfortunately every one has been re-cut (Fig 18.3). Such heads are not to be found at Gloucester, Hereford or Ledbury. A sketch of the priory, drawn by E.A. Freeman, provides details of the fenestration of the south aisle as it was in the mid 19th century. The original second and third windows from the east had been replaced after the 1699 fire with others of crude church-warden-gothic design. These in turn were replaced during restorations of the early 20th century (Fig 18.4).

Fig 18.2 Hereford Cathedral: central tower with cinquefoils within a roundel

The Conventual Lady Chapel

Popular devotion to the Virgin, due to Her powers of maternal intercession, reached new heights in the early 13th century. This found tangible expression in many of England's greater churches. The Lady Chapel at Hereford Cathedral, built c1220–40, is an early example. Characteristically, it projects eastward beyond the presbytery, in rectangular form. Locally, there were later examples at Tewkesbury and Great Malvern. At Gloucester the existing Lady Chapel, of 1468–82, replaced a 13th-century chapel.

In 1314, despite finding Reading Abbey owed more than £1,200, Abbot Nicholas of Whaplode had, by a series of economy measures, built up a large enough surplus to embark upon the construction of a handsome eastern Lady Chapel, which was demolished with the rest of the abbey at the Dissolution. Archaeological information on the chapel is extremely limited, as Reading Gaol, built in the 19th century, impinged on its foundations. S.W. Buckler's 'Notes on Reading Abbey', of 1824, describe the chapel as of five bays with 'the interior, as nearly as could be ascertained, about 60 feet by 20 feet within the walls'. Restricted evidence from excavations in 1971–3 suggests

Fig 18.3 Detail of ballflower and later crowned head on dripstone

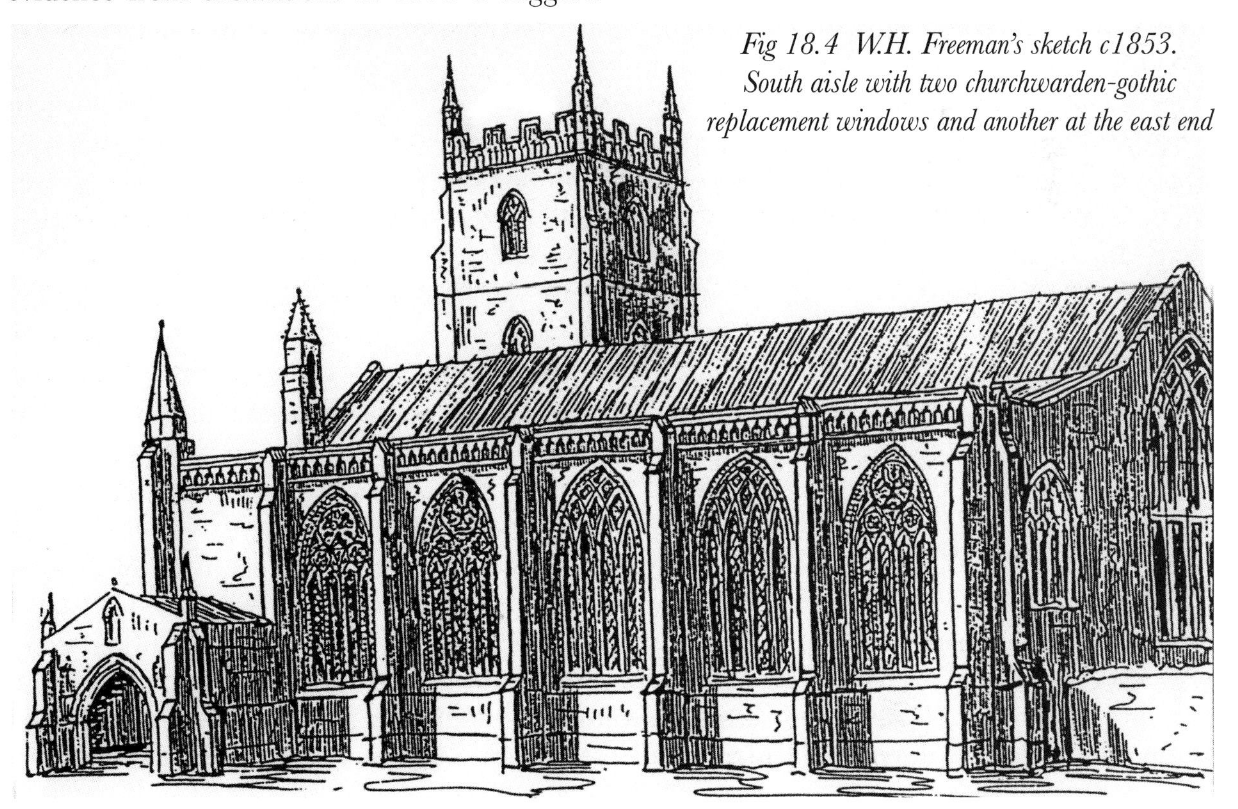

Fig 18.4 W.H. Freeman's sketch c1853. South aisle with two churchwarden-gothic replacement windows and another at the east end

the chapel might have been somewhat larger. Comparative measurements for Hereford Cathedral Lady Chapel are some 50ft by 35.[403]

The Leominster excavations of 1853 and 1932 revealed that a Lady Chapel, similar in plan to that of the mother church, had, as at Reading, replaced the small Romanesque chapel at the eastern end of the ambulatory. The foundations showed this was some 30ft wide, but no firm archaeological evidence was obtained as to its length, or date of construction (see Fig 7.4).

However, at Leominster, in contrast to Reading, there is considerable documentary evidence relating to the chantry within the Lady Chapel, especially as to its property, and thus funding. On 28 November 1331, for a fine of 5 marks, £3 6s 8d, Hugh de Radynges, chaplain, received a licence from the Crown to alienate in mortmain, to the 'dead hand' of the church, 240 acres of arable and other lands 'to fund two chaplains to celebrate divine service daily in the conventual church according to the appointment of the grantor'. This is the foundation document of the Lady Chapel built at the east end of the presbytery. A second Lady Chapel was established, within the parochial church, later in the century. Hugh's 240 acres represented but one of a considerable number of endowments, some very large but mostly small. In February following, William de Fynchamstede, prior, and John of Gloucester, sub-prior, granted the tenants of the priory some 433 acres of arable, 26 acres of meadow, 1 acre of pasture, 9½ messuages and 2 tofts in the fields of Leominster, Ivington, Stoke, Stockton, Priddleton in Humber and Miles Hope near Laysters, as well as several burgages within the borough, in 73 distinct lots.[404] The disparity between the 240 acres of the 1331 licence and the 433 acres of arable granted to the priory tenants in 1332 is to be explained in terms of the many other, individual, endowments received, such as that of Adam de Kynton, chaplain, c1336, of lands at Whyle in Pudlestone. Such endowments, listed in the third sequence of the Leominster Cartulary, are mostly undated. In May 1336 Hugh de Radynges obtained a further licence from the Crown to alienate in mortmain, for another major series of grants.

The largest endowment came on 28 April 1350, the worst of the great pestilence over, when a further licence to alienate was granted to William de Gorsynton, Thomas de Hompton and Adam de Salesbury. On this occasion we are given the names of the 26 donors of messuages, arable, meadow, pasture, more and wood in Leominster, Hope-under-Dinnmore, Ivington, the Hyde, Broadward, Luston, Lucton, Bircher, Yarpole, Hope's Wood, Miles Hope and Stockton. They included members of a number of prominent local families, such as Philip Romayn and William Lyulf from the borough, and Giles Hackluyt of Eaton, Walter Mapenore and John de Launde, lord of Whyle in Pudlestone, and Richard de Radyng and Walter de Ryere, chaplains. The earlier applications to the Crown for licence to alienate will have brought together similar series of grants.[405]

The custodians of the chantry kept full details of the conventual Lady Chapel's assets. These are to be found in the 'Collection' known as *Liber Cartarum Capellae Beatae Maria Monachorum Leomestrie*, HRO M31/8, which was copied by one of Coningsby's clerks from 'a small MS Vellum Ledger Book'. Of the 173 charters listed, the first 138 relate to property etc within the borough, the remainder to property outside. Very few bear a date.[406]

The 'Collection' includes details of a number of smaller endowments of the chantry. Hugh Lawlor's grant of a half-burgage in South Street to 'God, the Blessed Mary and the monastery of Leominster, for the health of his soul and those of his ancestors and successors', is characteristic.

	Messuage	Arable	Meadow	Pasture	More	Wood	Rents
Nov 1331[1]	3	240	10	3		40	16s
Feb 1332[2]	9½	433	26	1			
May 1336[1]		110	10	20		80	16s
Nov 1336[1]	14½	3	12				£2 0s
Apr 1350	6	360	24	10	10	18	£1 10s
Total	33	1,146	82	33	10	138	£5 2s

[1] endowment; [2] grant

CPR 1331, 221; 1336, 257; 1350, 495; 1376, 384; Domitian Aiii f196a; HRO M39/1/ff96b-112b

Table 9 Endowments of the Conventual Lady Chapel

His heirs and assigns could retain the property for so long as, at Michaelmas each year, they paid the sub-prior 12d 'for the freedom of the borough', and gave the chaplain and his successors 2lbs of wax for a taper to burn every Saturday, with six gallons of oil for one lamp to burn every day from morning to night at the altar of the Blessed Mary and another to burn all night on Fridays and Sundays at the Cross on the altar of St James. The chaplain, 'for the health of his own soul', was to make the said lamps ready. The charter ends with first a malediction and then a blessing. 'If anyone knowingly presumes to break, diminish or alter this my gift, let the highest judgements fall on them and they and their posterity be rooted from the earth nor come within the pity of the Mother of mercy. Whosoever preserve this my grant, the Lord prosper him hereafter.'

A typical lease is that of Richard de Henrethe who, as '*custos* of the altar of St Mary in the conventual church of Leominster', granted John Melide 'that house, with its appurtenances, which lies in West Street between the lands of William de Cholestre and Philip Mile, at a rent of 2s to be paid at the Annunciation of the Virgin Mary, and 18d at the feast of St Michael'. The lease, like so many, is undated, but internal evidence is of some assistance. A John Melide represented the borough in the 1314 and 1325 parliaments. Other charters record exchanges of property. Indeed, one of the very few dated charters, of 1343, is between Philip Romayn, Member for the borough in 1332, 1338 (twice), 1339, 1346 and 1348 (twice), and William Dumbleton, described as *custos*. As John of Gloucester was keeper, or prior, of Leominster until 1347, *custos* here refers to Dumbleton as keeper or guardian of the chantry of the Blessed Virgin.[407]

Dumbleton succeeded as prior, from 1348 to 1361. His election as abbot of Reading in autumn 1361 was in all probability as much the consequence of his success in raising funds for the Lady Chapel as for his leadership of the monastery and guardianship of its estates through the trauma of the Black Death. As abbot, Dumbleton proved to be both builder and man of prudence. A conspiracy by some Reading monks against him was investigated by the abbot of St Albans, who expelled some of the conspirators. Some went to cells of St Albans. Petitioning the Crown for licence to leave Reading and stay at Leominster 'with a few household servants', Dumbleton explained that he could 'not conveniently carry out works necessary for the repair of the church of Reading and his abbey, as well as his manors and granges, unless he acts prudently and moderates his expenses'.[408]

Fig 18.5 Leominster Priory: tomb recess in external south wall of south transept

Lay sepulture

For the Benedictines, lay burial within the monastic and parochial churches was welcomed as a means of rewarding patronage and attracting income by the appropriation of parish churches from lay rectors aspiring to such a privilege. Thus Joanna de Bohun, whose magnificent funerary monument can be seen in the Lady Chapel of Hereford Cathedral, had given its clergy the advowson of Lugwardine church with its chapels, to provide eight chaplains and two deacons to sing Masses to the Virgin, for the benefit of her soul, in 1327. At Leominster Priory the only remaining physical evidence of such lay sepulture is the decaying tomb recess in the south wall of the south transept (Fig 18.5). This was the tomb of a person of some substance. Despite its sad condition today, it was once a monument of quality, not only enriched with ballflower, indicating a date of c1330, but, as Morris points out, 'clearly related in its design to the tomb recess in the cathedral of John, brother of Bishop Richard Swinfield,' who had served as cathedral treasurer and precentor. The number of noble burials yet to be seen at the more remote Abbey Dore suggests that there would have been others within Leominster Priory. Was such an arrangement part of the relationship between the priory and the Mortimers of Wigmore?[409]

The Leominster monks exercised tight control over burials, within the parochial church as well as their own. In 1385, acknowledging that he had offended against the Lord and the church of Leominster in many ways, Robert Calderbroks came before the keepers, John Bray and Thomas Chaucumb, humbly and devoutly begging mercy. He had 'advised and assisted the burying of Thomas Power in Leominster church without licence and against the will of the keepers'. The 2s he had received for the burial he had given to John Dyer (the vicar) to be converted to their and other uses, 'to the peril of their souls'. On the other hand, in 1408, when Richard, son of Hugh de Wynnesley, 'came and begged licence of the keepers that his father might be buried in the parish church of Leominster, the same was granted because of the many benefits for which the said manor was beholden to Hugh'. Richard, who as bailiff returned himself as Member of Parliament, was evidently following in his father's footsteps. Ralph Hackluyt, who died in 1417, was equally acceptable to the keepers. A flat memorial stone in the chancel, with a man in armour and a woman 'scratched in black lines', bears his name and coat of arms: three battle axes or hatchets. A county family of standing, the Hackluyts of Eaton provided three sheriffs in the 14th century and two more in the 15th.[410]

The Parish Church

During the 14th century the parish church was drawn more deeply into the general administration of the diocese. The first reference to an ordination ceremony taking place at Leominster church was in 1366, when fifteen candidates were admitted to holy orders. In 1387 forty-two candidates, and in 1388 another forty-five, were ordained there by Robert of Archila, suffragan bishop during Bishop Gilbert's term of service as treasurer to Richard III. Four years later Bishop Trefnant admitted fifty-two ordinands to holy orders in the parish church.[411]

Increasingly, the episcopal registers provide more information on the state of both the church and its clergy. By 1347 there was a number of stipendiaries, priests who received fixed salaries for offering daily masses at chantries for the repose of the souls of the founders. On a recent visit Bishop Trillek, a man who devoted his reign to the wellbeing of his diocese, noted that they had refused to assist the vicar and his assistants in the performance of their parochial services. Instead they rudely occupied themselves with 'various insolences and enormities ill-befitting their order, to the diminishment of God's worship and harm to their souls', distracting some worshippers and offending others. Trillek required the prior, John of Gloucester, to make enquiries concerning these priests, and to compel the guilty to participate in the Divine Office by ecclesiastical censure. The same year, the vicar was commanded to announce sentence of greater excommunication against each of those 'sons of iniquity who had broken into the priory's treasury, stealing what money was there and then killing some of the prior's peacocks and stealing two of his swans'. The strictly liturgical dramas performed in Latin in church had by now developed an appealing, crude and comic side. At Leominster, however, they were castigated by Bishop Trillek as having 'degenerated into purely secular subject matter, leading to ribaldry and obscenity'. Thus the faithful, 'whose minds should be intent on solemnities and prayers, were deprived of devotions and drawn towards inanities to the wronging of God's name and perilous example'. The next year Trillek banned the performance of plays within the parish church, with the threat of anathema and excommunication for transgressors.[412]

Half a century later, in 1397, an episcopal visitation showed little change as far as the unbeneficed clergy were concerned. Several stipendiaries are named: William, chaplain of the chantry of the Blessed Virgin, William Crompe, William Casyn, Richard Pastay and John Grasley. None 'obeyed the vicar in the service of God and divine matters'. Further, William Crompe, priest, was 'a public trader in animals and sheep, buying and selling at profit'; William Casyn, priest, threatened 'any who uncovered his shortcomings' that he would 'reply likewise'; Thomas Whytebrede, chaplain, was 'incontinent with Alicia Taelour'; Walter Goodrich, chaplain, 'is a common merchant, who makes a profit of 5s from buying and selling 60 sheep'. All this should not be surprising. Such was the shortage of clergy after the Black Death that a multitude of laymen, many of them illiterate, came crowding into orders. The chantry chaplains were bound by custom to say masses for the dead after the offertory at the parochial mass. Their behaviour at the priory will have been due to their inability to say them early in the morning and spend the rest of the day on their outside interests.[413]

The Parochial Lady Chapel

Despite such lapses in church discipline, there is firm evidence of the piety of many of the principal residents of the borough. Support through endowments etc for the monastic Lady Chapel at the east end of the priory was not the only achievement of such piety. A chantry of the Blessed Virgin was founded within the parochial church sometime later. In November 1376 the Patent rolls refer to a priest who would celebrate divine service in 'the chapel of Our Lady in the church of Leominster according to the ordinance of the founders, their heirs and assigns forever'. A certain

William was the chaplain in 1397. The founders were John I, son of William, de Salesbury and Richard Lorimer, both of whom had represented Leominster at Westminster, together with John de Pyriton, Walter de Coumbe, Richard in le Wyche and Richard Lounteley. They paid the king 20 marks, £13 6s 8d, to alienate into mortmain 14½ messuages, 3 acres of arable, 12 of meadow and £2 in rents in Leominster, Hennor, Stretford and Eaton. This fine stands in marked contrast to that levied by the Crown 45 years earlier, in 1331, of a mere 5 marks, £3 6s 8d, for the alienation of 240 acres of arable. The ordinance of the founders was successful in ensuring that the townspeople would retain control of this chantry. Presentation to the chaplaincy of the parochial Lady Chapel, by the prior, was to be 'on the nomination of the twelve best and most worthy men of Leominster', in other words, the twelve capital burgesses. Both priory and conventual Lady Chapel were dissolved by Henry VIII in 1539, but the parochial chantry of the Blessed Virgin was not suppressed until 1547. The piscina and sedilia at the eastern end of the south aisle, it has been suggested, served this chantry (see Plate 8).[414]

Tile Fragments

During the restoration of the south nave and south aisle in 1878–9, George Gilbert Scott found tile fragments of some 50 widely differing designs. These he reset in the recess at the west end of the south nave. Hilary White published a short interim statement on these tiles in 1994. The collection deserves a wider and much more detailed description, discussion and illustrations than can be provided here, where space permits consideration of fragments (1) to (18) only.[415] Of these, tile (1) (Plate 16) is outstanding: a lion passant guardant within a pair of circles, with a wavy line between, the pattern outlined on a dark green background. Shattered into numerous pieces, it was successfully reconstructed by Scott. A similar design has yet to be found.

The 17 remaining fragments fall into three main groups: Chertsey derivatives, (2–6); heraldic tiles of the Bredon/Tewkesbury group, (7–12); and a Worcester group (13–17) (Fig 18.5). The five tiles of the first group are of considerable interest. They formed part of five different, four-tile compositions, derived from designs at Chertsey, Halesowen and Hailes abbeys, where the late-13th-century pavements have been described as having 'the most technically accomplished tiles of the Middle Ages'. Their lineage can be traced to designs produced, under Henry III's patronage, for Clarendon Palace and Westminster Abbey chapter-house. Most remarkable was a series of elaborate Chertsey roundels, depicting the Romance of Tristan and Isolde, the Labours of the Month, and the Signs of the Zodiac, within a patterned circular band or frame. These were set into a square by the addition of four corner sections, decorated with scrolls of vine foliage. Chertsey moulds, with roundels fired in one piece, were used in a similar way at Halesowen. Here the decoration of the circular band was developed, in some cases carrying an inscription, in others a procession of dragons. According to Eames, 'this is the only form of the dragon present on tiles in the British Museum's collection'. The most famous of the Halesowen roundels depicts the seated figure of Abbot Nicholas, with a tonsure, holding his crozier in his left hand and the church in the other. Here the circular band carries the legend in Lombardic capitals, 'This work Abbot Nicholas gave to the Mother of Christ, that he may flourish without confusion'.[416]

In the early 14th century such designs achieved wide popularity. To simplify production for a wider market, other tilers abandoned the roundel to produce a similar, square design, in four rather

Fig 18.5 Tiles fragments 1-6 (not to scale) *Eames' Design 1035 (courtesy BM)*

than five parts. Five Leominster tiles, two pairs (2–3 and 5–6) and a singleton (4), are derived from these Chertsey compositions. Of the first pair (2) has a startled face, with bristling hair, within the quadrant of the circle. Due to the tile's condition, it is difficult to decide whether the face is that of a man or lion. A design found at Hailes Abbey, and excavated at Bordesley in 1866, has a similar fierce mask with flowing hair within a band, with two pairs of fantastic animals confronting each other. The circular band on Leominster tile (2) carries four letters, in Lombardic capitals, with a pair of fantastic confronted animals, rather than the procession of dragons on the Chertsey tiles. On the outer edge is a spray of foliage, in a cruder form than the Hailes/Bordesley examples. On the second tile of the pair (3) a spray of five leaves replaces the face in the centre, and the band carries a procession of four fantastic animals. This is a mirror image of Eames' design 1035. A fragment of type (2) was found at Abbey Dore, and one of type (3) at Berrington Street, Hereford. The third Leominster example (4) is very worn. Here, rudimentary coats of arms replace the bands of Lombardic letters or fantastic animals.[417]

The second pair of Leominster tiles (5-6) bears quite different Chertsey/Hailes designs. In both cases the centre of the four-tile square would be occupied, not by a circle as in (2) and (3), but by a diamond. On the outer sides of each of the diamonds was a semi-circle, extended almost to form a horseshoe and containing foliage. Leominster tile (5) has a rabbit jumping beneath four leaves and four bunches of berries within the horshoe. On tile (6) there is instead a six-petalled flower. These designs are evidently derived from other tiles found both at Chertsey and, during the 1866 excavations, at Bordesley, where the horseshoe is punctured by quatrefoils, and an oak branch, with leaves and acorns, grows from the

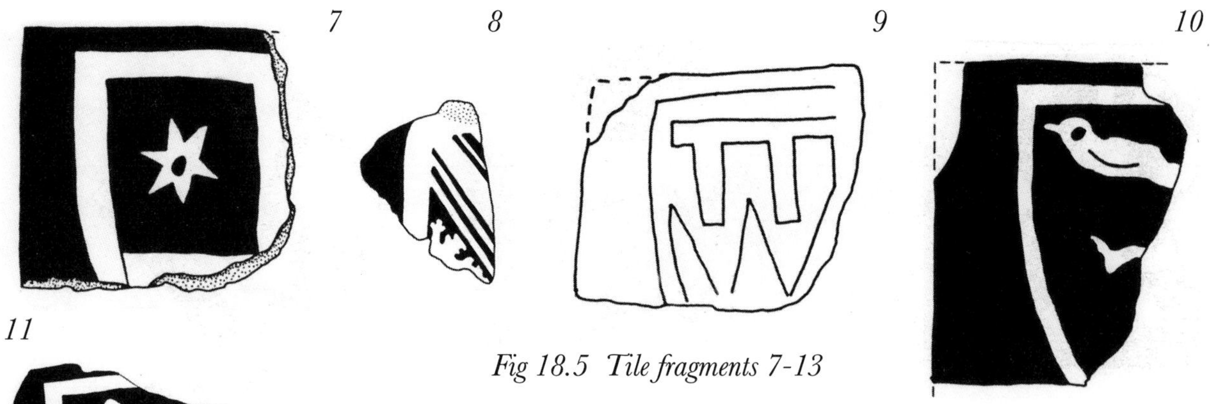

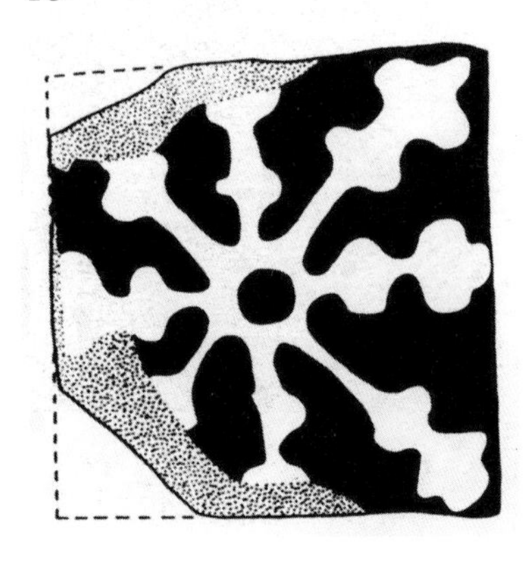

Fig 18.5 Tile fragments 7-13

central circle into the horseshoe, with a more delicate form of the decoration found on tile (6) in the corner. Fragments of (5) and (6) have been found at Tewkesbury, and of (6) at Berrington Street, Hereford.[418]

There are six heraldic tile fragments (7–12). Four coats of arms can be identified with a degree of certainty. The designs suggest that most are of the same group as some 40 or so 14th-century heraldic tiles in the chancel of Bredon church, together with others at Tewkesbury and elsewhere. This group of tiles has been discussed by Vince and Wilmott.[419] (7) Quarterly in the first quarter a mullet (star) of six pierced, the arms, as at Bredon, of Robert, Earl of Oxford, brother-in-law of Roger Mortimer, first Earl of March, hanged at Tyburn in 1330; (8) A bend cotised (placed between two bars), between six lioncels, as at Bredon, the arms of the de Bohuns, earls of Hereford; (9) Five fusils conjoined in fesse, a label of five points, for which Wilmott suggests at least five possibilities, also present at Tewkesbury; (10) The fourth is a cross patonce between five martlets, the arms of Westminster Abbey and, traditionally, Edward the Confessor, also at Abbey Dore. This is frequently found in mirror image, the swallows looking to the right rather than the left.

Tile (11) is more problematic. It has fleur-de-lys, in three rows of three, with a singleton below, seemingly a crude attempt at France, ancient: a field of fleur-de-lys. Also problematic is (12), the lower portion of a shield with a field checky, divided into contiguous rows of small squares, which would be emblazoned alternately metal (or fur) and a colour. If the whole field was checky, as at Bredon, this would be the Warenne, earls of Surrey, but there are numerous possibilities for lesser families. On the other hand, with a fesse (now lost) just above the break, this would probably have been the arms of the great marcher family of Clifford, checky a fesse, as found at Dore Abbey. Petrological analysis of the Bredon

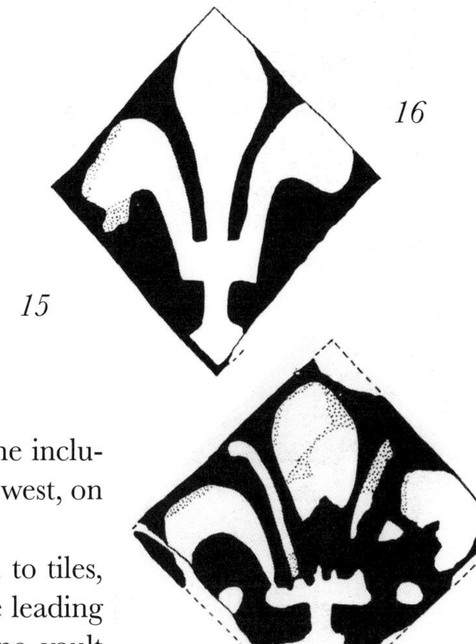

Fig 18.5 Tile fragments 14-18

and Tewkesbury group of tiles, with sandstone and limestone inclusions, is consistent with a source close to Hereford or further west, on the Welsh border.[420]

A third group, of five tiles (13–17), is similar in design to tiles, identified by Keen as 44–48, immediately above the passage leading from St John's chapel in Worcester cathedral. In the stone vault covered by these tiles are four *meurtrières*, murder holes, similar to those in front of the portcullis of a castle. As Keen points out, these tiles are of a different size and later than the main series in the cathedral, for which he proposed the date 1377–80. One further design rescued by Scott (18) has a circular frame, decorated with a knotted band and five-petal flowers.[421]

Excavations have provided further evidence. In the 2005 dig, hundreds of discarded fragments of broken medieval tiles were collected. The vast majority were cream and dark green, suggesting an original chequer board pattern. Some fragments, with decorative schemes, have yet to be fully analysed. One, DSCN0270, is similar to fragment (18) above (Fig 18.6).

When floodlighting was recently installed at the priory, Border Archaeology located an assemblage of high-status floor tiles close to the south-east corner of the priory. Laid in a line and uncemented, they were apparently used to create crude flooring, and were thus of secondary deposition. Analysed using x20 magnification, three fabric series were established. A Bredon type included border tiles, single and four-tile patterns, and heraldic designs. The Droitwich fabric tiles were oblong, rectangular, square and triangular in shape, with flower as well as fleur-de-lys decoration in repeating patterns and squares. Finally, the Malvern Chase tiles 'replicated 15th-century Bredon, Droitwich and Great Malvern specimens'.

Fig 18.6 Excavated tile fragment DSCN0270

Five fragments received special mention. Two had chevron borders around indiscernible pictorial designs; the third, 'a flower design within a double circle', could be a companion of DSCN0270 of the 2005 excavations. One heraldic tile is described as 'a checked pattern consisting of small squares, split in the centre by two horizontal lines', probably the checky a fesse of Clifford? Most important, however, is a green glazed tile with a yellow slip design portraying 'an upright man raising the palm of his hand behind a lion'. Unfortunately, none of these tiles has yet been returned to the parish or made available for public inspection.[422]

Episcopal Visitation of the Parish Church

In 1397 Bishop Trefnant conducted a triennial visitation to enquire into the manners of life of the clergy and laity of his diocese. Prior John Fifhyde and Sub-Prior John Chauncell availed themselves of this opportunity to present a written submission concerning the conduct of Reginald Pole, the vicar, his priests and the parishioners. The prior's first charge was that Pole and his parish priests, inflamed with pride, abused their almuces by wearing them not only in and about the church but also in the hustle and bustle of the town, thereby detracting from the dignity of cathedral and collegiate churches. Secondly, despite the bishop's ruling at his last visitation, Pole still refused to restrict the saying of the Mass of the Virgin to the period stipulated, between the 9th and 10th hours. He was thus continuing to disturb the monks at their High Mass. Thirdly, Pole refused to join the monks, properly habited according to ancient custom, in the conventual choir for vespers, masses and processions on the church's principal feasts. Fourthly, Pole's priests refused to take the oath of obedience to their rector, the abbot and convent of Reading. Finally, Pole was accused of taking the offerings of the faithful for himself, to the grave prejudice of abbot and convent. This is not altogether surprising. Maximum salaries for clergy, fixed by Parliament in 1362, were wholly inadequate in terms of post-Black Death inflation since 1349, and were not raised until 1414. As will be seen, Pole's successor, John Vir, a canon lawyer, brought this matter to a highly satisfactory resolution.

As to the parishioners, Fifhyde submitted that some had enclosed, with a barrier and wall, the altar of SS Mary Magdalene, Margaret and Katherine 'within the parish church', where on feast days the prior had been accustomed to celebrate solemn Mass, and the faithful, in great numbers, had made offerings. That was not all. The parishioners had removed from this altar the statue of St Giles, where many offerings had been made for the dead. These had included the bequest of a chalice, vestments and a missal for the officiating priests. The statue had been particularly fruitful for two reasons: because it was devoutly believed that all who were truly repentant, confessed their sins and abstained from further commission, like the king who had sought to shoot Giles's favourite hind, would be forgiven through the saint's merits; and because St Giles was held in especial veneration by the local smiths as their patron and intermediary.[423]

Trefnant found for the prior and sub-prior on all the issues raised, except the wearing of the almuces, which he held to be 'permissible for the glory of God'. The parishioners must remove the wall; the vicar should observe all the principal feasts in the customary manner, avoid clashing with the conventual High Mass, take the oath of obedience, and be content with 1d for a single mass, as laid down by custom.[424]

On Trefnant's arrival at Leominster on 5 June, the parishioners took the opportunity to present their grievances, not only against the rector, the abbot and convent of Reading, and their keepers, the prior and sub-prior, but also against the vicar and his clergy. They raised seven issues of default on the part of the abbot as rector. The first two related to the vexed problems with which Cantilupe had had to deal more than a century earlier: the parish clerk was unable to ring the bells at the set hours, as he ought, because the monks, with custody of the key, locked the doors. Further, the rector impeded and harassed the parishioners when they improved and renovated their parish church, 'as they should'.

Thirdly, the parishioners complained that the rector had for three years failed to provide a clerk to carry the bell and light before the vicar when he was conveying the body of Christ to the sick. It was the custom, they claimed, that the rector should provide water from Lugg Bridge, beyond the town on the Ludlow side, suitably blessed, and give the clerk a salary of 8s per annum. Fourthly, the church lacked a book for the office of burial. The current one was worn out through use. In times of plague sixteen or eighteen bodies had to be buried on the same day. Even two books, the parishioners maintained, would not suffice. Fifthly, the prior did not allow any parishioners to communicate in the parish church without first making an oblation of at least ½d. Trefnant's Register bears the terse comment, 'Forbidden for the future'. Sixthly, the two antiphons and two graduals in their church were unsuitable and insufficient for elderly priests, who found them too difficult to read. Finally they reported that, as the vicar's cattle fouled the churchyard where they were pastured, the clergy's silk vestments were unduly soiled during processions.[425]

Walter le Brut and Lollardy in the north-west of the county

The appeal of John Wycliffe as a religious reformer had been primarily academic. After his death in 1384, antipathy to the Church amongst humble folk was based firmly on the belief that 'no governance is to be held the law of God which is not grounded in holy scripture'. William Swinderby was 'perhaps the very greatest of the Lollard evangelists'. He was saved at the last moment from being burned at the stake at Leicester in 1382 only by the intervention of John of Gaunt. Swinderby recanted, but later retreated to north-west Herefordshire, not far from the priory's estates and within easy reach of the safety of the Welsh March. There he preached, amongst other places, at Kington, Whitney, Wigmore, Croft, Eardisley and at a small chapel at Newton in the Deerfold Forest. Persuaded by the promise of a safe conduct, Swinderby faced Bishop Trefnant alone in Bodenham church in June 1390. Nine months later he was tried at the cathedral for heresy. The charges included his belief that true contrition brought forgiveness without a word to a priest; that indulgences and pardons had no place in holy writ; that Christ came to save men, not to slay them, the reverse being anti-Christ; and his rejection of tithes and offerings to the members of the priesthood who had 'come to their benefices by simony, do not perform their office or were notorious fornicators'. Swinderby recanted once more.[426]

Trefnant now moved against Swinderby's companion and friend, Walter Brut. Of his early life little is known, other than that his proud claim to be of Welsh parentage, 'layman and husbandman', is well founded. His lands consisted of three messuages, with 120 acres of arable and five of meadow at Lyde Godfrey, now Lyde Arundel, Lower Lyde Court and Upper Lyde, or Lyde Prior, which had been granted to St Guthlac's, Hereford, in the 12th century.[427] His ability in spoken as well as written Latin, and his facility in dialectic suggest he had been a student at Oxford. If so, this would have given him adequate opportunity to immerse himself in Wycliffe's views. His career has been described in the *DNB*, by Emden and in the *ODNB*. In the first, 'Brit' is a fellow of Merton College, but this Emden rejects, claiming instead that certain astronomical calculations made by Brut in his *Testament*, submitted at his trial for heresy in Hereford, were consonant with his possible identity as author of *Theoremata planetorum*. This is discussed more fully in *ODNB*, where Walter 'Bryt' is 'astronomer'; but his authorship of *Theoremata planetorum* has been left 'an open question'. Such discussion, whilst important, excludes adequate exploration of Brut's Lollard views, of which there is generous record in his *Testament*, incorporated in Trefnant's Register for 1391 and which Foxe translates in his *Book of Martyrs*.[428]

What was effectively a show trial opened at Hereford Cathedral in October 1393, when Walter Brut presented himself before Bishop Trefnant, accused of clandestinely proselytising both nobles and the vulgar, with numerous heresies, including the assertion that the pope was anti-Christ and a denial of the Real Presence, that the sacrament was 'but symbol and memorial'. Ranged against him were 22 doctors of law and masters and bachelors of theology, including the Chancellor and former Chancellor of the University of Cambridge, the Master of New College, Oxford, the priors of Worcester Cathedral, St Peter's, Gloucester, and the Ludlow Carmelites, the Treasurer of St David's Cathedral, and the precentor of Hereford Cathedral.

Brut now publicly defended the beliefs for which Swinderby had been charged, which thus became the subject of a second accusation. Brut replied to both with his *Testament*, a lengthy document in Latin, some 73 pages in the printed version of Trefnant's Register. 'A remarkably wide-ranging and often extremely shrewd work of theological enquiry by a very searching Christian', this deserves broader consideration than it has yet received. Brut's ability to quote at length from the Bible, word for word on almost 200 occasions during his trial, his numerous references to the Old and New Testaments and the Apocalypse, on occasions ten or more to the page, together with his knowledge of canon law, showed that his Oxford days had not been wasted.

Brut's fundamental contention was that 'the head of the body of the church is one, which is Christ, and the head of Christ is God'. The pope's power was usurped, for 'the power to bind and to loose is not specially granted to Peter'. His claim to absolve from sin was not founded on scripture; it was on his own authority that he enjoined the sinner to penance. When, by selling pardons, the pope seduced men with promises to deliver them from death, this was the grievous sin of simony. Touching the Lord's Supper, Brut's position was similar to that adopted by Martin Luther some 120 years later. 'By the works of the law shall no flesh be justified. The just man shall live by his faith.' Thus Brut denied the mediatorial role of both the church and its priests. On the latter, he had much to say, asking 'do priests sin or not, who bargain for money to pray for the soul of a dead man or woman? Selling prayers is abominable.' Benedictions, exorcisms and hallowings with the use of holy water, together with images, oaths and tithes, were further objects of attack. Brut went on to the prophetic statement that 'temporal goods shall be taken away from the clergy for the multitude of their sins'. His belief that he did not dare exclude women 'from administering the body of Christ' has aroused considerable interest in our own day.[429]

Brut's judges took three days to reach their conclusions. The care with which they condemned his 37 'errors' indicates that Brut's charges had struck home. The Royal Council, fearing the social unrest that the trial could arouse, issued letters patent to fourteen of the principal figures in the county, including the sheriff and the mayor of Hereford. As Brut had already been the cause of troubles not only in the diocese but in neighbouring areas, the fourteen were commanded to be prepared to deal forcefully with any popular movements which threatened interference with the proceedings in the cathedral. The measures taken were effective. Brut stated publicly, at the cross in the cathedral churchyard, that he submitted to correction by his bishop, as a subject ought. The master of New College then preached a sermon on Romans 11:20: 'because of unbelief they were broken off by faith ... Be not highminded, but fear'.[430]

This was far from the end of the matter. The Lollard attack on the worldliness of churchmen fell on receptive ears. Walter, despite his very evident learning, sought to portray himself as a man of the people and a true Briton. Indeed, he had commenced his defence: 'I, Walter Brut, sinner, layman and Christian, having my offspring on both my mother and father's side as a Briton'. Conscious of the ultimate penalty, the stake, Brut crafted a well-judged defence, stressing the doctrine of Christian mercy: 'our offence against God is far more grievous than any offence of our brother against us. It thus behoves us to be merciful if we will have God's mercy.' 'Judge not that ye be not judged.' 'Thou shalt not kill and whomsoever shall kill shall be in danger of the judgement.' 'Love your enemies ... do good to them that hate you and pray for them that disrespectfully use you and persecute you.'[431]

Out of the hands of his captors, Brut seems to have lost sight of Christ's Sermon on the Mount, for his subsequent career, as yet undiscussed in the literature, reveals a very different man to that of the *Testament*. In 1394 he gathered a group of kindred spirits about him and, in the words of the prior of Leominster, 'had for three months made sundry affrays within the town against the peace of our Lord the King'. Brut's Leominster supporters were led by a certain Hugh Maune, whose servants, together with some of Brut's companions, assaulted William Lyulf, one of the prominent citizens, 'by force of arms, that is to say with swords, shields, bows and arrows, beating and maiming him'. Although difficult to identify, Maune was a man of some consequence in the shire. In 1388 he was a witness, with Kinnard de le Bere of Kinnersley and Walter Devereux of Weobley, to an agreement about the manor of Ashton. The two latter were both killed leading the Herefordshire levies at the battle of Bryn Glas near Pilleth. On the Friday following, having heard that Brut, Maune and others were approaching the town armed with coats of mail, plates, pallets, swords, bucklers, pole-axes, launcegayes and bows bent, with arrows in the same bows, the constables, Hugh Hackluyt and John Huntley, gathered a counterforce, including the sub-dean's servant, John Cook, and laid in wait to arrest the malcontents. Opening fire, they shot at Brut, smote him and left him for dead, with five arrow wounds. In the process they suffered two fatalities, John Cook, described as of the county of Berks, and Thomas Aubrey. Despite an arrest warrant, Brut effected his escape, no doubt into the marcher lordships, beyond the jurisdiction of English law. By August 1404 he was dead, probably killed supporting Owain Glyn Dwr.[432]

What is not fully brought out in most portraits of Brut is the strength of his local support. Swinderby's safe conduct to and from Bodenham was due to pressure on Trefnant from Brut's 'powerful friends amongst the gentry of the diocese'. Fear of the strength of such support is evident in the Council's mandate to the sheriff. This refers to 'an armed conspiracy', 'his adherence, attempting by force to defeat the bishop's purpose', and 'conventicles, assemblies or confederacies, by any colour, whereby the bishop and doctors might by any means be molested'. Brut's supporters amongst the local gentry included Sir John Clanvow of Cusop, Michaelchurch-on-Arrow and Ocle

Pychard, in whose literary works are Lollard resonances. Without the support of other manorial lords such as Sir Robert de Whitney, a relation by marriage of Clanvow, Swinderby would never have had the freedom to preach at Whitney, Almeley, Eardisley, Clifford, Kington and elsewhere. At Glyn Dwr's victory at Pilleth in 1402, Whitney was killed and Clanvow taken prisoner. If Brut was amongst those who lost their lives in the battle, it was on the other side.[433]

In terms of Brut's activities at Leominster, one of the prime movers may well have been Sir John Croft, who had married Janet, daughter of Owain Glyn Dwr. Croft's interest in the character of the clergy is indicated by his grant to Thomas Neel, deacon, in 1381–3 of an annual pension of £5 from his rents in Leominster. Relations between the Crofts and their neighbours, the priors of Leominster, had rarely been good. In 1382 Sir John had been excommunicated for unjustly detaining the tithes of Newton, one of the 39 places listed in Bishop Richard de Capella's charter of 1123 as being within the *parochia* of Leominster. At Croft Swinderby had preached openly, in the castle chapel, and had concealed himself to avoid Trefnant's citations. After the Leominster incident in 1394, Richard III took a personal interest in matters. Croft was apprehended, and the king ordered his constable at Windsor Castle to 'receive Sir John from one who shall deliver him on the king's behalf and keep him in custody until further orders'. The royal mandate was signed at Hereford. The following month Croft received a letter from Trefnant, making an appointment for him to renounce Lollardy. Croft replied with an expression of surprise at such a request. Only on 5 March following was Trefnant able to inform the king that Sir John, still in Windsor Castle, had sworn that he would 'neither read nor own English books extracted from holy scriptures according to the bare text, with evil intent, by certain persons called Lollards'. This is but the best recorded case against the prominent friends of Swinderby and Brut in north-west Herefordshire.[434]

Sympathy with the tenets of Lollardy remained embedded in this area. In 1391 Isabel Priestes of Almeley had to swear her repudiation of Lollardy on the Gospels. In 1433 John Vir, vicar of Leominster, had to enquire into further accusations of Lollardy, at Almeley. Three years later John Woodhulle, cleric of Almeley, publicly abjured his 'dyvers erroures and heresies' under fifteen heads, averring that 'John Wyclyf's opinions and his felawes are dampnable and to be reproved and his bokes dampned'. At Eardisley in 1505 John Croft made a further attack on the papal power of 'byndyng and lowsyng'. The Quakers established a firm hold in Almeley in the first half of the 17th century. This was to find physical expression in their Meeting House, built 1672. Further west in the Olchon valley was one of the earliest Baptist communities in the Marches and Wales. In the 1650s Leominster itself was to earn the title 'Little Geneva'.[435]

19 The Priory's Agrarian Economy in the 14th Century

1. *Herneys*, *Burys*, Customs and Services

Pope Nicholas's Taxation of 1291 records the details of the ecclesiastical taxation of one-tenth granted by the pope to Edward I to defray the expenses of another crusade. For this a new valuation of individual churches was made, which listed temporalities and spiritualities separately. The taxation is important for the priory estates, as it provides what it took to be the rental, probably the minimum, at which its manors and granges could be let. To take one example, it is known from other sources that the rental of Durham Abbey's estates between 1293 and 1297 was about £3,700, yet in this Taxation the temporalities were assessed at £620. At Leominster the Taxation credited the priory with a mere 46 'cattle' and 280 sheep, yet an Extent of 1327 indicates the total number of oxen exceeded 350, and of sheep some 1,250. The significance of Table 10 is therefore only relative.[436]

Earl Coningsby's *Register or Ledger Book of the Lands granted to the Tenants in Villeinage* is the only significant documentary source for the workings of the priory's manorial economy. It contains excerpts he had translated from the 14th-century halimote rolls of Leominster Priory into a ledger book in his Evidence Room at Hampton Court. As the title shows, it is restricted in the range of evidence that it provides, for Coningsby's selection of material was activated, not by antiquarian interests, but by his personal agenda. The copy of the original rolls, in the possession of Thomas Blount of Orleton in 1669, was probably Coningsby's source.[437]

In 1692 Coningsby bought three of Leominster's four ancient *herneys*, Stockton, Stoke and Ivington with Hope-under-Dinmore, from Major Wildman for £3,060. These were still administered by their halimote courts. Later, he purchased the large manor of Marden, immediately south of Hope and Hampton, from the Crown.

The earl suspected that, after the Restoration of Charles I, 'various tenures had been altered and that demesne and other lands of great value had been artfully withheld', to his prejudice. The *Register* was but part of a 'laborious collection' of orig-

	Carucates x 240 =	Acres	Carucate value	Total
Leominster	6	1,440	£1 0s 0d	£6 0s 0d
Ivington	4	960	£1 0s 0d	£4 0s 0d
Luston	3	720	£1 0s 0d	£3 0s 0d
Stockton	4	960	13s 4d	£2 13s 4d
Stoke	3	720	13s 4d	£2 0s 0d
Hope	3	720	10s 0d	£1 10s 0d
Bokland/Fencote	3	720	6s 8d	£1 0s 0d
More	2	480	5s 0d	10s 0d
Total	28	6,730		£20 13s 4d

Taxatio Ecclesiastica Record Commission (1802) 173

Table 10 Assessment of Leominster Priory: Pope Nicholas's Taxation of c1291

inal records, which he had amassed, relating to the three *herneys* and Marden. 'Deducing conclusions highly favourable to his purpose, he caused ejectments to be prepared against a considerable number of respectable families', all holding by copy of the Court rolls. They took their case to the Court of Chancery. On receipt of the Court's adverse judgement, the earl published a pamphlet, disparaging the Lord Chancellor. For this he was imprisoned for six months in the Tower, where he used the time to search for further evidence amongst the public records. Eventually, he abandoned his cause and destroyed much of the material, including virtually all copies of his monumental *History of Marden*.[438]

Coningsby's interest in the halimote rolls of the three *herneys* was the information they might provide about the services and payments due from the priory's villein tenants in the lands he had acquired. His *Register*, unlike the Leominster Cartulary, thus provides virtually no evidence as to the priory's freehold tenants or their landholdings. Nevertheless, considerable information on the general administration of the estates can be drawn from it. Some of the names and numbers of freehold tenants in 1431–2 can be found in a register of Reading Abbey, which was in the Wiltshire County Records Office.[439]

There are other drawbacks to the *Register*. The 756 extracts from the Leominster halimote rolls cover only the years 1330–1401. They are divided into two series, with a twelve-year gap, 1336–48. For the pre-Back Death era, 1330–6, there are 101 extracts, for the years 1348–1401 there are 655. However, the later sequence, on ff10–85b, precedes the earlier, on ff86–110. Both sequences are set out by *herneys* and townships within the *herneys*, but the order is far from chronological, and there is no complete annual sequence. The number of halimote extracts varies considerably between the four *herneys*: 364 for Ivington,[440] 162 for Stockton,[441] 141 for Stoke[442] and 89 for Luston.[443] The inclusion of Luston *herneys*, even with a reduced number of extracts, is indeed fortunate, for after the Dissolution these lands were in the hands of the Croft family. There are occasional intrusions of non-halimote material.

The extracts are all in translation, but one cannot always be confident about the clerk's translation of significant medieval terminology, nor his transcription of personal and place-names. The county owes a great debt to Mr Stephen Millett of Rhode Island who, after purchasing the *Register* and a number of other volumes of Herefordshire interest from a dealer who had acquired them at the sale of Hampton Court contents in 1972, generously donated them to the Herefordshire Record Office. Without the *Register* our knowledge of the medieval administration of the priory's four *herneys* would be thin indeed.

The *herneys*

The *Register* shows the priory's demesne lands being administered as four distinct *herneys*, centred on *burys*, or granges, at Stockton, Stoke (Prior), Ivington and Luston. These divisions of the Leominster estates probably originated in the earliest years of the minster, if not before.[444]

The townships and settlements that made up each of the four *herneys* are recorded in the halimote rolls extracts. Stockton *herneys* included lands at Brimfield, parts of Upton (Court?) and Drayton; at Middleton, parts of Miles Hope, *More* (Moor Abbey) and Overton; and at Kimbolton, parts of Hamnish, Over and Nether Bache, and nearby Grammanton.[441] The *herneys* of Stoke extended from Eaton in the northwest and Fencote (Abbey) in the north-east through *Bocland* (Buckland),

Fig 19.1 Cursneh Hill seen across the former meadow lands of Summergalls lying between the Lugg and Kenwater

Figs 19.2 Hope, the Bury: a) existing farm buildings; b)stone paving, measuring up to 56" x 63" x 5", serving as a fence, from earlier buildings?

Pyrtulton (Priddleton), Westwood and Risbury to *Wyggeton* (Wicton), south of Stoke. Within Ivington *herneys*, *Somergild* (Summergalls) lay to the west of Leominster Marsh, between Kenwater and Lugg. Meaning 'liable to seasonal flooding', it was an area of low-lying meadowland for the home farm.[445] Stagbatch, Cholstrey and *Cussenore* (Cursneh, Fig 19.1) lay between the Pinsley Brook and River Arrow, with *Bradeford* (Broadward) and part of Eaton further to the east. Ivington *bury* was between Arrow and Little Arrow. Brierley and *Waverton* (Wharton) lay due south of Leominster, on the north and east slopes of Ivington Hill and Brierley Wood; to the south-west lay *Over* and *Nether Hulle* (Upper and Lower Hill). There were also demesne tenants at *Orleton* (Aulden?) in Ivington, not to be confused with Orleton in Luston. The majority of the priory's demesne tenants in the more compact Luston *herneys* were at Luston itself, with others at Orleton, Bircher, Yarpole, Lucton and Eyton.

Hope-under-Dinmore, which is not mentioned in Domesday Book, is sometimes referred to in the *Register* as Hope. It has therefore to be carefully distinguished from Miles Hope, in the north of Stockton *herneys*, which does appear in Domesday. In the 12th century most of the highland about Dinmore, 3½ miles south of Ivington, was still very heavily wooded, but in the first decades of the 13th a considerable area was assarted. By 1330 the halimote rolls show that Hope-under-Dinmore had developed into a sub-manor of Ivington. It had its own *bury*, now Bury Farm (Figs 19.2a&b), in a small valley looking east, and under its wing were the settlements of Woodmanton and Winsley to the west, and to the north Newton and *Pirbryn* (Pervin), overlooking the Marlbrook (see Byant's Map on the inside of the front cover).

The *Burys*

The Extent of 1327, in the *Register*, provides detailed descriptions of the lands, staff and stock of the four *herneys*, and of Ivington's outlier at Hope-under-Dinmore and Stockton's at Moor Abbey. All but *More* were centred on a *bury.* At Leominster Priory this Old English term was retained in preference to the Anglo-French 'grange', and is still in use today, as at Ivington, Luston, Stockton and Stoke; Hope has apparently arrogated to itself the title of *bury*. 'Grange', on the other hand, was used by most monasteries to describe their outlying farms, and is the modern generic term. The *burys* provided the framework within which the priory's demesne lands were to be cultivated. Here, or at a nearby tree, the halimote court met every three weeks, or at such times as suited the abbot's keepers, the prior and sub-prior. The court's jurisdiction was twofold. It controlled all transfers of land within the manor. On taking a lease, tenants, whether freehold or villein, had to swear an oath of fealty to the abbot as their lord, and publicly acknowledge that they held their lands of him, with suit of court and all services as laid down by the custom of the manor in the court rolls. Secondly, the court administered manorial husbandry, not only of the common fields, but also of the pastures, mores, meadows, wastes and woods. This included stinting, the regulation of the dates and the number of animals, both in total and for individuals, for admission to the common lands, and the prevention and remedying of abuses and nuisances, as well as the maintenance of common ways.

Control of manorial husbandry lay with the *praepositus*, usually translated as reeve, but in the *Register* as overseer and occasionally by the more restricted term, pindar. Whatever the title, his was the difficult task of ensuring the lord suffered no loss, in the same way as the bailiffs of the borough and the manor foreign, but in a much narrower context. One of the priors had evidently treated the courts' annual selection process in a somewhat autocratic manner, for one of the court rolls laid down that the overseer could be elected to office only with his consent. On many manors freemen refused to serve, maintaining that 'by ancient custom the reeve must be of villein blood' and fearing that lawyers would thus find means of proving them to be villeins. At

	Wheat Load	Wheat Bushel	Cash s d	Cloth ells
Overseer/Steward				
Virgate holder:		8	3s 4d	
Customary:			10s	
Reaper:	4	4	3s	
Reaper's Servant:		1pw		
Carter:	4	4	4s	
Swineherd:	4	4		4
Shepherd:	4	10	4s	
Keeper of lambs:		10½		
Cowherd:	4	4	2s	4
Daya, dairymaid:	4	4	5s 5d	
Sub-daya:	2	11		3
Hedger:		6		
All servants:		(oats) 6		

Load: Horseload; pw: per week
Other individual payments given in text
HRO M31/1/f5v

Table 11 Leominster Manorial Extent, 1327: Stockton. Manorial Servants etc: Reumeration

Leominster, however, reeves were appointed from amongst the tenantry of the *herneys*, free or villein. They had small perquisites, and some were very successful. In 1372, after the death of his wife, Amy, William Robyns was granted all her lands and tenements, meadows, feeding mores and pastures in Stagbatch and elsewhere in the fields of Leominster. At the same time the keepers granted William that he 'shall be a free burgess of Leominster, to buy and sell there as the other burgesses do, without toll or custom for his life'. His £2 fine was paid on his account 'of the office of steward of Ivington'.[446]

At the large *herneys* of Ivington, the reeve received, if a freeman, 5s plus 4 horseloads and 4 bushels of wheat, one load of hay, and vesture of an acre; if a villein or customary, holding his land by custom of the manor, 5s, 8 bushels of wheat in autumn, one load of hay, and vesture of an acre, with a further 5s for 'service and pannage'. At Stockton, for a freeman, the payment was 3s 4d a year, eight bushels of wheat in autumn, one load of hay and vesture of one acre of wheat; a villein received 10s a year and was quit of all works due to the lord. The 1392 Ivington court rolls suggest that local custom also played a part. As overseer and pindar of Ivington, William Robyns of Stagbatch, native (villein) by birth and thus probably son of William Robyns above, was to pay only 16s rent for his native land and was free from 'the great works in autumn', but he had to perform *husbondrepes* for three days. This was the reaping service due from *husbondsmen*, the most substantial villagers, with houses, as opposed to the poorer sort, cotters or cottagers. If 'he shall be removed from said office', Robyns was to pay the full rent of £1 and perform the great works as before.[447]

Fig 19.3 Ivington Bury Gatehouse

The Extent shows that each *bury* had an establishment of cowherd, shepherd, swine-herd, reaper, carter, dairymaid and, at Ivington, a hedger, as at Stockton (Table 11). Normal remuneration for the principal servants was 4 horseloads and 4 bushels of wheat but almost all, except the carter, received supplements, either in cash or kind. Although there was a total of some 350 oxen on the demesne lands, the only reference to an ox keeper is at Hope. This was a seasonal post, for he received 'a bushel of corn each week from the hour he is sent to Hope until the feast of the Holy Cross'.

The *burys* had cowsheds, ox houses, sheep-cotes, piggeries, carthouses, barns and dairies, all about a courtyard. As with most monastic granges, the *burys* would have been enclosed by a ditch. Certainly the Moor Abbey complex was surrounded by a moat, part of which survives, and at Ivington the stonework of the lower part of the gatehouse giving access to the *bury* is probably medieval (Fig 19.3). As well as the buildings about the yard, each *bury* had a dove house. Another essential adjunct was the garden and orchard, providing herbs and fruit for the priory. Although not specified, the products are all carefully valued. Even at the small grange at Moor Abbey, the combined annual total amounted to 5s. At Ivington, Hope, Moor Abbey and probably elsewhere, the priory had its own vineyards.

Stockton, with its dove house, fishponds, mill and deserted medieval village sites, and probably a medieval barn, has been described as having 'the potential to add considerably to our knowledge of the form, function and development of a medieval grange'. The fishponds south-east of the *bury* are 'among the ten most important sets in the counties of Hereford and Worcester'. Now dry, they consist of two tanks, originally fed from the Cogwell brook, which also served the *bury* mill.[448] There was a further priory fishpond north-west of Stockton's manorial outlier at Moor Abbey. The site of the mill, on the Stockton or Cogwell brook, is no doubt indicated by the field-names Near and Far Mill Meadows on the tithe map. The clearly marked croft boundaries of the deserted medieval village, in all probability *la Towne* of the court rolls, lie to the south of Stockton Cross. The site has yet to be fully surveyed.[449]

The priory dove house is referred to in a lease of the demesne lands of 'le bury, Stockton' to Agnes Vale in 1554. It is a circular building of stone, with a conical clay-tiled roof and open hexagonal timbered lantern providing entry and exit for the pigeons. It is of at least two builds, for there is a step as the building line changes halfway up the wall, and was restored, in part, in the mid 18th century, the wind vane carrying the initials EB and the date 1759 (Fig 19.4). The timber potence arm, a revolving ladder consisting of a post secured on pivots in the centre of the floor

Fig 19.4 Stockton dovecote and barn

and roof cross-beam, provided the means of reaching the 500 or so nesting boxes of the interior, with their swabs and eggs. The potence was introduced from France only in the late 17th or early 18th century.[450]

The pigeon's unique capacity to produce crop milk frees it from the strict breeding seasonality, related to maximum availability of insects etc, of other birds. Its breeding season thus extends from March to September and occasionally other months. It thrives on the grain available amongst the stubble after harvesting. Two eggs are incubated in about two and a half weeks, by both parents. As the young quit the nest in about three to four weeks, up to eight swabs or eggs can be harvested annually from one breeding pair. The pigeons were also valued for their feathers and manure. The latter, held to be particularly strong, was frequently used as a leaven for the kitchen garden's dung hill. Almost as valuable as the pigeons, but much less frequently mentioned, were the rabbit warrens. There was a warren at Ivington, and presumably at the other *burys*. In 1385 the chaplain of 'Burle' (Birley) was found hunting coneys in Ivington Park with dogs, nets and ferrets.[451]

Water Mills

There were water mills in all the *herneys*. The majority will have belonged to the great manor of Leominster before 1123, for Domesday Book records eight mills at 73s and a further eight at £5 8s in 1066. Later, the priory's Cartulary records two more, as gifts of local landowners. Ralph de Pembridge gave Luntley mill, on Tippets Brook, a tributary of the Arrow. This Abbot Roger, 1158–65, granted to 'our servant' Baderon for a rent of 20s per annum, paid at the feasts of SS Peter and Paul, 29 June, and St Martin, 11 November. At Hennor, probably on the Stretford brook, John Thece had granted the priory 'all his mill, arable, meadow and pasture now in the tenure of Osbert Sturm, miller'.[452]

As these were a seigneurial monopoly, tenants were obliged to take their corn to be ground at the lord's mill. Thus at Middleton in Stockton Philip le Pinder agreed in 1359 'to pay the pence for grinding the grain with his neighbours'. In 1381 John of Stockton, on taking over the yardland or virgate late of Walter in *le Wiche*, accepted that he must grind his corn 'with his neighbours at the mill'. Cholstrey mill is defined in a lease of 1389 as 'a water mill with its half-yardland and suit of mill of the townships at Stagbatch and Cholstrey'. When, after the Black Death, Walter de Ponte took a half-yardland at Hope, for 9s 8d per annum he was able to compound for 'all services and customs', except suit of mill, the obligation to have his corn ground at the abbot's mill. Nevertheless, the decline of arable farming consequent on the Black Death led to a collapse in the profitability, and therefore the number, of mills. There are many references to the miller's customary tribute of eggs. In the 1327 Extent the millers at Stockton, Stoke and Hope paid 100 eggs yearly, but at Luston only 50.[453]

The significance the abbots of Reading attached to their tenants' obligation of suit of mill is illustrated by an agreement between Abbot Adam of Lathbury (1226–38), formerly prior of Leominster, and Hugh de Croft concerning the construction by the latter of a mill on the brook in Fishpool Dingle, the boundary between Hugh's wood at Croft and the abbot's at Highwood to the east, within his *herneys* of Luston. None of the abbot's men, nor tenants of their lands, was to come or be received at the mill. If any such were intercepted going to the mill, or were proved to have done so by the oaths of two law-worthy men, the said Hugh or his heirs should pay a fine of 6s 8d for every such occurrence. If they failed so to do, the abbot was accorded the right to distrain them, without any contradiction, of all their landholding at Wintercott, for each such occasion. Hugh was obliged to affix his seal to the document to give greater force to the agreement, in perpetuity.[454]

Being of timber, water mills and their working parts were particularly prone to decay. Medieval records contain many references to the need for maintenance, repair and reconstruction. In 1351, when John Ball assumed the tenancy, formerly held by Thomas *le Muleward*, of Hope water mill with a half-yardland, he undertook to 'maintain all mills, house pools, streams and everything belonging to the said lord's mill at his own charge and in as good or better state than he found them, and so to leave it the same'. John Grubbe and William Ball stood as sureties for his performance of this covenant. The court rolls for 1349 refer to a new mill at Stoke, serving the *herneys* of Stoke. In 1372 a lease of a pasture called Bilet at Eaton's More, Ivington, included 'the fishery at *Etonsmille* until the keepers build a (new) mill there'. By the Monday before Christmas 1391 this had been constructed. An 'Olde Mulle' is referred to 'near Leominster' in 1334 and, more precisely, at Cholstrey in 1355, presumably close to the site of what is now Cholstrey Mill Farm, on the Pinsley. In 1389, when Richard Mayons and Ralph, his son, leased Cholstrey mill, they paid 37s 10d annually, plus 2d for tithe, and presumably the customary 100 eggs. They were 'to keep all things in repair, make no waste in the trees there, except for housebote and heybote', house- and fence-building. Nor was it 'lawful for them to demise or let the premises without licence from the keepers'. The entry fine was £4, of which they paid 4d on entry, the remainder due at 3s 4d per annum over 24 years. Pledges for performance were Walter Bobbe, William Robyns, steward of Ivington, and William Baker.[455]

Fig 19.5 Croward's Mill: wheel and leat

Not far away, also in Ivington *herneys*, on the Lugg, was Crowford, later Crower's or Croward's, mill, to which tenants in Somergils owed suit in 1397 (Fig 19.5). This mill will also have served tenants in the Broad and part of the Marsh areas of Leominster borough. However, the 1327 Extent lists Crowford mill as part of Luston *herneys*, on the other bank of the Lugg. Here, in addition to rent and other services, the miller owed a customary payment of 50 eggs. As Crowford could hardly have served the priory's tenants living at Luston, one must assume there was an, unrecorded, mill on the brook flowing eastward through Luston to join the Ridgemoor brook just to the south of Eye. In 1571 the Marsh Mill was recorded as belonging to the halimote of Stockton, the rent being £10 13s 4d, the entry fine £42 13s 4d. Like Crowford Mill, it served the industrial area to the north of the borough. In 1592 there was conflict between the proprietors over the maintenance and repair of the weir that served both mills.[456]

Customs and Services

The *Register* provides details only of the priory's villein tenants. The Extent shows these customaries performing seasonal work, but not week work. The former was wide-ranging: sowing grain, mowing and collecting hay, and reaping the harvest in the open fields and meadows of the lord's demesne. 'The great works in autumn', as they appear in the halimote rolls, were primarily concerned with getting the lord's harvest home. These customs had various names, such as *husbonrepes* and *metebone*, from the Latin *messis*, harvest, hence harvest boon. Assistance was also required with the autumn and spring reaping, and haymaking.

On entry into a tenement or amendment of an agreement, a fine was due to the lord. In most cases, when the court rolls specified rent to be paid, it was accompanied by the formula, 'with all customs and services', that is as recorded on an earlier roll, these being detailed only when there was significant change to the terms of the tenancy. Thus at Ivington in 1331, for a messuage, 3 acres of arable and a portion of pasture called *Mondayeslond*, Nicholas son of Philip le Souter paid 13d per annum, sowed and reaped the corn, and gathered the lord's hay, as a *Mondayesman*. In 1334 at Ivington Walter *Affegrove* received a messuage, 3½ acres of arable and half an acre of meadow for which he paid 2s yearly; his services included three days' reaping in autumn, three days' mowing and two days' haymaking. Nevertheless entries in the Court rolls for the 1330s, that is prior to the Black Death, show that customary tenants with major holdings were already commuting such 'great works'.[457]

'Small customs' included such matters as more-rent, marsh-rent, woodpenny or *woodgavell* (the obligation to carry wood for the lord), *wintergavell* (a winter service or payment), *fleoc* (an unknown service or payment) and hundred silver (a contribution to the administration of the hundred court). Some tenants continued to be liable for *honeygavell*, the ancient honey rent. A list at the end of the Leominster Cartulary shows eight tenants paying the priory between ¾ and 4¾ gallons of honey, 19¼ gallons in all. Elsewhere William le Hide was able to commute the honey rent on his yardland to an annual payment of 1s 8d. At Aston in Stockton in 1334 Richard Lovyett was still paying *mulstonsylver*. After the Black Death commutation of such works and of 'small customs' became widespread.[458]

Dues required from his natives by the abbot as lord included the payment of heriot, the deceased tenant's best beast or chattel, before an heir could succeed to the estate. On the priory lands this applied on the death of either husband or wife; on the husband's death the lord chose before the wife, but on the wife's the husband chose before the lord. All married natives had to provide the priory with geese. At Ivington, Stockton, Stoke, Luston and Hope one goose was due from each couple, making a total of some 250 geese. A varying tribute of eggs was also due from overseers, reapers, dairymaids and millers: at Ivington five hens and 50 eggs each from the overseer and reaper, 100 eggs from the dairymaid and miller. At Luston, Crowford mill paid 50 eggs and the forester of Yarpole 50 hens and 300 eggs.[459]

To ensure that all could play their part effectively in the community's farming cycle, a court of the joint *herneys* of Luston, Ivington, Stockton and Stoke left a formal memorandum on their rolls

Fig 19.6 Ivington Bury: gatehouse and barns today

of the *principalia*, in English heirlooms, where 'loom' was the Old English for 'tool'. This provides a detailed picture of the essential requirements of village life. 'Every free man or native holding any native land of the lord shall leave (to his successor) after his death: his best waggon (or cart) with all its furniture, a plough with a harrow, one winnowing fan, the best bed with its furniture (viz 2 sheets and a canvas), the best brass pot, the best pan (or skillet) with a trivet, a *bylle* (billhook), and *barsax* (a plain knife or dagger?), *sykyll*, scythe, spade and *schowle* (shovel), a pair of cords for binding the waggon, a *pykegevell* (a pitching fork for sheaves), a table cloth, a towel, a table and, a little chest or box, 5 hens with a cock, five dishes with a platter, a cup, the best tub, the oven if there be one, a sack, a press, a sieve with a fan, a *trugge* (bushel), a hogshead (barrel), a tub (bowl) with a pail, a cooler, a *dongepyke* (a hopper), a *penetral* (probably a gimlet for boring small holes in wood), and if the land be sowed he shall leave his successor all the straw from the same land'.[460]

20 The Priory's Agrarian Economy in the 14th Century

2. Arable, Pasture, Meadow and Woodland

In recent research in Ireland, Charles Doherty has drawn attention to the distinctive ecclesiastical impact on land management where the church 'had control of manpower that must have been the envy of kings. It had established centres that exercised a strong gravitational pull (by contrast kingship was peripatetic). It was in a position to exploit fully technical innovations such as the heavy plough and the horizontal water-mill. It was thus the only organisation that could produce a surplus — particularly of grain.' As Blair points out, in the British world 'there are also signs ecclesiastical institutions developed a more organised, intensive and perhaps techonologically innovative estate-management regime'. With its extensive estates organised into four large *herneys*, Leominster should have been in a particularly good position in this respect, with its diverse lands affording a range of resources, especially timber and woodland pasture.[461]

The 1327 Extent provides details of the acreage of arable, pasture and meadow at each of the four *herneys*, and at the granges of Hope and Moor Abbey (Table 12). The overall percentage of arable (88%) and pasture/meadow (12%) is similar to the 85% and 15% of the 6,000 acres of the Hereford episcopal demesne, as described in the *Red Book*, and to that of the demesne lands of St Katherine's Hospital, Ledbury. Three fields are identified at each of the *herneys*. At the granges of Hope and Moor there were only two, and at the latter they were about a quarter the average acreage. Such a division reflects the three-season rotation of two crops and fallow, characteristic of lowland Herefordshire.[462]

However, the Extent may give a false impression of order and simplicity in terms of the operation of the three-field system. The 14th-century court roll entries, as copied into Coningsby's *Register*, indicate that the pattern of landholding and medieval fields at Ivington was much more complex than Table 12 suggests. The *Register* refers to 'the fields' in six of the townships within the *herneys* of Ivington. At *Bradeford* (Broadward) and Newton they are not named. There were three fields at Cholstrey, *Cosenore* (Cursneh), Walton and *Lusfield*; three more at Stagbatch, Longwall, Longmarsh and the Worthyn; at Brierley, West 'next the Wye', North and Park fields; and at Winsley, *Crassewall*, *Brunwalle* and Down fields.[463]

In Stoke *herneys* the 1349 halimote rolls record that William Mylns' arable was 'in the three fields of Fencote'. At Hope, however, Gray found evidence in the 1608–9 surveys of seven common fields, of which only two are mentioned in the Extent, and at Brierley of eleven, of which *Katchlowe* occurs frequently in the Ivington halimote rolls, but not in the Extent. As there are not a few references in the halimote rolls to closes and the exchange of lands between tenants, who are evidently anxious to consolidate their holdings, this may be evidence of subsequent fragmentation. These Jacobean surveys used by Gray are the only firm evidence of enclosure. What stands out

Herneys	Luston		Stockton		Stoke & More			Ivington* & Hope			Total	
	Acres	%	Acres	%	Stoke	More	%	Ivington*	Hope	%	Total	%
Arable	A1 150		A1 155		A1 142	A1 36		A1 144	A1 150			
	A2 140		A2 192 2s		A2 106	A2 34		A2 132	A2 120			
	A3 125		A3 208½		A3 145			A3 146				
Total	415	92	555½ 2s	93	393	70	90	422	270	81	2125½	88
Pasture	P1 15		P1 12		P1 6	P1 12		P1 16	P1 8			
	P2 8		P2 11		P2 10			P2 63				
			P3 1					P3 12				
								P4 6				
Total	23	5	24	4	16	12	5	97	8	12	180	7
Meadow	M1 12		M1 20		M1 6			M1 46	M1 3			
	M2 2				M2 14				M2 2			
					M3 4½				M3 12			
Total	14	3	20	3	24½		5	46	17	7	121½	5
Total	452		599½ 2s		433½ +82=515½			565+295=860			2427	

s selion; * except Rede and excluding Ivington Park

Luston: A1 Tuffenhull; A2 Breshull; A3 Wondesbach; M1 Fleta; M2 Calowcroft; P1 More; P2 Oxelesue
Stockton: A1 Whitebroc; A2 Conemers/Alvedon; A3 Red-weye/Stalling; M1 Eftey; P1 Bolingey; P2 More; P3 vivary
Stoke: A1 Milnefurlong; A2 Blackwardyn; A3 Oldstock Field; P1 Copenhall; P2 Eaton More & vivary; M1 Copenhall; M2 Arnehale; M3 Folkey
Hope: A1 Hhenhope; A2 Brounesfield; M1 next Lugg; M2 Folkey; M3 Cheney; P1 Grascroft
Ivington: A1 West; A2 against the Park; A3 Merell; M1 Enchenye; P1 Bungey; P2 Ivington More; P3 Middlemore; P4 Calvernoft
More: A1 Chantecroft; A2 Westfield & Ayeswoode; P1 More within the Close

HRO M31/1 f122-6

Table 12 Leominster Manorial Demesne, Extent of 1327: Arable, Pasture and Meadow

is the stress that tenants were placing on the consolidation of their pasture, and to a lesser extent meadow, at the expense of arable. This is only to be expected after the collapse of arable farming in the post-Black Death era.[464]

	Pasture		Mead	Arable
Hope	99¾	70%	18	25
Brierley	82½	75%	17½	10½
Stockton	33	59%	17	5¾

Gray (1969) 488, 522

Arable

In origin, the basis of land measurement was the quantity that could be ploughed in a certain time. Thus the carucate, hide or ploughland, which consisted of four virgates or yardlands, represented the land an eight-oxen plough team could till in a year, and the acre was as much as a yoke of oxen could plough in a day. As this depended on the nature of the soil, carucates, virgates and acres were all customary measures, and thus variable. The statute acre of 4,840 square yards was introduced by the *Composition of Yards and Perches* of c1266–1307, but made slow progress and had to be reintroduced by Edward III and Henry VIII. An extended note in Coningsby's 14th-century *Register* deals in detail with 'The Measure of an Acre', which includes 10x16 perches, 20x8 perches and 40x4 perches.[465]

In the early middle ages the virgate was probably 'the ideal family holding of rural society', but later the half-virgate filled this role. In Herefordshire the customary virgate or yardland was 60 acres. There is firm evidence for this on the manors of St Katherine's Hospital, Ledbury. Thus the Weston (Beggard) Court rolls for 1322 note that 'one virgate contains 60 acres and one noke is one quarter of a virgate', that is 15 acres. As late as 1497 the court rolls of another St Katherine's manor, Kempley in Gloucestershire, announce that 'one noke contains 15 acres and is thus a quarter part of one virgate'. This customary virgate of 60 acres also obtained on the neighbouring episcopal lands. Swithin Butterfield, who had the task c1580 of resurveying the bishop of Hereford's lands according to the statute acre, believed that the Herefordshire acre was two-thirds the statute acre. In Worcestershire and Warwickshire the virgate was commonly between 25 and 30 acres, with the majority of peasant holdings less than 15 or 20 acres. On the diverse Westminster Abbey estates, 'it was possible to have a large virgate or a small virgate, even where all virgates were in theory of the same acreage'.[466]

That the standard acre was employed in the priory estates seems unlikely. Table 14 shows the average holding for 94 of the peasants on the priory lands in 1431/2 to be 0.9 of a virgate, that is 54 acres. The probability is that these were Herefordshire customary acres, equivalent to 36 standard acres. Swithin Butterfield's experience suggests that such a reassessment of land areas was very difficult to implement; one can just imagine the suspicion of many peasant proprietors. If the statute acre was not introduced on the bishop's lands before 1580, what chance would the prior's surveyor have had in the 14th century?[467]

Grain production was limited to winter-sown wheat, which thrived on the heavy loams, and spring-sown oats, more tolerant of rain than barley. There is no mention in the *Register* of barley or rye, which only found favour in the sandy soils of the south of the county. The Extent makes no reference to peas or beans, although they do appear in the court rolls as crops produced by the villagers. Tithes paid to the priory from Newton were predominantly wheat and oats, but there were some pease and vetches.Generally the quantity of oats sown was greater that of wheat, varying between 5% and 20% more per acre. The yield cannot be established, as figures are available only for grain sown, by 'horseloads'. In describing most of the open fields, it is explained that the acreage given does not include the *Rede*, land recently won from the waste. In the case of Hhenhope field at Hope, we are told that the *Rede* was 7 acres and one selion, and that the quantity of wheat sown was 18 bushels, giving some 2½ bushels per acre. [468]

Harvest, the most critical time of the year, began about Lammas, 1 August, so-called from the *half maesse* or mass loaf, baked from the first ripe corn. Until harvest home, Michaelmas, 29 September, the demand for labour was intense. The reaper, the tenant in charge of harvesting, received the standard allowance of four horseloads and four bushels of wheat, with a payment of 3s. His servant, the *repreve*, an experienced hand leading the reapers, received one bushel of wheat per week during harvest time. In addition each autumn they were both given 5s for their 'service', and pannage. Six other, unnamed, officials, possibly team leaders, were also involved in the harvesting. Three received annually 13 horseloads of wheat, vesture of 3 acres, a number of sheaves in autumn, a bushel of *hopcorn* and another of *hopoaten*; the other three, evidently deputies, received half that quantity.

The Stoke entry gives details of 208 horseloads of grain and 26 'in profits' going to the Outer Court of the priory. 'At the coming of the abbot' 40 further horseloads were delivered. 'In augmentation' the baker received 104 horseloads, and for 'certain customs' 22 horseloads and two bushels. To the brewer went 156 horseloads and 18 'in profits'. At Stockton and Ivington the carter was granted four horseloads and four bushels of wheat, the standard wage of most servants of the *herneys*, but at Luston he received 4s yearly in addition, and had an under-carter to assist him at harvest time, who received 4s plus eight bushels of wheat. There were 'pairs of irons' for the subsequent ploughing of the fields at all five *burys*; Stockton, Ivington and Hope each had three.

Pasture

The Extent indicates the amount of pasture available for the different animals. In most of eastern and midland England the horse had become the favourite draught animal by the end of the 13th century. For the heavy soils of Herefordshire, however, even c1327, the ox remained the popular plough beast. This is evident from details in the Extent about demesne pasture. At Stockton 100 beasts, 20 cows and seven calves were kept in Ash Wood, with its 345 acres of woodland/pasture, and 20 oxen with two heifers on the 12 acres at Bolingey pasture (P1 on Table 12). The meadow of Ivington Park, which is not quantified, maintained '100 beasts and 10 -', evidently, as at Ash Wood, a further reference to oxen and cows, for sheep are dealt with separately. If this is the case, the park provided the equivalent of some further 90 acres of pasture. Large numbers of animals were being pastured in land termed in the one case 'wood' and in the other 'park', both in fact woodland/pasture, discussed below under woodland. The 63 acres of the drained lands at Ivington More (P2) sustained 80 oxen and cows, whilst the 18 acres at Middlemore (P3) and Calvernoft (P4) accommodated a further 20.[469]

At the other *herneys* the numbers were much smaller: at Hope 19 oxen on 8 acres of pasture at *Grascroft* (P1) and 'next the Lugg'; thirteen on the 6 acres of Copenhall (P1) pasture at Stoke; and at Luston thirteen on the 8 acres of *Oxelesue* (P2). Even within the close at Moor Abbey (P1) there were six oxen. The priory thus had more than 350 oxen, far more than was required for the priory's tables. At Bolton in the early 14th century, with thirteen to nineteen canons and five lay brethren, 80 head of cattle sufficed. By the 16th century Leominster's riverside pastures had become renowned for the fattening of cattle from Wales before they were sold on to the west midlands and, later, the London markets. It is probable, however, that in the early 13th century the priory's surplus was sold on as draught animals for the plough. With the Black Death and the decline of arable farming, this market collapsed.[470]

The precise number of cows cannot be readily established but was probably about 90, considerably smaller than of oxen. Vivaries are mentioned at Luston, Stockton, Stoke and Moor Abbey, but not at Ivington. From the context it is clear that the term 'vivary' is being used, not in the popular sense of fishponds, but as enclosures for cattle, with cowsheds, in close proximity to the *bury*. These were dairy cows, most of the milk being used for making cheese. Easily stored, it formed one of the staples of the medieval diet, especially during the hard months of winter.

At Luston, where there were 40 cows and calves in 15 acres in the More (P1), the cowherd received 3s and pasture for a calf in addition to his allowance of wheat. At Stockton, with 16 cows in the 11 acres of the More (P2) towards Eyam (Eye) and another acre at the vivary (P3), the cowherd received the standard payment of wheat, plus 4 ells of cloth. The 10 acres at Eaton More, with the vivary at Stoke (P2), accommodated 20 cows and two bulls. In addition to his wheat the cowherd was given pasture for a calf, but only 1s and 3 ells of cloth. There is no reference to cows at Ivington, other than those in the More with the oxen, but dairying was evidently important here, for the cowherd enjoyed the same terms as at Stockton, and the dairymaid had an assistant. At Moor Abbey a vivary is referred to, but there are no details of staff other than the keeper, *custos*, of the manor, who received the usual 4 horseloads and 4 bushels of wheat. Pope Nicholas's Taxation of 1291 credited the priory with a mere 46 'cattle'.[471]

The key dates in the annual cycle of the pasture were May Day and Martinmas. Over winter and during spring the cattle were either in the byres or found patches of rough grazing. On 1 May the pastures, now rich with grass, were thrown open until 11 November. The shepherd's calendar can be followed at Ivington. The flock spent the winter at the *bury*, in timber sheds to keep them warm. Here he and his dog had to keep good watch; on any occasion when he was obliged to leave the sheep he had to ensure 'a good keeper in his stead'. By January the flock would be at its lowest level. Traditionally the 'casting of the lambs' began on the feast of the Purification, 2 February, and with it the milking of the ewes, each providing about a litre a day. With weaning, after four to five months, milking ceased. From the feast of the Holy Cross, 3 May, to St Peter in Chains, 1 August, the park provided the flock with woodland/pasture grazing. From the Purification to Michaelmas, 29 September, harvest home, the shepherd had an assistant, the keeper of the lambs, who received 10½ bushels of wheat for his services. In June the sheep were washed. The meadows were thrown open at Lammas, and here the older and weaker ewes could be fattened, ready for slaughter. After the harvest had been gathered the flock was left on the stubble and folded overnight by the shepherd, now without his assistant, within hurdles stored at the *bury*. Their dung, although inferior to that of cattle, was a significant nutrient when trodden into the ground.

Sheep were valued not for their meat, but for their wool, skins and milk. With suitable nutrition, ten sheep could give as much milk and butter as one cow. The sheep milk the dairymaids also turned, principally, into cheese. The Ecclesiastical Taxation of 1291 records a total of 280 sheep on the priory demesne. The details provided by Coningsby's *Register* show this to be a gross miscalculation. There were 100 sheep at Stoke, 120 at Hope, 200 on pasture at Moor Abbey, 240 at Stockton, 300 at Ivington, a total of 960. The presence of a well-paid shepherd indicates that there was also a considerable, unspecified, number at Luston. There were shepherds at all four *herneys*, and at the granges of Hope and Moor Abbey. At Hope the shepherd's wheat allowance was merely 3 horseloads and 3 bushels, with 4s and a covering at the feast of the Conversion of St Paul, 25 January, when the sheep were folded at the *bury* and lambing was about to begin. The shepherds at the *herneys* received the standard wheat allowance, 4 horseloads and 4 bushels, with a supplement at Ivington of 4s, one ewe and one lamb, and an additional 6 bushels during the period of the casting of the lambs; at Stockton of a ewe and a lamb, and a further 6 bushels of wheat in the lambing season. At Luston the shepherd's supplement was comparable to that at Ivington, but at casting time he received a bell-wether. Usually castrated, this led the flock with a bell round its neck. On this basis, it can be assumed that the unspecified number of sheep at Luston was comparable to that at Ivington, some 300 sheep, thus raising the total of the priory's combined flocks c1327 to some 1,250, a small number compared to the 3,600 at Bolton in 1310/11. A list of the wages on the granges in 1407/8 illustrates how sheep farming on the priory estates was boosted after the Black Death (see Table 8).[472]

Meadow

Throughout the Middle Ages meadows were of even higher value than pasture. The principal food for overwintering animals, hay was a vital crop. Given its value as winter provender, and the extensive areas of flood land surrounding the minster, it is not surprising that from early times much effort had been expended on converting the marshy and damp ground of the mores to meadow, as well as pasture. Excavations just south of Dinmore Hill, at Wellington quarries, have provided evidence that this process began well before the Conquest. Of the 97 acres of pasture at Ivington, 75 were still called more at the time of the Extent.

By far the largest area of meadow belonging to the priory was at Ivington. The 46 acres of meadow at *Enchenye* produced 46 loads of hay. This was valued at 2s per load, even more than the legendary Volkey meadow by the Lugg at Hope, which commanded only 1s 9d per load. Elsewhere in the Leominster *herneys* the price of hay ranged between 1s 8d and 1s 6d. Table 13 analyses the quantity and quality, in terms of value, of the hay harvested on the meadows of the four *herneys*. The most valuable meadows were not those that produced the highest quality hay, but those which produced the greatest quantity per acre.

Herneys	Meadow	Acres	loads	yield	price/ load	income per acre	total income
Stockton	Eastey M1	20	25	1.25	1s 8d	2s 1d	£2 1s 8d
Ivington	Encheney M1	46	46	1	2s 0d	2s 0d	£4 12s 0d
Hope	Cheney M3	12	12	1	1s 8d	1s 8d	£1 0s 0d
	Volkey M2	2	3	1.5	1s 9d	2s 7½d	5s 3d
	Next Lugg M1	3	4	1.3	1s 9d	2s 4d	7s 0d
Luston	Callowcroft M2	2	2	1	1s 6d	1s 6d	3s 0d
	Fleta M1	12	24	2	1s 4d	2s 8d	£1 12s 0d
Stoke	Copenhall M1	6	9	1.5	1s 6d	2s 3d	13s 6d
	Arnehale M2	14	18	1.3	1s 7d	2s 0½d	£1 8s 6d
	Folkey M3	4½	4	0.9	1s 8d	1s 6d	6s 8d
Total		121½	147				£12 9s 7d

18½ acres under 2s an acre. The table assumes loads are equal — HRO M31/1 ff122-6

Table 13 Leominster Manorial Demesne, Extent of 1327: Value of Hay from the Meadows

The annual cycle of the meadows began with their closure, to promote spring growth, at Candlemas, the feast of the Purification of the Virgin, which was celebrated with candles on 2 February. Mowing for all with meadow rights, and for those owing services of mowing and haymaking, began on the Feast of the Nativity of St John, 24 June. On completion of the mowing, traditionally at Lammas, 1 August, the meadows were thrown open to all with grazing rights, for their animals to gain what benefit they could from the stubble, at the same time enriching the soil with their manure.

The meadow services due from the natives, as those for ploughing the arable and reaping the harvest, were dictated by manorial custom. When Walter Affegrove took on the lands in Ivington formerly tenanted by Margery Ross, his services included mowing the meadow for three days and making hay for two, as recorded in the court rolls. At Luston the villein tenant of every yardland had to carry two loads of hay to the *bury* court. Until 1349 the general obligation for the Leominster customaries was, according to the extent of their lands, to mow for one or more days, and to carry the hay. Such long-established customs were to be severely challenged by the acute labour shortages resulting from the Black Death.[473]

The banks of the Lugg in Luston and the Ivington townships of Brierley and Pervin were also valued for the provision of flax, which grows best in a cool, moist temperate climate. Its production and manufacture was one of the few cottage industries of which there is record. Dense sowing encouraged slender, unbranched stems, which the womenfolk harvested, pulling them out of the ground by the roots. They were laid out to dry before being retted, steeped in a nearby stream, to rot away the fleshy parts. They were then rubbed vigorously and beaten to separate the fibres, which were then hung up in strikes. When thoroughly dry, they were combed out in preparation for spinning. The finer fibres were made into thread for weaving into linen, the heaviest into canvas, for such domestic use as shirts and towels, smocks and board cloths. The flax seed was also used, for the production of linseed oil. At Selby flax and hemp production was linked, and in 1416–17 the Benedictines sold their tithes of both commodities for a total of £1. At Leominster there is also reference to tithes of hemp.[474]

Woodland

Assarting

For the sixteen 'members' of the great manor of Leominster, Domesday Book gives the composite figure for woodland of 'six leagues long and three leagues wide', far more than is found in any other Herefordshire entry. It then provides details of assarting: from land 'reclaimed from the woodland (for the plough) comes 17s 4d'. In the former, large Leominster manor of Much Marcle, '58 acres had been reclaimed from the wood'. Only at two other places within the county is assarting recorded, the Lacy manors of Weobley and neighbouring Fernhill, where it gave merely enough land, in each manor, for another plough.

The earliest record of large-scale assarting in Herefordshire is in the grants of Robert of Ewias and Robert de Tregoz to Ewyas Harold Priory. Conditions for assarting in a big way began in 1198, when Abbot Adam I of the Cistercian house at Dore persuaded Richard I, desperate for money, to sell him first 300 acres for £200 and then a further 200 acres of the Forest of Treville. All the tall trees Adam, we are told, sold in Hereford for three times the purchase price, thereby

Fig 20.1 Assarted land about Hope, Dinmore Woods beyond

creating fertile arable land 'as flat as a threshing floor'. Despite the vicissitudes suffered in John's reign by almost all monasteries, above all the Cistercians, a survey of 1213 shows Dore holding more than 1,200 of the 2,000 acres of Treville. As these events were well publicised by Giraldus Cambrensis, they must have had a profound impact on both landlords and tenants in Herefordshire and were probably the stimulus for assarting on the priory's lands.[475]

Today the only major area of woodland on the former priory estates is about Hope-under-Dinmore. In the first decades of the 13th century there are records of extensive assarting on the priory's lands in three of the four *herneys*: Stockton, Ivington and Luston. Although Stoke is not mentioned, two of the three major field names are indicative: Blackwardyn Field, of 106 acres, from the Old English *wordign*, 'enclosures', and Oldstock Field, of 145 acres, from Old English *stocc*, 'land with tree stumps left standing on it'. These probably represent assarting in the pre-Conquest period, as do *Worthyn* fields at Stagbatch and Fencote.

Woodlands at (Miles) Hope and about Tenbury were the subject of a lengthy dispute between the abbots of Reading and Walter II de Clifford. One of the greatest of the marcher barons, and lord of Tenbury, Walter was sheriff of Hereford in 1195 and 1205. The Leominster Cartulary includes a copy of the final concord drawn up before the royal justices at Gloucester in 1203, whereby Walter quitclaimed 540 acres of woodland in (Miles) Hope to Abbot Elias (1200–13), who in turn quitclaimed his rights in *Tametebury* (Tenbury) woods to Walter. Further north Miles of Hope received 100 acres of 'our wood of Hope' at an annual rent of 12s. These lay between the water of the *vivarium* of the *bury* at (Miles) Hope and the water of the mill at *Laston* (Leysters?). For an additional 108 acres for assarting in the same wood Miles paid 13s annual rent and, for the total 208 acres, an entry fine of £4.[476]

In the Cartulary this is followed by a series of charters of Abbot Elias relating to woodland for clearance and cultivation. To William, priest of Bodenham, he granted 51 acres in 'our wood of *Dunem'(ore)* next to the wood of our lord the king', at Marden. At their southernmost extent, marked today by the parish boundary between Hope and Dinmore, the priory lands marched with that section of the large royal manor of Marden, west of the Lugg, referred to in a charter of Richard I as 'our wood of *Mawerthene*'. This area was the subject of another grant by Abbot Elias, to Thomas of Eyton. He was granted 36 acres for assarting and cultivation in Dinmore Wood, for an annual rent of 16s and £1 6s 8d for entry. Twenty-four acres were 'adjacent to the wood of William the priest', presumably of Bodenham. Elias also granted Robert de Furches 74 acres of 'waste' at *Winnesleg* (Winsley), one and a half miles due west of Hope. This was defined as 'next to the boundary between St Peter of Leominster (the priory) and St Aethelbert of Hereford (the dean and chapter) in *Dunemor*'. The tithes of this relatively small piece of land had been assigned by the Commandery of the Hospitallers of St John in Dinmore to the Chapter of Hereford Cathedral for brewing beer. Today, the land north of the parish boundary, other than Plock Wood, is almost devoid of woodland. The early-14th century Winsley House is described by Thomas Blount as having above the porch a tau cross 'bearing in old characters *Per signum Tau libera nos Domine*' and on a tie-beam in the hall '*bendy of five pieces* haply the arms of Wyndelsey'. In the 14th century Winsley House passed to the Beringtons.[477]

Elias' grants of woodland for assarting were not restricted to the southern limits of Dinmore. A charter for John of *Pirbyn* (Pervin) refers to land already asserted out of Brierley or Pervin woods, a few hundred yards east of Ivington's iron-age camp. In the north-west he permitted assarting about Gattertop and Upper Hill in *Bosco nostro de Craswelle*. Here John de Hull received 30 acres for 5s and Nigel *de Hulla* 42 acres, with 8 acres of pasture at Brierley, for 12s 8d a year, with £1 entry fine. Within the ten years 1203–13 Elias had granted some 430 acres of wood and 'waste' about Dinmore Hill for cultivation.[478]

Assarting also took place in Luston *herneys* during Elias's abbacy. Six acres at *Luggofre*' were granted to William, priest of Ashton, and a further 16 acres to William de *Kingeslene* (Kingsland), the former paying 18d, the latter 2s 6½d annually. The place-name *Luggofr*' suggests a site on the bank or ridge of the Lugg, as at Tars Coppice and Wood in Lucton, where the land rises to 124m. Elias granted 82 acres for assarting, 30 at *Loch'ofr*' and 52 at *Norhleg*', to Thomas Pachet. The charter gives no hint as to situation or even the *herneys*, but the place-name *Loch'ofr*' looks very much like scribal error. If this refers to *Luggofr*' then at least 152 acres had been asserted in Luston *herneys* in the same ten years. With the Dinmore assarts, this gives a total of some 600 acres.[479]

Parkland, Underwood, Woodland/Pasture and Timber

General evidence as to Leominster's woodlands is found in the Extent. This gives detailed information on the quantity of woodland at the *herneys* of Stockton, Luston, Ivington, and its outlier, Hope. Although Stoke woodland is not mentioned in the Extent, a number of its court roll entries refer to 'Fencote in Westwood', and Pope Nicholas's Taxation, 1291, includes £1 income from *Westwode*. The Leominster Cartulary provides more details. A series of four charters, c1186–1211, relate to the sale by Adam *le Buteler* and William, his son, to the abbot of Reading of that part of *bosco meo de Westwde* lying between *Risnebruggebeche* and the lands of William de Parco for £30; and to William's grant of his demesne wood and that of his tenant, Adam *de la Grene*, for a further £16 13s 4d. No acreage is given. Westwood, like the woodlands at Ivington in 1327, is referred to as 'park' in a Stoke court roll of 1376.[480]

Ivington Park is described as 360 acres where 'they may fell every year 40 acres of underwood at 6d per acre, in all 20s'. Trees cropped as underwood, *subboscus*, were species that regrew rapidly, either by sending up shoots from the stumps or stools as coppice, or from the roots as suckers. Grown in compartments based on the annual cycles, they were cut close to the ground on a regular rotation. At Ivington and Stockton this was every five years, at Hope every six. If practice at Ivington mirrored that at the comparable area at Stockton, where 40 acres were cut each year using a five-year cycle, this would signify some 200 acres of underwood at Ivington. According to Price, writing in 1795, as timber oak, ash and elm prevailed in Herefordshire, but birch, lime, hedge maple etc could also be coppiced. Underwood, coming principally as rods and poles, had many and varied uses. Hazel and willow were of especial value for wattle-infilling for the virtually universal timber buildings, and as spars or rods for thatching, hurdles and fencing. Most importantly, underwood provided firewood. Cattle, sheep and especially deer were rigorously excluded from the underwood by banks, ditches and fences.[481]

The halimote rolls illustrate the importance of underwood to the villager. In his old age Hugh *le Wynde* conveyed 9 acres of freehold at Brierley to John *le Wynde* who, the court insisted, was to make careful provision for Hugh's food and accommodation, including 'all the underwood of the hedges, but not to dig the hedges'. At Eyton in 1352 the court made provision for the orphan, Thomas *Polle*. His guardian was to have custody of Thomas' lands for three years, after which he had to quit them 'as well wooded as he received them'. The quantity of underwood required for an average family for a year is reflected in a corrody granted to William *le Hounte* at Hope in 1379. In return for his grant to the priory of a meadow, William was to receive 3 horseloads of good, pure wheat, well winnowed or fanned, 1 horseload of oats containing 16 bushels, and '4 cartloads of underwood to be delivered to him by the bailiff then in our wood'.[482]

In Ivington Park there was also a considerable amount of woodland/pasture, grassland with trees and bushes on which animals were regularly grazed. Often the trees were pollarded, cut at some 8ft to 10ft above ground level, to prevent the animals from browsing the young shoots. Pollarding is now mostly restricted to willow. Parkland grazing at Ivington maintained '100 oxen, 10 cows and 300 sheep from Holy Cross (3 May) until St Peter in Prison (1 August)'. In addition the park provided three loads of hay, suggesting 3 acres of meadow. Valued at 1s 8d per load, it could not rival the hay of neighbouring *Enchenye* at 2s.

In the 345 acres of wood and pasture at Ashwood, in Stockton *herneys*, 'they may fell, within five years, 60 acres of underwood at 4d per acre, the whole 20s'. Here 100 oxen, 7 heifers and 20 calves were maintained from Holy Cross, but only until the Nativity of St John, 24 June, not St Peter in Prison. The remaining 285 acres included wood/pasture for a similar number of cattle to that at Ivington Park, but there is no reference to the pasturing of sheep. This may well be included in the bland phrase that 'in the pasture of the said manor they may keep 180 sheep, or 240 if the common of the Lord Prior could be recovered' from Brian de Brompton. Here, timber trees remained readily available. As late as the early 1530s Mr Cholsey, 'late prior, caused 100 trees to be hewed for repairs together with 28 loads of hewn timber'. Ashwood was, apparently, still well named. The favoured timber for musical instruments, to Thomas Smyth, c1534, went 'ash for making a pair of organs' for the priory.[483]

Unlike Ivington and Westwood in Stoke, Ashwood is not referred to as parkland in the Extent. However in 1422 John Bengz and Maud, his wife, 'our servants', were granted the custody, as overseers, of 'our park of Aschewood for life with all fees lawfully belonging to the same'. John was also to receive 1 bushel of wheat per week, together with 'the boughs, crops and bark of all trees in the said park'. The name is perpetuated by two farms, Upper Ashwood Park Farm, about a mile north of Ashton, and Ashwood Park Farm, a mile further north along the road to Brimfield, and also as Park Wood. Ashwood will have extended along the pronounced ridge stretching north-east from Ashton to Upper Drayton. It remains heavily wooded from Park Wood to Ashton, as does the southern part of the ridge, from Ashton to within 500ft of Stockton Cross. 'Redwood containing by estimation (at the Dissolution) 40 acres' was also in Stockton *herneys*. 'The herbage and pannage of the said wood be of the yearly rent or value of £1.[484]

At Dinmore were four distinct areas of woodland. The overall acreage of underwood was much smaller than at Ivington and Stockton, and a six-year rather than five-year rotation was practised, but the annual value per acre was considerably higher. At Middleover and Plotswood 55 acres were harvested over six years as nine-acre compartments, with a sale price of 4s 6d per acre; and at Birchover were 4 acres of underwood, sold 'within six years' at 6s per acre. By contrast, between 1203 and 1213 Abbot Elias had received from Agnes of Newton for 54 acres — 30 in *Birchofr'*, 16 at *Middelofr'*, 6 at *Wlfputte* and 2 at *Bakenhope* — an annual rent of 10s, that is 2d per acre, with a 40s entry fine. The site of Birchover, occasionally *Birchour*, is identified in a charter of Stephen, son of Reginald of Newton, as lying between Winsley and Newton.[485]

Hope also provided the most valuable of all woodland commodities, timber. This came from trees of at least 2ft in girth. The woodland entries for this grange illustrate the fundamental distinction between the production of underwood, on a short cycle, here of six years, and of timber, with a cycle of up to some 60 to 100 years. Timber was required primarily for structural work in buildings, and was often selected on site. Oak, the most common of English woodland trees, was the most suitable, but elm, with twice the growth rate, was preferred where it was necessary to resist damp. The wide-spreading parkland oak was not as useful for construction as its taller and straighter, tight-growing counterpart. The timber woods described at Hope were relatively small in area and would probably have provided the valuable standards that would be squared off with the adze. 'Against the court', that is the *bury*, were 39 acres, but no underwood. Towards the west the foreign wood contained 16 acres, also providing timber.[486]

Pannage, pasturage for pigs, was another valuable woodland resource. After the pigs had been allowed on the stubble, the mast harvest would be abundant, for the pigs to be fattened up for some six weeks prior to slaughter. Only at Hope are pigs recorded: 'feed for 30 hogs, the pannage is worth 7s 6d'. However swineherds are mentioned in the Extent. At Ivington and Stockton they received the standard 4 horseloads and 4 bushels of wheat, with 4 ells of cloth and one *purtell*, but at Luston merely 2 horseloads and 11 bushels, plus the cloth and *purtell*. The inclusion of swineherds at these three *herneys* in a list of wages of the workers of the manors of the demesne in 1407/8 confirms that they were charged with the care of the pigs of the demesne, not those of the villagers (see Table 8).

The Extent makes no reference to woodland in Luston *herneys*, other than that 'the forester of Yarpole pays 50 hens and 300 eggs'. However a court roll of 1408 records that John Fifhyde and William Belle, keepers of the manor, leased the pasture in our Park of *Oker* with the woods, for his life, to William Legat, paying the exchequer of Leominster 6s 8d yearly. Legat was to preserve the said park in quiet and free from disturbance, and be answerable to the keepers for *tac* (a customary fee for the right to keep swine) and *poundlac* (possibly the duty to keep the pound locked) under the penalty of being fined at the will of the keepers; 'if by any colour he makes any destruction, to his own profit, which shall be found by his neighbours to the value of one farthing he shall satisfy the lord with 1½d'. He was to close and impale the park at his own charge, with underwood to be delivered to him by the sub-dean, having the boughs and wood for the fences freely given by the sub-dean. The keepers were to have the other boughs and William was to have free access to his

Fig 20.2 Highwood Bank and Fishpool Dingle from Bryant's map

pasture in the park. 'If he be deficient two weeks in his rent they may enter and expel him.' William gave no fine because of the expenses he would incur with the enclosure.

Also in Luston *herneys* was the Highwood, which on Bryant's *Map of Herefordshire* (1836) has become 'Bircher or Highwood Common' (Fig 20.2). The name lives on in Highwood Bank, above Fishpool Valley, north-west of Croft Castle, Highwood Farm and Highwood House. In 1411 Thomas Andrewe, king's servant, yeoman of Henry IV's chamber, was granted the keepership of the *Highwode* of Leominster as a corrody for life, with the due wages, fees and profits as Walter Lyngeyn, deceased, had of the grant of King Edward III. There are records of despoliation in 1534, not only the removal of eight trees from Highwood, but also in *Luctonswode*, where Sir Richard Croft, died 1562, who had bought 16 acres at 16s an acre, sold them for 24s. Croft had also purchased a further 20 acres and seven timber trees, at a price unknown. This may be a reference to Oaker Wood, the only large wood in Lucton, for it was bounded on the north by Croft parish. At the same time 16 timber trees at Redwood in Stockton were 'lost'.[487]

Some details of Farlow, the priory's one distant estate (see Fig 5.2), are to be found in the 1327 Extent. It describes a toft with 40 acres of arable, 3 of meadow and one of more, all valued at 4d an acre, and a mill worth 10s, totalling £1 1s 4d. Eight messuages, two half-yardlands, 43 acres and two selions brought in £1 14s 7d; a further two messuages and 27 acres, 9s 7d, and two messuages in decay, with two half-yardlands, 13s 8d. The total value was £3 19s 2d.[488]

21 The Black Death, 1349

The Black Death was the great divide in English medieval history. The key contemporary source is the *Chronicle* of Henry Knighton of St Mary's Abbey, Leicester. He describes how, at the height of the pestilence, in 1349, 'there was a great cheapness of all things, owing to the general fear of death. Sheep and oxen strayed through the fields and crops for lack of keepers.' By the following autumn, however, 'a reaper was not to be had for less than 8d a day with his food, a mower for less than 12d with his food ... necessaries became so dear that what previously had been worth 1d was now worth 4d or 5d. Those who had let lands on yearly labour services (to villeins) were obliged to relieve and remit these services, excusing them on easier terms lest their houses should be irreparably ruined and the land remain completely uncultivated.' Concisely, there was an abundance of land and an acute shortage of labour.[489]

Edward III's response was an ordinance in June 1349, which sought to bind the able to their work, and their wages to their 1346 rates. Parliament recapitulated this in 1351 as the Statute of Labourers, 'against the malice of servants which were idle and not willing to serve after the pestilence without taking excessive wages'. Carters, ploughmen, shepherds, swineherds, dairymaids and others should receive only livery and wages as in 1346, eg mowers of meadow no more than 5d an acre or a day, reapers of corn 2d in the first week of August, 3d in the second and so on, and less in the country where less was wont to be given, without meat or drink or other courtesy to be demanded, given or taken; 2½d for threshing a quarter of wheat or rye, and 1½d for a quarter of barley, beans, peas or oats — 'if so much is given'. The first offence against the Statute brought 40 days' imprisonment. In a vain attempt to ensure compliance, commissioners were appointed, with powers to bring offenders before the local justices. On 1 May 1356 William Gorsynton, recorded as a bailiff of Leominster in 1347, John Gour of Pudlestone and Thomas de Hompton were appointed as commissioners within the abbot of Reading's liberty of Leominster. Against such powerful economic forces, these measures proved, for the most part, ineffective.[490]

Current estimates put the population decline at some 30–50%, with considerable local variation. Both the incidence and the subsequent impact remain matters of debate. The halimote rolls do not provide the basis for any statistical details of fatalities. Furthermore, the pre-Black Death halimote extracts for 1330–6 are thin on villein customs and services, and details of commutation. Thus comparison of the economic conditions of the customary tenants in the pre- and post-plague eras is difficult.

Work on the bishopric of Worcester estates indicates a 42% decline in tenant numbers, a figure that includes some recovery in the aftermath. In Hereford diocese the most valuable evidence comes from the details of clergy institutions in Trillek's episcopal Register. Averaging six a year in 1346 and 1347, there were 160 in 1349. First evidence of the plague comes from the south-east, about Ross and the Dean Forest, in January and February. By April it had reached Ledbury. The first clerical death in the north-west, of Hugh de Brut, was at Knill on 30 May, followed by Richard de

Hull at Brampton Bryan on 22 June and Brut's successor at Knill, John de Baderon, on 4 July. The peak was reached in July and August, when there were institutions at Stockton, Aston, Pembridge, Eardisland, Dilwyn, Sarnesfield, Hampton and once more at Knill. There were institutions at Monkland on 1 September, Weobley on 11th and Yazor on 17th. The last in the Leominster area was at Lyonshall on 3 November. As compared with the eastern areas of the county, Leominster and the north-west apparently got off lightly, apart from the six parishes about Pembridge.[491]

Prior William Dumbleton and his sub-prior, John de Sutton, both survived the plague. Dumbleton was elected abbot of Reading in autumn 1361, and on his death in 1369 was succeeded by Sutton.[492] Of the fate of their fellow monks we have no knowledge. Due to the death of so many priests at Reading Abbey, where there had been 65 monks in 1305, the pope was requested in 1354 to permit the ordination of 30 monks, each five years under the canonical age of 25. It has been suggested that, overall, the numbers in English religious houses were reduced by about a half. Although the Black Death will have had a dramatic impact on the *Opus Dei*, we are much better informed about its impact on ecclesiastical economies. The court rolls of Hereford Cathedral and episcopal estates provide a wealth of information. As landowners, dean and chapter were squeezed by the acute labour shortage. At Hereford Cathedral, where at least eight of the canons had died, their income was reduced by half. As an economy measure, the bishop abandoned his palaces at Bishops Frome, Bromyard, Colwall, Ledbury and Ross.[493]

The Stockton halimote rolls of 1 May 1349 carry poignant references to the earliest victims. Fellow villagers moved quickly to secure the better lands, without payment of entry fines. On that day Hugh Walkelyn took, in exchange for his own lands, 21 acres of arable of divers tenants in Kimbolton 'until some of their heirs come and pay their fine for the aforesaid lands, which done the exchange to be void'. At Middleton John de Roke acquired 6 acres of the lands formerly held by John de Leys, Richard Wylkins, John le Rede and Dom Henry, the chaplain. By 1350, when Simon Wodehale took, in exchange, 19 acres of land formerly held by Hugh atte Roke, Thomas Baymont, John of Eston, Henry Pachelor, Jeffery le White, and Nicholas de Haton, he had to pay 'to the Lord's purse (as entry fine) 6s 8d, on Michaelmas and Christmas next coming'. William le Kyng obtained 18 acres of the arable of Jeffery le White, William Holder, John atte Stele and Thomas Lacy on similar terms. Seven yardlands and two half-yardlands changed hands at Stockton *herneys* halimote in October 1349, but these were not exchanges. Two widows, a widower, a son and a daugter were amongst those who paid from £6 13s 4d to £2 for a yardland, and £5 for a half-yardland. Two of the women negotiated the inclusion of a licence to marry.[494]

The Luston halimote rolls for 1359 have the same saving clause, in one case relating to a tenant who had fled to, what he hoped would be, a better life. Prior Dumbleton's grant to Hugh Holle and Richard atte Barre of land in Lucton, for their respective lives, ended with the formula, 'if William atte Barre does not return to these parts'. As late as 1367 the Stoke halimote granted Richard Aylmond a yardland only 'until the heirs come and fine with the said keepers and take the said land'. Two years later at Brierley a grant of a tenement and close was still qualified, 'if none come'. On occasions, sureties had to be given that the incoming tenant would not depart. Thus, Walter atte Grene, having provided two sureties, was granted the late Godman Brown's half-yard-land at Cholstrey, under penalty 'that he shall not leave the said lands during his life'. Other entries indicate the lord fulfilling his duties as guardian of orphans, widows etc. An orphan's land was granted to a neighbour, with the responsibility of caring for the heir until he came of age. Thus at Bircher, before the plague, William, heir of Edith de Lee, was given into the custody of neighbours with his mother's lands, 'because he is a boy within age and unable until thirteen years to pay the fine and perform the services due'.[495]

The post-Black Death halimote rolls illustrate Dumbleton's and Sutton's response to the disaster. All landowners sought to retain as many tenants as possible, in a labour market that had suddenly become extraordinarily fluid. Where there was surplus land, some survivors had a firm interest in remaining, if the terms on offer were reasonable. Others, with smaller holdings, sought to improve their lot by negotiation with their lord or, like William atte Barre, by departure to pastures new.

Leasing

The bishops of Worcester and many other major landowners, religious and lay, reacted to the labour shortage by cutting back drastically on the direct exploitation of their lands, running down their demesne lands by leasing, thus minimising the problems of costs and shortages of labour. The beneficiaries were the knights, yeomen and prosperous peasants who took up the leases. During the last years of the 14th century, it has been suggested, 'landlords nearly everywhere had ceased to farm their own land'. Some of the greatest Benedictine houses, such as Christ Church, Canterbury, Westminster and Durham, made a determined effort to maintain villein tenure and labour services, but by 1416 even Durham had leased all but two of its greater manors.[496]

Coningsby's *Register* contains numerous references to the leasing of the priory's demesne to customary tenants, in both small and large quantities, but, given his interests, none to freehold tenants. In 1357, 46 selions 'of our demesne' were leased out at Hope, and in 1363 four acres of 'our demesne lands in Birchore field'. By 1366 the process had spread to Ivington, where 33 acres of 'our land' were leased. In 1371–2, 394 selions were leased in Lynacre's Furlong and *Kacheslowe* and Cornmarsh fields, with 38 selions at Bromefeld in Overhill. Some leases, optimistically, were for only twelve years; others, more realistically, for life, as with 6 acres of demesne in Crossenore (Cursneh) field in 1369. Leasing of the demesne was one response taken by the priory's keepers. Another was an increasing emphasis on wool production, discussed later (see Chapter 23).[497]

Commutation

Commutation of services and customs to regular money payments had been well established by the 1330s for some customary tenants with larger holdings. After the Black Death the amount to be paid became the subject of intense negotiation between keepers and villeins. At Stockton in 1370 widow Alice Reynard, who paid 8s annual rent for her late husband's half-yardland, was happy to commute her 'great works in autumn', three days' *husbonrepes* and carrying corn and seed, to a payment of 6s 8d at the feast of St Peter in Chains, 1 August.[498]

However, a considerable group of villein tenants had not commuted even by the early 15th century. A number of these staged a strike against their labour services. In 1410 William Wall of Stagbatch, Hugh Baldwyn, William Baret, John Baker, John Huggyns, Roger Comber, with others, who were summoned by William Bobbe, pindar of Ivington, to do their autumn works of reaping in the week before St Peter in Chains, 'did not perform the said works, wherefore the lord is much damaged'. On another occasion the case of John de la Ree, who had not performed his service for two years, was transferred from Westminster, where he was represented by his own attorney, to the abbot's liberty at Leominster, where the abbot's bailiff was ordered to 'exhibit speedy justice to the two parties'.[499]

In 1401–2, when most 'great customs and services' had been commuted, a quite unusual range of services is recorded in one of the last entries in the *Register*. At Ivington Walter atte Walle, who held a messuage and a half-yardland, was to sow one *fithur* (balk or unploughed ridge?) and a half with half a bushel of his own corn, work 16 days of the Great Custom, reaping the lord's corn in autumn, reap 5 days for *husbenrepes* and half a day for *metebone*, reap one ridge and a half at his own cost, carry one ridge (*rug*) and a half, carry a load of the lord's corn to the lord's barn of Ivington, carry a load of tithe to the lord's barn, mow 3 days for the lord, pay 3d *mershrent*, 3d *lammasgavel* and 5 eggs, one goose and 2 hens. Not mentioned, but certainly included, would have been suit of mill. In addition to his half-yardland, Walter held 16 acres of arable, 4 acres of meadow and three pastures, including one called 'lambland', for which the rent was £1 10s 2d yearly. Whether he preferred to use surplus money to acquire further land, or paid some smallholders to undertake his customs and services at a competitive rate, must remain a matter of conjecture. This appears to be an example of the villein Walter striving to make good.[500]

As with commutation of services and customs, entry fines also dropped. In 1350 comes first evidence of 'wine to enter'. By 1366 a flagon of wine for entry becomes a common feature, and so it continues up to one of the last Ivington entries, in 1400. On one occasion in 1369 four flagons were paid. As to the nature of this wine, whether it was of the grape or other fruit, one can only speculate. However, the idea of a wide range of small villein vineyards seems improbable.[501]

Servile Tenure and Manumission

For the villeins of the priory, as elsewhere, conditions of tenure improved after the Black Death. Rather than following immemorial custom, rents and entry fines came to be regulated by the state of the local land market, the so-called land-labour ratio. Two other liabilities, by the mid 13th century important tests of customary status, were beyond the scope of such regulation. The first was heriot, payment of the deceased's best chattel. Originally an animal, with the increasing affluence of many villeins, after 1349 this could well be a much more valuable material object. The second liability was merchet, the arbitrary amount exacted from villeins for permission for their daughters to marry. By the 15th century heriot and merchet were an easy means for acquisitive lords to squeeze large sums from wealthy villeins. Some manorial lords thus became especially anxious to preserve evidence of their more affluent servile families, those who could be most profitably exploited. In 1415 the earl of Mowbray claimed certain prosperous burgesses were his villeins who had absconded, and in 1445 Sir John Fastolf claimed that William Heyne, a wealthy mill-owner of Castle Combe, his villein by birth, had goods to the value of £2,000. For the right to marry and re-enter her husband's mills etc, the widow and her second husband eventually paid Fastolf £100 and £40 respectively.[502]

At Leominster the prior's attitude to villein marriage became more relaxed under the immediate pressure of population collapse. In 1349 John Underwode was granted a messuage and a noke on the basis that 'he shall take a wife after these presents'. At Stockton in 1368 a man, granted his widowed mother's lands, was given licence to marry 'wherever he pleases'. At Ivington in 1375

William Adys was licensed to marry the widow of the late John Oddale, with the provision that, if she predeceased him, he would retain her land. When Alice Wakelyn was granted the lands of the late William Nyeborn, she also was granted the right to marry 'wheresoever she pleases', apparently on the basis that the husband would join her on her lands at Wharton.[503]

In the long run, however, the priors were surprisingly successful in their efforts to retain villeinage and thus payment of heriot and merchet in a market where there was a glut of land. Part of their success may be attributed to the weaker bargaining position of tenants in a lordship close to the borders of Wales, where population movement, if it was to bring material advantage, had to be to the east. Given the intimate relations between Leominster, with its tradition of burgage tenure, and the lands of the foreign beyond, marriages between townspeople and those of villein birth were a persistent problem. Thus William Wall of Stagbatch, native of the lord abbot, had to pay merchet of £2 for a licence for Margaret, his daughter, to marry a burgess.[504]

The results of Dumbleton's and Sutton's policies in the years immediately after the plague are evident in a survey of the priory's tenants taken in 1431/2. In the four ancient *herneys* the priory had retained a remarkably high percentage of customary tenants: 48% overall, 58% in Stockton, 67% in Ivington, Luston 47%. Only at Stoke, where they represented a mere 19%, were the villeins heavily outnumbered. This was to provide the abbots with welcome income from more affluent villeins seeking manumission. At the grange of Hope, vigorous assarting in the early 13th century had attracted free men and their families into 'new lands'; there were eleven free tenants but only one villein. As one would anticipate, there is evidence of a general increase in the size of tenant land holdings (Table 14).[505]

The first recorded manumission on the priory lands was in 1376, when the Hope halimote rolls recorded that Walter Peion of Priddleton 'shall, during his life, be quit from all services and customary works and from all servitude, nor shall it be lawful for any keeper of Leominster to take, seize or withhold any of the chattels, lands, tenements or cattle purchased by the said Walter, by reason of his servile condition. He has liberty to dispose of all his lands, goods and chattels during his life without contradiction from the abbot and convent of Reading and their keepers.' The other side of this bargain is not expressed on the rolls. Walter would have had to pay well to be quit of his servitude and the potential threats to his possessions.[506]

There is a list of the manumissions of the priory's villeins in the Coningsby *Register*, and another in a Reading cartulary, formerly in the Wiltshire Record Office. Of these the earliest record is in 1394/5, when Joanna, daughter of John Ball, villein of Stagbatch, had to pay for manumission on becoming the wife of Thomas Blewet, burgess of Leominster. Later cases provide instructive documentation. The abbots of Reading, whilst publicly expressing a high moral stand on 'servitude', were yet pursuing

	Tenants	**Holdings in virgates**					
		2½	2	1½	1	½	¼
Middleton	12				8	4	
Priddleton	9				4	5	
Luston	33	1		4	19	9	
Ivington	12				12		
Stoke	16		2	2	5	7	
Hope	12				7	3	2
Total	94	2½	4	9	55	14	½

Total 85 virgates; average 0.9 virgate — Wilts CRO D1/19

Table 14 Landholdings, 1431/2

policies to secure its retention. In 1434 Abbot Thomas 'manumitted and made free from the yoke of servitude William Legat of Luston (park-keeper of *Oker*) and John, his first born, together with any offspring after the dates of these presents to be begotten. So that neither we nor our successors shall have any right or claim on the said William and John and their offspring in their goods and chattels by reason of any servitude by us demanded or challenged'. In the same year Thomas Adys of Ivington and John, his son, were 'freed and delivered from the yoke of servitude'. Twelve years later, Abbot John manumitted Richard Adys of Ivington and Richard, his son, and in 1456-7 Thomas Grubbe of Stoke. In none of these cases are details given of the fee imposed, but payments for manumission continued to be a profitable matter. However, a year before the priory's dissolution Cromwell's agents were able to report that the Leominster estates were 'a royal rich country' for there were many 'bondsmen'. As late as 1557, 'in consideration of his services in the office of steward of the lordship of Leominster, and all of the Queen's lands in Herefordshire', John Poule of Leominster and his heirs, 'villein regardant to the Crown', was granted 'all such liberties and franchises within that borough as other lieges enjoy'.[507]

Wages at the *burys* and granges in the early 15th century

The list of the wages of those employed at the various granges 1407/8 provides valuable evidence as to the changes that had taken place in the economies of the *herneys* and their subsidiaries since the Black Death. Comparison with Table 8 shows contraction in the number of families at the granges, and increased payments to the remaining officers. In 1327 cowherds, receiving 2s, were to be found at each of the *herneys*, with a vivary at Moor Abbey. In 1407 there were only two, at Ivington and Luston, each receiving 4s. The Grange or home farm at Leominster had the full range of staff, except for cowherd, and the only stock-keeper and carter. On the other hand, there was now a shepherd at each of the eight granges — the entry 'O this year' against the More in Stoke *herneys* suggests that a shepherd was usually found there also — and at all but the Leominster Grange, the home farm, and possibly Stockton, he was at the top of the hierarchy of farm workers, receiving 6s. In addition to the shepherd at Ivington *herneys* in 1407 the list of wages refers to one receiving the same 6s wage at the Hyde, which lay to the west of Ivington, three-quarters of a mile south-east of Stretford. Here the shift to sheep farming occurred within eight years of the Black Death, as the Ivington halimote rolls refer in May 1357 to Thomas de Comynhope, 'shepherd', with Alice his wife, living in a messuage and close, formerly Hugh de Hyde's.[508]

This represents a new area opened up for sheep farming, and a marked change in the priory's economy. Before the Black Death stock-rearing on the rich pastures of the Lugg and its tributaries had been of major importance, as evidenced by the 350 oxen of the 1327 Extent. The oxen were evidently sold on as draught beasts in an area where they had yet to be supplanted by the horse. The burgeoning demand for grain of the early 14th century was brought to an abrupt halt in 1349. Demesne farming was now at a discount, and with it the emphasis on stock-rearing. The result of the decline in the demand for grain was a rapid shift to sheep-rearing, to meet an ever-increasing demand for wool of the highest quality from the rapidly growing English and overseas cloth trade. However, there is evidence that the market for cattle 'fattened' on the rich meadows of the Lugg and Arrow and their tributaries revived in the 15th century, to rise to new peaks in the 16th and 17th.[509]

22 The 15th Century: Glyn Dwr's Revolt, the Priory and the Parish Church

Documentary sources become thin by the 15th century. Extracts from the halimote rolls in Coningsby's *Register* terminate in 1401 with entries for Ivington on the Monday before Michaelmas, and Brierley on the Sunday before the feast of St Luke. Otherwise there are only a few random entries. The Leominster Cartulary includes sections in 15th-century hands, but most relate to the preceding centuries. The name of only one of the priors and sub-priors between 1428 and 1511 is known.[510] The episcopal registers are the single major documentary source for the conventual and parish churches. To these the building history of the parish church and properties within the town provide a valuable supplement. In addition, as the Wars of the Roses were, in some respects, an extension of marcher rivalries, Leominster, briefly, entered the pages of the nation's history, due to its proximity to the scene of three vital battles: Glyn Dwr's victory at Bryn Glas in 1402, Henry VI's rout of the Yorkists at Ludford bridge, 1459, and the future Edward IV's victory over the Lancastrians at Mortimer's Cross in 1461.

The Revolt of Owain Glyn Dwr, 1400–13

The 15th century did not open well for Leominster or its priory. Forfeiture of the estates of three of the greatest marcher lords, and the death of two others — Roger Mortimer, third earl of March, killed in Ireland in 1398, aged only 24, and John of Gaunt in 1399 — created a political vacuum in Wales of which Owain Glyn Dwr was not slow to take advantage. On 16 September 1400, at his manor of Glyndyfrdwy, he was proclaimed Prince of Wales. He immediately burned Ruthin, and ravaged Denbigh, Rhuddlan and other English boroughs in the north-west. In 1402 Owain captured Reginald de Grey, lord of Ruthin, for whom Henry IV quickly paid a ransom of 10,000 marks, £6,666 13s 4d. On 22 June that year Owain overwhelmed the Herefordshire forces at Bryn Glas near Pilleth, overlooking the Lugg, 12 leagues from Leominster. The carnage, we are told, was 'horrendous'. Their leader, Edmund IV Mortimer, brother of the fourth earl, was captured, with Thomas Clanvow of Ocle Pychard, and eminent members of the Herefordshire gentry were killed, including former sheriffs Walter Devereux of Weobley and Kinnard de la Bere of Kinnersley, and Robert Whitney. A local, but unsupported tradition, reported by Price in 1795, records that, soon after Bryn Glas, Glyn Dwr 'made himself master of Leominster and confined Mortimer in the (abbot's) dungeon in that town. He then wreaked his vengeance on the Ecclesiastics who had favoured the cause of the English ... laid the priory of Leominster under heavy contributions'.[511]

Fearing Mortimer, uncle of the well-guarded earl of March, as a potential Yorkist claimant to his throne, Henry IV refused to find his ransom. On 30 November Mortimer therefore allied with Owain, marrying his daughter, Joan. Other Herefordshire gentry also took Owain's daughters to wife: John Scudamore of Kentchurch married Alice, Sir John Croft married Janet, and Sir

Richard Monnington a fourth. On 13 December Mortimer wrote to a number of his powerful neighbours to announce that he had joined Glyn Dwr in his struggle to obtain 'his right in Wales'. Owain's policies now included the securing of the English throne for Mortimer. This formed part of the Tripartite Indenture between Owain, Mortimer and Hotspur. If their combined forces were successful, all lands west of the Severn and Mersey were to go to Owain, whilst the Percys would have all lands north of the Trent. The rump of England would remain for Mortimer, as English king. Rumours were rife of large sums of money being despatched by 'certain English monasteries' to Wales. Leominster, with its history of close relations with the Mortimer family, was, of course, a prime suspect.[512]

Transposing the battle of Pilleth to 'Severn's sedgy bank', in *Henry IV Part 1*, Act 1 Scene 3 Shakespeare encapsulates the position of both sides in an exchange between Hotspur and Henry:

Henry: That we at our own charge shall ransom straight
His (Llywelyn's) brother-in-law, the foolish Mortimer;
Who, on my soul, hath wilfully betray'd
The lives of those that he did lead to fight
Against the great magician, damn'd Glendower,
Whose daughter, as we hear, the Earl of March
Hath lately married. Shall our coffers then
Be emptied to redeem a traitor home?
Shall we buy treason, and indent with fears,
When they have lost and forfeited themselves?
No, on the barren mountains let him starve;
For I shall never hold that man my friend
Whose tongue shall ask me for one penny cost
To ransom home revolted Mortimer.

Hotspur: Revolted Mortimer!
He never did fall off, my sovereign liege,
But by the chance of war: to prove that true
Needs no more but one tongue for all those wounds,
Those mouthed wounds, which valiantly he took,
When on the gentle Severn's sedgy bank,
In single opposition, hand to hand,
He did confound the best part of an hour
In changing hardiment with great Glendower.

Four weeks after the battle at Bryn Glas, the royal Council licensed 'the good men of Leominster, situated on the frontiers of the Marches of Wales, to fortify the town with walls, pales and ditches for defence against the Welsh rebels, and to compel all men of the town to contribute to the expense according to their means'. Though lacking for a town wall, there is archaeological evidence for the line of the town ditch. However, 14th-century pottery found in the ditch indicates that this, not surprisingly, predates the 1402 licence.[513] A proclamation in that year, rendering all trade with the Welsh illegal, was a dead letter. Most people in the marcher counties, concerned far more with profits than with patriotism, smuggled large quantities of goods, including oats and other grains, beer, malt and fish, over the frontier. In 1403–4, in defiance of royal authority, the men of Hereford and Salop even negotiated a local truce with Glyn Dwr, for which they paid a handsome sum. In October 1404, cattle were still being bought from the Welsh. Trade flowered probably as never before.[514]

In April 1403 the 15-year-old Henry of Monmouth, the future Henry V, was appointed his father's lieutenant in Wales with a force of some 20 knights, 50 men-at-arms and 2,500 archers. In early May he laid waste to Owain's manor houses and lands at Sycharth and Glyndyfrdwy and garrisoned the royal castles, but otherwise achieved little. This is hardly surprising, given his desperate lack of financial support. In 1404, 'to pay for men-at-arms to abide in and safeguard the borders of Wales and to resist the Welsh rebels should they invade the realm', Henry IV borrowed a total of 200 marks, £133 6s 8d, from certain abbots and priors having lands in Wales and the Marches. The sums levied provide a revealing hierarchy: Hereford Dean and Chapter £40 (30%); Malmesbury Abbey £30 (22%); Leominster Priory £20 (15%); Lanthony Secunda, at the Hyde, Gloucester, and Wigmore Abbey £13 6s 8d each (10%); Deerhurst £8 (6%); Wormsley £5 (4%); and Llanthony Prima, in the Honddu valley, a mere £4 (3%).[515]

Prince Henry brought his household to the March in the spring, and spent most of his time at Hereford and Leominster, presumably at the priory. Nevertheless, until 1408 his father, Henry IV, was constantly plagued by plots and threats of plots. Rumours of the 'large sums of money being sent from religious houses in England to Wales, and of some English commanders in Wales acting as double agents' continued, 'possibly not without some kernel of truth'. Given the long and intimate connection between the Mortimers of Wigmore and the priors of Leominster, such as the siege of Hereford in 1264 and the prior's support for Roger III de Mortimer imprisoned in the Tower in 1322, it would be hardly surprising to find Leominster amongst such 'religious houses'. In August 1405 a French expedition landed in Wales, and a combined force marched across Glamorgan to take up position on Woodbury Hill, eight miles from Worcester. 'With a better organised commissariat, they might have marched on into the Midlands.' On the other hand, with the death of Owain's brother, and the capture of his son, brother-in-law and secretary, support in Wales began to crumble. On Henry V's accession, in 1413, generous terms brought rapid returns, but Owain was never taken, despite rumours of refuge at Monnington, Croft and elsewhere in Herefordshire.[516]

Demographic Decline

The Welsh threat removed, the dominant features of life on the Marches until the accession of Henry Tudor as King Henry VII in 1485 were the long-term impact of the Black Death and subsequent outbreaks, and, from c1450, the political instability arising from the conflicting claims of Lancastrians and Yorkists to the throne. In assessing demographic decline, not only the major outbreak of 1349 and the Grey Death or Plague of Children of 1361–2 but later, more localised, outbreaks have to be taken into account. High mortality was characteristic of the 15th as much as the second half of the 14th century, for by 1400 the plague had become endemic, particularly in towns. In larger towns, such as Oxford, property on the principal streets remained tenanted but in the back streets fell into decay. Thus to build his New College William of Wykeham was able to buy the sites of 30 houses very cheaply. Merton College garden was formed in a similar way. Here property values did not rise until the late 16th century. For example the rent of one property, 11 marks (£7 6s 8d) in 1293, was 6 in 1357, fell to 3 in 1393, rose to 7 in 1426 but was only 4½ marks (£3) in 1460. Many other large towns, such as York, Lincoln, Scarborough, Boston, Coventry and Winchester, suffered in the same way as Oxford. This Dobson has described as 'the ubiquity of the urban malaise', but other towns 'were emphatically not in general decline'. In some counties, such as Staffordshire, an overall contraction in the number of towns is notable, and the role of the smaller market town is now being explored.[517]

The same forces were at work in the Herefordshire market towns. Here contraction took place from the periphery, with the market-place or -places remaining relatively vibrant. At Ledbury, where statistical evidence is available, a comparison of households by streets in 1288 and 1597 shows there was a contraction of some 63% in New Street, 54% in Bye Street and 41% in the Homend, but an increase of 35% close to the High Street, in the Southend. In the market-place itself, an increase from 26 tenancies to 58 households was achieved by fragmentaion of burgage plots. Topographical evidence indicates that, after the population collapse following the Black Death, the borough did not recover to its 1285 bounds until the end of the 18th century.[518] For Leominster no such data is available, but what evidence there is suggests that it did not follow the same pattern.

The parish churches of Herefordshire's towns and villages symbolise the economic prosperity enjoyed by the county during much of the pre-plague era; also, in most cases, the subsequent decline. Ledbury is again a good example. The flourishing character of its economy, as marketing centre for the surrounding agricultural area, is reflected in the architecture of its parish church, for which, as at Leominster and elsewhere, funding was of course local. The aisled and cruciform minster of c1100 was redeveloped c1190, a three-stage detached tower added in 1230–40, and a north aisle in 1230–60. Finally, that 'conscious masterpiece', the outer north chapel, was added c1300–40. After that there was nothing, until c1500. At Bromyard the only late medieval addition was a stair turret. At Ross, the church is almost wholly late 13th/early 14th century. At Kington post-plague work is also negligible, a two-bay arcade in the south chapel. The widespread prosperity of the early years of the 14th century is underlined by the range and quality of work at Pembridge, Dilwyn, Kingsland, Allensmore, Marden, Madley and Eaton Bishop, in particular the glorious stained glass of c1330–50 in the two last. In stark contrast is the dearth of perpendicular work within the county, other than at the cathedral — and Leominster's parochial church.

Not all parts of the country suffered from the 'urban malaise'. During the mid 14th century, cloth replaced wool as England's principal export. English wool exports c1300 were some 30,000 sacks, but fell in the 15th century to some 10,000. Cloth exports, on the other hand, rose by 50% in 40 years, from 40,000 fully finished cloths in 1400 to 60,000 in 1439. Cloth-production, the transformation of the raw material into the finished product, was centred on East Anglia, especially Suffolk, parts of the Cotswolds, the south-west, especially Somerset, and the West Riding. The manufacturing towns tended to be new and relatively small, such as Lavenham, Long Melford and Hadleigh in Suffolk; Northleach and Chipping Campden in the Cotswolds; Castle Combe, Tiverton and Totnes in the south-west; and Halifax, Leeds and Wakefield in the West Riding. They exemplify the close relationship between the prosperity of the surrounding countryside and urban growth in the late Middle Ages.[519]

The great 'wool' churches, many built virtually anew in the 15th century, such as Woodbridge, Blythburgh and Southwold in Suffolk, Fairford in Gloucestershire, Steeple Ashton in Wiltshire, and Mells and Bishop Lydiard in Somerset, point up the difference between such cloth-manufacturing counties and most of Herefordshire. At the cathedral the only major works of this period are the building of the cloisters, which took almost 80 years to complete, 1412–90, and alterations to the south transept, to provide a setting for Bishop Trefnant's tomb, illumined by a six-light window above. The great west window was added by Canon Lochard in 1435, ultimately serving to weaken the Romanesque façade and its, later, west tower. Otherwise, there were only the intimate, but very beautiful, chantry chapels of bishops Stanbury, 1470–80, and Audley, 1492–1502. At Leominster, however, the 15th-century enhancements of the parochial church, the great west window and the west tower, suggest that the borough's economy was buoyant.

The Great West Window

Leadership and finance for enhancement of the parish church had to come from the parishioners, especially the small group of wealthy burgesses. By 1413 relationships between the bailiff and commonalty of Leominster and the abbot of Reading and his keepers at Leominster had changed. The former were now self-confident enough to challenge their lord by claiming ownership, rather than mere rights of pasture, of the 24 acres at Portmanmore. Clearly one of the borough bailiffs had failed in his duty to challenge this encroachment on the abbot's liberties. The abbot, through his keepers, was obliged to bring an action to recover seisin at Hereford's August assizes, where bailiff and community were commanded, 'on the part of our lord the king, that you and everyone of you cause full seisin to be given to the said abbot without delay. Fail not.'[520]

Construction of the large west window for the south nave and a west tower at the end of the Romanesque north nave represents the third and final stage in the aggrandisement of their parish church by the borough's governing elite. Window and tower are vivid evidence of the wealth to be found in what, compared with Hereford, was but a small market town. As with the Decorated work of the south aisle, the inspiration came from St Peter's Abbey, Gloucester, where in the 1420s Abbot John Morvent rebuilt the west end. There the dominant feature was the great west window, well illustrated in an anonymous water colour (Plate 17a). Two great mullions,

Fig 22.1 Great west window with Gloucester-style buttresses

in the form of flying buttresses, divided it into three sections, each of three lights. The design was based on the even larger, mid-14th-century window at the east end, some 72 by 38ft, about the size of a tennis court. This also was divided by two considerable mullions, but here into sections of four, five and four lights. To protect this vast area of glazing from strong easterly winds, the mullions had been buttressed.

Given such august lineage, the Leominster architect would have had no doubts about adopting such flying buttresses for his own west window. At the priory the outer sections are also of three lights but the central section of merely two. Originally, these would have been filled with the remarkable stained glass of the era, and on sunny afternoons the parish's south nave would have been suffused with its colours. Given Leominster's reputation during the Commonwealth as 'little Geneva', it is hardly surprising that every trace of the original glazing has been lost (Fig 22.1 & Plate 17b).

Fig 22.2a&b Lintel of 15th-century processional doorway, internal view above and external below

The West Tower

Many parish churches had bell towers by the 13th century. These were certainly getting grander in the 14th century. The magnificent west tower at the neighbouring, and rival, borough of Weobley had been built c1330–40. Of five stages, with a richly decorated spire supported by four flying buttresses, it dominated the whole of its district and the nearby section of the route leading from Wales into Leominster via Hay and Sarnesfield. As to the date of the priory's west tower, the only evidence is architectural. Rivalry with Ludlow, where St Laurence's tower was completed 1461–73, could well have been the stimulus.

To provide support for Leominster's new tower, considerable building work had to be undertaken on its substructure. On the east side the arch was strengthened, from ground to arcade level, by the insertion of a new arch. This gave an unrestricted view from the west portal right down the earlier nave. On the south, west and north the new tower stands not on, but within the Romanesque structure. To achieve this, internal supporting arches were built against the earlier Romanesque work at the second stage. Externally, the tower is thus set back from the west façade. The tower completed, the Leominster burgesses could at last look their neighbours from Ludlow, and Weobley, in the eye.

Further works were undertaken by the monks, who rebuilt the doors and passageway of their processional entrance at the western end of the north aisle. This gave access to and from the cloister. The reasons for reconstruction are not known. The stepped passageway is now blocked. The only visible evidence today are the lintels on the inner and outer face, to the left of the new doorway giving access to the toilets etc (Figs 22.2a&b and see Fig 7.1).

John Vir

If Gloucester's new west window was built in the 1420s, then Leominster's was probably constructed in the late 20s or early 30s. This suggests it was the brainchild of John Vir, the most remarkable of all the men to hold the office of vicar of Leominster prior to the Dissolution. He succeeded Reginald Pole in 1423 and held the post for 43 years. Held in high regard by the local gentry, Vir had been presented to the chapelry of Hampton Wafre by Sir Rowland Lenthall in 1428. According to Leland, Sir Rowland, knighted at Agincourt in 1415, 'took many prisoners there, by which prey he began the new building'. The chapel, mostly of the 15th century, is within Hampton Court (Fig 22.3), for which Lenthall received licence in 1435 to crenellate, and to empark 1,000 acres. Vir also held the rectory of Hopton Wafers, Salop.

Shortly after institution as vicar he was appointed, with the bishop's commissary, to hold an enquiry into the complaint by Edmund Mortimer, fifth earl of March, about the state of Chirbury Priory, Salop. Bishop Spofford's mandate was 'to punish, and reform faults and scandals there'. The prior had to resign. Two years later, Vir and the bishop's vicar general held an enquiry into irregularities and mismanagement by the abbot of Wigmore. Here flagrant abuses were revealed: daily services were ignored; dilapidations had mounted to £100; the legality of the abbot's election was challenged; and two monks who had sought a general chapter to remove the abuses had been expelled. These are but two local examples of the serious lapses in monastic discipline in the diocese during the era. Perilous misconduct was also found at Limebrook and Aconbury. Of the quality of monastic life at Leominster we have no evidence before 1448.[521]

Fig 22.3 Hampton Court Chapel today

Lollardy was not dead in north-west Herefordshire. After his appointment as bishop's proctor, that is his proxy in ecclesiastical matters, one of Vir's first tasks in 1430 was to hold an enquiry into accusations of heresy at Almeley.[522]

The problems Reginald Pole had experienced with regard to his emoluments as vicar came to a head in 1433, when Bishop Spofford, with the consent of both parties, adjudicated between vicar and abbot as to the vicar's emoluments. Abbot and prior, John Hasley, now met more than their match. A canon lawyer, with all the experience gained as bishop's proctor, Vir presented a lengthy written statement of his case to Spofford. Vir then ensured that Spofford's decision was reproduced, *in extenso*, in the episcopal register. It occupies four and a half pages of close print in Canon Bannister's 1917 edition. The provisions include payment by the rector to the vicar each year, in perpetuity, of £20, two wagon loads of hay and two more of firewood, the lesser tithes of apples and all fruit of the trees in the town of Leominster and the villages of Stoke and Docklow, plus 6d for each office of the dead, 3d for each anniversary mass for the dead, and half the oblations made by the faithful at the Corpus Christi Mass.

Of the other provisions, one of the most significant was that the vicar and his two chaplains enjoyed the right to eat with the prior, at midday as well as in the evening, on the occasion of all the numerous principal feasts observed by the priory. On earlier occasions, when the principal feasts had been referred to in the episcopal registers, only the most important, such as Christmas, Epiphany, Easter and Pentecost, had been named, the remainder dismissed as 'the rest'. On this occasion, Vir insisted that each of the principal feasts was named and placed in sequence. Thus we have firm evidence that the feasts of St Edfrith, the minster's Columban founder, and another of Leominster's saints, Aethelmod, were still being celebrated by Edfrith's Benedictine successors almost eight centuries after his arrival on the banks of the Lugg. The position of these two feasts in the sequence shows that they conform to the dates given in Leominster's Anglo-Saxon calendar: Aethelmod's, 9 January, is between Epiphany, 6 January, and St Vincent, 22 January; Edfrith's feast, 26 October, between the feast of the relics, 10 October, and SS Simon and Jude on 28 October.[523]

Conflict between Priory, Parish and Vicar

In 1425 Richard Plantagenet, duke of York, inherited the earldom of March on the death of Edmund, the 5th earl. Leominster, like most of Herefordshire, became a stronghold of the Yorkists. It was probably from Richard that Henry VI learned in February 1448 that all was not well at Leominster Priory. It was no doubt on his advice that the king appointed Walter Devereux, the local Yorkist leader, with John Norroys, a member of the royal household, as wardens. 'Wastes, dilapidations and alienations had taken place through the negligent and improvident governance of certain monks, late custodians of the priory, so that the resources of the monastery and manor suffice not for the payment of debts incurred.' They were to enquire into 'all the destructions, damages, burdens and excesses committed upon the priory's manor and all goods withdrawn therefrom'. The names of the guilty were to be established. No further payments were to be made except for the sustenance of the monks and their servants, and hospitality was now to be restricted to genuine guests, the poor and pilgrims. At Leominster, as at other local monasteries, relations and friends were apparently being accommodated.[524]

That long source of controversy between monks and parishioners, the ringing of parochial bells, arose once more. Both sides could muster powerful arguments, as in 1276, when Bishop Cantilupe expressed surprise that 'the bells provided at the cost of the parishioners are never rung nor allowed to be rung'. The monks, however, maintained that the tolling of the parochial bells, presumably in the new west tower, was a gross interference with the holy office.

The parishioners of Leominster were not alone in their conflicts with the monks. Throughout the country, similar battles were being fought at Benedictine and Augustinian houses with parochial naves. Probably the most notorious case was at Wymondham, Norfolk. In 1249, when the central tower became dangerous, the monks temporarily took over the parishioners' western tower. On the return of their bells to the lantern tower, they walled up the parochial tower. Archbishop Arundel empowered the parish to 'find, place, keep and have sufficient bells in the same'. The parishioners, insisting the old one was too low for the bells to be heard, built the present great west tower c1445. At 140ft in height, it quite overshadowed that of the monks.[525]

At Leominster problems relating to the collection of ecclesiastical taxation arose once more in the 15th century. In August 1404, when the new bishop, Robert Mascall, had just been consecrated in Rome, a royal mandate was sent to the guardian of the see. This pointed out that the prior of Leominster had been appointed as a collector 'without mature deliberation'. 'Letters patent of the late king produced in Chancery' showed that the prior 'could not undertake or answer for such a charge' without consent from Reading. The abbot had acted quickly, requesting formal inspection of Richard II's charter and 'plainer declaration that the monks of Leominster were quit of collections, accounts and levyings of tenths, quotas, subsidies, charges and impositions whatsoever granted by the king to the clergy' — for a fine paid at the king's chamber. Henry IV therefore discharged the prior from such duties, but the issue did not go away, despite such 'plainer declaration'. In 1524 collection of royal tenths was part of a formal agreement between abbot and bishop. For almost three centuries it had remained a profound irritant. The abbot standing firmly by his principles and charters, the bishop, in one of the poorest of English dioceses, had but few adequately equipped clerics to ensure that ecclesiastical taxation was secured to the satisfaction of the royal clerks.[526]

A Leominster Missal and Breviary (Plates 2 and 3)

Amongst the extensive collection of early Leominster borough records at the Herefordshire Record Office are the Registers of Pleadings of the Court of Record for 1555–64. These were, and continue to be, wrapped up for their protection in ten folios of a late medieval missal. The majority of these folios are in very good condition, but those on the outside are faded and dirty. The Latin text is in black, with highlights in red, and initials are blue on a red background, textured with foliage patterns. One folio has musical notation on both sides. Two further folios, with notation, are from a Breviary, with services for the eve of the Nativity and Christmas Day.[527]

It is fortunate indeed that one of the folios establishes that they came from a missal of the Hereford Use, the modified form of the standard medieval Roman rite as used in Hereford diocese. Variations between the Uses were mostly in matters of detail. The principal diocesan Uses were those of Salisbury, York, Hereford and Lincoln. In March 1542 in Canterbury Province, all clergy under the archbishop's jurisdiction were ordered to adopt the Use of Sarum. Later it was commanded that 'henceforth, all the whole realme shall have but one use', ie of the 1549 Prayer Book. The principal monastic orders also had their own Uses. Thus William of Wicumbe's labours at Leominster included the correction of a Collectar, giving the daily prayers for the celebrant, 'according to the Use of Reading', derived from Cluny.[528]

Inclusion of the feast of the Translation of the Relics of St Thomas Cantilupe, on 25 October (Fig 22.4c), proves that this missal conformed to the Hereford rather than the Reading Use. Although no date is given, it is confirmed by the preceding festival, of St Romanus, on 23rd. In 1320, after years of preliminary discussion, Pope John XXII canonised Thomas Cantilupe and announced that his feast should be held on 2 October. This was recognised by the Salisbury and other Uses. However, Cantilupe was not translated from his tomb, still to be seen in the north transept, to the shrine in the middle of the Lady Chapel, until 1349. The translation was celebrated only in the Hereford Use. That these folios were used to wrap the earliest records of the borough court, sitting in the Frere Chamber of the former priory, strengthens the belief that the folios were from a discarded missal of Leominster parish church.[529]

There are only four manuscript copies of missals according to the Hereford Use: British Library Additional MS 39675 of c1320–49; Bodleian Library, University College, Oxford MS 78a of c1400–25; Downside College MS 48243, attributed to the early 15th century; and Worcester Cathedral MS F161, of the 15th century. None is perfect. The first, originally at Hereford Cathedral, was acquired by the Catholic family of the Beringtons of Winsley, near Hope-under-Dinmore; but after the death of Thomas, c1820, it eventually passed to E.S. Dewick, who gave it to the British Museum. The Worcester missal, a particularly fine copy, is written in a bold, expert liturgical hand, some pages having large initials and full borders in gold and colours, with foliage and knotwork.[530]

The only printed text of the Hereford Use is an edition of 1874, reprinted from the Rouen edition of 1502. Edited by W.G. Henderson, it has been described as 'not outstanding', but 'sufficiently workable to establish the order of Mass'. Space permits but a brief introduction to the text of these folios. The following analysis of their contents owes much to a colleague on the Hereford Diocesan Advisory Committee, Rev Ian Gibbs of Munslow.[531]

The first folio relates to *Benedictio Aquae*, the blessing of the salt and water, customarily sprinkled over the people before High Mass, and used at blessings, burials, dedications, exorcisms and for the church stoup at the entrance. The blessing took place on Sunday, before Terce, by a priest dressed in alb and amice at the lectern in the middle of the choir. 'I exorcise thee, O creature of salt, by the living God ... who commanded thee to be cast into the water by Elisha, the prophet, that the barrenness of the water might be healed, that thou mayest become salt exorcised for the salvation of them that believe ... and all that take thee; and from that place where thou shalt have been sprinkled, let every delusion and wickedness, or craft of devilish cunning, when adjured flee and depart'. After two collects, the priest cast salt into the water in the form of a cross. This passage from the missal ends with the singing, as the water was being sprinkled, of the antiphon, 'thou shalt purge me O Lord with hyssop and I shall be clean; thou shalt wash me, and I shall be whiter than snow'.

The nine subsequent folios include sections from both the Temporale, the observances of the church year, the variable parts of the Mass, and the Sanctorale, the feast days of particular saints, all fixed. The first of the folios of the Temporale provides details of the Midnight Mass and Dawn Mass for the Nativity, Christmas Day. Differences are slight between the six folios of the Temporale and Henderson's text, but more evident between the latter and the last four folios, the Sanctorale, of which the first records the feasts between 22 and 26 July: Mary Magdalene and Abbot Wandrille,

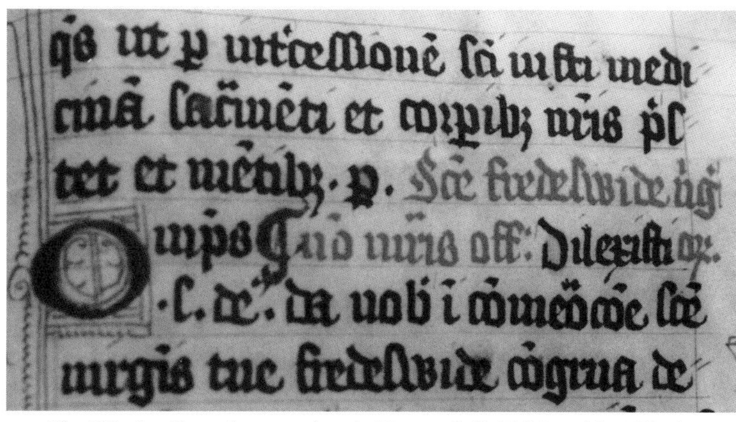

Fig 22.4a Leominster missal. Feast of St Frideswide, Virgin, legendary West Saxon princess, founder of double monastery on site of Christ Church Cathedral, Oxford (19 October)

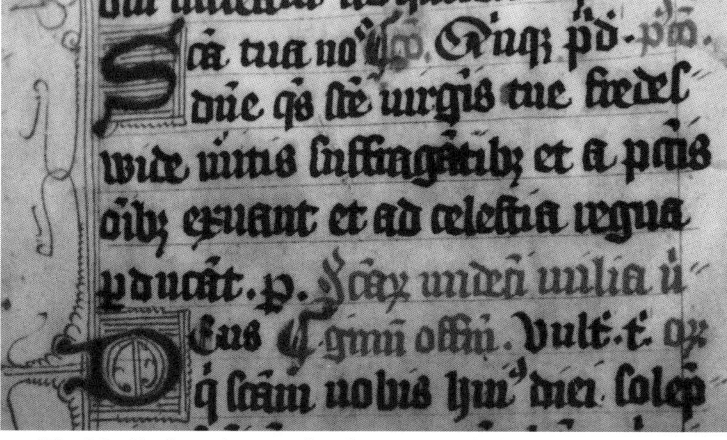

Fig 22.4b Leominster missal. 11,000 virgins, companions of the British princess Ursula on pilgrimage to Rome. They won their crowns of martyrdom at the hands of Huns at Cologne, AD238. (21 October)

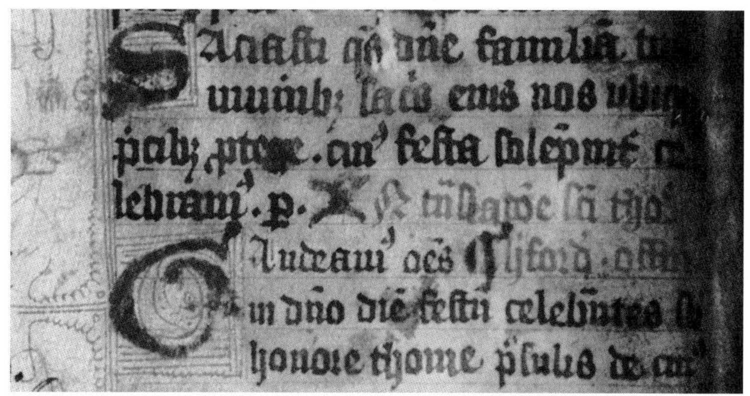

Fig 22.4c Leominster missal. Feast of the Translation of St Thomas of Hereford (25 October)

22nd; Apollinaris, 23rd; Vigil of James the Great and Feast of Christina, 24th; principal feast of James the Great and feasts of Christopher and Cucufato, 25th; and Anne, mother of Mary, 26th. It is significant that the Hereford Use recognised the principal feast and vigil of James the Great. Despite frequent conflicts with the monks of the priory, the parishioners also participated in the vigil of their mother house's major saint, whose hand was enshrined by the high altar at Reading, a ceremony that will have been introduced into the conventual and parochial church soon after Henry I's gift to Reading Abbey of St James's arm in its precious reliquary.

The second and third Sanctorale folios provide texts for the feasts of the Assumption of the Virgin, 15 August, and Her Nativity, 8 September. The final folio includes the feasts of the Archangel Michael, 16 October, Luke the Evangelist and the Commemoration of Justus, 18th, Frideswide, 19th, (Fig 22.4a) the 11,000 virgins, 21st, (Fig 22.4b) Romanus, 23rd, and the Translation of St Thomas of Hereford on 25 October (Plates 2c&d). Consideration of two feasts may help to date the missal. In 1480 the Convocation of Canterbury petitioned their archbishop to prescribe the observance of five feasts, including the Translation of St Aetheldreda, foundress of Ely, on 17 October and the feast of St Frideswide, patron of Oxford, on 19 October. Thus, whilst the presence of Frideswide might suggest a post 1480 date for the missal, the absence of the Translation of St Aetheldreda raises doubt. Moreover, in many instances prescribed feasts 'had been celebrated locally for a long time', as the latter at Oxford and the former at Ely. The adoption of new cults owed more to a slow process of 'germination, initial extension and wider popularity', than to official decrees. The inclusion of one feast and omission of the other therefore suggest a date prior to 1480.[532]

Confirmation comes from the other Hereford missals. Downside College MS 48243 has been attributed to the early 15th century on the basis of Ker's identification of the handwriting of some folios as that of John Grasely, who was ordained priest in Hereford between 1410 and 1412. This manuscript also includes Frideswide whilst excluding Aetheldreda. The British Library missal, Additional MS 39675, could take the date back much further, for it includes the principal feast of Thomas of Hereford, but not the minor feasts of his Deposition and Translation. This indicates that it was written after 1320, but before 1349. As this manuscript also includes Frideswide's feast, all that can be said with confidence about the Leominster missal is that it was written after 1349, the Translation of St Thomas, but before the 1480 petition for the inclusion of Aetheldreda.[533]

The two further folios, used to enrol borough records of the mid 16th century, never formed part of the missal (Plate 3). Each has one-third cut off. With considerable notation, they came from a Breviary, a book for choral or private recitation of the canonical hours. They include services for the Vigil of the Nativity, 24 December, and for Christmas Day: 'Today the King of heaven has for us deigned to be born of a Virgin'. Is it a coincidence that the missal's first folio and these from the Breviary all relate to services for Christ's Nativity, and that in the Sanctorale of the missal we find the feasts of the Assumption and Nativity of the Virgin, as well as of Anne, her mother?

The Leominster Chalice

The west window and tower were not the only major lay contributions to the parish church. At the very end of the 15th century, or more probably in the early 16th century, a silver gilt chalice, 8½ inches high, 4½ inches across the base with a bowl 5½ inches in diameter, was presented to Leominster church. It has been described by W. St John Hope, the first person to catalogue all the English medieval chalices and patens, as 'without question the most elaborate and splendid English chalice now remaining'. For Charles Oman, a more recent authority on English church plate, it is 'amongst the beautiful examples of the English late medieval goldsmith's work'. Around the broad, conical bowl is a band, with the inscription in bold Gothic lettering: *Calice(m) saluta(ris) accipia(m) et nom(in)e d(omi)ni invocabo*, 'I will take the cup of salvation and call upon the name of the Lord', Psalm 116:13. Between each word is a conventional leaf. The hexagonal stem is encased in pierced Gothic tracery, some of it in the Decorated style, with small buttresses at the angles. Its knop has six lobes, decorated with lozenges containing a five-leafed flower, originally enamelled in transparent blue. Both above and below the knop are six pieces of pierced tracery.

The foot has six incurved sides bearing, alternately, the Gothic monograms IHC and XPC. One of the IHC monograms is, however, an insertion. It replaces the plaque of the Crucifixion or crucifix, which was always engraved on one of the compartments of the foot (Fig 22.5b&d). At the celebration of Mass, this was held facing the priest. The compartment was probably removed prior to the visit in 1553 of Edward VI's commissioners, who would otherwise have categorised the chalice as a 'superstitious object', and confiscated it. Beneath the monograms are three further

Fig 22.5a An engraving of the Leominster Chalice

Fig 22.5b The Leominster Chalice showing the replacement encurved side

Fig 22.5d The Bacton Chalice showing what the replaced encurved side of the Leominster chalice may have looked like

Fig 22.5c The Bacton patten with vernicle and chalice with crucifix and foliate feet

Fig 22.5e The Leominster paten showing vernicle

bands of decoration, the upper being of small, pierced quatrefoils. Originally each of the six points of the foot would have been decorated with a small, and vulnerable, ornament, usually in the form of conventionalised leaves. As can be seen on the engraving (Fig 22.5a), these were cut off the Leominster chalice, probably because one or two had been broken off. The Bacton chalice, stylistically of the same group, but only 5¾ inches high and simpler in design, the bowl having no inscription, retains both the base compartment, with the original engraving of the Crucifixion, and its six feet in the form of leaves (Fig 22.5c). Confusingly, the term 'knop' may originally have been applied to the feet.

The dating of the Leominster chalice is dependent on style, for there is no hallmark or maker's initial. For St John Hope it was 'probably c1500', for the Royal Commission, 'late 15th century'. On the other hand, Charles Oman dates it as 1510. Yet he admits that, of all the chalices within its group, 'only three are hallmarked and these range between 1494 and 1507'. The Reformation brought production to an end. Many were melted down and replaced by a 'fayre, decent or comely' communion cup. Leominster is unusual in having both a medieval chalice and an Elizabethan cup, hallmarked 1576.

There was also a paten of similar date. The edge of its rim carried a double row of engraved zigzags. Each of the spandrels of the base, which sinks into a sexfoil, was engraved with oak leaves and acorns about a rose. In the centre of the sexfoil, within a circle, is the vernicle, the impression of Christ's face left in the napkin on which He wiped His face on the way to Calvary (Fig 22.5e). After the Black Death, this became a very popular subject throughout Europe. Although the majority of English late-medieval patens are engraved with the vernicle, differences in its representation are quite considerable. Having weathered the threat of Edward VI's Commissioners, Leominster's chalice and paten were stolen from the priory in March 1996 during a church festival. Thieves, hiding in the priory after nightfall, smashed open the reinforced display case. The chalice was restored to the priory after its discovery on the altar of a Cotswold church. The paten has not been recovered.[534]

23 The 15th Century: Trade and Civil War

Leominster Ore

The 15th century witnessed a dramatic change in the range of wool prices. In 1343 the gradation of English wool prices had been gentle; by 1454 it was very steep. Generally the price of wool had fallen considerably, due to increased production and a subsequent reduction in quality. In consequence, sheep farming had become 'a counsel of despair'. For the very best wool, however, demand intensified as selection procedures became more sophisticated. In 1454 Parliament drew up a list of suggested minimum export prices. The wool of 'Hereford in Leominster' now commanded £13 a sack; next came Leominster 'Soke' (lordship) and Shropshire March £9 10s; Cotswold wool was £8 6s 8d. All other English wools, including 'rest of Hereford', were under £6 a sack, many £4 or less. This ranking was maintained in the 16th century, as Table 15 shows, and as confirmed in a list of selling prices of English wool at the Calais Staple during Edward VI's reign, 1547–53. Whilst most of Herefordshire was pushed into severe economic depression, by the mid 15th century the pre-eminence of Leominster's wool was a major stimulant to the local economy.[535]

The high quality may in part be explained by the extraordinary conservatism of the priory's agrarian practices. An entry in a manuscript of the Biddulph Phillips collection in the Herefordshire Record Office informs us: 'Our wool about Lemster Oar and Canon Pyon for it has been sold above 30s, equals if not exceeds the Aquilian or Tarentine Wool in ye South of Italy, tho' it cost not so much Charge and Curiosity in ye ordering of it, for there ye Shepheards covering their Sheep with Skins to preserve the wool from the injury of Bushes, weather and dirt. Here we only house them by Night, both Winter and Summer, which with the Vertue of the Soyl and hard fare upon the fallow fields, produces ye desired Effect for if these fine-woll'd Sheep be put into Pasture Grounds to Feed that Wool will grow courser, as their Flesh grows fatter'. This statement is confirmed by entries in Coningsby's *Register*. The emphasis placed by the priory on the production of high quality wools can be detected in the Ivington halimote rolls after the Black Death when, in 1372, Walter atte Walle was granted 4 acres of arable from the priory's demesne with the proviso that it was 'not lawful to feed sheep or lambs on the said land under penalty'. The fallow of the former demesne, now leased out, was reserved for the abbot's flocks. The apparent conservatism of the priors of Leominster who, retaining bondsmen, could continue the old rotation in open fields, may be explained by their need for large

	Price per stone	
	Previous	1536
Leominster	6s 8d	9s or 9s 3d
March	6s	7s 6d
Cotswold	5s or 5s 3d	7s and above
Berkshire	4s 6d and 4s 9d	6s 8d
'Young Cottes' (Cotswold)	4s	6s
Lynsey and Casten (Kesteven?)	2s 8d	5s
Holland and Rutland	2s 4d	4s 8d
Norfolk	1s 6d or 1s 8d	3s 4d

L&P Henry VIII, X, No 247

Table 15 English Wool Prices, 1536

tracts of fallow. Elsewhere, as pastures were improved, so fineness of wool declined, and this at a time when the rise of worsted textiles had a dramatic impact on wool supply. The 'New Draperies' needed long fibre wool, and demand from Flemish and Italian manufacturers of high quality cloth remained high. Thus in 1457–8, 2,000 sacks of 'Lempster', Marches and Cotswold wools were being exported, under royal licence, by Roger Gentyle and his associates through 'the straits and mountains of Marrock' to the city of Milan.[536]

'Ore' is a term usually meaning 'respect, reverence, honour or glory'. In this context it is transferred to a locality. There has been much debate about the precise location of Leominster Ore. In his *Glossographie: Hard words now used in England* which, as he explains, had 'taken up the vacancy of above twenty years', Thomas Blount defines this term: 'The end of, extreme part. A Region Land or Country: Thus Lempster Ore is that fertile part of Herefordshire which lyes about two miles round that Town.' From the Dissolution the term 'ore' became synonymous with the lordship of Leominster, as in 'a Survey of the Lordship of Leominster alias Leominster Ore belonginge to the Lord Duke of Buckingham'. In 1651 the same title was used in a survey and valuation for 'the right honorable Coll. Henry Marten, esq', and in a 1718 reference to the 'Petty Tithes' of 'Leominster Ore' held by lease from the bishop of Hereford.[537]

In the 17th century, however, subject to fierce competition from the wool of the merino sheep of the Spanish high meseta, the price of fine English wool began to fall. Ironically, this was when Leominster Ore, taken up by the poets, began to enter the world of legend. For Camden in 1586 the shire 'now glories chiefly in its wool (commonly call'd Lemster Ore) which (excepting that of Apulia and Tarentum) is by all Europe accounted the best'. In *Cheape and Good Husbandry* (1615) Markham claimed that from the ore 'a thread could be drawn as fine as silk'. In the *Poly-Olbion* (1622) Drayton asked:

> 'Where lives the man so dull on Britain's farther shore
> To whom did never sound the name of Lemster Ore
> That with the Silke-worm's web for smallness doth compare?'

In *Hesperides* Robert Herrick speaks of 'a bank of mosse spungie and swelling' and as 'farre more Soft then the finest Lemster Ore'. For Thomas Fuller, in his *Worthies of England*, 'as for the wool in this county it is best known to the honour thereof by the name of Lemster Ore, being absolutely the finest in this county and indeed all England'.[538]

Cloth and Other Trades

The fineness of Leominster ore may have caught all the headlines, but it was on drapery that the town's economy principally flourished. As Leland put it, 'the town by reason of theyr principall wolle usyd great drapinge of clothe and thereby it flourished'.[539] As late as 1722, William Stukeley described Leominster as 'a town of brisk trade in manufactures of their admirable wool in hat-making, leather, and many others; it lies in a valley luxuriant above measure. Three rivers of very swift current go through the town, besides others very near: nor will the industrious inhabitants suffer the water-nymphs that preside over the steams to be idle: for with mills, and machinery of various contrivance, they make them subservient to many uses in the way of their trades'.

Leominster's fulling mill, c1193, had been one of the earliest in the country. Fuller, in various forms, was one of the most common occupational surnames of the town throughout the Middle Ages. The 1235 Worcester charter identified cloth, wool and wool thread as three of the borough's four principal exports (see p172). Of the nine principal trade guilds or 'Occupations' in the borough, four regulated the cloth trades: the fellowships of the Walkers (Fullers) and Dyers, the Weavers, Mercers and Taylors. Each trade guild operated its own apprenticeship system, and controlled entry into the mystery and the quality of its craftsmanship. The 'Occupations' were responsible for the maintenance of nine of the stone bridges giving access to the town: for example the Mercers maintained the Pinsley bridge, the Walkers and Dyers the Red Crosse, and the Tanners the Kenwater bridge.[540] A Leominster speciality was the soft woollen plush fabric called camlet or chamlet, probably from the Arabic *khamlat*. Its popularity is confirmed by one of Edward IV's sumptuary laws, 'touching the wearing of inordinate or excess of apparel, according to degree'. This enacted, in 1482, that 'no yeoman of the Crown nor none other shall, under the degree of esquire or gentleman, wear in their doublets damask or satten, nor gowns of chamlet upon pain to forfeit for every default £2.'

The town also grew rich on the fattening of stock, principally brought in from Wales. A reference to 'Fattyngmore' pastures at Ivington in 1450 and elsewhere at earlier dates is indicative. The first full reference is as late as 1556, when more than half the cattle sold at the fair came from Wales, one-third from Radnorshire, others from as far away as St David's, Pembroke and Carmarthen. Taking the Roman road to Llandrindod, they then travelled across the easy, droving country of the 1,500ft high Mynydd Eppynt to the upper Wye and thence via Painscastle, to be fattened on the rich meadows of the Lugg and Arrow and their tributaries. The stock was then sold on, principally to the west midlands. It is highly probable that this represents the revival of the much earlier trade, as evidenced by the 350 oxen in the Extent of 1327 and of which the first reference is probably the tribute of '25,000' oxen paid by the Welsh princes to King Athelstan c927. By Elizabeth's reign, royal commissioners were resorting to Leominster to buy fattened oxen for the royal court, paying £7 10s per head, a further £1 if the ox was stall-fed. For Speed, c1610, 'no place in England yieldeth better conditioned cattle' than Herefordshire. The soil, Stukeley found, was 'luxuriant above measure: trees of all sorts flourish prodigiously: we were surprised at the extravagant bulk of plants, leaves of dock as big as an ordinary tea-table, comfry leaves as long as my arm … borage quite grown out of cognizance'.[541]

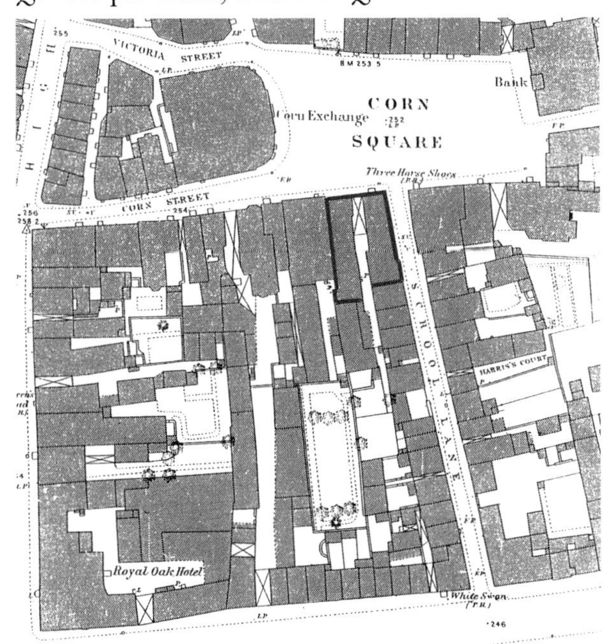

Fig 23.1 Showing 15th-century School Lane development between Corn Square and Etnam Street

Urban Development

The prosperity of the prior's borough in the 15th century is still evident in its townscape. At Oxford, as elsewhere, the many lands and buildings remaining unoccupied demonstrated the depressed level of the property market. Two major developments at Leominster bear witness to a vigorous demand for property within the town.

The first was at School Lane. This is much narrower than the roads of the 12th-century town plan, and connected Etnam Street with the major market centre, known as *Corncepyng* in the Middle Ages. It was the result of speculative development in the 15th century, as its buildings testify. When, in the early 12th century, the first burgage plots were established, a small series was laid out on the south side of *Corncepyng*. This extended back to the northern line of what later become Etnam Street. In the 15th century a series of contiguous

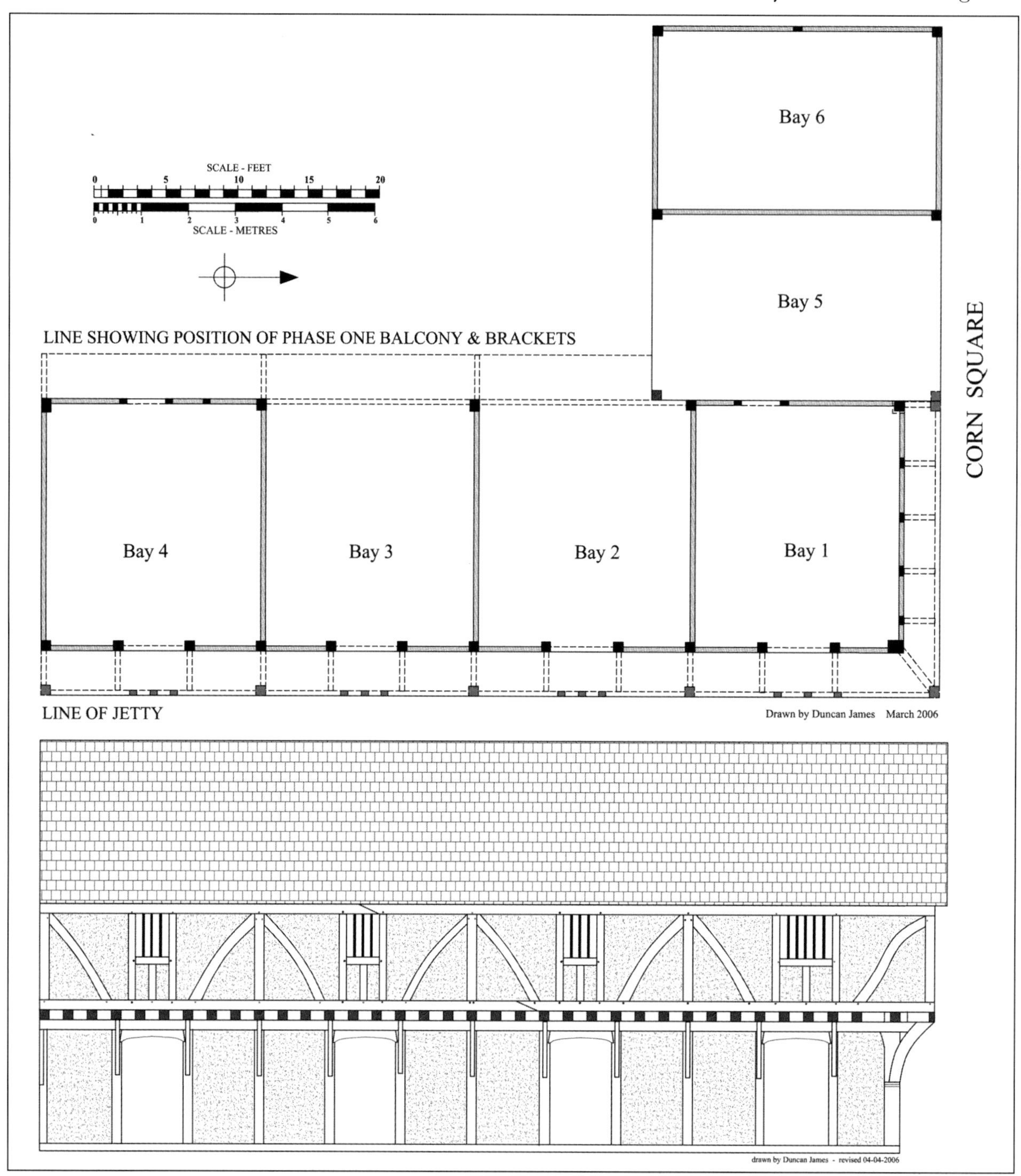

Fig 23.2 Original ground plan of 16, 16a and 17 Corn Square and partial reconstruction of east elevation of no.16 (School Lane façade)

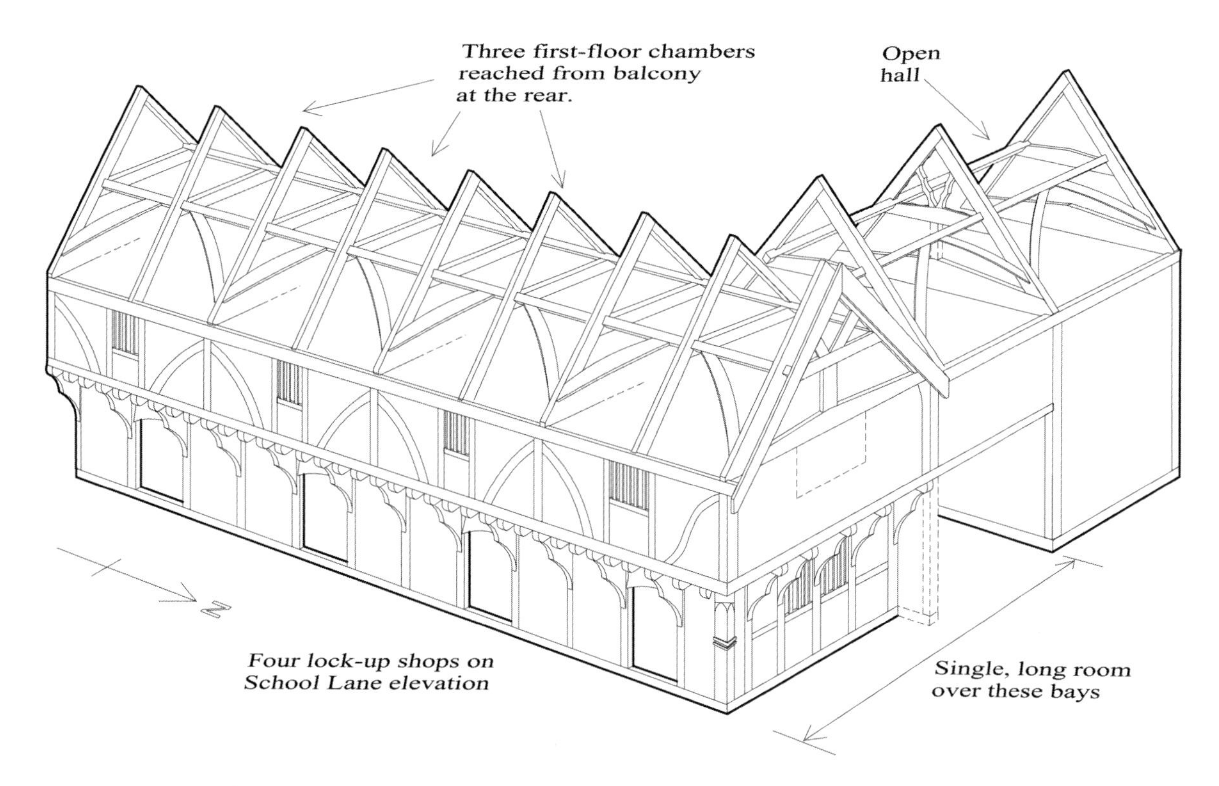

Fig 23.3 Three-dimensional sketch of 16, 16a and 17 Corn Square and School Lane elevation

plots on this site were brought into single ownership as a result of purchase and/or exchanges. These would have ranged from the site of the Three Horseshoes on the east to 17 Corn Square on the west, permitting the creation of School Lane, and the construction of new properties at either side of its northern end (Fig 23.1).

The buildings at the north-west end of School Lane, which also extend westwards as 16, 16a and 17 Corn Square, have been examined in detail by Duncan James. As a result, he has been able to establish the mid 15th-century layout. This was L-shaped, consisting of a four-bay structure under a single gable along School Lane, and another, two-bay range under one roof, now 16a and 17 Corn Square. The former consisted of four shops of identical ground plan at street level. Each measured 17ft deep by 15ft wide with a central, shuttered display area on the front, and an additional doorway at the rear. Above were four more chambers, slightly larger than the shops, as they were jettied some 3ft over the lane on twelve handsome, cusped brackets. Access was from a balcony at the rear, which overlooked an open courtyard. At the angle of School Lane and Corn Square, beneath the dragon beam, a diagonal bracket springs from a moulded capital on the corner post. The overhang then extended at right angles under the gable along the Corn Square frontage. Later the jettying was underbuilt, as we see it today. The gable end of 16 Corn Square retains its original, foiled and sub-cusped bargeboards. No. 17 had no jetty, as it formed a small, single-bay open hall (Figs 23.2–23.4).

Three of the four chambers above the shops were identical, but that on the corner extended by one bay over 16a Corn Square to the west. Although the roof timbers are smoke-blackened, it

Fig 23.4 Postcard of 16, 16a and 17 Corn Square showing lateral brackets, jettying and cusped bargeboards

was not a hall open to the roof, but a two-bay upper chamber. The blackening probably came from the use of a brazier. At this upper level, the wall between 16a and 17 Corn Square is of particular interest, as it has a cusped truss of unusual form, a tie-beam (closed) truss, with the cusping visible only from the hall side. The western wall of 17 is of the same, mid-15th-century date as the east range, confirming that the site was developed all at one time. Access to the courtyard was between nos 16 and 17. Gabled attics, with zigzag decorated bargeboards and square braced panels below, were added to 16a and 17 in the 17th century. Subsequently the façades of all three buildings were altered to give an appearance of unity. The Three Horseshoes on the north-east corner of School Lane, built somewhat later, formed an essential part of the development. Here again, the first floor originally projected on both its principal façades.

From the earliest times, this square had been *Corncepyng*, the corn market, where all grain was sold. The borough records carry frequent references to the Corne Markett House shown on Gallier's 1832 plan (Figs 23.5 and 23.6). In 1605 a Barley Market House was built. Thus there was provision for the two principal grains of the locality. Yet in the Middle Ages, as in the 16th and 17th centuries, the covered housing available for grain on market days proved inadequate. The jettied timber buildings of the square was therefore provided with pentices. Attached to the first-floor overhang, they extended outwards some 6ft, to provide farmers with a convenient place to store their sacks. As rent for the pentice, the householders had a wooden scoop with which they extracted one full measure from each sack. This rent would supply most families with bread corn for seven days, till the next market. Such pentices disappeared in the 18th century, with turnpikes, and grain sale by sample.[542]

At a time when the triangular market area between High Street and Drapers Lane had long been filled with encroaching buildings, the incentive for the School Lane development was the provision, on a prime site in the market-place, of four shops, with three workshops above. Furthermore, School Lane created a short cut to Corn Square, thus extending the catchment area for its shops to people living in lower Etnam Street.

Abbey Cottages at Tewkesbury represent a similar, if considerably larger development than 16-17 Corn Square. Here a terrace of 23 timber buildings was constructed, probably in two stages, along the Church Street side of the abbey precinct. Each had a shop at the front, some 11ft 6in by 8ft, and an inner open hall, rising two stories, measuring 11ft 6in by 10ft. Steps gave access to a first-floor bedroom over the shop. The lean-tos or pentice chambers to the rear of the terrace are most likely later additions. Despite these differences, Duncan James has found constructional links between the Leominster and Tewkesbury developments, the most important being the roof, with clasped purlins and diminished principals, not native to Herefordshire.[543]

What is the origin of the name School Lane? The upper two-bay room over 16 and 16a Corn Square may have been built as a schoolhouse. On the other hand, such an extensive and carefully planned development suggests institutional initiative, as at Tewkesbury. Here the strongest candidate would be the *custos* of the conventual Lady Chapel, acting with or for *Magister Alexander, rector scolarum*, a figure referred to in the 14th-century accounts of the *custos*.[544]

Before 1485, demand for properties led to the development of two new suburbs outside the Town Ditch and bars, on the west. Significantly, these extended along the two major roads from Wales to Leominster, the king's highways via Cholstrey and via Monkland. In effect they formed

Fig 23.5 Leominster Corn Exchange, 1850, the replacement for Corn Market House

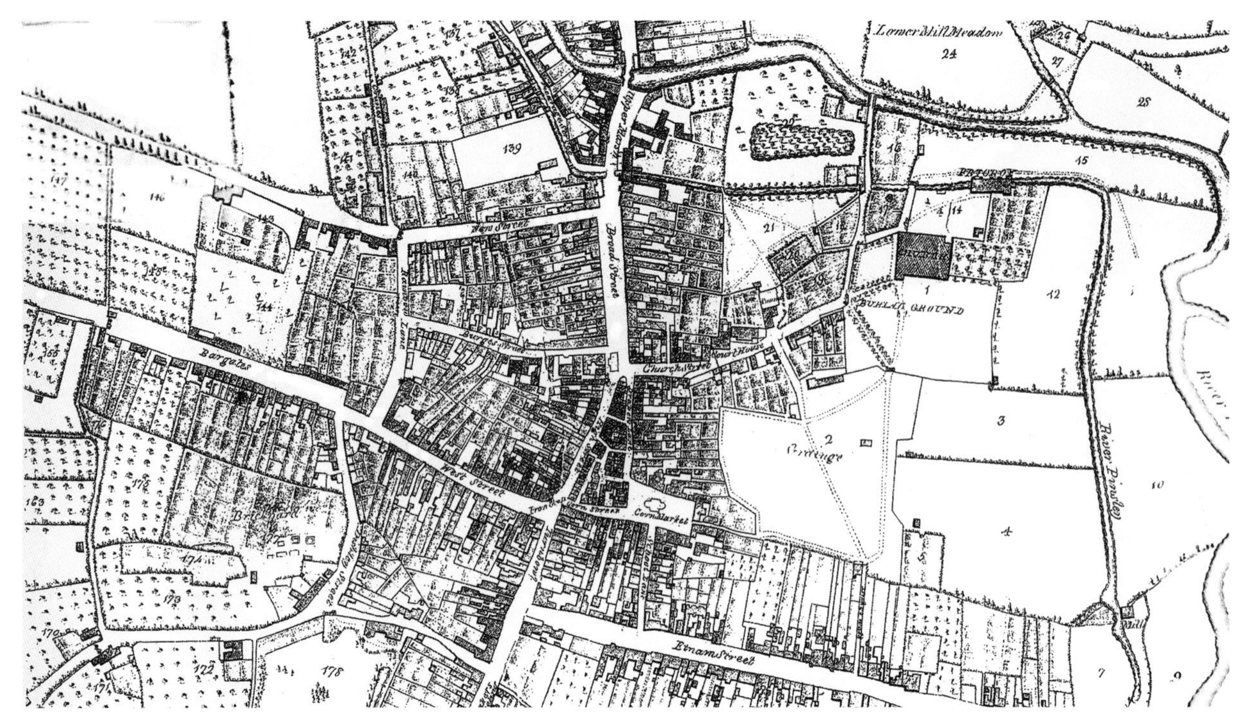

Fig 23.6 Gallier's plan showing the expanding suburbs to the west with the notable wide market pace along Bargates inside the the West Bar, which is clearly marked

extensions to West and New Streets. Within the West Bar, a wide new market-place had already developed, somewhat similar to that at Moor Street outside the north gate and walls in Chepstow (Fig 23.6). Much of the Bargates market area was destroyed when Leominster's western inner ring road was constructed.[545]

Duncan James's work shows that 15th-century development was in no way restricted to the two areas mentioned. There is abundant evidence of the redevelopment of individual plots throughout the borough. Only two buildings, behind 40 Broad Street, have so far been tree-ring dated, giving dates of 1463 and 1500. They are part of a complex that included 44 Broad Street, originally a four-bay, two-storey range, jettied over the Pinsley. 5 High Street is of especial interest, as it contains the remains of a high-status building of late medieval form, evidently replacing earlier encroachment on the wedge-shaped market between High Street and Drapers Lane. At present there is little archaeological or documentary evidence as to the date of this market encroachment. However, at Ledbury it began well before c1285, at which time the *Red Book* shows that there were up to 14 permanent booths in the Butchers' Row along the west side of the market-place. Reference to *selda edificata* occurs in both the early section of the Leominster Cartulary and the records of the *custos* of the Lady Chapel. 3 Church Street, Leominster, has the substantial remains of a late medieval shop with great chamber over. 20/22 Draper's Lane is a large, two-storeyed medieval shop with access to private accommodation from the side alley. The top storey was added in the 17th century. Grafton House, Burgess Street, is a small hall-house with axial upper and lower ends. Unusually, the building was jettied and included a central first-floor room, the small open hall being set back towards the rear of the building. 25–29 Bridge Street is a late medieval open hall-house with cross wings to the north and south, with contemporary, richly carved, bargeboards (Fig 23.7).[546]

Fig 23.7 25–9 Bridge Street showing late medieval bargeboards and elaborate cusp and tracery decoration. Quatrefoils at base

The Yorkist Victory

With no clear-cut law of succession, Richard Duke of York had the strongest claim to the throne, so long as Henry VI had no children. Richard had succeeded as sixth earl of March through his mother, Anne Mortimer, sister of Edmund, fifth earl. Walter Devereux, the duke's principal agent in the county, had been appointed royal administrator of Leominster Priory in 1448 to stem the 'wastes, dilapidations and alienations'. Earlier he had served as a close adviser to the duke, in Normandy and Ireland. Walter had become lord of Weobley, with its castle, in 1437 and held the constableship of Wigmore Castle for Richard. In 1447 he was one of the two Members for Herefordshire, representing the Yorkist interest, and in 1448 sheriff. His daughter, Anne, married 'the most influential Welshman of his generation', William Herbert, lord of Raglan castle and eventually earl of Pembroke. John Weobley, Devereux's agent at Hereford, played skilfully on the internal divisions between the oligarchs and the humble tradesmen who strongly resented their exclusion from power. At mayoral and parliamentary elections, violence flourished. In 1448 Weobley appeared in the city with 30 armed supporters, and in 1450, 200 of his men invaded the Tolsey.

Devereux's agent at Leominster was Hugh Shirley. A burgess and elector in 1449, he was elected as Member for Leominster in 1450, 1460 and 1472. It is unlikely that Shirley went to the extremes taken by John Weobley at Hereford. Nevertheless, he received a royal pardon in 1452. Denounced in Parliament as 'maintaining robbers and peace-breakers' in 1455, he was pardoned again, as 'gentilman', for 'all treasons, murders, rapes of women, rebellions, insurrections, felonies, champerties, maintenances, embraceries, trespasses, offences, negligences, extortions, misprisions, ignorances, contempts, forfeitures and deceptions', and in December 1459 for 'all treasons, insurrections etc', a reference to his participation on the Yorkist side at the battle of Ludford Bridge.[547]

The night before the rout of Richard of York's forces at Ludford Bridge, on 12 October 1459, Henry VI rested at Leominster, enjoying hospitality at the now reformed priory. Shirley represented Leominster in the 1460 parliament when Richard claimed the throne. Before the year's end Duke Richard was dead, the consequence of his foolhardy attack on much stronger Lancastrian forces, at Wakefield. In February 1461, however, his son, Edward Duke of York won the decisive victory over the house of Lancaster at Mortimer's Cross. Owain Tudor, grandfather of Henry VII, surrendered. Next day Duke Edward found his revenge for his father's death at the battle of

Wakefield. Owain was executed in Hereford's market-place. His head was placed on the market cross, his body buried at the Grey Friars'. The next month Edward was crowned Edward IV.[548]

Following the Yorkist triumph, Hugh Shirley was amply rewarded: 6d a day (£9 2s 6d a year) as yeoman of the Crown, and £10 a year from the earldom of March. He was escheator of Herefordshire 1461–4 and again in 1474. Thomas Shirley, probably Hugh's son, was returned as Member for Leominster in 1467. Hugh was elected again in 1472, when Thomas was the abbot's bailiff and returning officer. Another Hugh Shirley was returned in 1491. Apart from the events of 1448, there is no record of the priory for some half-century. John Schakendon, referred to in 1467–8, is the only prior so far identified between 1428 and 1511. Under Edward IV (1461–83) law and order in the March deteriorated even further. The Herbert and Vaughan families openly defied all authority until 1479, when Herbert Vaughan was forced to give up his earldom of Pembroke. Even the dispatch of Edward IV's son to Ludlow castle and, at least initially, the accession of Henry VII made little impact.

The Maid of Leominster

The scandalous story of the Maid of Leominster probably befits these times. It is recounted by no less a person than Sir Thomas More:

> I remember nowe what a worke I have herde that was at Lempster in ye kynges fathers dayes. The pryour brought pryvely a straunge wenche in to the chyrche that sayd she was sente thither by god and wolde not lye out of the chyrche. After she was grated within yron grates above in the rode lofte where yt was byleved she lyved withoute any mete or drynke only by aungels fode. Dyvers tymes she was houseled in syght of the people with an hoste unconsecrate and all the people lokyng upon. There was a devyce with a small hair that conveyed the hoste from the paten of the chalyce out of ye pryours handes in to her mouth as though it came alone. So all the people, not of the towne onely but also of the countrey aboute, toke her for a very quycke saynt. Dayly (they) sought so thycke to se her that many that coulde not come nere to her cryed out alowde 'Holy mayden Elyzabeth helpe me' and were fayn to throwe theyr offryng over theyr felowes heddes for prece. Now lay ye pryour with holy mayden Elyzabeth nyghtly in ye rode lofte tyll she was after taken out and tried in ye kepyng by my lady the kynges mother. And by the longyng for mete with voydaunce of that she had eten (which had no saintly savoure) she was perceived for no saynt and confessed all the matter.
>
> 'What came of the pryour?' quoth I, 'It had ben grete almes if the pryour and she had ben burned togyther at one stake.' Quoth he, 'that can I not tell but I wene he was put to suche punyshment as the pore nonne was'.[549]

More refers to these events as taking place in the reign of Henry VII, 1485–1509, but of the names of the priors during this period there is no record.

24 The Decades leading to Dissolution

What is known of priors Worcester and Cholsey indicates that they were men of a very different character to their predecessor, responsible for the maid of Leominster outrage. Thomas Worcester, prior by 1511, was the only man to hold this office of whose student years we have knowledge. He was ordained priest in 1505 in Magdalene College chapel, by Richard Mayhew who had been consecrated Bishop of Hereford at Lambeth Palace the previous year. Mayhew however retained his vice-chancellorship of Oxford University until 1506, and the presidency of Magdalene College until 1507, in which year he finally retired to his diocese. Thomas Worcester studied logic, philosophy and then theology for eight years at Canterbury College, Oxford, where he was resident from 1504-9. He was awarded his degree of Bachelor of Theology in 1508. The college accounts record his annual payments of 10s in 1504–5 for a little room near the privy, 10s in 1506–7 for a chamber in the garden, and 8s in 1508–9 'for a chamber on the steps of the garden chamber'. In 1511 Worcester, as prior, was licensed by Mayhew to undertake a pastoral role outside the walls of his monastery, to hear confessions and enjoin penance throughout the extensive Leominster deanery, essentially the area of the Anglo-Saxon *parochia*. In practice he probably fulfilled this role merely at the churches and chapels within the *herneys* of his priory, at Ivington, Stockton, Stoke and Luston, places he would be visiting in the normal course of his temporal duties as the abbot of Reading's deputy.[550]

Henry Bray was Thomas Worcester's sub-prior after 1510. He owned a copy of *Speculum Spiritualium* printed in Paris in 1510. His choice is interesting, for the book included tracts by Richard Rolle, the hermit mystic of Hampole, a man with a marked antipathy to the liturgical prayers of the Benedictines. All such outward music, he believed, disturbed inward harmony. 'Those who enjoy the fervour of sweetly flowing devotion flee from such roaring. Those who hear celestial sound no longer concord with corporal clamour. They hear unwillingly even the solemnities of the psalmodists.' Bray's book is now in the Bodleian Library as part of the University College Collection. The inscription reads, *Iste libellus pertinet ad dompni Henrici Bray, custos ordinis Leominstris*, that is sub-prior.[551]

An entry in the episcopal register for 1515 raises the question as to whether Worcester was absent from Leominster or whether, as so many other priors before him, he was at loggerheads with the parishioners. Thomas Hare, chaplain of the parochial chantry of the Blessed Virgin Mary, resigned on 11 May. After seven weeks had passed and no candidate been presented by the patrons, the abbot and convent of Reading, Bishop Bothe presented Richard Benson, 'by lapse'. On Benson's resignation, in 1518, the bishop's register records that Thomas Lee was presented by the abbot and convent of Reading, carefully noting that this was 'on the nomination of the twelve men of Leominster', in accordance with the original terms of the chaplaincy's foundation. It is highly likely that Bray's failure to present was his unpreparedness to formally accept the nomination by the twelve, the capital burgesses of the borough. Early in February 1519 'Thomas Worcester, monk of Reading', was elected abbot. By 28 July 1520 he was dead. His successor, Hugh Cooke, or Faringdon, was to be Reading's last abbot and was to die a death of 'quite incomparable heroism or, as some would call it, obstinacy'.[552]

The only documented visit of an abbot of Reading to the priory was that of Cooke in 1522. However, the 1327 Extent records, under Stoke *herneys*, the customary delivery of 40 horseloads of wheat 'at the coming of the abbot', suggesting that in the early 14th century such visits did take place. When the clergy — Master Richard Hall, vicar, John Dyer, Christopher Morys, Henry Dyer and John ap Howell, chaplains, John ap Jenkyn, curate of Stoke (Prior) and Robert Baudewyn, chaplain of Bromfield — received the abbot at the parish church, according him full episcopal honours, the bishop's officers regarded this as an insult to the cathedral church and episcopal see of Hereford. In consequence, each had to perform penance at the feast of St Thomas, 2 October, offering a wax candle costing 1d at the saint's shrine in the cathedral's Lady Chapel, singing *Iste Confessor*, with versicle and prayer. By 1529 Richard Hall, the vicar, was in further trouble. His parishioners complained to Bishop Bothe, who raised the matter immediately. 'Although the care of their souls is entrusted to you, on principal feasts of your church to the diminution of divine worship, and the grave peril of your soul, you send your parishioners to the services in the conventual priory church.' One assumes that the parishioners were obliged to stand in the north and south transepts on these occasions. Unable to bear such neglect, Bothe instructed Hall, and his priests, clerks and ministers, to sing divine service on all the principal feasts with the organ and 'all possible solemnity to the praise and glory of God Whom everything that hath breath is bidden to praise'.[553]

Priors Cholsey and Reading

The last but one of Leominster's priors was Prior Cholsey. He seems to have been blissfully ignorant of the impending storm. From Ashwood in Stockton, Cholsey had 28 loads of timber hewn for repairs, as well as ash for Thomas Smyth to make a pair of new organs.[554] By contrast John Reading, his sub-prior, was not only aware, but determined to exploit the new political situation to the full. The Royal Council had not yet decided on the outright dissolution of the monasteries. Rather, its policy was one of 'seeking out weaknesses wherever they were to be found', to effect the surrender of carefully chosen monasteries. In many this policy was already leading to the sale of moveable goods, and the proliferation of new leases of their lands. [555] In this John Reading was in the van.

To supervise the troubled territory of the English border counties and Wales, a Council in the Marches of Wales had been established in 1476. In 1525, in an attempt to revive the Council's authority and to establish good order, quiet and tranquillity in the March, Cardinal Wolsey despatched the 9-year-old Princess Mary Tudor, with her household, to Ludlow, with John Veysey, bishop of Exeter, as the Council's president. This had an immediate, if unexpected, impact on Leominster Priory. Removed from the capital, several of the princess's household servants, accustomed to good living, suddenly found themselves without a livelihood. Prior Cholsey was thus required to take a number of them 'unto your convenient finding'. Veysey proved totally inadequate for his task as president. As Thomas Croft put it, although there had been one hundred murders in the Marches and Wales since Veysey's appointment, not one murderer had been punished. Veysey was replaced in 1534 by Rowland Lee, who had entered Wolsey's service in 1528, and had been highly successful in bringing about the dissolution of a number of minor monasteries. He then became one of Henry VIII's principal agents for relations with the monasteries and the conduct of the royal divorce. Having 'directed' the election of a number of new priors and abbots, he was rewarded in 1534 with the bishopric of Coventry and Lichfield. Four months later he took up office in Ludlow. 'Stowte of nature, not affable to anye of the walshrie, an extreme severe ponisher of offenders', Lee ordered numerous public hangings, including members of the gentry, at Ludlow and elsewhere.[556]

After Lee's arrival a report was submitted to the Council at Ludlow, describing in great detail 'the evil demeanour of a monk at Leominster', Sub-Prior John Reading, who had embezzled from the church a silver gilt pyx and censer, a pair of cruets, ten of the best copes, three coats of tissue, that is cloth interwoven with gold or silver, from the image or Our Lady, and the parcel-gilt front of St Edward's shrine. From the prior's house he had taken a parcel gilt salt cellar, a great maser, a standing cup of silver gilt, a dozen silver spoons, a pair of great andirons worth 2 marks (£1 6s 8d), and most of the kitchen stuff and napery. He had despoiled the priory of 36 acres of woodland and more than 250 trees in Hopeswood, Ashewood, Luctonswood, Redwood and Highwood, for his own benefit.

Counterfeiting the abbot of Reading's exchequer seal, the sub-prior had extorted more than £34 from his poorer tenants by issuing false leases etc. In addition, his outstanding debts amounted to £103 17s 10d. These included £1 3s 4d to Roger Williams, curate of Lucton and Eyton, for wages and half a bible; £5 to John Power, schoolmaster, his wages for almost four years; to George Patis, curate of Kimbolton, his wages of 13s 4d; to William Raynold 3s 4d 'for keeping of Stockton pool'; and £1 to Thomas Smith, still outstanding for Prior Cholsey's pair of organs. More surprisingly, 'to my lord Ferrers' his fee of £2 10s had yet to be paid; to the high sheriff he owed £1; to his under-sheriff 6s 8d; and to the constable 3s 4d.[557]

Bishop Lee immediately recognised in Reading, whom Price refers to as John Glover, a man who would do his business. Leominster, valued at £448 in 1535, was the richest monastery in the March after the other Benedictine houses at Shrewsbury, £532, and Chester, £1,003. To the chagrin of Abbot Hugh Cooke of Reading, Lee evidently secured Cholsey's resignation and thus the priorship for Reading. In November Lee wrote to Thomas Cromwell about John Reading as 'the poor prior of Leominster who, through the provocation of his abbot, was enjoined to keep the cloister as a conventual monk of small reputation. I advise you that the said prior is of as good reputation as the abbot of Reading ... I beg therefore that he may have your lawful favour and to be at liberty as other heads of religious houses'.[558]

Cromwell himself intervened. His agents reported in 1538 that 'the whole lordship is by year £700, as I was told by the prior, but the common people say it is 1,800 marks (£1,200). The abbot and prior have wasted the woods and the tenants make no repairs but I beg your Lordship's favour for the prior Reading who will show you great money etc. With the prior there are here Sir Robert Worralle, priest, and John Ynke, his bailey of Lemster, who can give your Lordship further instructions. There are many bondsmen belonging to the Lordship and it is a royal rich country.'[559]

Prior John Reading, finding himself obstructed by Abbot Cooke, wrote to Cromwell. 'Please direct my master the abbot (of Reading) to pay me at least £100, your letter to be his discharge.

You shall have £40 of it. Touching the seal of mine office that unjustly is withholden from me, please let it be restored or allow me to use another, and you shall have half the profits that shall arise thereby. My master, the abbot, has made the chief and richest of the bondsmen of Leominster free and taken the profits to himself which ought to have gone to the priory. My predecessors have had authority to manumys them; and if you will comfort me to use the same you shall have half the profits.' There is record of only one manumission during Chosley's priorate, of John, son of John Poll of Ivington, in 1523/4 'Scholar and Bachelor of Arts at Oxford'. Between 1535/6 and 1537/8, during Reading's priorate, there were at least five manumissions: John, son of Thomas Bubbe of Kingsland, William Wynde, Thomas Wanklayne, Richard Poll of the Hyde, Ivington, and William Wall.[560]

In a final attempt to ingratiate himself with Cromwell, Prior Reading wrote in November 1539, praying 'take no displeasure (that) I write so boldly to you. ... If the King will take his pleasure of the house of Leomstre — as it is supposed His Grace will of that and many more — unless he appoints it to his son, our Prince (Arthur), it were a goodly thing for your Lordship or your son. There is not such another turf within the realm worth 1,000 marks rent (£666 13s 4d) as lying all within five or six miles compass so that one bailey could gather the whole rents. I pray God send you a merry and a joyful Christmas and so many.' The letter ended abruptly, without a signature.[561]

The Dissolution

In 1539 Henry VIII took the major monasteries into his own hands. The certificates of regulars and chantry priests living within the diocese record the fate of some of Leominster Priory's monks and its parochial chantry priests. They include details of only three monks; others may have returned to family homes in or about Reading. Thomas Cherne, 'late of the cell of Reading, of honest life', and Hugh Rumsye of Ivington, 'late of the priory of Leominster', received the usual pension of £5, but Walter Broughton of Ludlow, 'late of the house of Reading', only £2 16s 8d, 'out of the cell of Leominster annexed to Reading'. Like the other two, he never married. The pension of Robert Worrall, who had been presented to the vicarage of Lyonshall in 1520 by James Worrall of

Fig 24.1 The excavations in 2005 showing four postholes for scaffolding used to aid the demolition of buildings about the south-west corner of the cloister

Leominster, and thirteen years later to the parochial Lady Chapel, was £6. Thomas Sebright, 'late chantry priest of the Trinity service', enjoyed the standard £5 pension, but his colleague, Philip Nicholas, 'formerly of the service of our lady of pity' and 'of honest name, living at Leominster and never married', received a mere £1 19s 10d.[562]

Fig 24.2 Sketch by W.H. Freeman c1853 showing the end of the north wall of the aisle prior to Scott's replacement of the north-east bay, with Tudor window (Fig 24.3)

Fig 24.3 Leominster Priory: three light window of c1540 inserted to light the parochial altar

Of Prior John Reading's fate nothing is known. At Leominster dissolution was a farce; at Reading it was high tragedy. The distinguished abbot, Hugh Cooke or Faringdon, firmly maintained the papal supremacy. For thus denying the newly-established royal supremacy he was tried for treason, found guilty, hanged, drawn and quartered. The parts were left in chains outside his own abbey gate. So began the age of plunder.

Henry VIII wanted money, and quickly. The monastic church — the eastern end, transepts and crossing, together with the easternmost bay of the north aisle, with its processional door that the monks had used for entry into the cloister — and all the conventual buildings about the cloister came down immediately. Four postholes for the scaffolding for the demolition work about the south-west corner of the cloister were revealed during the 2005 excavations (Fig 24.1). The site became a quarry for building materials. Details are recorded in the borough chamberlain's accounts. One entry, for 1557, reads: 'Item. Paid for the carriage of iiij lodes of Stone out of the Priory to the bridge ... ijs'. The choir, transepts and crossing quickly disappeared but the parish church to the west, with its two naves and two aisles, remained in use. The only decorated masonry now left from the monastic church is some half dozen or so pieces of chevron ornament above an arch in the annexe of the Grange (see Fig 10.6).

Ownership of the priory nave passed to the parish. The demolition of the crossing and transepts of the conventual church left all the east end of their church open to the elements. A new eastern wall was quickly erected in order that the church could remain in use. Freeman's sketch of c1853, of the Romanesque nave looking east, shows the perpendicular east window built at the end of that nave c1540 (Fig 24.4). This was described by the Royal Commission in 1934 as 'four trefoiled lights with vertical tracery in a two-centred head, with a

Fig 24.4 Sketch by W.H. Freeman c1853 showing the Ramanesque 'Nave looking east' with its east window of c1540 and Tudor window to the north

moulded label'. This evidently had counterparts at the end of the south nave and south aisle, but after the disastrous 1699 fire the former was replaced with church warden gothic fenestration, as were the second and third windows from the east in the south aisle (see Fig 18.4). There was further restoration work on the east windows in the last century (Fig 24.5). Those in the south nave and south aisle were replaced in 1923, and subsequently the 16th-century Perpendicular window of the north aisle gave way to the present one, of Romanesque design. Only in the eastern wall of the north aisle is there considerable evidence of the re-use of the Romanesque ashlar work from the demolished eastern end of the priory church (Fig 24.6).[563]

As the shading on one of Freeman's sketches shows, the easternmost bay of the Romanesque north aisle was not rebuilt until the mid 19th century, by George Gilbert Scott. However, a three-light Tudor window was inserted into the north wall of the Romanesque nave to provide additional illumination for the altar. This window is still *in situ* (Fig 24.3).

Fig 24.5 Leominster Priory: east end showing the windows restored in the 20th century

Fig 24.6 Leominster Priory: east end showing re-used Romanesque ashlar work

25 Epilogue

The *Herneys*

After more than four centuries, the ancient lordship of Leominster was once more in the hands of the Crown. Continuity was a major characteristic of the post-Dissolution era. The lordship continued to be administered through the halimotes of the four *herneys*, as under the priory and the minster church. Initially there was some degree of confusion, until leases were renewed at former rents. Details preserved in a number of cases are valuable for the light they throw on the way the priory's estates were administered in the late 15th and first half of the 16th century, a period for which there is virtually no other evidence.

Fig 25.1 Ivington Mill today

The site etc of the late priory was leased in 1540 to George Cornewall, with two meadows called *Somergilds*, an orchard, a pasture beyond the water of *Pynnysley*, a garden called Horsewall and a fishery within the pale, at a rent of £7 3s 4d. Luston *bury*, with the tithes of corn, flax, bees and apples, a cottage next the orchard, a pasture called *le Cowlesowe* and the farm stock there, was granted to Robert Brothar on a 21-year lease, for a fine of £13 6s 8d and annual rent of £27 7s 10d. Ivington *bury*, with pasture and pannage of the park and heath, *Fattyngmore* pasture, Ivington mill, the tithes of corn and flax of Ivington, Bricrlcy and Pervin, of wool, geese, pigs and pigeons of Ivington, Brierley, Stagbatch, Cholstrey and Wharton, and of wools and lambs of *Redyngs* Place, Leominster, and West *Harnes*, together with farm stock and implements, was initially leased to Simon Hyett, for a fine of £20 and rent of £46 13s 4d. Stockton *bury*, its demesne lands, dove house, *le Myll crofte* and tithes of Stockton halimote, were granted in 1554 to Agnes Vale at a rent of £20 3s 4d. Woods, wards, marriages, mines and quarries were excluded.[564]

Luston *herneys* was eventually detached from the so-called 'Lordship of Leominster alias Leominster Ore'.[565] After a decade in disgrace, Sir James Croft was restored to royal favour in 1572, as Controller of the Household, and was granted 'reversion and rent of the site of the Manor of Luston called "le Bury" and lands (named) in Luston ... for life, with remainder to Edward Croft, his son and heir apparent, in tail male'.[566] The family had held the manor of Yarpole since 1361; with the grant of Deerfold forest and of priory lands in Kingsland they were now able to consolidate their hold on the north-west of the county.

The three other *herneys*, Ivington, Stockton and Stoke (Prior), were retained by the Crown. In 1620 they were leased to James I's favourite, George Villiers, who was made Duke of Buckingham in 1623. Parliament granted his manor of Leominster in 1650 to the regicide, Colonel Henry Marten. At the Restoration in 1660 it was returned to the second duke, who sold it to Major John Wildman in 1675. A speculator in forfeited lands, Wildman plotted not only against Cromwell, but also against Charles II c1681. He sold the three *herneys* in 1692 to Thomas Coningsby, who incorporated them into his Hampton Court estate. However the court books show that they were administered through their ancient halimotes or courts baron until at least the mid 19th century, when records terminate.[567] Thus institutions apparently fashioned for the Saxon minster continued to serve new masters. Coningsby's decision to have a considerable number of the halimote rolls transcribed into his *Register* preserved these rich records of the 14th century for posterity.

The Borough

For the burgesses, dissolution of the priory brought emancipation from the abbot of Reading, their lord for four centuries. With that bond had come economic advantages, such as 'freedom from tolls, customs and exactions in all markets and fairs whatsoever, by land and water, over bridges and seaports' throughout the whole of England; but also constraints. Now the borough faced a legal void. Uncertainty came to an end only in May 1554 when Mary Tudor was 'pleased to make, bring and create the inhabitants (of Leominster) into a Body Corporate and Politic'. Continuity was the dominant theme of her charter. It retained the system of government 'since time immemorial' of a bailiff and twenty-four burgesses. The bailiff was to be elected from 'one or more discreet and substantial persons' amongst them, and any vacancy amongst the twenty-four was to be filled by their nomination of a fellow townsman. The Court of Record was to meet every other week 'in the Forbury Yate-house', where the arms of the abbot and convent were replaced by those of the Crown. Bailiff and burgesses were to continue to enjoy their Friday market, and were granted two two-day fairs. The borough retained its court of sessions, gaol, coroner and community seal. It was also to have a free grammar school. Reform of the Marian charter's provisions came only in 1835, with the Municipal Reform Act.[568]

'*The Coming of Edfride*': A Secular Poem

The minster's early-11th-century prayer book is firm evidence that Edfrith, as well as Merewalh and Eafe's youngest daughter, Mildgith, was honoured in Leominster almost a century before Mildburg's *Life* was written for the newly founded Cluniac monastery at Much Wenlock. His festival, on 26 October, in the Calendar, and his name in the longer litany, in company with Aethelmod, Haemma and Guthlac, provide the wider context. Despite the, initially, unsympathetic attitude of Reading's Benedictine abbots, remembrance of Edfrith's mission remained the leitmotif of Leominster's history. In 1290 his festival became the borough's great autumn fair. By the early 14th century, Bishop Orleton had his own copy of *The Legend of St Etfrid*, transcribed from the Mildburg Life. The 1433 list shows that 26 October remained one of the principal feasts of the conventual church.[569]

Continuity characterised not only the administration of the *herneys* and borough government, but also the Edfrith tradition. This was now transformed into the foundation legend of the borough. By the opening years of the 17th century, it was circulating about the town as a poem in English. Part of this poem, written in what he termed a 'medieval monastic hand', was published by Blacklock in 1893. It told how the Lord bid Edfrith to go south 'and preache his Gospel at Ridgmouth'. How 'the Kinge baptised by Edfride gave to build a church thyrtie plowlands ... a goodlie Church was shortelie plight. The Towne with buildings did increase, inhabitants did multiplie. And Edfride ruled the Church in peace, full fiftene yeres and thene did die.' In 1980, when the full document was given to the Herefordshire Record Office, it emerged that Blacklock had omitted the last third of the poem, and that script, vocabulary and text show the poem to be a work of the early 17th century.[570]

The poem incorporates wild anachronisms and local mythology, but details indicate the date of its composition. It refers to Sir Philip Hoby, one of the agents through whom the borough sought its 1554 charter, and to the borough's apprentices' charity, founded according to the terms of the will of Bishop John Scory, who died in 1585. When the poet comments, 'greate commanders rule arighte; inferiors follow in delighte; subjects follow kings' example, ffor kings are Gods to the people', he is reaffirming James I's dictum that kings are God's 'vicegerents on earth, adorned with some sparkle of divinitie'. The poem was written to foster civic pride by stressing the august origins and great antiquity of Leominster, with its minster church that antedated the cathedral. It was both a pæan to the town and a sermon to its people.

The text of *The Legend of St Etfrid* on which the author relied was a 13th-century copy. It tells us, 'that nighte Edfride lodged abroade, in open field nere Ridgemouth banke', a spelling consistent with the place-name *Reodesmuthe*, as it appears in the 13th-century Mildburg *Life* and the early-14th-century *Life of Edfrith*. Later versions, such as Tynemouth's abridgement and Capgrave's edited version in the *Nova Legenda Angliæ* of 1516, refer to Edfrith resting at *Redeswode*.[571] Thus the author of the legend had access either to one of the earlier copies of Mildburg's *Life*, or to a later, and freer, metrical rendering, in the vernacular, based on them.

The author was almost certainly John Hackluyt of Eaton, son or grandson of Thomas Hackluyt, Clerk to the Council in the Marches, Leland's informant on his visit to Leominster 1535–43. In 1592 John claimed to have found 'a brassen plate on the south wall of the church', with an inscription in Saxon characters. This recorded, amongst other things, the gift by the Mercian prince, Kenelm, died 812 or 821, of all his lands, 'but only Kingsland and also my Kenelmworth I do not give', to the church 'my foremost fathers did build'. John had strong antiquarian interests and knowledge of Bede, the Anglo-Saxon Chronicle and Old English. The 'brassen plate', we are told, could 'hardly be seen for four layers of whitewash'. It was, no doubt, John's fabrication. Kenelm, most renowned of West Midland saints, was buried at Winchcombe Abbey. His *Life*, written at the request of the monks, described how on the death of his father, King Coenwulf, in

821 he had been murdered by his jealous sister, Cwenthryth — whose eyes subsequently fell out. Evidently Hackluyt's intention was to link Edfrith and Merewalh in the 7th and the nunnery in the early 11th century with the popular history of the Mercian royal family of the 9th century, by referring to Kenelm's maintenance of the royal lands about Kingsland where, he had told Leland, 'Kynge Merwald sometyme lay'.[572]

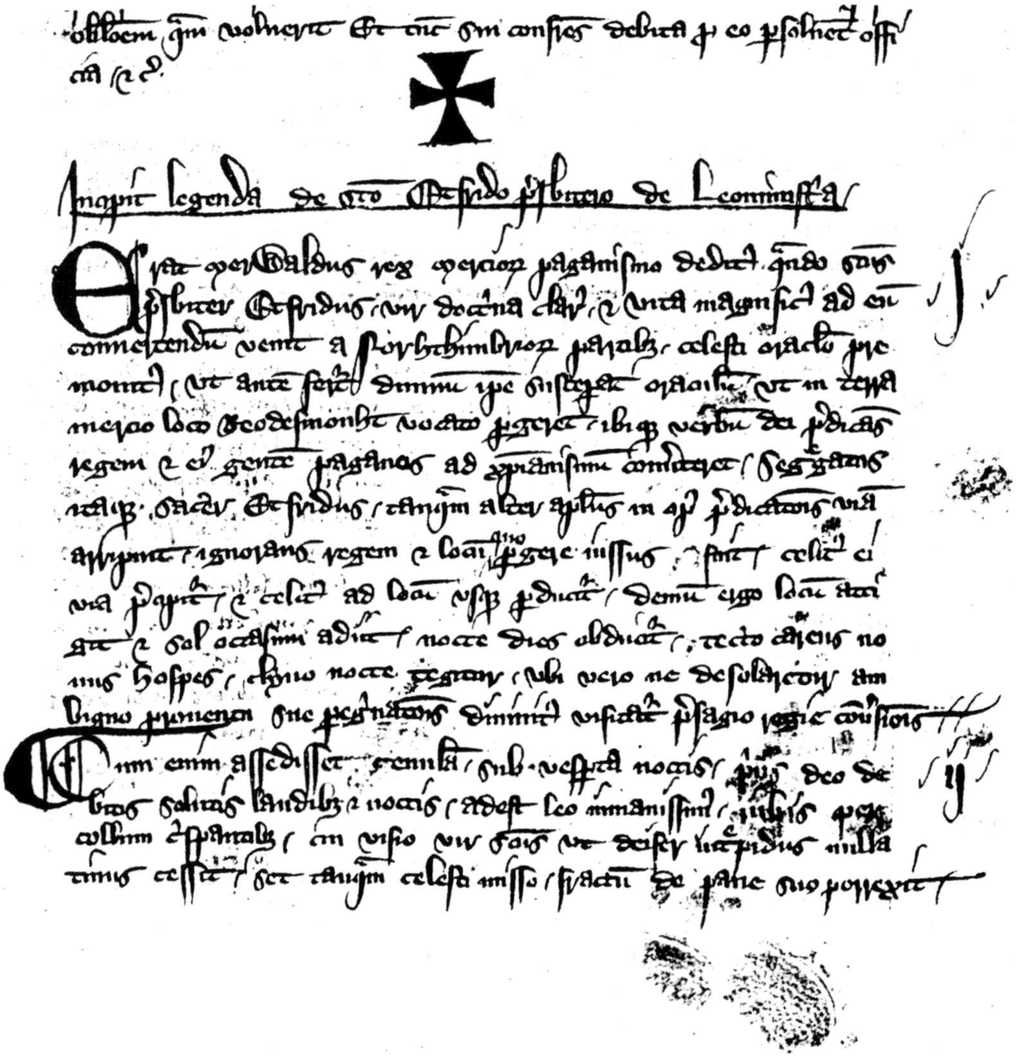

Fig 25.2 BL Harley MS 2253 f1.32r The Legend of St Etfrid, Priest of Leominster
(complete with flaws in the vellum on which it was written)

Appendix 1

'Helper of those who toil'

	Adiutor laborantium,	Helper of those who toil,
	bonorum rector omnium,	Ruler of all the good,
	custos ad pro pugnab(c?)ulum	Custodian of the ramparts
	defensorque credentium,	Defender of the believers,
5	*exaltatu(o?)r humilium,*	Exalter of the lowly,
	fractor superbientium,	Breaker of the proud,
	gubernator fidelium,	Governor of the faithful,
	hostis inpoenitentium,	Enemy of the impenitent,
	iudex cunctorum iudic(i)um,	Judge of all judges,
10	*Castigator errantium,*	Chastiser of those who sin,
	Casta uita uiuentium,	Pure life of the living,
	Lumen et pater/luminum,	Light and father of all lights
	Magna luce lucentium,	Shining with great brilliance,
	Nulli negans sperantium	Denying to none who hope
15	*Opem atque auxilium,*	Your help and succour,
	Precor ut me homunculum	I pray that me, little man
	Quassatum ac miserrimum	Broken and wretched,
	Reigantem per tumul(t)um	Rowing through the storm
	Seculi istius infinitum	Of this infinite age,
20	*Trahat post se ad supernum*	That Christ may draw me after Him
	Uite portum pulcherrimum.	To life's high celestial haven,
	Xriste (me per?) infinitum	... an incessant
	Ymnum sanctum in seculum	Holy hymn forever.
	Zelo/subtrahas hostium	Take me from the envy of enemies
25	*Paradisi in gaudium.*	Into the joy of Paradise.
	Per te, Christe Ihesu, qui iuius et regnas.	Through you, Jesus Christ, who live and reign.

(Contractions removed)

BL Cotton MS Galba Axiv ff20r-21r

Appendix 2

Sumer is icumen in

Latin text and translation

Perspice christi cola, que dignacio
celicus agricola, pro vitis vicio filio
non parcens exposuit, mortis exicio
qui captivos, semivivos, a supplicio vite donat
et secum coronat, in celi solio

Pay heed, Christian, what an honour!
The heavenly farmer, because of a flaw on the vine
[his] son did not spare but exposed to the destruction of death;
He to the half-living captives [of hell] gives life
and crowns [them] and himself on the throne of heaven.

References

Abbreviations used

ASC	*Anglo-Saxon Chronicle*
ASE	*Anglo-Saxon England*
BHL	*Bibliotheca Hagiographica Latina: Antiquae et Mediae Aetatis* 2 vols, Soc Bollandists (Brussels, 1898-1901)
BL	British Library
Brut	*Brut y Tywysogyon or The Chronicle of the Princes, Red Book of Hergest Version* ed.T.Jones (1955)
CCR	*Calendar of Close Rolls 1227-1500*, PRO (1902-55)
CChR	*Calendar of Charter Rolls 1226-1516*, PRO (1903-27)
CDI	*Calendar of Documents relating to Ireland* 5 vols, ed H.S.Sweetman (1875-86)
CIPM	*Calendar of Inquisitions post Mortem* PRO 14 vols (1904-54)
CPR	*Calendar of Patent Rolls 1216-1557*, PRO (1901-39)
Domitian Aiii	BL Cotton MS Domitian Aiii: 'The Leominster Cartulary'. Details given only if not in *RAC* I or II
DBG	*Domesday Book. 15: Gloucestershire* ed J.S.Moore (1982)
DBH	*Domesday Book. 17: Herefordshire* ed F.&C.Thorn (1983)
DNB	*Dictionary of National Biography* (Compact ed, 1975)
EH	Bede *Ecclesiastical History*
EHD	*English Historical Documents c500-1042* ed D.Whitelock (2nd ed, 1979)
GP	William of Malmesbury: *The Deeds of the Bishops of England (Gesta Pontificum Anglorum)* trans D.Preest (2002)
Gesta Regum	William of Malmesbury: *Gesta Regum Anglorum* I, ed R.A.B.Mynors, R.M.Thomson & M.Winterbottom (1998)
HBS	Henry Bradshaw Society
H&CG	*Historia et Cartularium Monasterii Sancti Petri Gloucestriae* ed W.H.Hart, RS 33, 3 vols (1863-7)
HD&CA	Hereford Dean & Chapter Archives
HRO	Herefordshire Record Office
John of Worcester	*The Chronicle of John of Worcester. II The Annals 450-1066* ed R.R.Darlington, P.McGurk & J.Bray (1995); *III The Annals 1067-1140* ed P.McGurk (1998)
Lapidge (1991)	*Anglo-Saxon Litanies of the Saints* ed M.Lapidge, Henry Bradshaw Soc 106 (1991)
Life	*Life of St Mildburg* (*Vita Sancte Milburge verginis*) BL Add MS 34633 ff206r-15v
LL	*Liber Landavensis* ed J.G.Evans (1979)
Lloyd	J.E.Lloyd *A History of Wales …to the Conquest* 2 vols (3rd ed, 1939)
L&P, HVIII	*Letters and Papers of Henry VIII* PRO 23 vols in 28 (1862-1932)
Monasticon	*William Dugdale: Monasticon Anglicanum* ed J.Caley et al, 6 vols in 8 (1817-30)
Muir	*A Pre-Conquest English Prayer Book (BL MSS Cotton Galba Axiv and Nero Aii (ff3-13)* ed B.J.Muir, Henry Bradshaw Soc 103 (1988)
New Groves	*New Groves Dictionary of Music* 2nd ed (2001) ed S.Sadie & J.Tyrrell
ODNB	*Oxford Dictionary of National Biography* (2004)
OV	*The Ecclesiastical History of Orderic Vitalis ed M.Chibnall, 6 vols (1969-80)*
RAC	*Reading Abbey Cartularies* ed B.Kemp, 2 vols (1986-7) includes Domitian Aiii
RCHM	*Royal Commission on Historical Monuments: Herefordshire* 3 vols (1931-34)
Reg	*Registers of the Bishops of Hereford* Cantilupe Soc (Hereford, 1907-21)
Rot Litt Claus	*Rotuli litterarum clausarum* ed T.D.Hardy, I (1833)
RRAN	*Regesta Regum Anglo-Normannorum 1066-1154* 3 vols: II *1100-35*, ed C.Johnson & H.A.Cronne (1956); III *1066-1154*, ed H.A.Cronne & R.H.C.Davis (1968)
RS	Rolls Series
Rule	P.Delatte *The Rule of St Benedict. A Commentary* trans J.McCann (1950)
Rushforth	R.Rushforth *An Atlas of Saints in Anglo-Saxon Calendars* ASNC Guides, Texts & Studies 6 (2002)
S	P.H.Sawyer *Anglo-Saxon Charters: An Annotated List & Bibliography* (1968)
TNA	The National Archives
TWNFC	*Transactions Woolhope Naturalists Field Club*
VCH	*Victoria County History*
Wormald	*English Kalendars before AD 1100*, Henry Bradshaw Soc 72 (1934)

1. BM Add MS 34,633 f207r-208v
2. A.J.M.Edwards, 'Odo of Ostia's History of the Translation of St Milburga and its Connection with the Early History of Much Wenlock Abbey' (unpublished University of London MA thesis, 1960); idem, 'An Early Twelfth-Century Account of the Translation of St Milburga of Much Wenlock' *Trans Shropshire Archaeol Soc* 67ii (1962-3) 134-51. For the Gotha codex, P.Grosjean in *Analecta Bollandiana* 58 (1940) 90-103
3. BL Harley MS 2253, f132r; H.Pawsey, 'The Legend of St Etfrid of Leominster' in A.Malpas et al *The Early Church in Herefordshire* (Leominster, 2001) 14-40; Lincoln Cathedral MS 149, ff 83v-93v; Lambeth Palace MS 94, ff 169r-169v
4. W.A.Chaney *The Cult of Kinship in Anglo-Saxon England: The Transition from Paganism to Christianity* (1970) ch5; *EH* II, 14, 20
5. *EH* II, 14; III, 21, 24
6. Nero Aii f7v & Galba Axiv f93v published in *A Pre-Conquest English Prayer Book* ed B.J.Muir, HBS 103 (1988) 12, 126
7. P.Busby, D.Hurst, E.Pearson & B.Watson, 'The evaluation of the western cloister walk Leominster Priory, Herefordshire: an interim report', *West Midlands Archaeology* forthcoming
8. Alex Bayliss revised report, March 2006
9. *Facsimile of British Museum MS Harley 2253* ed N.R.Ker, Early English Text Society 255 (1965) articles 98, 18, 116; *Reg Trillek* I, i-iii, 96-7; *Reg Spofford* 163; HRO AG
10. *Anglo-Saxon Wills* ed D.Whitelock (1930) 54-60; *Rhigyfarch's Life of St David* trans J.W.James (1967) xi, 8, 33; V.Watts *Cambridge Dictionary of English Place-Names* (2003) 370
11. S677; text translated in *EHD* I, 514-16; H.P.R.Finberg *The Early Charters of the West Midlands* (2nd ed, 1972) no 418; *Gwaith Iorwerth Fynglwyd* ed H.Ll.Johnes & E.I.Rowlands (1975) 54, 114; R.J.Thomas *Enwau Afonydd a Nentydd Cymru* (1938) 157-8; *The Itinerary of John Leland* ed L.Toulmin Smith, 5 vols (1966) II, 75; III, 42
12. See p37
13. See p245
14. A.H.Smith *English Place-Name Elements 2* EPNS 26 (1956) 42-3; M.Gelling *Place-Names in the Landscape* (1984) 54-6
15. D.Lewis, 'Leominster' *Current Archaeology* 195 (Dec-Jan 2004/5) 1214-7; I.Burrow& C.Dyer in *Bordesley Abbey: The First Report on Excavations, 1969-73* ed P.Rahtz& S.Hirst, BAR 23 (1976) 120, 132
16. D.Hill & M.Worthington *Offa's Dyke. History and Guide* (2003) 139-43; P.White et al *The Arrow Valley, Herefordshire: Archaeology, Landscape Change and Conservation* (2003) 47
17. C.Thomas *Early Christian Archaeology of North Britain* (1971) 38; A.MacDonald, 'Adomnán's Monastery of Iona' in *Studies in the Cult of St Columba* ed C.Bourke (Dublin, 1997) 40-3
18. C.G.Brown & A.E.T Harper, 'Excavations on Cathedral Hill, Armagh, 1968' *Ulster J of Archaeol* 47 (1984) 109-66; D.Brook, 'The Early Christian Church east and west of Offa's Dyke' in *The Early Church in Wales and the West* ed N.Brooks & A.Lane (1992) 77-89.
19. C.Thomas, see n17, 29-31, 212-13, fig 7; F.McCormick, 'Iona: The Archaeology of the Early Monastery' in Bourke, see n17, quoting 'H.King pers. comm.'; Nancy Edwards *The Archaeology of Early Medieval Ireland* (1990) 104-12; A.O.Anderson & M.O.Anderson, ed & trans *Adomnán's Life of Columba* (1961) I, 3, 14a, 15b.
20. J.Barber, 'Excavations on Iona' *Proc Soc Antiq Scotland* 111 (1981) 282, 380; F.McCormick, 'Excavations at Iona, 1988' *Ulster J Archaeol* 56 (1993) 78-108; Anderson & Anderson, see n19, II, 29; A.McDonald, 'Aspects of the Monastery and Monastic Life in Adomnán's Life of Columba' *Peritia* 3 (1984) 271-302; R.Meens, 'Ritual Purity and the Influence of Gregory the Great in the Early Middle Ages' in *Unity and Diversity in the Church* Studies in Church History 32, ed R.N.Swanson (1996) 31-43
21. D.O'Sullivan, 'The Plan of the Early Christian Monastery on Lindisfarne: A fresh look at the evidence' in *St Cuthbert, His Cult and His Community to AD1200* ed G.Bonner *et al* (1989) 125-42, Fig 11; D.O'Sullivan & R.Young *Lindisfarne, Holy Island* (1995) 40-2, Plan 21; J.Blair, 'Anglo-Saxon Minsters. A Topographical Review' in *Pastoral Care before the Parish* ed J.Blair & R.Sharpe (1992) 231.
22. R.J.Cramp, 'Monastic Sites' in *The Archaeology of Anglo-Saxon England* ed D.M.Wilson (1976) 241-6; C.A.R.Radford, 'Glastonbury Abbey before 1184: Interim report on the excavations 1908-64' in *Medieval Art and Architecture at Wells and Glastonbury*, Brit Archaeol Ass Conf Trans for 1978 (1981) 113-14; *Med Archaeol* 23 (1979) 243; P.J.Ellis, 'Excavations at Silver Street, Glastonbury, 1978' *Proc Somerset Archaeol Nat Hist Soc* 126 (1982) 17-24; *ASC* 'A' *sa* 688; W.Rodwell, 'Churches in the Landscape: Aspects of Topography and Planning' in Faull (1984) 18-21; P.Leach & P.Ellis, 'The Medieval Precinct of Glastonbury Abbey – some new evidence' in *In Search of Cult: Archaeological Investigations in honour of Philip Rahtz* ed M.Carver (1993) 119-24. Brief summaries of excavations between 1904 and 1964, together with detailed plans of the town centre precinct and excavations at the abbey are to be found in M.Aston & R.Leech *Historic Towns in Somerset* (1977) 57-65; S 227 in *The Early History of Glastonbury: De Antiquitate Glastonie Ecclesie* ed & trans J.Scott (1981) 90-1; H.Woods, 'Excavations at Glastonbury Abbey 1987-1993' *Proc Somerset Archaeol Nat Hist Soc* 138 (1995) 7-73; P.Rahtz *Glastonbury* (1993) 92-3. For comparative dimensions of predominantly curvilinear banks and ditches, J.Blair *The Church in Anglo-Saxon Society* (2005) 198, n74
23. The exception is R.Morris *Churches in the Landscape* (1989) 110-11; Muir (1988) see n6, 127; J.Hillaby 'Early Christian and Pre-Conquest Leominster: an Exploration of the Sources' *TWNFC* 45 (1987) 630-5 esp omissions in both Leominster & 'Glastonbury' calendars, 4-7, in Table 6, p631
24. Blair (1992) see n21, 231-5; idem (2005) see n22, 196-8;

T.A.Hall *The Minster Churches in the Dorset Landscape* BAR, Brit S 304 (2000) 49-78
25. R.Shoesmith *Hereford Excavations* 2 (1982) figs 131, 134, 135, 136; J.Hillaby, 'The Norman New Town of Hereford' *TWNFC* 44(ii) (1983) 181-95; idem *Ledbury. A Medieval Borough* 3rd ed (2005) 1-8, 14, 24-7
26. Blair (2005) see n22, Ch 5, 'Monastic Towns? Minsters as Central Places, c.650-850'; Hillaby (2005) see n25, 19
27. H.P.R.Finberg, 'St Mildburg's Testament' and 'The Princes of the *Magonsaete*' in Finberg, see n11, 197-224; M.Gelling *The West Midlands in the Early Middle Ages* (1992) 81-3; K.Pretty, 'Defining the Magonsaete' in *The Origins of the Anglo-Saxon Kingdoms* ed S.Bassett (1989) 171-83
28. M.L.Faull, 'The semantic development of OE walh' in *Leeds Studies in English* 8 (1975) 32; *EH* III, 7; Gelling (1992), see n27, 81; idem, *Signposts to the Past* (1978) 93-5
29. J.E.Lloyd *History of Wales from the earliest times to the Edwardian Conquest* 2 vols (3rd ed, 1939) I, 185-91; *EH* II, 20
30. E.Ekwall *English River Names* (1928) lviii-lix, 108, 383; K.Jackson *Language and History in Early Britain* (1953) but note Gelling (1978), see n28, 90; B.Coplestone-Crow *Herefordshire Place-Names* BAR British Series 214 (1989) 11 & map 4 for the region called *Lydas*
31. The irregularity of the Severn boundary is analysed by S.Bassett, 'Church and diocese in the West Midlands: the transition from British to Anglo-Saxon control' in Blair & Sharpe, see n21, 35-9; H.P.R.Finberg, 'Bishop Athelstan's Boundary' in Finberg, see n11
32. See Chapter 5, Fig 6.3 & Table 5
33. J.Blair, 'Minster Churches in the Landscape' in *Anglo-Saxon Settlements* ed D.Hooke (1988) 35, 40-50; idem, 'Anglo-Saxon Minsters: A Topographical Review' in Blair & Sharpe, see n21, 230-1; *Leland's Itinerary* see n11, II, 74. For Marden, K.Ray, 'Archaeology of Three Early Churches of Herefordshire' in Malpas, see n3, 129, 132-3
34. S677; P.White et al, see n16, esp 43-8
35. The Hereford episcopal lists of BL Cotton MS Vespasian Bvi f108v & Cambridge Corpus Christi College MS 183, 63v are in J.Hillaby, 'The Origins of the Diocese of Hereford' *TWNFC* 42i (1976) 23; R.I.Page. 'Anglo-Saxon Episcopal Lists' *Nottingham Medieval Studies* IX (1965) 71-95; X (1966) 2-24
36. *Life* f207r; D.Rollason *The Mildrith Legend* (1982) 80, 82; B.Thorpe *Florentii Wigorniensis: Chronicon ex Chronicis* 2 vols (1848-9) I, 265; P.Sims-Williams *Religion and Literature in Western England, 600-800* (1990) 39-53; Gelling (1992) see n27, 82-5
37. Gelling (1992), see n27, 82-3; Coplestone-Crow, see n30, 12-13.
38. Finberg, see n11, nos 413, 421; S 677, 1462; *EHD* I, no 135, p556; *ASC* 'D' *sa* 1016; J.Whybra *A Lost English County. Winchcombshire in the Ten and Eleventh Centuries* (1990) 106.
39. Rollason (1982) see n36, 9-68
40. *Life* f208v; *Laws of the Earliest English Kings* ed & trans F.L.Attenborough (1922) 78-9
41. *Life* ff208v-209r
42. S.Hollis, 'The Minster-in-Thanet Foundation Story' *ASE* 27 (1998) 41-64
43. BL Cotton Caligula Axiv ff121v-124v; Hollis, see n42; S86, S87, S91. Texts in B.Thorpe *Diplomatarium Anglicum Aevi Saxonici* (1865) 25-6, 30-3; Hillaby (1987) see n23, 582 & Table 1
44. BL Cotton Caligula Axiv
45. S1798; Finberg, see n11, 197-216; Coplestone-Crow, see n30, 11-13
46. *HE* III, 15; IV, 2 & 3; *Vita Mildrethae* summarized by Rollason (1982) see n36, 77-9. Both sisters were buried at Peterborough.
47. Finberg, see n11, 204-6; Hillaby (1976) see n35, 28, 33-6; *Brut y Tywysogyon: Chronicle of the Princes, Red Book of Hergest Version* ed T.Jones (1955) *sa* 729, 760 on the battles of Pen-coed in Deheubarth and at Hereford.
48. Hillaby (1976) see n35, 16-52; idem, 'Leominster and Hereford: The Origins of the Diocese' in *Hereford Medieval Art, Architecture and Archaeology* Brit Archaeol Ass Conf Trans 15 (1995) 1-4, 11-13
49. *Leland's Itinerary* see n11, II, 66. For the translation of Bishop Cuthbert's epitaph on the 'high roofed mausoleum', *Deeds of the Bishops of England* trans D.Preest (2002) 202-3. The Hereford Cathedral tradition remained that Mildfrith was its founder, M.R.James, 'Two Lives of St Ethelbert, King and Martyr' *Eng Hist R* (1917) 221, 244. Indeed, the interior of the chapter house of c1336-48 was decorated with five trefoil-headed panels. The first was decorated with paintings of King Mildfrith, together with the cathedral's patron, St Ethelbert. G.Marshal *Hereford Cathedral: Its Evolutuion and Growth* (1951) 116
50. For fuller discussion see p41, n109; Hillaby (1987) see n23, 634-5
51. BL Nero Aii f5r; Galba Axiv no 61 f93v & no 103 in Muir (1988) see n6, 7, 126, 190; *Reg Swinfield*, 124-5; BL Egerton MS 3031 ff6v-8v
52. D.W.Rollason, 'Lists of Saints' Resting-Places in Anglo-Saxon England' *ASE* 7 (1978) 61-93
53. S677; RAC I, no 354; see Table 3.3 & p45 Finberg, see n11, no 418
54. *Leland's Itinerary* see n11, II, 74. For the Athelstan cult, below pp37-9
55. See Chapter 25; *ASC* 'A' 918; 'D', 915; J.Hillaby, 'Burgred. The Severn Stoke Coin Hoard and the Demise of the Mercian Kingdom' *Trans Worcs Archaeol Soc* 3S 17 (2000) 125-48
56. Blair (2005) see n22, Map 35, pp296, 306
57. *The Bosworth Psalter* ed F.Gasquet & E.Bishop (1908) 152; 'About an Old Prayer Book' in E.Bishop *Liturgica Historica* (1918) 384-91 is the remarkable, and heart-warming, account of Bishop's discovery of Galba Axiv in the British Museum.
58. *A Catalogue of Manuscripts containing Anglo-Saxon* ed N.R.Ker (1957) 198-201
59. R.Rushforth *Atlas of Saints in the Anglo-Saxon Calendar* Anglo-Saxon, Norse & Celtic Guides, Texts & Studies

6 (2002), 26; R.A.Banks, 'Some Anglo-Saxon Prayers from British Museum MS Cotton Galba Axiv' *Notes and Queries* 210 (June, 1965) 207-13; A.McIntosh, 'Wulfstan's Prose' *Proc Brit Acad* 35 (1949) 110-13

60. Muir (1988) see n6, xii; Hillaby (1987) see n23, 628-54; idem, 'The Early Church in Herefordshire: Columban and Roman' (2001) in Malpas, see n3, 41-76; R.Rushforth, see n59, 26-7; Blair (2005) see n22, 151-2; idem, 'A Handlist of Anglo-Saxon Saints' in *Local Saints and Local Churches in the Early Medieval West* ed A.Thacker & R.Sharpe (2002) 507, 527, 537
61. Galba Axiv, ff 6v, 53v, 89v, 85r, 125v
62. Muir, no 60
63. Ker (1957) see n 58, 198-201; D.Dumville, 'On the dating of some late Anglo-Saxon Liturgical Manuscripts' *Trans Cambridge Bibliographic Soc* 10 (1991) 46-7; *Anglo-Saxon Litanies of the Saints* ed M.Lapidge, HBS 106 (1991) 69-70; R.Priebsch *The Heliand MS: Cotton Caligula A.VIII: A Study* (1925) 26-7; Muir (1988) see n6, nos 86-103
64. Muir (1988) see n6, xiii-xiv, nos 5, 6, 77. For Athelstan, see pp37-9
65. Lapidge (1991) see n63, 69-70; Muir (1988) see n6, nos 1, 10
66. A.L.Meaney, 'Variant versions of Old English medical remedies' *ASE* 13 (1984) 240-1
67. Ker (1957) see n58, 198-201; Muir (1988) see n6, xiv-xv, nos 1-4, 9-10, 40, 61, 65, 71, 81
68. Muir (1988), see n6, nos34, 70; M.L.Cameron, 'The Sources of Medical Knowledge in Anglo-Saxon England' *ASE* 11 (1983) 135-55
69. Muir (1988) see n6, nos 73, 86, 93; Domitian Aiii f118. For David's cult, p37. *Reg Spofford* 163
70. Blair (1992) see n21, 246; J.Williams *Historical and Topographical View of the Ancient and Present State of Leominster* (1808) 193; HRO M31/9/3 f19; T.G.Blacklock *The Suppressed Benedictine Minster and Ancient and Modern Institutions of the Borough of Leominster* (repr 1999) 8, 9, 179
71. For *parochia* below pp59-60 & Fig 6.3; Domitian Aiii f119r; Hillaby (2001) in Malpas, see n60, 61-4
72. R.A.Banks, 'Some Anglo-Saxon Prayers from BM Cotton Galba A.xiv' *Notes and Queries* 210 (1965) 207-13
73. *Regularis Concordia* trans T.Symons (1953) 41-6
74. Muir (1988) see n6, no 68; S.L.Keefer, 'The Veneration of the Cross in Anglo-Saxon England' in *The Liturgy of the Anglo-Saxon Church* ed H.Gittos & M.B Bedingfield, HBS Subsidia V (2005) 143-84
75. Muir (1988) see n6, nos 81, 71, 73
76. *Liber Sacramentorum Gellonense* ed A.Dumas (1981) 452-9; *Gregorian Sacramentary* ed H.A.Wilson, HBS 49 (1915) 220-5; *Missal of Robert of Jumièges* ed H.A.Wilson, HBS 11 (1896) 274-9; *The Portiforium of St Wulstan* ed A.Hughes, HBS 89 (1958) 163-7; Galba Axiv ff118v & 119v
77. J.Blair, The Anglo-Saxon Church in Herefordshire: Four Themes' in Malpas (2001) see n3, 4; for the Irish priests, K.Hughes, 'Evidence for contacts between the churches of the Irish and English from the Synod of Whitby to the Viking Age' in *England before the Conquest* ed P.Clemoes & K.Hughes (1971) 49-67; Sims-Williams, see n36, 108-9, 113-14, 183-7; Text translation and commentary on the *Amra* are in T.O.Clancy & G.Márkus *Iona: The Earliest Poetry of a Celtic Monastery* (repr 1997) 96-128
78. Muir (1988) see n6, no 14; J.F.Kenney *Sources for the Early History of Ireland: Ecclesiastical* (repr 1979) 264; Clancy & Márkus, see n77, 39-68
79. *The Irish Liber Hymnorum* II, ed J.H.Bernard & R.Atkinson, HBS 14 (1898) 23-6, 140-69 comments on the manuscripts of the *Altus Prosator* and provides prefaces for the *Altus* and *Adiutor Laborantium.*
80. J.Stevenson, '*Altus Prosator*', *Celtica* 23 (1999) 326-68; F.G.E.Raby *Oxford Book of Medieval Latin* Verse (1959) 458; W.F.Bolton *A History of Anglo-Latin Literature, 587-1066* (1967) 40
81. B.J.Muir, 'Two Latin Hymns by Colum Cille (St Columba)' *Revue du moyen age latin* 39 (1983) 205-9; Bishop, see n57, 386; Muir (1988) see n6, no 15; Clancy & Márkus, see n77, 69-80
82. Muir (1988) see n6, no I, June & Nov; N.Netzer *Cultural Interplay in the Eighth Century: The Trier Gospels and the Making of the Scriptorium at Echternach* (1984); R.Rushforth, see n59, 13-14, Table VI: June
83. Muir (1988) see n6, no 31, xxvii, xxix, xxx: Basle MS Avii.3; BL MS Harley 2965 *An Ancient Manuscript of the eighth or ninth century: formerly belonging to St Mary's Abbey (Winchester)* ed W.deGray Birch (1889); Cambridge University Library MS L1.1.10 *The Prayer Book of Aedeluald the Bishop, commonly called the Book of Cerne* ed A.B.Kuypers (1902); K.Hughes, see n77, 49-67; idem, 'Some Aspects of Irish Influence on Early English Private Prayers' *Studia Celtica* 5 (1975) 48-61
84. Muir (1988) see n6, no 26
85. Muir (1988), see n6, no 16
86. W.H.Frere *Studies in Early Roman Liturgy 1: The Kalendar* Alcuin Club Coll 28 (1930) 7-83; Gasquet & Bishop, see n57, 152, 149; M.Perham *The Communion of Saints* Alcuin Club 62 (1980) 1-44
87. Frere, see n86, 44-9; *EH*, IV, 1, 18
88. Nero Aii, ff5r (May) & 6v (August); R.Rushforth, see n59, Table V: May
89. See p23 & n55
90. Details of the 20 calendars in Table 2 are drawn from *English Kalendars before AD 1100* ed F.Wormald, HBS 72 (repr, 1988); Muir (1988) see n6, nos 1, 61, pp 3, 7, 12, 126; Lapidge (1991) see n63, 166, lines 198-200
91. Muir (1988) see n6, nos 40, 61; Lapidge (1991) see n63, 69-70, 157-71
92. Galba Axiv, f93v; Muir (1988) see n6, 126, no 1 (May and October); Lapidge (1991) see n63, 170, 166, lines 199-200; J.Blair, 'Handlist of Anglo-Saxon Saints' in Thacker & Sharpe (2002) see n60, 527, 537; *Reg Swinfield* 124-5; *CChR* 1290, 356; Ker (1965) see n9, xxi-xxiii, articles 98, 18, 116; *Reg Spofford* 162-3; HRO AG 25
93. Rollason (1978) see n52, 90; Muir (1988) see n6, 126, no 1 (January); Lapidge (1991) see n63, 166, line 198; Blair

in Thacker & Sharpe (2002) see n60, 507; BL Egerton 3031, 6v-8r; *Three Chapters of Letters relating to the Suppression of the Monasteries* ed T.Wright, Camden Soc OS 26 (1843) 227; John Freeman quoted in F.&C. Thorn *Domesday Book. Herefordshire* (1983) notes to 1.10a Leominster; *Cambridge Dictionary of English Place-Names*, see n10, 29; *An Anglo-Saxon Dictionary* ed J.Bosworth & T.N.Toller (1964) 1013; Gelling (1978) see n28, 187-8; idem (1984) see n14, 211-18; E.M.Leather *Folk-Lore of Herefordshire* (repr 1973) 149; *Leland's Itinerary* see n11, II, 74; OED use 4a

94. *Reg Swinfield* 124; *Reg Spofford* 162; BL Egerton 3031, 6v-8r; T.Wright (1843) see n93, 227
95. Muir (1988) see n6, 123-4; Lapidge (1991) see n63, 162, lines 50, 52
96. D.W.Rollason, 'The Cults of Murdered Royal Saints in Anglo-Saxon England' *ASE* 11 (1983) 4-5, n17; C.A.R.Radford, 'The Church of St Alkmund, Derby' *Derbys Archaeol J* 96 (1976) 26-61; J.Bacon *Liber Regis* (1786) 363
97. Muir (1988) see n6, 126; Lapidge (1991) see n63, 166, lines 227, 229; L.Fleuriot, 'Les Evêques de la *Clas Kenedyr*, évêche disparu de la région de Hereford' *Etudes Celtiques* 15 (1976-7) 15-16; A.W.Wade-Evans *Vitae Sanctorum Britanniae et Genealogiae* (1944) 68-9, 314, 317; G.H.Doble *St Suliau and St Tysilio* (1936); Coplestone-Crow, see n30, 109, 130, 179
98. 435-43; Muir (1988) see n6, 126; Lapidge (1991) see n63, 166, lines 229-32
99. Muir (1988) see n6, 126; Lapidge (1991) see n63, 167, line 241; S.Baring-Gould & J.Fisher *The Lives of the British Saints* (1907-13) IV, 279-82; III, 43; *Reg Swinfield* 238-9; *Reg Trefnant* 178, 186, 189; *Reg Stanbury* 180; *Reg Myllyng* 197-8; *Reg Bothe* 332, 367; Blair (2001) in Malpas, see n77, 5
100. Muir (1988) see n6, 128; Lapidge (1991) see n63, 169, line 347; Rollason (1982) see n36, 86
101. BL Egerton 3031 f6v; T.Wright (1843) see n93, 226; *Reg Spofford* 162; Domitian Aiii, f74v-5r; *Royal and other Historical Letters illustrative of the Reign of Henry III* ed W.W.Shirley, RS 27ii (1866) 156-7; *Gesta Regum* 811
102. Muir (1988) see n6, no 1 (March); B.Yorke *Nunneries of the Anglo-Saxon Royal Houses* (2003) 103, n217. What appears to be *Ventana* (Winchester) is in the text, but 'is so badly damaged that more cannot be made of it', Muir (1988) see n6, xiv, 166. Above all, neither Calendar nor relic list bear any Winchester imprint, Table 2.
103. *Gesta Regum* 822-3; W.G.Hoskins *Devon* (1959) 219; *Reg Swinfield* 124-5
104. C.N.Brooke *Saxon and Norman Kings* (1967) 119-24; Muir (1988) see n6, nos 1, 40, 61; Lapidge (1991) see n63, 159 line 72, 165 line 174
105. Muir (1988) see n6, no 1; G.H.Doble *The Saints of Cornwall* 4 (1965) 132-66; idem, 'The Relics of St Petroc' *Antiquity* 13 (1939) 403-15; P.Grosjean 'Vies et miracles de S Petroc' *Analecta Bollandiana* 74 (1956) 131-88; D.H.Farmer *The Oxford Dictionary of Saints* (1980) attributes Nero Aii to Truro on the basis of the 23 May feast of St Petroc. *Gesta Regum* 807-9, 815; M.Lapidge, 'The Cult of St Indract at Glastonbury' in M.Lapidge *Anglo-Latin Literature 900-1066* (1993) 419-52
106. Muir (1988) see n6, no 5; W.H.Stevenson, 'A Latin Poem addressed to King Athelstan' *Eng Hist R* 26 (1911) 482-7; M.Lapidge 'Some Latin Poems as Evidence for the Reign of Athelstan' in idem (1993) see n105, 49-86
107. *ASC* 'D' 926; *Gesta Regum* I, 216-17; J.E.Lloyd (1939) see n29, I, 335-6, 353; H.R.Loyn, 'Welsh and English in the Tenth Century: The Context of the Athelstan Charters' *Welsh History R* 10 (1980-1) 283-301
108. *Reg Swinfield* 124-5
109. *Leland's Itinerary* see n11, II, 74. For Thomas Hackluyt see p261; *Anglo-Saxon Charters V: Charters of Shaftesbury Abbey* ed S.E.Kelly (1996) xiii-xv; Hillaby (1987), see n23, 664-5; *ASC* 'E' *sa* 979 (978); Yorke, see n102, 76-7
110. Table 6; BL Egerton 3031 ff6v-8r; T.Wright (1843) see n93, 226; Lapidge (1991) see n63, 169, lines 339, 340 and note
111. Whitelock, see n10, 54-6, 163-7; *John of Worcester* II, 582-3
112. J.E.Lloyd (1939) see n29, II, 357-71; *John of Worcester* II, 548-51; *ASC* 'C' *sa* 1046
113. *The Lives of Women Saints of our Contrie of England* ed C.Horstmann, Early English Text Soc 86 (1886) 102-8; Symons, see n73, 2
114. *John of Worcester* II, 548-9; *Hemingi Chartularium Ecclesiae Wigorniensis* I, ed T.Hearne, 2 vols (1723) I, 275-6
115. For Henry I's reasons for foundation and the foundation charter, *RAC* I, pp13-19, 33-6 and Ch 6
116. R.V.Lennard *Rural England, 1086-1135* (1959) 400-1, n5; followed by P.Stafford, '*Cherchez le Femme*. Queens, Queens' Lands and Nunneries: Missing Links in the Foundation of Reading Abbey' *History* 85 (2000) 9-10; S.Foot *Veiled Women* 1 (2000) 103-7; below Ch 4
117. Fencote, assessed with Bokland at 3 hides, was within the *herneys* of Stoke in 1291. For Stafford, see n116, 10, 'Leominster revenues were being shared equally between queen and nuns'.
118. *ASC* 'C' & 'D', *sa* 1052, 1055; *Brut sa* 1063; J.E.Lloyd (1939) see n29, II, 364-5, 370-1
119. HRO BN30/2 Letter of The Rev S.Woodhouse, Archdeacon of London, of 16 December 1970 to Norman Reeves (Notebook 2); N.Reeves *The Town in the Marches* (1973) 30-1
120. J.Hillaby, 'Weobley Castle, Borough and Church: the de Lacy and de Verdun Legacies, 1066-1377' in *Looking beyond the Castle Walls: the Weobley Castle Project* ed G.H.Nash & B.Redwood BAR 415 (2006) 77-142 at 84-121 & Fig 5.4; VCH *Hereford* I, (1908) 272-80
121. F.W.Maitland *Domesday Book and Beyond* (1960 ed) 145-6
122. *EH* V, 23; Bede: 'Letter to Egbert' *EHD* I, 734-5; Finberg, see n11, nos 1-4, 73, 180, pp204-6; *The Early Charters of the Thames Valley* ed M.Gelling (1979) nos 310, 677
123. Not included by D.Knowles in *The Monastic Order in England* I (1963) Appendix VI

124. F.M.Stenton *First Century of English Feudalism* 2nd ed (1961) 43 n2; VCH *Hereford* I, 284-5; A.H.Smith *The Place-Names of Gloucestershire* 2, English Place-Name Soc (1964) 206-7; C.S.Taylor, 'Berkeley Minster' *Trans Bristol Gloucs Archaeol Soc* 19 (1894-5) 70-84; 18 (1893-4) 132; B.R.Kemp, 'The Churches of Berkeley Hernesse' *Trans Bristol Gloucs Archaeol Soc* 86 (1967) 96-110; J.Blair, 'Secular Minster Churches in Domesday Book' in *Domesday Book. A Reassessment* ed P.H.Sawyer (1985) 104-42; J.Blair, 'From *Hyrness* to Parish: The Formation of Parochial Identities' in Blair (2005), see n22, 426-504
125. B.Kemp, 'Some aspects of the *Parochia* of Leominster in the 12th Century' in *Minsters and Parish Churches. The Local Church in Transition 950-1200* ed J.Blair (1988) 83, n5
126. *Llyfr Iorwerth* ed A.R.Williams (1960) 60; G.R.J.Jones, 'Multiple Estates and Early Development' in *English Medieval Settlement* ed P.H.Sawyer (1979) 9-34; idem, 'Continuity despite Calamity ...' *J of Celtic Studies* 3i (June 1981) 1-30; idem, 'Early historic settlement in border territory. A case-study of Archenfield and its environs' *Recherches de Géographie rurale* ed C.Christians & J.Claude (Liège, 1979) 117-32; idem, 'The Pattern of Settlement on the Welsh Border' *Agr Hist Rev* 8 (1960) 66-81; *Anglo-Saxon Towns in Southern England* ed J.Haslam (1984) 129-32 on Amesbury as 'proto-urban settlement'; S.C.Stanford *Croft Ambrey* (1974) esp Chs 12-14, 'Regional and Local Setting' and figs 2&3; idem *The Archaeology of the Welsh Marches* (lst ed, 1980) Chs 6 & 8
127. Orderic Vitalis *The Ecclesiastical History* ed M.Chibnall, VI (1978) 294-306; RAC I, 14 n1; C.Coates *History and Antiquities of Reading* (1802) 244-5
128. *Brut* sa 1116 & 1121; *Regesta Anglo-Normannorum* II, ed C.Johnson & H.A.Cronne (1956) nos 1292-5
129. *RAC* I, no 1; *Monasticon* IV, 40-1; D.Dumville, 'The Foundation of Cholsey Abbey' in idem *English Caroline Script and Monastic History* (1993) 79-85. For the earlier monasteries of Reading and Cholsey see P.Stafford, 'Cherchez la Femme: Missing Links in the Foundation of Reading Abbey' *History* 85 (2000) 4-27; R.H.D.Gem in *Ethelred the Unready* BAR 59 (1978) 107-9
130. C.Warren Hollister *Henry I* (2001) 413
131. K.J.Conant *Carolingian and Romanesque Architecture 800-1200* (2nd ed, rev 1978) 200; J.Hunt, letter describing 'Old Barn at Cholsey, Berks', *Gentleman's Magazine* 86 (Feb 1816) pl 1, 105; W.Horn, 'The Great Tithe Barn of Cholsey, Berks' *J Soc of Archit Historians* 22i (March 1963); T.Wright *History of Ludlow and Neighbourhood* (1852) 495 reports in an appendix, 'a great barne in Lempster fired by a comet, burned fifteen days'. His information came from parchment rolls of Mrs Davies of Croft Castle.
132. J.Evans *The Romanesque Architecture of the Order of Cluny* (1938) 16-32; K.J.Conant, 'The Theophany in the History of Church Portal Design' *Gesta* 15 (1976) 200
133. *Gesta Regum* 746-7
134. W.Farrar, 'An Outline Itinerary of Henry I' *Eng Hist R*, 33 (1919) 519-21; *Regesta Anglo-Normannorum* I, 165-6; J.B.Hurry *Reading Abbey* (1901) 40-1
135. *Brut sa* 1121
136. *RAC* I, pp13-19, no 1
137. B.R.Kemp, 'The Monastic Dean of Leominster' *Eng Hist R* 83 (July 1968) 505-15; J.Price *An Historical and Topographical Account of Leominster, and its Vicinity* (1795) 251-5; *Taxatio Ecclesiastica ... Auctoritate P. Nicholai IV c1291* Record Commission (1802) 173, 159; *Reg Bothe* (E.Foxe, 1535-8) 366
138. The first two cartularies are discussed in *RAC* II, pp1-8; *CR* 1231, 507; B.R.Kemp, 'The Foundation of Reading Abbey and the Growth of its Possessions and Privileges in the twelfth century' (unpublished University of Reading PhD thesis, 1966); idem (1988) see n125
139. *DBH* 1.10a-38
140. Domitian Aiii f118
141. HRO M 31/9/1: West *Herneys* 1334 ff100, 101; Ivington 1350 ff47; Stockton 1349 f10; Luston 1349 f9; Stoke 1349 f86 and see Ch 19
142. *RAC* I, no 2; H.M.Cam *Liberties and Communities in Medieval England* (Cambridge, 1963) 71-3, 109; *Rolls of the Justices in Eyre ... for Lincolnshire 1218-19 and Worcestershire 1221* ed D.M.Stenton, Selden Soc 53 (1934) xlvii, xlix; HRO M31/9/3 f15
143. Domitian Aiii, f59v; *RAC* I, no 354; *Monasticon* IV, 56 no II. For detailed discussions of the spiritualities of Leominster Priory, Kemp (1966), see n138, 151-210; idem (1988) in Blair, see n125, 83-95; idem, 'Hereditary Benefices in the Medieval English Church: A Herefordshire Example' *Bull Inst Hist Research* 43 (May 1970) 1-15
144. Blair (2001) in Malpas, see n77, 5; Kemp (1988) in Blair, see n125, 85, Fig 20
145. See p45; VCH *Hereford* I, 274-5
146. *RAC* I, nos 174, 340; Kemp (1988) in Blair, see n125, 83-96
147. *Monasticon* IV, 53-4; K.M.Morgan, 'An Edition of the Cartulary of Leominster Priory up to the mid Thirteenth Century' (University of Cardiff MA thesis, 1972) follows the old foliation; *RAC* I, pp1-13. Detailed discussion of the temporalities and spiritualities of Leominster Priory will be found in Kemp (1966) see n138
148. Domitian A.iii, f95; BL Egerton 3031, f63; Harley 1708, f17
149. Prior Walter's seal as papal judge delegate in 1220 is attached to TNA E 329/186. Luke 15:11, 'For whosoever exalteth himself shall be abased; and he that humbleth himself shall be exalted'; *Catalogue of Seals in the PRO: Monastic Seals* comp R.H.Ellis (1986) I, 51, M478; *Heads of Religious Houses in England and Wales, 940-1216* ed C.N.L.Brooke & V.London (1972) 42, 71
150. See p27; BL Domitian Aiii, f118; *RAC* I, no 340
151. J.Harper, 'Echoes from the Stones' in Malpas, see n3, 86
152. Blacklock, see n70, 57
153. Knowles (1963) see n123, 148-9
154. Muir (1988) see n6, nos 81, 71, 73
155. E.A.Freeman, 'Leominster Priory Church' *Archaeol Camb* NS 4 (1853) 9-33; idem, 'Excavations at Leominster Priory Church' *Archaeol Camb* NS 4 (1853) 180-8; idem, 'Excavations at Leominster Priory Church' *Archaeol J* 10

(1853) 109-15; idem, 'Excavations at Leominster Priory Church' *Ecclesiologist* 14 (1853) 143-9; *Hereford Times* 5 Feb 1853: 'Excavations in the Priory Garden ...'

156. S.Harrison & M.Thurlby, 'An Architectural History' in *A Definitive History of Abbey Dore* ed R.Shoesmith & R.Richardson (1997) figs 19, 25; RCHM I, dated plan at end of volume; M.F.Hearn, 'The Rectangular Ambulatory in English Mediaeval Architecture' *J Soc Archit Historians* 30 (1971) 187-208
157. C.F.Slade, 'Excavations at Reading Abbey, 1971-73' *Berks Archaeol J* 68 (1975-6) 29-70; 'Medieval Britain in 1971' *Medieval Archaeology* 15 (1971) 171, R.A.Rutland, 'revealed part of the east end ... of the abbey' and concludes 'the plan would thus match that at Leominster'
158. *RCHM* III, 111; E.A.Freeman *Archaeol J* 10 (1853) see n155, 111
159. Conant (1978) see n131, 139-53, 157-75 for the pilgrimage churches
160. M.Thurlby & R.Baxter, 'The Romanesque Abbey Church at Reading' *Windsor: Medieval Archaeology, Art and Architecture of the Thames Valley* BAA Conf Trans 25, ed L.Keen & E.Scarff (2002) 282-303; see p72 & n165
161. B.R.Kemp, 'The Miracles of the Hand of St James' *Berks Archaeol J* 65 (1970) p.1-19; idem *The Hand of St James at Reading Abbey* Reading Medieval Studies 16 (1990); K.Leyser, 'Frederick Barbarossa, Henry II and the hand of St James' *Eng Hist R* 90 (July, 1975) 481-506; F.Arnold-Foster *Studies in Church Dedications* 3 (1899) 17
162. C.Coates, see n127, 240-3; Hurry, see n134, 27-31;D.Bethell, 'The Making of a Twelfth-Century Relic Collection' in *Popular Belief and Practice* ed G.J.Cumming & D.Baker, Studies in Church History 9(1972) 63, n1&2; *RAC* I, nos 42, 43, 44, 46;
163. J.Hillaby, 'St Oswald, the Revival of Monasticism and the Veneration of the Saints ...' *Trans Worcs Archaeol Soc* 3S 16 (1998) 80, 109; *The Vita Wulfstani of William of Malmesbury* ed R.R.Dartington, Camden Soc 40 (1928) 203-4; A.T.Bannister *The Cathedral Church of Hereford. Its History and Constitution* (1924) 167-75; R.C.Finucane *Miracles and Pilgrims* (1977) Chs 4, 6, 10.
164. *Reg Swinfield* 124-5; *Monasticon* V, 56; G.H.Doble, 'The Leominster Relic List', *TWNFC* (1942) 58-65; Hillaby (1987) see n23, 625-8
165. BL Egerton 3031, ff6v-8v; T.Wright, (1843) see n93, 225-7; Bethell, see n162, 61-72; P.J.Geary *Furta Sacra: Theft of Relics in the Central Middle Ages* (rev ed, 1990)
166. *Reg Swinfield* 124-5
167. Domitian Aiii f74r; *Monasticon* IV, 56; J.Barrow *English Episcopal Acta VII: Hereford 1079-1234* (1993) no 32; J.Hillaby, 'The Saint that never Slept: Robert de Bethune, 1131-48' *Report of Friends of Hereford Cathedral* 46 (1980) 21-40; Blair (2001) see n77,
168. Domitian Aiii f74r; *Vita Wulfstani* see n 163, c10
169. Domitian Aiii f74v-75r; Shirley, see n101, 156-7; F.C.Cowley, 'A Note on the Discovery of St David's Body' *Bulletin Board of Celtic Studies* 19 (1960) 47-8
170. *L&P, HVIII* 7, no 1678; see p255
171. *CChR 1290*, 356; *Reg Trillek* i-iii, 96-7; Ker (1965) see n9, article 116; *Reg Spofford* 160-5
172. *Archaeol J* 41 (1884) 374-414; 42 (1885) 96-119, 215-46, 331-69, 440-68; 43 (1886) 53-88, 290-305, 403-22
173. See p159 & fig 15.11
174. M.R.James *Abbeys* (1926) 60
175. Domitian Aiii f74r; Monasticon IV, 56 no III; Barrow, see n167, no32
176. *RAC* I, nos 360, 364; *Reg Trefnant* 140
177. William of Wycumb, '*De Vita Roberti Betun Episcopi Herefordensis*' in *Anglia Sacra* 2, ed H.Wharton (1691) c21-3; 'The Anglo-Norman Chronicle of Wigmore Abbey' ed & trans J.C.Dickinson & P.T.Ricketts *TWNFC* 39iii (1969) 421-7
178. Blacklock, see n70, 61
179. G.F.Townsend *The Town and Borough of Leominster* (1863) includes a chapter, 209-28, on the priory church by E.A.Freeman. The nave arcade is described on 217
180. E.Roberts, 'On Leominster Priory Church' *J Brit Archaeol Ass* 27 (1871) 438-45
181. *RCHM*.III, 112; A.Clapham *English Romanesque Architecture after the Conquest* (1934) 79
182. J.Bony, 'French Influences on English Gothic Architecture' *J Warburg & Courtauld Institutes* 12 (1949) 5, n1; G.Zarnecki, 'The Romanesque Sculpture of the Welsh Marches' in *Medieval Art: Recent Perspectives* ed R.Owen Crocker & T.Graham (1998) 73; Conant (1978) see n131, 283-91; N. Pevsner *Herefordshire* Buildings of England (1963) 225, 23
183. *Congrès Archaéologique de France* 77 (1910) I *Angers et Saumur* 48-54; Hillaby (1987) see n23, 664-5, 48-54
184. *OV* VI, 278; *RRAN* II, nos 1580, 1581, 1687, 1691
185. J.T.Smith, 'The Norman Structure of Leominster Priory Church' *Ancient Monuments Soc Trans* 11 (1963) 97-108; A.H.S.Megaw, 'Byzantine Architecture and Decoration in Cyprus: Metropolitan or Provincial?' *Dumbarton Oaks Papers* 28 (1974) 77-9, plates 27, 29, 31; A.Stylianou & J.A.Stylianou *The Painted Churches of Cyprus* (1985) 382-94; J.P.McAleer *The Romanesque Church Façade in Britain* (1984) 597, n180; Pevsner *Herefordshire*, see n182, 225n. See also M.Thurlby's note, 'Leominster Priory' in Brit Archaeol Ass Conf Trans 15 (1995) see n48, 23-4
186. RCHM III, 222-3
187. J.T.Smith, see n185, 97-108; A.Clapham in *RCHM* III, 111; idem, see n181, 41, 61
188. G.Zarnecki *Regional Schools of English Sculpture in the Twelfth Century* unpublished London PhD thesis (1950) 358, 359 n1; *Cistercian Abbeys of Britain* ed D.Robinson (London, 1998) pp.113, 132-3, 140.
189. Thurlby & Baxter, see n160, 298-30
190. P.Kidson & P.Murray *A History of English Architecture* (1962) 37; J.P.McAleer, 'Southwell, Worksop, and Stylistic Tendencies in English Twelfth-Century Façade Design' in *Medieval Architecture and its Intellectual Context* ed E.Fernie & P.Crossley (1990) 61-72; *RCHM* II, 100-1
191. J.Hunt, 'Sculpture, Dates and Patrons: Dating the Herefordshire School of Sculpture' *Antiq J* 84 (2004) 360;

Zarnecki (1950) see n188, 358-61; Conant (1978), see n131, 204, 358-61

192. D.Kahn *Canterbury Cathedral and its Romanesque Sculpture* (1991) 48 fig 49; *Corpus of Anglo-Saxon Stone Sculpture IV. South-East England* ed D.Twiddle, M.Biddle & D.Kjölbye-Biddle (1995) 179-81, ill 183-91
193. D.M.Robinson *Chepstow Castle* (1986) 5; R.C.Turner et al, 'The Great Tower, Chepstow Castle, Wales' *Antiq J* 84 (2004) 223-317; see also D.Bates, 'William the Conqueror, William fitz Osbern and Chepstow Castle' and R.Turner et al, 'The Norman Great Tower' in *Chepstow Castle, its History and Buildings* ed R.Turner & A.Johnson (2006) 15-42; E.Fernie *The Architecture of Norman England* (2000) 82; G.Coppack, 'The Round Chapel of St Mary Magdalene' in *Ludlow Castle: Its History and Buildings* ed R.Shoesmith & A.Johnson (2000) 145-54
194. E.Gethyn-Jones *The Dymock School of Architecture* (1979) 17-19
195. K.J.Conant, 'Supplement to Cluny: Les Eglises ...:' *Speculum* 45 (i) (1970) pl XVI showing full-size reconstruction of Cluny sanctuary at Fogg Museum; Conant (1976) see n132, figs 10 & 11
196. BL Cotton Vespasian Aviii f2v in *The Golden Age of Ango-Saxon Art, 966-1066* ed J.Backhouse et al (1984) no 26, pl IV; *The Church of Haghia Sophia at Trebizond* ed D.Talbot Rice (1968) 177-8; Stylianou, see n185, 157-85. George Zarnecki draws attention to a 'late Anglo-Saxon wooden casket in the Cleveland (Ohio) Museum of Art on which an Ascension is carved, and above Christ in a mandorla supported by four angels, a separate scene' in 'The Future of Shobdon Arches' *J Brit Archaeol Ass* 141 (1993) 87 n8
197. T.S.R.Boase *English Art 1100-1216* (1953) 83; C.Heighway & R.Bryant *The Golden Minster... of St Oswald at Gloucester* CBA Research Report 117 (1999) 154-7, fig 4.7; M.P.Brown *The Book of Cerne* (1996) 119-20, 174
198. A de Vita et al *Libya: The lost cities of the Roman Empire* (Cologne, 1999) Lepcis Severan Basilica, 122-7; R,Cramp *Corpus of Anglo-Saxon Stone Sculpture. County Durham and Northumberland* (1984) nos 525 & 526, I.i 16, 114-15, I.ii, pl 98, nos 525-6; D.M.Wilson, *Anglo-Saxon Art from the Seventh Century to the Norman Conquest* (1984) 54-6, Figs 49, 50, 74, 78, 79; W.G.Collingwood, 'Anglian and Anglo-Danish Sculpture in the West Riding' *Yorks Archaeol J* 23ii (1914) 133-5, 224-6; idem *Northumbrian Crosses of the Pre-Norman Age* (1927, rep 1989) 41-2
199. T.S.R.Boase, 'Fontevrault and the Plantagenets' *J Brit Archaeol Ass* 3S 34 (1971) 1-10
200. William of Newburgh, *Historia* ed R.Howlett RS 82i (1884) 105; W.L.Warren *Henry II* (19797) 60-2
201. McAleer, see n190, 61-72; Sims-Williams, see n36, 91, 157-8, 169-70
202. *John of Worcester* III, *sa* 1139-41, 269-79
203. *Letters and Charters of Gilbert Foliot* ed A.Morey & C.N.L.Brooke (1967) 390, no 340; *RAC* I, no 328; BL Harley MS 1708, f120v; full text, D.Walker, 'Charters of the Earldom of Hereford, 1095-1201' *Camden Soc* 4S 1 (1964) no 25; *Monasticon* IV, 56
204. See Ch 1, pp5-10
205. L.Fullbrook-Leggatt, 'The River Twyver and the Fullbrook' *Trans Bristol & Gloucs Archaeol Soc* 83 (1964) 78-84
206. E.Ekwall *English River-Names* (1968) 310; *Historic towns Atlas* 1, ed M.D.Lobel (1969) Reading maps 2 & 3; J.Bond, 'Monastic Water Management in Great Britain' in *Monastic Archaeology* ed G.Keevil, M.Aston & T.Hall (2001) 93-9
207. Busby et al, see n7
208. R.Shoesmith, 'Archaeology, 2000: Leominster, Old Priory' *TWNFC* 50i (2000) 101
209. *Rule* c22
210. J.P.Greene *Medieval Monasteries* (1992) 119-22 & figs 2 & 54
211. Busby et al, see n7
212. D.Knowles *The Monastic Constitutions of Lanfranc* (1951) 1-49; M.Gibson *Lanfranc of Bec* (1978) 146, 173-4; A.Coates *English Medieval Books: The Reading Abbey Collections from Foundation to Dispersal* (1999) 118-19. William of Wycomb will have copied details of library procedure in the *Customary* recorded by him with a stylus in the *Collations* of Odo of Cluny, see p143
213. *Rule* 315
214. D.L.Brown & D.Wilson, 'Leominster Old Priory: Recording of Standing Buildings and Excavations, 1979-80' *Archaeol J* 151 (1994) 308-68; *RCHM* III, 114-15; W.Stukeley *Itinerarium Curiosum* (2nd ed, 1776) I, 72, pl 1
215. R.K.Morris, 'Mouldings and Other Architectural Elements' in Brown & Wilson (1994), see n214, 330-3; Hillaby (2006) see n120, 108-14
216. *Cal Papal Registers I. 1198-1304* ed W.H.Bliss, PRO (1893) 282
217. Especially amongst the Benedictines 'we find the superior's apartments constitute a distinct building, nearly always close to the conventual dormitory and reredorter', J.C.Dickinson *Monastic Life in Medieval England* (1961) 42
218. Brown & Wilson, see n214, 342
219. Knowles (1963) see n123, Ch 20 esp 350
220. *Cal Liberate Rolls* 1232, 191
221. R.W.Morant *The Monastic Gatehouse* (1995) 24; Blacklock, see n70, 68-9
222. Domitian Aiii, f118
223. M.Gelling *Place-Names of Berkshire* 1 (1973) 171-2. For subsequent history, Blacklock, see n70, 69, 72-3; Morant, see n221, 6-12, 37-41
224. *CCR* 1231, 507; Blacklock, see n70, 193-4. The old gaol was pulled down in 1753, when a new gaol was built in New Street; HRO Borough Chamber Minutes III, 23 April 1753
225. *CCR* 1248, 91; 1275, 206; 1282, 172; 1346, 8-9
226. *CPR* 1293, 7; 1400, 229; *L&P, HVIII* 4ii, no 4313 (14); 5, no 80 (34)
227. *CPR*, 1339, 223
228. HRO M31/8/1 f115v
229. HRO M31/8/1 f115v

230. Stukeley, see n214, I, 72; Price, see n137, 80; Blacklock, see n70, 70-1
231. *RAC* I, no 224
232. Domitian Aiii ff67v-8v; Barrow, see n167, nos 301-3
233. *Leland's Itinerary* see n11, II, 70
234. Domitian Aiii ff113r-16v
235. Domitian Aiii ff112r-15r
236. J.R.H.Moorman *Church Life in the Thirteenth Century* (1946) 357; 14 College Green, Gloucester, listed SO 8318 NW
237. W.H.StJohn Hope, 'Kirkstall Abbey' *Proc Thoresby Soc* 16 (1907) 60-3 & Historical Ground Plan; idem, 'Fountains Abbey' *Yorks Archaeol J* 59 (1900) 388-93; G.Coppack, 'Thornholme Priory: the development of the monastic Outer Court' in *The Archaeology of Rural Monasteries* ed R.Gilchrist & H.Mitum, BAR Brit S 203 (1989) 185-222; J.P.Greene *Medieval Monasteries* (1992) 154-7
238. Hurry, see n134, 40-2
239. *CPR* 1223, 386; 1226, 58, 81; 1232, 4; 1233, 25; *CCR* 1231, 506; 1233, 262, 263; *LibR* 1232, 191
240. J.Hillaby *St Katherine's Hospital, Ledbury c1230-1547* (2003) 43; D.Walker *Charters of the Earldom of Hereford*, Camden Misc 22, Camden Soc 4S 1 (1964) no 52 not to be confused with the earl's much more important grant of Broadward, see *RAC* I, nos 327, 328
241. HRO M31/9/116b; M31/9/115a
242. *CCR* 1318, 599; 1376, 464; 1384, 448; *L&P, HVIII* 4(i), no 4096
243. HRO M31/9 f115; M/31/9 f116; M31/9/120; Price, see n137, 164-5; Townsend, see n179, 41-2; Hurry, see n134, 73-4
244. J.Bond *Monastic Landscapes* (2004) 183
245. J.H.Tillotson *Monastery and Society in the late Middle Ages: Selected Account Rolls from Selby Abbey 1398-1537* (1988) 23, 179-87, 189-91
246. HRO M31/9/1 f59; *L&P, HVIII* 15, nos 63, 117; Ch 19
247. Knowles (1963) see n123, 456-65; I.Kershaw *Bolton Priory: The Economy of a Northern Monastery, 1286-1325* (1973) 148-58; Tillotson, see n245, 161-3, 169-71. 190-1
248. *DBH* 1.10a, 1.21, 1.28; *RAC* I, nos 328, 330; Busby et al, see n7
249. *Rule* 66
250. D.Knowles *The Religious Orders in England. III: The Tudor Age* (1979) 260-4
251. Kershaw, see n247, 133; for Redyng see n241
252. HRO M31/9 f37
253. *L&P HVIII* 16, no 947 (21); Townsend, see n179, 84 quoting T.Wright (1852) see n131, 495
254. W.Horn, see n131
255. S 677; *EHD* I, 514-16; Lord Rennell, 'The Boundaries of the Saxon Manor of Staunton-on-Arrow in a Charter of King Edgar of 985' *TWNFC* 36iii (1960) 279-91
256. HRO M31/9/4/1-5; but in 1572 a rent of £10 13s 4d and a fine of £42 13s 4d was paid by Francis Lovell for the two 'Marshe mylls' in Stockton *halimoot*, *CPR* 1572, no 2529
257. J.P.Greene, see n237, 98-9; StJohnHope, see n237, 63 & plan; HRO M31/9/1 f116r
258. Tillotson, see n245, 143. Selby pittancer's accounts for 1441-2 describe the renewal of a malt kiln house, 106-7. Blacklock, see n70, 72-3 refers to 'a Kilgo or large Kiln for drying Hops ... with a wide ditch along the east side' (of the Grange).
259. J.Bond, 'Production and Consumption of Food and Drink in the Medieval Monastery' in Keevil et al, see n206, 65-8; idem (2004), see n244, 153-70; Tillotson, see n245, 163-4, 192-3
260. C.H.I.Homes, 'Herefordshire Vineyards' *TWNFC* 41i (1973) 9-13; Tillotson, see n245, 72-3; M.Faraday *Ludlow 1085-1660. A Social, Economic and Political History* (1991) 107; Hillaby (2005) see n25, 67-8. For general accounts: Bond (2001) see n206, 68-70; idem (2004) see n244, 165-70
261. Tillotson, see n245, 196, 201, 220, 233, 254
262. *Welsh Verse* trans T.Conran (2003) 183-6
263. Reg *Trillek* 109-10; HRO A63/1/305; Bond (2004), see n244, 153-65
264. HRO M31/9/1 f5v; J.Langdon *Horses, Oxen and Technological Innovation* (1986) 142-56
265. BL Egerton 3031 f12v; *English Benedictine Libraries: The Shorter Catalogue* ed R.Sharpe, J.P.Carley, R.M.Thomson & A.G.Watson (1996) B71, B75, B76 lists all the Reading and Leominster items, as does A.Coates, see n212, 25-36; S.Barfield, 'Lord Fingall's Cartulary of Reading Abbey' *Eng Hist R* 3 (1888) 113-25
266. *Reg Trillek* 96-7
267. Sharpe et al, see n265, 454-63; A.Coates, see n212, 25-36. An excellent description and discussion of Reading Abbey library's catalogue and books is provided by C.de Hamel *A History of Illuminated Manuscripts* (1986) 76-81
268. Muir (1988) see n6, nos 81, 71, 73, 63; Sharpe et al, see n265, no 65
269. Numbers in brackets indicate line of entry, starting with coloured capital letter, in Fig 13.1; those in 2nd column are shown as eg 2.1; Sharpe et al, see n265, no 39
270. Sharpe et al, see n265, B74.1-22, B75 nos 2, 14, 13; J.R.Liddell, 'Some notes on the Library of Reading Abbey' *Bodleian Quarterly Record* 8 (1935) 385-416
271. *Rule* c42; Sharpe et al, see n265, 33-41
272. Eusebius *History of the Church* trans G.A.Williamson (1965) 239-40
273. L.Bouyer *The Spirituality of the New Testament and the Fathers* (1968) 282
274. C.Stancliffe, 'Sedulius *fl.* 7th-8th cent' in *ODNB* (OUP, 2004) (http://www.oxforddnb.com/view/article/50134, accessed 1 June 2006)
275. L.M.Davies, 'Sedulius Scottus *fl.* 840x51-860x74' in *ODNB* (OUP, 2004) (http://www.oxforddnb.com/view/article/50134, accessed 1 June 2006)
276. Lapidge (1993) see n105, 27, 33; M.Gretsch, 'Aethelwold's translation of the *Regula Sancti Benedicti* and its Latin Exemplar' *ASE* 3 (1974) 125-51
277. D.Dumville *English Caroline Script and Monastic History* (1993) 8 n4, 10-11
278. A.Gransden *Historical Writing in England c550-c1307* (1974) 297-307; *Bibliotheca Hagiographica Latina* II

(Brussels, 1990-1) 1184-93

279. Muir (1988) see n6, no 70; *Leechdoms, wortcunning and starcraft of Early England* ed I.Cockayne, RS 35 (1863-7) II, 294-7; Sharpe et al, see n265, no 40
280. S 167; *Landboc sive Registrum de Wincelcumba* ed D.Royce, I (1892) 18-21; W.Levison *England and the Continent in the Eighth Century* (1946) 253-9
281. Finberg, see n11, 200-16
282. Sharpe et al, see n265, no 16, suggest *The Guthlac Role* ed G.F.Warner, Roxburghe Club (1928) or the 11th-century Old English *Life*, BL MS Cotton Vespasian, Dxxi from Rochester Cathedral
283. Lapidge (1991) see n63, 159 line 69, 166 line 197; Hillaby (1998) see n163, 96-105
284. Muir (1988) see n6, p5; *Reg Spofford* 162. See p73
285. Lapidge (1991) see n63, 159 line 81, 167 line 260; R.Rushforth, see n59, 32-3 and Table V
286. Muir (1988) see n6, 7; Lapidge (1991) see n63, 166 line 213
287. *Reg Swinfield*, 124; Muir (1988) see n6, nos 98, 103; BL Egerton 3031, f6v; T.Wright (1843) see n93, 226
288. A.Coates, see n212, 116 n19, 169; H.E.Allen *Writings ascribed to Richard Rolle of Hampole and Materials for his Biography* (1927)
289. N.R.Ker *Medieval Libraries of Great Britain* (2nd ed, 1964) 114, and *Supplement to 2nd edition*, ed A.G.Watson (1987) 44; F.Madan, 'The Literary Work of a Benedictine Monk at Leominster in the Thirteenth Century' *Bodleian Quartlery Record* 4 (1923-5) 168-70; A.Coates, see n212, 61-5
290. BL MS Royal 8 Exviii ff94-6; F.Liebermann '*Annales Radingenses*' in *Ungedruckte anglo-normannische Geschichtsquellen* (Strassburg, 1879) 9-12; G.F.Warner & J.P.Gilson *Catalogue of Western Manuscripts in the Old Royal and Kings Collections* 1 (1921) 260; 'Annals of Tewkesbury' in *Annales Monastici* ed H.R.Luard, RS 36, 1 (1864) 43-5; Gransden, see n278, 405 n13, 29 n6, 30 n9
291. N.R.Ker *Medieval Manuscripts in British Libraries* II (1977) 934-9; R.M.Woolley *Catalogue of the Manuscripts in the Lincoln Cathedral Library* (1927) 102-17; R.M.Thomson *Catalogue of the Manuscripts of Lincoln Cathedral Chapter Library* (1989) 115-20: MSS 149 &150; N.R.Ker, 'Medieval Manuscripts' in *A Catalogue of Gloucester Cathedral Library* comp S.M.Eward (1972) no 1
292. B. Kemp, 'The Seals of Reading Abbey' *Reading Medieval Studies* 14 (1988) 139-62; Hurry, see n134, 94-8; R.H.Ellis, see n149, 75. There is a fine Reading Abbey seal at Hereford Cathedral Library, J.W.Leigh, 'Archives and Seals of Hereford Cathedral' *TWNFC* (1901) 112 & figs 21
293. The contents of Harley 978 are listed in A.Coates, see n212, 162-3
294. A.Taylor & A.Coates, 'The Date of the Reading Calendar and the Summer Canon' *Notes and Queries* 243 (1998) 22-4; P.M.Lefferts, 'Two English Motets on Simon de Montfort' *Early Music History* I (1981) 203-5
295. C.Hohler, 'Reflections on some manuscripts containing 13th-century polyphony' *J Plainsong and Medieval Music Soc* 1 (1978) 2-38
296. For E.Sanders, 'Wycombe, W. de' in *New Groves Dictionary of Music and Musicians* 2nd ed, ed S.Sadie & J.Tyrrell (2001) William of Wicumbe was 'at Leominster probably in the later 1270s'. In this he is followed by N. Losseff *The Best Concords: Polyphonic Music in Thirteenth-Century Britain* (New York, 1994) 68 who refers to 'both men returning to Reading from their service at Reading's cell at Herefordshire'.
297. The responsories are listed in P.M.Lefferts, *The Motet in England in the Fourteenth Century* (1986) 162-5, Table 26 'The *LoHa* Index'; B.Schofield, 'The Provenance and Date of *Sumer is icumen in*' *Music Review* 9 (1948) 81-6; Hohler, see n295, 13; L.Dittmer 'An English Discantum Volumen' *Musica disciplina* 8 (1954) 19-58
298. Hohler, see n295, 19 and Losseff, see n 296, 64-5, 74, 82; *RAC* II, nos 667-87, 786-94; Dittmer, see n297, 19-45
299. A.Coates, see n212, 61-5. The death of 'Th. then dean' in 1245 is recorded by the brief annals in Oxford, Worcester College MS 213; Sharpe et al, see n265, 461; Kemp (1968) see n137, 507 quoting BL Cotton Domitian Aiii f96v; Madan, see n289, 168
300. M.Bukofzer '*Sumer is icumen in*: A Revision', *California University Publications in Music* 2 (Berkeley, 1944) 79-114; A.Coates, see n212, 61-5
301. *Reg Cantilupe* 265
302. See n297 on the responsories
303. Schofield, see n297, 83; A.Coates, see n212, 163
304. D.Wulstan, '*Sumer is icumen in* – a perpetual puzzle canon?' *Plainsong and Medieval Music* 9i (2000) 1-17
305. See p158
306. Dittmer, see n297, 37. His belief that W de Wic was the Worcester canon, Winchcombe, led Dittmer to claim that this 'evidence seems to show conclusively that this type of Alleluia (setting) came from Leominster/Worcester and was represented also in Reading'. Giraldus Cambrensis *Opera* VI (1869) 189-90; Wulstan, see n304, 12-13, 'East & West' 62-93; Losseff, see n296, 69
307. J.Handschin, 'The Summer Canon and its background' *Musica Disciplina* 3 (1949) 55-94 at 65; *The Lais of Marie de France* trans G.S.Burgess & K.Busby (2nd ed, 1999) 24-5
308. Domitian Aiii, f62v-63r; *RAC* I, nos 358, 359
309. Domitian Aiii, f69r; *RAC* I, no 364
310. For detailed discussion of the priory's chapelries, Kemp (1988) in Blair, see n125, 83-95 and idem (1966), see n138, 198-210; Domitian Aiii, 67v-18r; Cotton MS Vespasian xxv, 220r-21v; RCHM III 147-8, 77-8, 43, 25
311. Hillaby (2005) see n25, ch 4; J.Bilson, 'Notes on Blyth Priory' *Yorks Archaeol J* 20 (1909) 447-54; for Dorchester Abbey, J.Sherwood & N.Pevsner *Oxfordshire* Buildings of England (1974) 579-80; F.H.Fairweather, 'Some additions to the plan of the Benedictine Priory Church of St Mary, Blyth, Notts' *Antiq J* 6 (1926) 36-42; VCH *Nottingham* 2 (1910) 83-8
312. A.G.Edouart, 'The Priory Church of Leominster' *TWNFC* (1892) 289; Domitian Aiii, f69v; *Monasticon* IV, 57

313. E.Sears *The Ages of Man: Medieval Interpretations of the Life Cycle* (1986) 54-63, 144-53
314. G.McN.Rushforth, 'Wheel of the Ten Ages of Life in Leominster Church' *Proc Soc Antiq* 2S 26 (1914) 47-60; BL Arundel MS 83 f126v; L.F.Sandler *The psalter of Robert de Lisle in the British Library* (1999 ed) 40, pl 4; A.Malpas, 'The Wheel of Life Painting in Leominster Priory Church' in Malpas, see n3, 89-98; R.E.Kraske, 'Piers Plowman and Local Iconography' in *J Warburg & Courtauld Inst* 3 (1968) 164-7
315. D.Verey & A.Brooks *Gloucestershire 2: The Vale and the Forest of Dean* Buildings of England (2002) 554
316. *RAC* I, nos 62, 63
317. D.Knowles *Religious Orders* 1 (1948) see n250, 55-63; Knowles (1963) see n123, 431-9
318. *CPR* 1223, 386; 1226, 58, 81; 1231, 506; 1232, 4, 25; *CLR* 1232, 191; *CCR* 1233, 262-3
319. *Monasticon* I, 539
320. *RAC* I, nos 73, 82
321. *CPR* 1275, 81, 128; 1285, 197; RAC I, nos 83, 92; *Re21Swinfield* 165-8
322. J.Hillaby 'Aaron le Blund and the last Decades of the Hereford Jewry, 1253-90' *TWNFC* 46iii (1990) 462-70; *Reg Swinfield* 168-9; *RAC* I, nos 92, 93, 98, 99, 100; Hurry, see n134, 37-8; *Documents... General and Provincial Chapters of the English Black Monks 1215-1540* III, ed W.A.Pantin, Camden Soc 3S (1937) no 210
323. Knowles (1963) see n123, 372-4, 653; C.R.Cheney *Episcopal Visitation of Monasteries in the Thirteenth Century* (2nd ed, 1983) 17-36
324. *Reg Cantilupe* 46-9, 116-17
325. I am grateful to Christopher Dalton for sharing his expert knowledge on this subject.
326. *Reg Cantilupe* 46-9
327. *Calendar of Ancient Correspondence concerning Wales* ed J.G.Edwards (1935) 69; *Reg Cantilupe* 95, 263-5, 269-70, 296
328. *Reg Cantilupe* 79, 81-8; *Records of Reading* ed J.M.Guilding, 1 (1892) 280-2; N.C.Trenholme *The English Monastic Boroughs* (Columbia, Mo, 1927) 19-22
329. *Reg Cantilupe* 218; *Reg Swinfield* 31-2
330. For the complex story of the sale of May see I.B.Cowan & D.E.Easson *Medieval Religious Houses, Scotland* (2nd ed, 1976) 59-60
331. *Reg Swinfield* 27-32, 38-41; *Reg Cantilupe* xiv, n2, 263-7, 269-72
332. *Reg Cantilupe* 200-2, 265-7, 296
333. For the conflict with Peckham, R.C.Finucane 'The Cantilupe-Pecham controversy' in *St Thomas Cantilupe, Bishop of Hereford: Essays in his honour* ed M.Jancey (1982) 103-24 and D.L.Douie *Archbishop Pecham* (1952) 192-201
334. *Register of John Peckham* ed C.Trice Martin, RS 77ii (1883) 505-7, 624-5
335. *RCHM* III, 115, pl 140 and J.W.Tonkin, 'The Forbury Chapel, Leominster' *TWNFC* 40ii (1971) 265-7 provide architectural descriptions. For completion Martin, see n334, 624-5
336. *Reg Swinfield* 14-15, 108-10
337. Domitian Aiii, ff66v-67r; *RAC* I, nos 361, 362, 363; *Reg Swinfield* 30; Barrow, see n167, nos 308, 362
338. *Reg Swinfield* 131-2, 149-50
339. Douie, see n333, 156-7; J.R.H.Moorman *Church Life in England in the Thirteenth Century* (Cambridge, 1946) 343-4
340. A.Coates, see n212, 120; *RAC* I, p28
341. *RAC* I, no 361; Barrow, see n167, xlvi-iii
342. *RAC* I, no 362-4; Barrow, see n167, no 308; *Reg Swinfield* 30, 64
343. *CCR* 1233, 255; *CPR* 1268-9, 253, 265, 308, 319, 328, 331, 349, 369, 415, 437; H&DCA, 2647
344. *Reg Trillek* 303-4; *Reg Gilbert* 33-4, 40-1, 59-60; *CPR* 1384, 454; HRO M31/9/1 f129; *CCR* 1384, 363, 593; L&P HVIII, 3, no 2415
345. See pp13-14; Hillaby (2005) see n25, 108; *Bromyard: A Local History* ed J.Hillaby & E.Pearson (1970) 1-2, Map 1 & Pl 1; Hillaby (2003) see n240, 62-4
346. J.Hillaby, 'The Boroughs of the Bishops of Hereford in the late 13th century, with reference to Ledbury' TWNFC (1970) 10-35; idem (2005) see n25, Chapters 1-6
347. *RAC* I, no 34; *Rot Litt Claus* I (1218) 355; *Curia Regis Rolls* 14, no 595
348. Domitian Aiiiff 119r, 120v; D.Walker, 'Hereford and the Laws of Breteuil' *TWNFC* 40i (1970) 55-65; Hillaby (2006) see n120, fig 5.3, 96-103, 105-6
349. A.Ballard *British Borough Charters 1042-1216* (1913) 30, 44, 68, 104 for the early charters of Pembroke, Haverford, Drogheda, Trim and Kells; for Drogheda, Trim and Kells *Chartae, Privilegia et Immunitates: Transcripts of Charters etc ... to Bodies Corporate (in Ireland)* Irish Record Commission (Dublin, 1829-30) 10; G.MacNiocaill *Na Burgéisí* I (Dublin, 1964) 74-5, 124-5, 172-3, 327 and the context J.Hillaby, 'Colonisation, crisis management and debt: Walter de Lacy in the Lordship of Meath' *Ríocht na Midhe* 8iv (1992/3) 25-9
350. M.R.G.Conzen, 'The Use of Town Plans in the Study of Urban History' in *The Study of Urban History* ed H.J.Dyos (1968) 113-30; idem, 'Alnwick: a study in town plan analysis' in *Trans Institute of Brit Geographers* 27 (1960) 3-48
351. Hillaby (1970) see n346, 10-35
352. For the topography of Reading *Historic Towns Atlas* 1 (1969) ed M.D.Lobel, 'Reading' and C.Coates' 1802 plan of Reading (Fig 16.1). The market stalls or booths came to be referred to as *selda* or *schopa*. There are references to these at Reading in *RAC* I, 844, 861, 865, 875, 878, 911, and in the *Liber Cartarum Capellae Beatae Maria Monachorum Leomestrie*, HRO M31/8, see p188
353. Domitian Aiii ff101v-2r, grant by Philip Talecurteys of a burgage in West and in New Street; Blacklock, see n70, 154-6
354. HD&CA 2181 provides the date 1186; illustrated in Hillaby (2005) see n25, 30
355. HRO M31/9/1 f4; Domitian Aiii ff 93v, 100, 122, 125-6; A.Ballard & J.Tait *British Borough Charters 1216-1307* (1923) 70-84; HRO Leominster Enclosure Act 1808; Ballard, see n349, 63

356. According to J.H.Bloom *English Seals* (1906) 221 the iconography of the Borough seal is 'typically 13th century', but lettering is not thoroughly reliable, P.M.Barnes & L.C.Hector *Guide to Seals in the Public Record Office* (2nd edn 1968) 22-3
357. *Red Book* HRO HE/1/133677 ff123-7; Hillaby (2005) see n25, 31, 36
358. *RAC* I, no 2
359. *RAC* I, no 659; VCH *Berkshire* I (1972) 63-4
360. Townsend, see n179, 51-2; HRO M31/9 f129
361. E.M.Carus Wilson, 'An Industrial Revolution of the Thirteenth Century' *Economic History Review*11 (1941) 39-60 omits Leominster from her list of fulling mills before the reign of Henry III; *Agrarian History of England and Wales, 1042-1350* ed H.E.Hallam (1988) 668-77 at 669
362. *RAC* I, no224; Domitian Aiii f46, charter of abbot of Reading leasing the mill to Philip Marshall; E.J.Kealey *Harvesting the air: windmill pioneers in twelfth-century England* (1986) 207, n11; TNA CP 40/41; RCHM III, no 20 on map p117
363. *FR* 1305, 520; *CCR* 1337, 149; *CPR* 1337, 480-3; E.B.Fryde, 'The Wool Accounts of William de la Pole' in idem *Studies in Medieval Trade and Finance* (1983) IX, 9; T.H.Lloyd *The Movement of Wool Prices in Medieval England* Ec Hist R, Supplement 6 (1973) 9-13; *CCR* 1342, 505
364. *History and Municipal Documents of Ireland* ed J.T.Gilbert, RS 53 (1870) 3-48; *Register of the Abbey of St Thomas, Dublin* ed J.T.Gilbert, RS 94 (1889) 109, 203, 383, 391, 404
365. HRO M31/9/3 ff17, 19; *CPR* 1294, 113; *Calendar of Inquisitions Misc* II, no 1065
366. For the Marian charter, *CPR* 1554, 395-8; for members for Leominster borough, *History of Parliament: House of Commons, 1386-1421* 4 vols (1992) ed J.S.Roskell et al. Vol 1, 436-8 discusses Leominster constituency; Vols 2-4 provide brief biographies of members. For the subsequent period, J.C.Wedgwood *Biographies of the Members of the Commons House, 1439-1509* (1936). The names of electors, returning officers etc, from 1422, are in TNA C219/-; R.&C. Botzum *The 1675 Thomas Blount Manuscript History of Herefordshire* (Lapidge Publications HR1 2LR, nd) 21. Further evidence as to the borough oligarchy can be found in the details of commissioners to collect the lay subsidy in the Calendars of Fine rolls.
367. *Reg Mascall* 155
368. *Reg Mascall* 146, 149, 153, 155; see p192
369. HRO M31/9/1 f5 58a, 3, 91b
370. HRO M31/9/1 ff 2, 47a, 104; Price, see n137, 214-15
371. For Blount of Orleton, Botzum, see n366, 17 and HRO B56/12 and *The Correspondence of Thomas Blount (1618-1679) a Recusant Antiquary* ed T.C.G.Bongaerts (Amsterdam, 1978)
372. *Pleas before the King or his Justices, 1198-1212* I, ed D.M.Stenton, Selden Soc 67 (1948) 55-8; R.B.Pugh *Imprisonment in Medieval England* (1968) 90, 93, 100
373. For Iter rolls from 20 Nov 1291-19 Nov 1292, HRO M31/9/3 ff12-42; HRO M31/9/3 ff 15
374. HRO M31/9/3 ff 12, 13, 16
375. HRO M31/9/3 f28; Price, see n137, 211-13
376. HRO M31/9/1 f2; Price, see n137, 211-15; *Monasticon* IV, 59
377. *RAC* I, no 136
378. T.Rymer; *Foedera* Ii (1816) 107-8
379. Domitian Aiii, ff73v, 74v; Oxford, Worcester College MS 213; A.Coates, see n212, 71, 155 (no 62)
380. J.E.Lloyd (1939) see n29, II, 669-76; *CCR* 1231, 588
381. Domitian Aiii f76v; *Monasticon* IV, 56 trans in Townsend, see n179, 269; 'Annals of Tewkesbury', see n290, 80. See p137
382. For the role of de Lacy and the politics of Herefordshire in this era J.Hillaby, 'The Hereford Jewry, 1179-1290. Part II: The Clients of the Jewish Community, 1179-1253' *TWNFC* 45(i) (1985) 210-39; J.E.Lloyd (1939) see n29, II, 670-1
383. *FR* 1305, 520; for the Moniwords Hillaby (1990), see n322, 461-2, 464-5; R.Johnson *The Ancient Customs of the City of Hereford* (1882) 230
384. Shirley, see n101, 156-7
385. *Rot Litt Claus* I, 355b; *Curia Regis Rolls* 14 (1961) 595; *CCR* 1237, 2-3; *CChR* 1335, 342
386. *Rot Litt Claus* I, 390b; *Monasticon* IV, 42, no xi; 57, xii; *RAC* I, no 72; *CChR* 1281, 253; *CChR* 1282, 261; *Placitorium ... Abbreviatio* (Record Commission, 1811); *CChR* 1290, 356
387. J.Hillaby, 'The Jewish Community at Hereford and its Clients, 1179-1253' *TWNFC* 44iii (1984) 358-419; idem (1990) see n322, 482-3, 486
388. *Annales Monastici*, ed H.R.Luard, RS 36, IV (1869) 448-9; *Flores Historiarum* II, ed H.R.Luard, RS 95 (1890) 486-7; *Metrical Chronicle of Robert of Gloucester* ed W.A.Wright, RS 86 (1887) II, lines 11062-107, 11138-85, 11234-307; *CPR* 1265, 425; *CCR* 1265, 115
389. *Cal Misc Inq* I, no 291; F.Noble, 'Herefordshire and Simon de Montfort: 1265' *TWNFC* 38ii (1965) 111-18
390. *CPR* 1265, 425; 1263, 299; *CCR* 1265, 115
391. TNA KB 26/174 & 175; *Plac Abbrev* see n386, 159; Johnson, see n383, 79: the visit of John le Gaunter, chief bailiff of Hereford, to negotiate in 1287
392. *RAC* I, no 72; BL Harley MS 1708, f120r; *CChR* 1282, 261; *Plac Abbrev*, see n386, 206; *CChR* 1281, 253; *CChR* 1290, 356
393. Faraday, see n260, 133 & n200; *CPR* 1349, 319; J.Bathhurst & E.J.L.Cole, 'Leominster Fair, 1556' *TWNFC* 42i (1976) 72-88
394. R.M.Haines *The Church and Politics in 13th-century England. The career of Adam de Orleton c1275-1345* (1978) 143 &n43
395. *CCR* 1280, 10; J.Barker *The Tournament in England* (1986) 53, 71, 95, 145-9
396. Barker, see n395, 66-7; J.E.Morris *The Welsh Wars of Edward I* (repr 1969) 181, 306
397. J.G.Edwards, see n327 (1935) 126-7; *Calendar Welsh Rolls* PRO, 1282, 276; 1283, 281; R.R.Davies *The Age of Conquest: Wales 1063-1415* (1991) 349-53; J.E.Lloyd (1939) see n29, II, 761-4

398. R.R.Davies (1991), see n397, 364-5, 368-70, 386; *History of the King's Works* I, ed H.M.Colvin (1963) 358, 369n, 381, 397n, 398; *Reg Swinfield* 443-5; *Reg Orleton* 51-2; *CPR* 1317, 659, 664 *Le Neve: Fasti Ecclesiae Anglicanae, 1300-1541. II Herefordshire Diocese* comp J.M.Horn (1962) 17
399. See pp229-31
400. Pevsner *Herefordshire*, see n182, 226; Freeman (1863) in Townsend, see n179, 224
401. *Wells Cathedral: A History* ed L.S.Colchester (1982) 73; RCHM *City of Oxford* (1939) plates 92 & 94
402. R.K.Morris, 'Decorated Architecture in Herefordshire: Sources, Workshops, Influence', unpublished London University PhD (1972), copy in Hereford Cathedral Library; idem, 'The Local Influence of Hereford Cathedral in the Decorated Period' *TWNFC* 41i (1973) 48-67; idem, 'Ball-flower Work in Gloucester and its Vicinity' in Brit Archaeol Ass Conf Trans 7: *Medieval Art and Archaeology at Gloucester and Tewkesbury* (1985) 93-8
403. C.A.Buckler, 'Notes on Reading Abbey', BL Add MS 36400 quoted in C.F.Slade, 'Excavations at Reading Abbey, 1971-73' *Berks Archaeol J* 68 (1975-6) 42, 47, 50
404. Domitian Aiii 200r. Charters relating to the grants to the conventual Lady Chapel will be found in the 3rd sequence. It commences on f137 with an index relating to some 123 items, including the charter of November 1331 and May 1336. HRO M31/9/1 ff96b-100a, 110b-12b; *CPR* 1331, 221; 1336, 257
405. *CPR* 1350, 495
406. HRO M31/8 ff1-174
407. HRO M31/8 ff58, 92-3. Other exchanges include HRO M31/8 ff16-17 and 78-9.
408. Pantin, see n322, 52; *CPR* 1364, 504
409. R.K.Morris (1973) see n402, 55
410. HRO M31/9/1 ff 120b, 96a; Wedgwood, see n366. Acting as bailiff of the liberty Richard Wynnesley returned himself as MP in Nov 1422, Sept 1427 & Jan 1442, TNA C219/13/1; C219/13/5; C219/15/2; Townsend, see n179, 233
411. *Reg Lewis Charlton* 102; *Reg Gilbert* 176-7, 179-81; *Reg Trefnant* 194-5
412. *Reg Trillek* 106-7, 109-10, 141-2
413. HD&CA 1779 f15v; A.T.Bannister, 'Visitation Returns of the Diocese of Hereford in 1397, Part III' *Eng Hist Rev* (Jan 1930) 99-100; A.H.Thompson *The English Clergy* (1947) 143-7; K.L.Wood-Legh *Perpetual Chantries in Britain* (1965) 182-95, 203-7
414. *CPR* 1376, 384; Bannister (1930), see n413, 99; *Reg Bothe* 331; Wilts CRO D1/19 f71v; Townsend, see n179, 230
415. Hilary White, 'The Floor Tiles' in Brown & Wilson, see n214, 357
416. E.S.Eames *Catalogue of Medieval Lead-Glazed Earthenware Tiles in the ... British Museum* 2 vols (1980) I, 10-12, 67-8, 141-71, 172-81, 202-3; II, designs 519, 858-68, 1033-6. A copy of the *Catalogue* is held in the Local Reference section at Malvern Public Library. E.S.Eames *Medieval Tiles. A Handbook* (1968) 7-10, 14. For plates of the Chertsey circular pictorial tiles, idem *Medieval Tilers* (1992) 42-9
417. P.B.Chatwin, 'The Medieval Patterned Tiles of Warwickshire' *Trans Birmingham & Midland Archaeol Soc* (1936) 1-41; his Fig 5.1, similar to Leominster (2), is the same as Eames' design 1036 from Hailes, a derivative of the Chersey 4-tile design 1033. 'Its elaborate stiff-leaved foliage, probably designed not later than the 1280s, seems to have persisted in use well into the 14th century', Eames (1980) see n416, I, 165-7. A.Vince, 'The Medieval Floor Tiles' in *A Definitive History of Abbey Dore* ed R.Richardson & R.Shoesmith (1997) 80-4, figs 51-6, 59; *Hereford City Excavations 3. The Finds* ed R.Shoesmith (1985) fig 63.8
418. Eames (1968) see n416, fig IV.4, and compare design 2721 with Leominster tile (5); A.G.Vince & T.Wilmott, 'A Lost Tile Pavement at Tewkesbury Abbey and an Early Fourteenth-Century Tile Factory' *Antiq J* 71 (1991) 138-73, nos 61, 62; for fragment (6) Shoesmith (1985) see n417, fig 63.12
419. The Leominster tiles (7-12) represent Vince & Wilmott nos 51, 12, 48, 36a, 46, 17, see n418
420. Vince & Wilmott, see n418, 140-1, nos 17, 39; C.E.Keyser, 'Bredon Church, Worcestershire' *J Brit Archaeol Ass* NS 18 (1912) 1-12
421. L.Keen, 'The Medieval Decorated Tile Pavements at Worcester' in *Brit Archaeol Ass Conf Trans* 1 (1978) 151, 156-7; see also Eames (1980) see n416, designs 2284, 2126, 2147
422. Herefordshire SMR 31935
423. *Reg Trefnant* 140-1
424. *Reg Trefnant* 142-3
425. HD&CA 1779, f15v; Bannister (1930) see n413, 99, 100
426. *Reg Trefnant* 231-78, 365-94; *The Acts and Monuments of John Foxe* ed S.R.Cattley, III (1837) 107-14. K.B.McFarlane in *John Wycliffe and the Beginnings of English Nonconformity* (1952) 114-20; H.G.Bull, 'The Lollards in Herefordshire' *TWNFC* (1869) 168-83
427. *CPR* 1404, 412; Coplestone-Crow, see n30, 166-7
428. A.B.Emden *Biographical Register of the University of Oxford to AD 1500* 3 vols (1957-9) I, 270-1; *Reg Trefnant* 278-359; Cattley, see n426, IIIi (1855) 131-88
429. Recently le Brut, his trial and Lollard views have attracted considerable attention: A.Hudson, 'The Problems of Scribes: the Trial Records of William Swinderby and Walter Brut' *Nottingham Med Studies* 49 (2005) 80-9; D.Aers, 'Early Wycliffite Theology of the Sacrament of the Altar' in idem *Sanctifying Signs: Making Christian Tradition in Late Medieval England* (2004) 67-82; A.Hudson, '*Laicus Litteratus*: the paradox of Lollardy' in *Heresy and Literacy 1000-1530* ed P.Biller & A.Hudson (1994) 222-36; M.Aston, 'Lollard Women Priests?' in idem *Lollards and Reformers: images and literacy in late medieval religion* (1984) 52-9
430. *CPR* 1393, 354-5; *Reg Trefnant* 359-405
431. Matthew: 5.21&44
432. Townsend, see n179, 32-6; *CPR* 1393, 319, 354-5; *CCR* 1398, 305. For Hugh de Maune see also *CCR* 1380, 469; 1388, 622; *CPR* 1404, 412

433. K.B.McFarlane *Lancastrian Kings and Lollard Knights* (1972) 160-6, 197-208, 230-2; *Reg Trefnant* 178. See pp229-39
434. *Reg Trefnant* 147-50, 251, 257; *CCR* 1394, 314
435. *Reg Trefnant* 145; *Reg Spofford* 153-7; J.Thomas *History of Olchon Baptist Church* (1790)
436. *Taxatio*, see n137, 174, 159 for details of spiritualities. Full details of the 1327 Extent will be found in HRO M31/9/1 ff 122-6 but the contents are summarised in Price, see n137, (Luston) 150-3, (Stockton) 155-8, (Stoke) 162-4, (Hope) 166-9, (Ivington) 176-9
437. *Monasticon* IV, 52
438. Hereford City Library LC942.44: 'Earl Coningsby's Case relating to Lempster' (1721); T.Coningsby *Collections concerning the Manor of Marden* (1722)
439. Wilts CRO D1/19 f87r-90v
440. HRO M31/9 ff47-85
441. HRO M31/9 ff10-29
442. HRO M31/9 ff29-38, 86-91
443. HRO M31/9 ff39-46
444. G.R.J.Jones (1960) see n126, 80; idem '... A case-study of Archenfield' (1979) see n126
445. After the Dissolution, when it was leased for 21 years to George Cornewall in 1540, it is referred to as two distinct holdings, 'Somergilds superior' and 'inferior', *L&P, HVIII* 15, no 942 (34); *CPR* 1557, 491. A.T.Bannister *Place Names of Herefordshire* (1916) 181 refers to 'Summergild' as a pasture, but as a tributary of the Lugg, the river-name means 'brook dry in summer', Ekwall (1928) see n30, 383
446. HRO M31/9/1 f58a
447. HRO M31/9/1 f78a
448. Report of Robert Sherlock, inspector at the Stockton planning appeal, 11 May 1993; *CPR* 1554, 196
449. Herefordshire Millennium Air Survey: Stockton HRO 99 Mb0703, 00 Mb1055-9
450. I.R.Stainburn *A Survey of Dovecotes in the Old County of Herefordshire* (1979) no 7
451. HRO M31/9/1 f121a; T.Williamson *The Archaeology of Rabbit Warrens* (2006)
452. Domitian Aiii f118r, 91r
453. HRO M31/9/1 ff21, 27, 74, 66, 123-4
454. Domitian Aiii f88
455. HRO M31/9/1 ff 69, 32, 59, 76, 53, 74, 79. For Stoke and Eaton mills see also Domitian Aiii ff80v, 93r
456. HRO M31/9/1 f124; *CPR* 1572, no 1905; HRO M31/9/1 f80
457. HRO M31/9/1 ff107, 100
458. HRO M31/9/1 ff 16, 33. For the 19¼ gallons of honey Domitian Aiii f253v quoted in *A Roll of Household Expenses of Richard de Swinfield* 2 vols ed J.Webb, Camden Soc OS 59&62 (1853 & 1855) II, ccxii n3
459. HRO M31/9/1 ff122-4
460. HRO M31/9/1 f9
461. Blair (2005) see n22, 253-4 quoting C.Doherty, 'Exchange and Trade in Early Medieval Ireland' *J Soc of Antiqs of Ireland* 110 (1980) 67-89 and idem, 'Some Aspects of hagiography as a Source for Irish Economic History' *Peritia* 1 (1982) 318
462. HRO M31/9/1 ff 122-6; Hillaby (2003) see n240, 51; Hallam, see n361, 414-21
463. HRO M31/9/1 ff 47, 53-4, 61, 66, 71-3, 77-8
464. HRO M31/9/1 f32a; H.L.Gray *English Field Systems* (1969) 448, 522
465. R.E.Zupko *British Weights and Measures* (1977) 20-1; HRO M31/9/1 f6
466. B.Harvey *Westminster Abbey and its Estates in the Middle Ages* (1977) 208-9; Webb, see n458, I, 7, 38; R.H.Hilton *A Medieval Society* (1975) 115
467. P.Williams *Bromyard. Minster, Manor and Town* (1987) 4; idem *Avenbury and the ruined church of St Mary* (2000) 21
468. HRO M31/9/1 ff 122-6
469. HRO M31/9/1 ff 123-5; Price, see n137, 177
470. Kershaw, see n247, 152-3
471. HRO M31/9/1 ff 122-6; *Taxatio*, see n137, 174
472. *Walter of Henley and other Treatises on Estate Management and Accounting* ed D.Oschinsky (1971) 338-9; HRO M31/9/1 ff 122-6; *Taxatio*, see n137, 174; Kershaw, see n247, 80-5; Bond (2004) see n244, 57-9
473. HRO M31/9/1 ff 93, 100-1
474. *L&P, HVIII* 15, nos 63, 117; *Bartholomew Anglicus: The Encyclopedia on the Properties of Things* ed R.Steele (1893) 106; Tillotson, see n245, 156. In the post-Dissolution era the watering of hemp in the 'lytell Lug' was prohibited, as a nuisance, 'under the payne of every deffault, vj s viijd', as was the washing of linen, Blacklock (see n70) 213.
475. *Giraldus Cambrensis: Opera* ed J.S.Brewer, RS 21iv (1873) 186-96; J.Hillaby, 'The House of Houses: the Cistercians of Dore and the Origins of the Polygonal Chapter House' *TWNFC* 46ii (1989) 227-31
476. Domitian Aiii ff 93v, 126v; for the Clifford family's other local interests, Hillaby (1985) see n382, 246-51
477. Domitian Aiii ff 124r, 124v, 125v-6r; W.Rees *A History of the Order of St John of Jerusalem in Wales and on the Welsh Border* (1947) 40 quoting BL Harley 6203; Botzum, see n366, 81; RCHM III, 70; *CCR* 1488, 100; *Charters and Records of Hereford Cathedral* (1908) ed W.W.Capes, 33-4
478. Domitian Aiii ff 124r, 125v, 127r; HRO M31/9/1 ff 55a, 58b
479. HRO M31/9/1 ff 123, 124, 125, 127
480. *Taxatio*, see n137, 173; Domitian Aiiif83-84v; HRO M31/9/1 f36
481. HRO M31/9/1 ff 122-6; Price, see n137, 208
482. HRO M31/9/1 ff 50b, 46b, 75
483. HRO M31/9/1 123r-125v; *L&P HVIII* 7, no 1678
484. HRO M31/9/1 f115
485. HRO M31/9/1 ff122, 125, 86
486. HRO M31/9/1 ff122
487. *CPR* 1411, 290; *L&P, HVIII* 7, no 1678
488. HRO M31/9/1 f122r
489. *Chronicon Henrici Knighton* ed J.R.Lumby, RS 93 II (1895) 58-65, trans in *The Peasants' Revolt of 1381* ed R.B.Dobson (1970) 59-63
490. *25 Edward III*, stat 2, cc 1-7 trans Dobson (1970) see n489, 63-8; *CPR* 1356, 392

491. C.Dyer *Lords and Peasants in a Changing Society: The Estates of the Bishopric of Worcester 1680-1540* (1980) 145-9, 209-11, 236-9; *Reg Trillek* 373-82; W.J.Dohar *The Black Death and Pastoral Ledership: The Diocese of Hereford in the 14th Century* (1995) 37-55 considers the reliability of institutions as evidence for mortality rates. The only other detailed evidence of mortality in the county is for the manors of Woolhope and Norton Canon, Hallam, see n361, 447-9. Reliability is discussed by J.Aborth, 'The Black Death in the Diocese of Ely: the evidence of the bishop's register' *J Med Hist* 21 (1995) 275-87.
492. HRO M31/9/1 ff48-9; *RAC* I, p29
493. *Cal Papal Regs* I, see n216, 282; Capes, see n477, x, 226-9; Hillaby (2005) see n25, 74
494. HRO M31/9/1 ff 11, 14
495. HRO M31/9/1 ff 43, 119, 60, 51, 104
496. M.McKisack *The Fourteenth Century* (1962) 340-4; R.A.L.Smith *Canterbury Priory* (1943) 126-7; Harvey, see n466, 246-61; R.B.Dobson *Durham Priory, 1400-1450* (1973) 272-5
497. HRO M31/9/1 ff 54, 58-60, 65
498. HRO M31/9/1 f10
499. HRO M31/9/1 f134
500. HRO M31/9/1 f93b
501. HRO M31/9/1 ff 49, 63, 82, 60
502. K.B.McFarlane *The Nobility of Later Medieval England* (1973) 221; R.H.Hilton *The Decline of Serfdom* (2nd ed, 1983) 52-5
503. HRO M31/9/1 ff 24, 57, 73
504. HRO M31/9/1 f91
505. Wilts CRO D1/19 ff87r-90v. See also C.Dyer *Standards of Living in the Later Middle Ages* (1989) 118-27 & Table 8
506. HRO M31/9/1 f56b
507. Wilts CRO D1/19 ff 18r, 69v; HRO M31/9/1 f121; CPR 1557, 390
508. HRO M31/9/1 ff 5, 47
509. *The Original Writings and Correspondence of the two Richard Hakluyts* ed E.G.R.Taylor, Hakluyt Soc 2S 76 & 77 (1935-6) 1 and documents 57, 62 & 63 includes a letter from Richard Hakluyt to Lord Burley, 1589, where he describes buying 'certeyn oxen of great bone to feede' in his 3 great fields at Eyton; he was to receive £7 10s for 7 such oxen from the royal purveyor, and £8 10s for stall-fed oxen, illustrating how many of the best beasts were bypassing the market due to direct purchase by major purveyors. Bathhurst & Cole, see n393, 72-88; *Agrarian History of England and Wales* IV, ed J.Thirsk (1967) 541
510. Domitian Aiii, ff183-247; HRO M31/9/1 f84
511. R.R.Davies *The Revolt of Owain Glyn Dŵr* (1995) 102-26; idem *The Age of Conquest. Wales 1063-1415* (1991) 443-59; J.E.Lloyd *Owen Glendower* (1931) 49-53; *Monasticon* IV, 52 quoting Price, see n137, 81 on Mortimer's imprisonment in the prior's Leominster gaol.
512. *Original Letters Illustrative of English History* 2S, ed H.Ellis (1927) 24-9; R.R.Davies (1995) see n511, 163-70, 179-80
513. *CPR*, 1402, 139; V.Buteaux *Archaeological Assessment of Leominster* Central Marches Historical Towns Survey (1996) 9 quoting N.Napthan et al *Evaluation at Bargates, Leominster* (1994) H&WCC Archaeol Services internal report 287
514. J.H.Wylie *History of England under Henry the Fourth* 4 vols (1884-98) III, 4-6
515. *CCR* 1404, 395; R.R.Davies (1995) see n511, 242-3
516. R.R.Davies (1995) see n511, 191-6, 293, 304-10
517. J.Bolton, 'The World Upside Down' in *The Black Death in England* ed M.Ormrod & P.Lindley (1996) 26-40; H.E.Salter *Medieval Oxford* Oxford Hist Soc 100 (1936) 87-9
518. Hillaby (2005) see n25, 27-42
519. RCHM I-III (1931-34) for the county's ecclesiastical architecture; R.K.Morris (1973) see n402, 48-67; *Id*, 'The Masons of Madley, Allensmore and Eaton Bishop' *TWNFC* XLI(ii) (1974) 180-97; *Id*, 'Pembridge and Mature Decorated Architecture in Herefordshire' *TWNFC* XLII(ii) (1977) 129-53; *Id*, 'Late Decorated Architecture in Northern Herefordshire' *TWNFC* XLIV(i) (1982) 36-58; H.J.Powell, 'The Perpendicular Style in Herefordshire' *TWNFC* XLIII(iii) (1981) 298-306 lists parochial work of the period. Bolton, see n517, for the economy of towns, their 'Prosperity or Decline' 65-70; J.G.Oliver, 'Churches and Wool: a study of the wool trade in 15th century England' *Hist Today* I (Sept 1951) 5-12; P.J.Bowden *Wool Trade in Tudor and Stuart England* (1962) 47 indicates centres of the English wool textile industry c1500; R.Gottfried *Bury St Edmunds and the Urban Crisis, 1290-1539* (1982) analyses the town's success as a textile centre
520. See p170; HRO M31/9/1 f4
521. *Reg Spofford* 39, 47, 58, 64-79, 80-3, 98, 108, 125, 216-17, 223-4, 350, 354; *Leland's Itinerary*, see n11, II, 72; *Reg Stanbury* 182
522. *Reg Spofford* 152
523. *Reg Spofford* 160-5
524. *CPR* 1448, 142; for Devereux see p251
525. H.Harrod, 'Some particulars relating to the church of Wymondam' *Archaeologia* 43ii (1871) 264-72; J.G.Tansley Thomas *A Brief History of Wymondham Abbey* (nd). For monastic plan A.New *Guide to the Abbeys of England and Wales* (1985) 459
526. *CCR* 1404, 350-1; *CPR* 1404, 474; *Reg Mascall* 115-16; *Reg Bothe* 161-2; HRO M31/9/1 f134
527. HRO S67/2/1/68 ff1r-2r; S67/2/3/1 ff1r-4v; S67/2/3/2 ff1r-2v; S67/2/3/3 ff1r-2v; S67/4/1/1 ff1r-2v
528. J.W.Joyce *England's Sacred Synods* (1967) 409
529. HRO S67/2/3/3 f2r&v
530. For University College, Oxford MS 78a: J.J.G.Alexander & E.Temple *Illuminated Manuscripts in Oxford College Libraries, the University Archives and the Taylor Institution* (1985) no. 422; Downside MS, Ker (1977) see n291, 454-9; Worcester MS, R.M.Thomson *Medieval Manuscripts in Worcester Cathedral Library* (1977) 455-8
531. The text of the folios will be found in *Missale ad usum percelebris ecclesiae Herefordensis* ed W.G.Henderson (1874, repr 1969) xliv-xlvii, 13-15, 51-2, 60-1, 172-4, 186-7, 287-90, 303-5, 318-22, 344-7; J.Harper *The Forms and Orders of Western Liturgy from the Tenth to the Eighteenth Century* (1991) 216-18

532. C.Wordsworth & H.Littlehales *The Old Service Books of the English Church* (1904) 190-3; R.W.Pfaff *New Liturgical Feasts in Later Medieval England* (1970) 1-8, 47. For the 11,000 virgins see J de Voragine *The Golden Legend* trans W.G.Ryan, II (1993) 256-60
533. Ker (1977) see n291, 455; *Reg Mascall* 146, 149, 152; G.Warner *Catalogue of Editions to the Manuscripts in the British Museum* (1916-20) 455-8
534. O.Morgan, 'An Ancient Silver Chalice preserved at Leominster' *Archaeologia* 35ii (1853) 489-90; W.St John Hope & T.M.Fallow, 'English Medieval Chalices and Patens' *Archaeol J* 43 (1886) 137-61, 364-402; B.S.Stanhope & H.C.Moffatt *The Church Plate of the County of Hereford* (1903) 9-10, 105-7; W.W.Watts *Victoria & Albert Museum. Catalogue of Chalices* (1922) 25-7; C.Oman *English Church Plate, 597-1830* (1957) Pl 6, 42-6, 302; 'Thieves plunder Priory treasure' *Hereford Times* 26 April 1996
535. *CCR* 1337, 149; *Rotuli Parliamentorum* V (1783) 274-5; *L&P, HVIII* 10, no 247; T.H.Lloyd, see n363, 9-13; J.H.Munro, 'Wool price schedules and the qualities of English wools in the later Middle Ages' *Textile History* 9 (1978) 118-69
536. HRO B56/13/93; M31/9/1 f58b; *CPR* 1457, 238-9, 246, 310
537. Bongaerts, see n371, 5, 24-31, 67-8; HRO A63/I/306, 305, 391, 395
538. W.Camden *Britannia* I (1586) 690; G.Markham *Cheape and Good Husbandry* (1676) 85; M.Drayton *Poly-Olbion* (1622) vii, 104; *The Poetical Work of Robert Herrick* ed L.C.Martin (1956 ed) 165; T.Fuller *Worthies of England* (1662) 33
539. *Leland's Itinerary*, see n11, II, 74; Stukeley, see n214, I, 72
540. See p173; HRO Leominster Court Leet Rolls 1577/8-1578/9; Blacklock, see n70, 212
541. Bathhurst & Cole, see n393, 72-88; Stukeley, see n214, I, 72
542. C.Heath *Historical and Descriptive Accounts ...of Monmouth* (1804) 103-4
543. *VCH Gloucestershire* 8 (1968) 129-30; Buildings of England *Gloucestershire 2: The Vale and Forest of Dean* ed D.Verey & A.Brooks (3rd ed, 2002) 735-6
544. HRO M31/8 ff72, 119
545. *CCR* 1485, 417
546. Hillaby (2003) see n240, 34; HRO M31/8 f10; BL Harley MS 1708, f48
547. CPR 1448, 142; R.L.Storey *The End of the House of Lancaster* (1986) 228-30; for Devereux R.A.Griffiths *Reign of King Henry VI* (1981) 362, 566, 593, 671-2, 710-11, 748, 770, 780
548. 'Gregory's Chronicle' in *The Historical Collections of a citizen of London in the fifteenth century* ed J.Gairdner, Camden Soc NS 17 (1876) 211; H.T.Evans *Wales and the Wars of the Roses* (1915) 69-80
549. *Complete Works of Sir Thomas More 6. A Dialogue concerning Heresies* ed T.Lawler et al (1981) 86-8
550. *Reg Mayhew* 241, 101; Emden, see n428, III, 2086; A.Coates, see n212, 93-4 & n29; *L&P HVIII* 3i, 342
551. Oxford, Bodleian Library, University College MS d6; *English Writings of Richard Rolle* ed H.E.Allen (1988) xli-lviii; A.Coates, see n212, 116, 169
552. *Reg Mayhew* 277, 283; *Reg Bothe* 331; *L&P HVIII* 3i, 342, 370, 388; J.Youings *The Dissolution of the Monasteries* (1971) 80
553. *Reg Bothe* 135, 245. For the list of principal feasts see *Reg Spofford* 162-3
554. See p220
555. Youings, see n552, 67-70
556. P.Williams *The Council in the Marches of Wales under Elizabeth* I (1958) 11-21, 33-5; *L&P, HVIII* 14, no 4096
557. *L&P, HVIII* 7, no 1678(i-v)
558. Price, see n137, 82; *L&P, HVIII* 7, no 1449
559. *L&P, HVIII* 13, no 1263
560. Wilts CRO D1/19 ff28, 29v, 69v
561. *L&P, HVIII* 14ii, no 620
562. HD&CA 5602 (microfilm); also F.C.&P.E.Morgan, 'Some nuns, ex-religious and former chantry priests living in the diocese of Hereford (c1554)' *TWNFC* 37ii (1962) 135-48; *Reg Bothe* 333, 348
563. D.Brown & L.Templeton *Archaeological Assessment at Leominster Priory* (1995) 7.2
564. *L&P, HVIII*, 15, nos 34, 63, 117; *CPR* 1554, 196; 1557, 491
565. HRO A63/1/305, 306, 391, 395
566. *CPR*, 1559, 40, 113; 1572, 373. For the extraordinary career of Sir James Croft, d1590, see O.G.S.Croft *The House of Croft Castle* (1949) 56-81
567. HRO A63/I/391, 306, 305, 394 which rental covers the years 1696-1718 and 1776-1854 for the burys of Ivington, Stocton and Stoke
568. *CPR* 1554, 395-8; Price, see n137, 220-51
569. Muir (1988) see n6, no 1 (October) & no 61; Lapidge (1991) see n63, 166 lines 198-200, 169 line 347; *CChR 1290*, 356; BL Harley MS 2253 ff 132r-3r; Ker (1965) see n9, art 98; *Reg Spofford* 163
570. HRO AG 25
571. *Life* of St Mildburg, BL Add MS 34,633 f207v; BL Harley MS 2253 ff 132r; Ker (1965) see n9, art 98
572. For Thomas and John Hackluyt see Taylor, see n509, 2S 76 (1935) 1-7; J.Weever *Antient Funerall Monuments* (2nd ed, 1767) 584-7 reproduces this 'choice piece of antiquity' 'in John Hackluyt's own handwriting'; *Gentleman's Magazine Library: Archaeology Pt II* ed G.L.Gomme (1886) 273-6; '*Vita et Miracula S. Kenelmi*' in *Three Eleventh-Century Anglo-Latin Lives* ed & trans R.C.Love (1996) lxxxix-xc, 52-65; *Leland's Itinerary*, see n11, II, 75

Index

Notes: page references in bold type refer to Figs, Illustrations, Tables and their captions. Pl refers to Plates.